EASTERN BENGAL BALLADS

Eastern Bengal Ballads
Mymensing

(Ramtanu Lahiri Research Fellowship Lectures for 1922-24, in two Parts)

Vol. I : Part I

Compiled and Edited by
Dineshchandra Sen, Rai Bahadur, B.A. D.Litt. (Hons.)

Forward by
The Right Hon'able Lawrence John Lumley Dundas,
Earl of Ronaldshay
Late Governor of Bengal

GYAN PUBLISHING HOUSE
NEW DELHI-110002

Eastern Bengal Ballads Mymensing

ISBN: 81-212-0906-4 (Set)
ISBN: 81-212-0907-2 (Vol. I)

Published in 2006 in India by
Gyan Publishing House,
5, Ansari Road, Daryaganj, New Delhi-110002
E-mail: books@gyanbooks.com

Laser Typesetting at: Vinayak Printers, Delhi
Printed at: Salasar Imaging System, Delhi

Dedication

To

The Hon'ble Justice SIR ASUTOSH MOOKERJEE, Kt., C.S.I., M.A., D.L., D.Sc., Ph.D., etc.,

President, Council of Post-Graduate Teaching in Arts, Calcutta University.

Esteemed Sir,

I take the liberty of dedicating to you this treasure of the old songs of Mymensing, dearly prized by me, as without your patriotic advocacy of the cause of our vernacular in the face of the great impediments and difficulties with which our Alma Mater *is beset at this moment, there would never have been any chance of their being collected and published.*

In these ballads, the most prominent feature is the presentation of the Bengali woman in a variety of aspects, true as truth itself and vivid as life. When face to face with danger, she often appears like the awe-inspiring and implacable goddess Kali, fiercely dancing on the funeral pyre or riding the storm. In the quieter moments of life, she is like the harvest goddess Laksmi—an embodiment of feminine grace and modesty and of all that is noble and good in the domestic region. In her great trials, she reveals the shining qualities of her character like gold purified by fire; and when complications arise turning her life into a problem of insoluble difficulty, her sweet voice is heard murmuring evermore the tale of her devotion like the voice of the goddess Ganga from the matted locks of Siva. She proves by her character that the deities worshipped by Bengali Hindus are born of the exalted human ideals of Bengal. Though she belongs to the age gone by, there is nothing that is crude about her,—she is fresh as a flower blown to-day. Absolutely free from all mere conventionality, she sings, lark-like, a free song in the infinite space of her heavenly virtue, showing the supreme triumph of love over all material forces. She is a voice from the past that is true for all ages; and though she hails from this tropical region of Bengal and has derived from its soil the warmth and geniality of her nature, her grand outbursts of noble indignation and her fierce revenge when wronged are like the storm-wind of the equinox. In some cases, however, she is a picture of patient suffering,—bearing without protest or complaint those ills which would chill the very life-blood of others. In these cases she still displays the saving graces of love and faith,—her spirit being akin to the frozen north, hallowed and redeemed by a mellow solar light. Everywhere she makes a universal appeal by the intensity and directness of those humane qualities which will be appreciated wherever truth and devotion are prized. She is the eternal symbol of love and sweetness, of strength and resignation—a mute sufferer of the persecution that has ever been the lot of the beautiful and the true in all ages—like a flower torn by wanton hands or broken by the storm—who, nevertheless, has always won and will never cease to win the admiring love of gods and men.

In these days, Sir, when in the more favoured soil of cultu e and liberty women are strenuously fighting for an equal footing with men in every respect, one wonders if the fair ones are resolved, like the old Siva in a well-known mythological tale, cnce more to reduce the god of love to ashes by the dart of their indignant glances. Until, however, that result is achieved, marriage-laws may alter and political hobbies may prevail, but the two sexes will continue to be inevitably linked by the freaks of that lively deity who presides over the human heart. These ballads shew the ever-conquering power of love,—marriage laws playing a mere subservient part in them. They belong to no church or temple but voice the eternal truths of humanity and as such are not, I venture to hope, likely to clash with the ideas of the advanced womanhood of our own times, who carry the banner of liberty and individualism.

I hope the interest of this book will be sustained in the future volumes containing more of these ballads.

Yours respectfully,

DINESH CHANDRA SEN.

Calcutta, the 23rd September, 1923.

FOREWORD

The Bengali language in its present form is a thing of recent growth. It has been fashioned gradually during the past one hundred years. Less than a century ago the committee of Public Instruction with Macaulay at its head declared that the vernacular language contained neither the literary nor the scientific information necessary for a liberal education. Nor was this all. For not only was the Bengali language of that day considered by Englishmen to be inadequate to the needs of the times, but it was also looked down upon by cultured Bengalis themselves; and it is on record that a suggestion made by an Englishman, Mr. Adam, that some at least of the lectures to be delivered in the educational institutions which were then being established might be given in Bengali, was vetoed by the Indian members of this committee on the ground that anything said or written in the vernacular would be despised in consequence of the medium through which it was conveyed. With these estimates of the vernacular language of Bengal less than a hundred years ago, contrast the description of it given recently by Mr. J. D. Anderson as "one of the great expressive languages of the world capable of being the vehicle of as great things as of any speech of men."

A language capable of undergoing so great a transformation in so short a time must, surely, have been sound at the roots. What of the seed which was garnered and cultivated by those great gardeners in the philological field—Rajendralal Mitra, K. M. Bannerji, Ramkamal Sen, Isvar Chandra Gupta, Bankim Chandra Chatterji, Dinabandhu Mitra, Akshay Kumar Datta, to mention but a few? It is a matter of common knowledge that such vernacular literature as flourished at the beginning of the 19th Century was in verse rather than in prose and was the possession of the masses rather than of the classes. A peculiar interest attaches, therefore, to any specimens of this literature which can now be collected. I have just read Rai Bahadur Dinesh Chandra Sen's translation of a ballad of Eastern Bengal entitled "Mahua." Here is a delightful specimen of the seed from which modern Bengali has sprung. It is charming in English ; but from the point of view from which I have written above, it is the language in which the ballad is sung that is of a paramount interest and importance.

Mahua is but one of a large number of ballads now being collected, arranged, translated and commented on with the untiring interest of the enthusiast and the skill of the expert scholar, by Rai Bahadur Dinesh Chandra Sen. And it is obvious that in addition to the philological interest attaching to such a collection it must possess also a special interest in respect of its subject matter. And here the Englishman unacquainted with the technique of the Bengali language can appreciate the ballads to the full in their English translation. For it is in such compositions that one finds sketched with an unconscious and for that reason, perhaps, an all the truer pen, intimate pictures of the life of a people. And since these ballads are believed to cover a period of roughly three hundred years from the 16th century onwards, they should throw much light surely upon the political history of Bengal. For it was during this period that Moslem influence was pushed eastwards, the Moslem capital transferred by Nawab Islam Khan from Rajmahal to Dacca, and colonies of Moslem feudal barons planted out in the eastern districts. In short these ballads should prove a mine of wealth alike to the philologist and the historian and last, but not least, to the administrator who seeks to penetrate the inner thought and feeling of the people.

RONALDSHAY.

CONTENTS

BALLADS

List of Illustrations

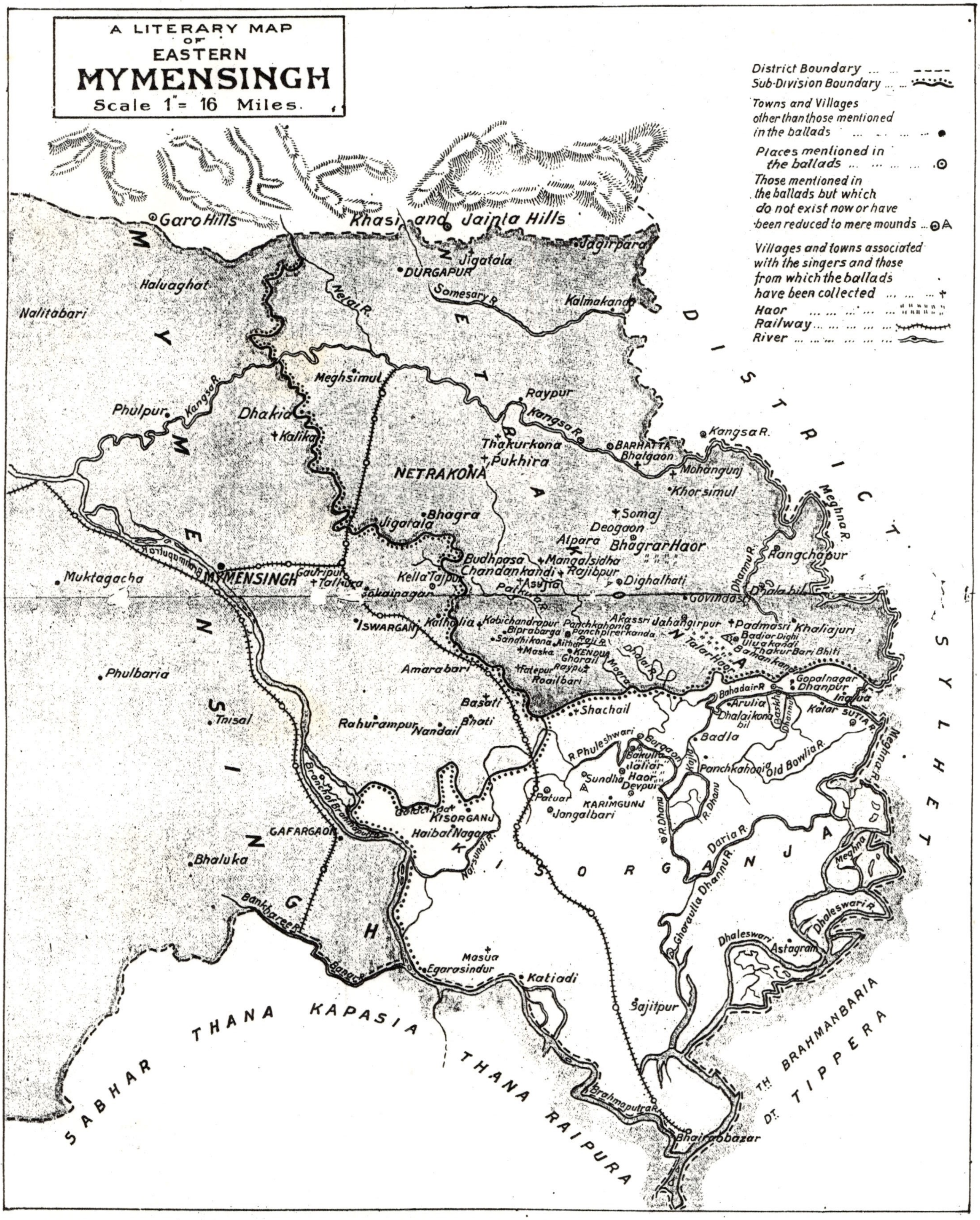

COST BORNE BY Dr A.N. TAGORE C.I.E. CALCUTTA.

LITHO BY BENGAL ART STUDIO & PRINTING LTD, CALCUTTA.

INTRODUCTION

How these ballads came to be known.

The first notice of some of the ballads appeared in the Bengali Journal the "Sourabha"

It was during the years 1912-1914 that my attention was first drawn to the poetical treasures of Mymensing by several articles, published in the 'Sourabha'—a local magazine of that district. These articles were written by one Chandra Kumar De, hitherto but little known in the field of Bengali letters. The Bengali style of his articles seemed to me to be singularly happy and his literary gifts of a promising nature. And what was more, I found in him one who keenly appreciated the beauty of the indigenous rustic songs of his district.

The articles that attracted my attention were upon some 'Kabi' songs of Mymensing, called by Chandra Kumar by the poetic name of "Mālir Jogān" (supply of the flower-seller), published in the 'Sourabha' of Baisakh, 1320 B. S. (April, 1913).

Then I began to search the back numbers of the magazine and became a habitual reader of Babu Chandra Kumar's contributions that appeared in the later issues of the journal. The story of Kenaram—the robber, which formed the subject of one of these articles, particularly interested me. Chandra Kumar quoted only a few extracts from the original ballad, and this only served to rouse my curiosity all the more. He latterly contributed a series of articles to the same journal on the "Vidyasundar by 'Kabi Kanka." This discovery was indeed an acquisition to our old literature, as the poem proved to be the earliest Bengali 'Vidya-sundar' yet known. But the life of Kabi Kanka itself, embodied in a supplementary song from which Babu Chandra Kumar had also made some extracts, possessed a unique and thrilling interest. The freedom breathed in the tale from the stereotyped literary canons of the Renaissance-school revealed a new feature which took me by surprise. The touching account that the writer of these articles latterly gave of the love between the poetess Chandrávati and Joychandra from an old ballad also struck me very much, and I longed to read the original poem from which the writer had given no extracts in his article. From his short summary, however, I gave an account of Chandrávati—the poetess, in my work called 'the Bengali Ramayanas.' Some of the European scholars took an interest in this account of mine and wrote complimentary things about Chandrávati. M. Jules Bloch, in a private communication dated the 10th March, 1921, wrote to me as follows: "I have just finished the romantic story of Chandrávati. May I congratulate you on the good and well-deserved luck of having discovered her after so many others and having added that new gem to the crown of Bengali literature?" Sir George Grierson referred to Chandrávati in his review of my 'Bengali Ramayanas' published in the Royal Asiatic Society's Journal (pp. 135-39; June, 1921) in the following words:—

Chandrávati.

"Space will not permit me to mention all Krittibasha's successors. Each had its own excellences and defects. I, therefore, confine myself to calling attention to the incomplete Ramayan of the Mymensingh poetess Chandrávati. In another poem she tells her own beautiful and pathetic story[1] and there can be no doubt that her private griefs, nobly borne, inspired the pathos with which her tale of Sita's woes is distinguished. It is interesting that like one or two other authors she ascribes Sita's banishment to Ram's groundless jealousy. A treacherous sister-in-law, a daughter of Kaikei, named Kukua, persuaded Sita much against her will to draw for her a portrait of Ravana. She then showed

[1] It was not Chadrávati who told her tale of disappointment in love. The poet Nayan Chand wove the story into a song. This will be seen from the colophon in the poem itself, the text of which is published separately.

this to Ram as a proof that his wife loved and still longed for her abductor. This story was not invented by the poetess. It must have been one of those orally current but not recorded by Valmiki or by the writer of the 7th book of the Sanskrit poem, for it re-appears in the Kasmiri Ramayan to which I have previously alluded."

Mr. W. F. Stutterhein, Hon. Secretary to the India Society for Holland, addressed me a long letter on this topic in January 1923, drawing attention to the fact that the accounts of the birth of Sita and of the jealousy of Kukua as given by Chandravati also occur in the Javanese and Malaya versions of the Ramayana. He put to me a score of queries in respect of these indigenous Ram-stories enquiring particularly as to the causes of their deviations from the epic of Valmiki.

It appeared from these that my short notice of the Mymensing poetess had already interested some of the foreign scholars.

The short extracts and notices given by Chandra Kumar, could not, as I have said, satisfy my curiosity and I longed to have a sight of the original poems. I wrote to Babu Kedar Nath Majumdar, editor of the 'Sourabha' making enquiries about Chandra Kumar De. I was informed by him that Chandra Kumar was a man of little or no education but possessed fine literary talents. He was so poor that he and his wife passed many a day of the year without meals. I was further informed that at the time he was suffering from a serious nervous prostration which threatened to affect his brain.

Chandra Kumar De—the discoverer of these ballads.

There was hardly any other man in the district of Mymensing that I knew of, who could give me a clue to the treasure of the indigenous ballads of the place. So, for sometime I could not find any opportunity for proceeding with my researches in that field.

Towards the middle of the year 1919, however, I heard that Chandra Kumar had recovered his health to some extent and was thinking of coming down to Calcutta for medical treatment. I forthwith wrote him an appreciative letter showing him sympathy and asking him to see me when he would come to our metropolis. I said in my letter that I would possibly be able to render him some help in the matter of his medical treatment. He wrote me a touching letter describing his pitiable condition and thanking me for my proferred help. He was so poor that he had to sell a few silver ornaments of his wife—her whole property, to meet the expenses of his journey from Mymensing to Calcutta.

He came to Calcutta sometime before the Pujas in that year and saw me at my Behala house. I found him a lean sickly looking young man, 30 years old, greatly dejected in spirit owing to his chronic illness and poverty. I introduced him to Kaviraj Jamini Bhusan Ray, M.A., M.B., a member of the Senate, who kindly took up his treatment, free of charge, and to Babu Gopal Das Chaudhuri, Zemindar of Sherpur who gave him free board during his stay at Calcutta.

A brief notice of his life may be of some interest to my readers, as he is the discoverer of this lyrical treasure of his country, though he took up the subject seriously in his hands later on at my initiation.

Chandra Kumar was born in the small village of Aithor (P.O. Kendua) in the district of Mymensing, in February, 1889. His father Ram Kumar De owned a few acres of land in that village, and this was all on which the little family depended for their maintenance. Ram Kumar was too poor to send his son to school. So Chandra Kumar had to be satisfied with a bare knowledge of the Bengali alphabet, picked up from a village Pathsálá. His mother Tara Sundari died when he was quite young and later on the Zemindar of the village forcibly snatched away the few acres of land from Ram Kumar. "So shocked was my father," writes Chandra Kumar, "by this disaster that he actually succumbed to it. I saw his face pale with grief at the loss of this only source of income, and shortly after he died, leaving me an orphan."

Chandra Kumar got a post, not long after, in the shop of a village grocer on Re. 1 a month, but was dismissed on the plea of incompetence and inattention. Next he was engaged by a man, who owned some lands in the locality, as rent-collector on Rs. 2 a month. "This post," says Chandra Kumar, "brought me in to direct contact with the peasants of a few villages near my home. They sang the *baramashi* songs and ballads which were never written but were preserved merely by oral recitation and singing from generation to generation. As I heard them sung in chorus, my heart thrilled with emotion." By his own efforts he mastered Bengali and wrote several interesting articles on his favourite subject—the rural songs of Mymensing, in the local journal 'Sourabha.' The editor, Babu Kedar Nath Majumdar, encouraged Chandra Kumar in his literary attempts, and later on Babu Bijoy Kumar Lahiri, a Zemindar of Kalipur, Mymensing, became his friend and sponsor and engaged him as his office clerk on Rs. 8 a month. "I was attacked with dysentery about this time," writes Chandra Kumar, "and a village quack gave me some drugs which brought on me an attack of insanity. I remained insane for two years. My love of the rural songs of my district is due to my intimacy with the peasants of my country and I cannot help thanking my quondam master, the village-landlord, who had given me the post of a *tahasildar* on Rs. 2 a month, affording me an opportunity to mix with the poor rural people of my district so closely."

When I met Chandra Kumar in August, 1919, I asked him whether he could help me in securing the songs and ballads of his district. He seemed to have a higher respect for the classical Bengali works of Mymensing like Chandi by Durgaram and Mansar Bhasan by Dwija Bangsi, than for the unassuming songs of the rustic folk which I prized so much. I did not encourage his predilection for Sanskritic poems, but insisted on his collection of indigenous songs. He told me that it was a very difficult affair to achieve success in that direction. These songs, generally speaking, were not reduced to writing. Stray portions of the poem were to be collected from individual rhapsodists of the countryside, whose ancestors had been their custodians during bygone ages. I gave him a promise of pecuniary help, and on returning home he sent me an instalment of songs. This comprised the 'Vidyasundar' of Kanka—the poet and the half-finished Ramayana of the poetess Chandrávati.

It was a task of infinite trouble and worry to which I had appointed Chandra Kumar. In the very frail state of his health he had to travel in the marshy lands of the district, collecting songs from professional singers. In most cases they observed a scrupulous reserve in respect of their songs and were by no means inclined to disclose them to people outside their own family. It was only possible to have these poems collected by a person like Chandra Kumar, who had literally fallen in love with them and was inspired by a truly patriotic zeal to recover the lost gems of his country's literature. No other man that I knew of was capable of collecting these rare poems of which the texts with English translations and summaries are going to be published now in the present series.

Chandra Kumar De was paid for his labours for sending the first instalment of his songs by the University of Calcutta, and under the auspices of the Hon'ble Sir Asutosh Mookerjee, whose zeal in the cause of the furtherance of Vernacular literature is well-known, the Syndicate offered him a post, for one year for the present, on a small pay, so that he might go on collecting these songs all the months of the year. At first Chandra Kumar hesitated to accept the post on the ground of his ill health. He feared lest he might not prove equal to the task or failed to render a good account of himself by steady and regular work. But at last on my repeated assurance that the University would not be hard upon him, in case he fell ill, he accepted a post on Rs. 50 a month. This pay included his travelling expenses and incidental charges for the collection of poems. He was appointed in March 1921 and has now served more than a year. His term was extended to one year more by the Senate on the expiration of the first year and I am glad to say that he has worked with a conscientiousness and energy during this time which have done him a great credit. His ill health has not deterred him from sending me new songs and ballads regularly, the rare poetic excellence of which, apart from their historical and philological value, has been a perfect surprise to me and to those who have heard them recited. But on this point I will speak later on.

Babu Chandra Kumar travelled in many villages of the districts of Mymensing and Sylhet such as, Samaj, Mohonganj, Khorsimul, Pukhuriá, Pauchkahania, Nasir-uljiral, Fatehpur, Baniachong, Mangalsiddhi, Bhatergaon, Dattanoaja, Hatiwar, Telighati, etc., from each of which he got portions of poems and stray songs which he subsequently put in their proper place while compiling a whole ballad. He writes from his native village—Aithor—on the 30th May, 1921 :—

"It is a great inconvenience that one individual singer is scarcely found in this district who knows a whole poem. It is to be recovered from various persons living in widely distant places, so that a long journey is required to get hold of a whole poem. Disappointments are sometimes faced in the course of such searches. It often turns out that after a long and difficult journey the man sought for is not found at his place or that the information previously obtained, of his knowing a particular poem or song proves untrue."

It is not possible to make previous engagements in such cases; the singers are to be attacked on the spot without notice. For, they generally try to avoid those who approach them for the songs. Sometimes he had to travel on foot 35 or 40 miles a day, conveyances not being available as the village-roads are *kancha* and unfit for traffic or carriages of any sort. In May, 1921, he suffered a good deal in the course of his travel owing to the Railway strikes. While engaged in this arduous work grim poverty often stared him in the face, the thought of the liquidation of his debts hanging heavy on him. He wrote to me sometime ago :

"I have no home, I live in another man's house with my wife." The pathos of this short sentence will be realised by all Bengalis, for, there are few men in this country, who however poor, do not own a few huts to call by the dear name of 'home.'

Struggling with poverty, ill health and domestic trouble and anxieties he has done for our literature what I consider to be really yeoman's service. He has been instrumental in discovering a find which is likely to prove a unique treasure to our literature. No praises are too high for the songs and ballads that he has sent me, as the readers will themselves judge from the texts herein published.

At each stage of his travel Chandra Kumar reports to me the progress of his work. On the 30th of May, 1921, he sent me the whole of the interesting poem of Kenaram—the robber, only short extracts from which had appeared in the "Sourabha." The complete songs of 'Mahua' and 'Adhua Sundari O Surat Jamal" were sent on the 6th May, 1921. Previous to his appointment under the Calcutta University, he had sent me Vidya Sundar by Kabi-Kanka, the *baramashi* of Lila and the Gopini Kirtan by the poetess Sula Gáyin. These he had collected in April, 1921. Chandra Kumar secured some exquisite Kabi songs chiefly on Radha Krishna from one Satis Chandra

Das, a merchant of Kalipur in his district. He sent me 'Bheluá Sundari' in two parts on the 6th April, 1922, and Asamá on the 13th June, 1923.

A list of poems collected up to now. I have received from him up to now the following poems on various dates :

List.

		Lines.
1.	Mahua by Dwija Kanai	755
2.	Malua	1,247
3.	Jay Chandra and Chandrávati by Nayanchand Ghosh	354
4.	Kamalá by Dwija Ishan	1,210
5.	Dewan Bhábná	378
6.	Kanka and Lila by Raghusut, Damodar, Nayanchand and Srinath Baniya	1,122
7.	Dewana Madina by Mansur Bayati	758
8.	Rupavati	493
9.	Kenaram by Chandrávati	1,054
10.	Kajalrekha	480
11.	Dewan Masnadali (excluding prose matter) ...	877
12.	Feroj Khan	960
13.	Bhelua Sundari	1,402
14.	Jiralani	828
15.	Madan Kumar-O-Madhumala (excluding prose portion)	96
16.	Vidya Sundar by Kavi Kanka	1,489
17.	Ramayana by Chandrávati	747
18.	Kavi songs	660
19.	Radha Krishna and Jatra songs (spoiled by worms) about	620
20.	Asama Sundari	527
21.	Gopini Kirtan by Sula Gayan	1,060
22.	Dewan Manhar Khan	880

We have altogether received 17,297 lines of these old songs and balladas up to now.[1]

[1] Slight discrepancies between the numbers of lines given on this list and those stated in the preface to the ballads are due to omissions in counting the preliminary hymns in some cases and in others owing to printing errors which were left unnoticed during the revision of proofs. But as the original texts are published separately, the readers will be able to calculate the numbers accurately if necessary.

I would not have been more pleased if these lines were all gold. The songs, perfectly artless, written mostly by Hindu and Muhammadan peasants, often show the real heart of poetry and some of them at least, I believe, will rank next only to the most beautiful of the Vaisnava songs in our literature.

II

Eastern Mymensing

Early History.

But before we dicuss the merits of these ballads, it is necessary to say a few words about the political and cultural history of Eastern Mymensing, from which most of these beautiful specimens of our old rural literature have been recovered. The Eastern part of Mymensing, indeed the whole of the kingdom of Pragjotispur of which it once formed a part, acknowledged the sovereignty of the Gupta kings in the 4th century A.D. During the best days of the Pal kings, Pragjotispur had acknowledged their sway, but with the decadence of their power it gradually separated itself from the great empire and asserted its political independence in a complete manner.

The Sen kings, along with their new conquests, carried their propaganda of converting the whole country into the Brahmanism of the new order; but Eastern Mymensing, had for a long time, remained true to the throne of Pragjotispur. When the latter power decayed in the thirteenth century, this part reduced itself to several small principalities ruled by the Rájvansis, the Hajangs and the Koches who were generally known to the Hindus by the common name of the "*Kirats*." They had a seat in Jangalbari in the Kishoreganj sub-division, where the last Rajvansi chiefs, Lakshan Hazra and Ram Hazra, were ousted of their dominions by Isha Khan about 1590 A.D. In the north one Vaisya Garo, another chief of that semi-Aryan tribe, ruled till the thirteenth century and was overthrown by one Someswar Pathak—a Brahmin chief, the founder of the present family of the Maharajas of Susang Durgapur. Someswar is said to have come from Kanoj in 1280 A.D. The great river Someswari still bears the name of the tutelary goddess of this Brahmin conqueror. At a place called Garh Jaripa near Serpur, Dalip Samanta, another Rajvansi chief, ruled in the 15th century; the ruins of his fort are still to be seen and called Jaripá, a corruption of the word Dalip. This Rajvansi chief was killed by Majlish Humayun, a general of Firoj Shah in 1491 A. D. The other towns which formed administrative centres in Mymensing under these semi-Aryan chiefs till the 15th century were Bokainagar, Madanpur and Khalijuri.[1] Eastern Mymensing, called Muzzambad by Mahomedans, extended up to Laur in Sylhet, and was finally conquered by Husen Saha in 1513.

From the south of the Garo Hills where begin the territories of the Rajas of Susang to the northern frontiers of the district of Dacca comprising Kapasia, Bhowal and Dhamrái, the vast tract of country was thus for long ages swayed by the Kamrupa Rajas, and the religion of the people was old Hinduism broadened by Buddhist ideas. I have already referred to the fact that this kingdom gradually made itself free from Kamrupa and resolved itself into small fragments ruled by the various tribes of the Koches. But they remained true to the ancient culture disseminated by the Hinduism of the pre-Renaissance type. Bhowal and Kapasia, the original seats of the manufacture of the Dacca muslin, were ruled by the Koch king Sisupal in the 11th century. Savar was snatched away from the Rajvansis by the ancestors of Haris Chandra probably in the 12th century, as we learn from an inscription of Mahendra, his son, published in the Dacca Review of 1920. Dhamrai was ruled about this time by Jasapál whose name is associated with the celebrated god Jasa Madhab of that ancient town.

[1] Kedar Nath Majumdar's History of Mymensing, p. 28.

The priestly religion dominated over by Brahmins, regarded as demi-gods,—based on caste-orthodoxy and Kulinism and founded by the Sen dynasty, could have no access into the Eastern part of Mymensing. In fact, the enemies of Ballal Sen often took refuge in these regions of Eastern Bengal for protection. It is well-known that Ballal Sen was opposed by his own people in his autocratic ways of re-building the caste system. The Barendra Brahmins refused to recognise his new order of Kulinism.[1] The Suvarna-Vaniks openly assumed a hostile attitude as will be seen from the testimony of the Ballal Charit. The king incurred the displeasure of his own son Laksman Sen by his attempts to raise a woman of the Dom caste, named Padmini, to the status of the chief queen. We find from the traditions current in the countryside and from numerous Sanskrit *slokas*, said to have been interchanged between the father and the son, that Laksman Sen headed a party against his royal father and fled to Eastern Bengal and remained there for some time to escape from the wrath of his infuriated father. Ballal had tried to persuade the principal citizens of some of the higher castes recognise the Dom woman Padmini as his chief queen, by taking food cooked by her. Those who carried out the royal order got thrones of solid gold as reward. They were branded as "Svarnapithis" or "Owners of golden thrones" by the more respectable and orthodox of the Hindu community and lost their status in society inspite of the patronage accorded to them by the monarch. This is mentionod in the Kabikanthár, Chaturbhuj and other old genealogical works written in the 16th century. "**वल्लालस्यान्नदोषेण**"—"Branded by infamy for taking food at the palace of Ballal"—is a line which we often come across in those genealogical books. It is found in an old document dated **1132** A.D., mentioned by Babu Kedarnath Majumdar in his History

[1] "বারেন্দ্র কায়স্থ, বৈদ্য, বারেন্দ্র ব্রাহ্মণ। বল্লাল মর্য্যাদা নাহি লৈল তিন জন।" কুল প্রবাদ।

of Mymensing (p. 25) that one Ananta Dutta settled in the village of Kastul in the Subdivision of Kishoreganj to escape from the persecution of Ballal Sen. A stanza in this interesting document runs thus :—

> " चन्द्रर्त्तुंशून्यावनिसंख्यशाके
> वल्लालभीत: खलु दत्तराज: ।
> श्रीकण्ठनाम्ना गुरुणा द्विजेन
> श्रीमाननन्तौ विजह्नौ च वङ्गम्" ॥ [1]

Thus it will be seen that the whole of Eastern Mymensing with the hilly lands dotted over by Bhowal, Savar and Dhamrai in the district of Dacca, were under the sway of of the Rajvansis, the Garos and other tribes whose culture and civilisation were quite different from those of the school dominated over by the Brahmins established by the Sen dynasty. These semi-Aryan tribes were a powerful and peace-loving people and loved art and literature. Some scholars have tried to prove them to be identical with the Panis of Rig-Veda known in history as Phœnicians. Mr. Nagendranath Vasu in his history of the Kamrup Rajas has, I believe, very ably started and established this theory. It was due to their encouragement that Dacca *muslin* owed its high excellence in ancient times. They were great traders and held liberal views on religious matters as will be observed from the fact that though Hiuen Tsung was a Buddhist zealot, he was invited by Bhaskar Burman of Kamrupa, a Hindu of Hindus, to visit his capital. The big cannon of Dacca called Jhumjhum Khan and its twin brother, Kalu Khan now lost in the Buriganga, had been probably manufactured in the royal factory of some Raja of these tribes, though they were latterly possessed by Moslem chiefs and adopted Muhammadan names.

[1] In Saka 1061 (1139 A.D.) Ananta Dutta, a prince of the Datta family, left Banga (Bengal, in which Eastern Mymensing was not included at that time) for fear of Ballal Sen, with his Guru Srikanta.

The Brahminic Literature.

We have been taking a survey of the political history of these places chiefly with the purpose of showing that the culture disseminated there was found materially different from and opposed to the dogmas of the Renaissance Brahmins.

The Hinduism or more properly speaking Brahmanism planted by the Sen kings with the help of the Kanoj Brahmins emphasised devotion to God and altogether ignored *Karma* (action). The Brahmins went so far as to say that one could not commit so many crimes in his life as might not be expiated by merely uttering the name of God once in a devout spirit. By accentuating devotion they lost sight of the ethical side of religion without which the ordinary machinery of social life could not work. The Brahmins enacted rules for *Gauridán*—or marriage of daughters eight years old and left no field to the bride or bridegroom for selection by mutual choice. They laid down strict rules in regard to taking meals, for fast and vigil, which are no doubt important and essential for purely spiritual purposes, but they disregarded secular ideas in the most uncompromising tone and left no door open for romance in matters between the sexes. Above all, they enforced strict obedience to Brahmins who were to be held even higher than the gods. In fact the old social fabric was now reconstructed mainly on the basis of a reverence to the Brahmins verging on worship.

In the Vernacular literature from the 14th century down we find Brahminic ideas of the above type fossilised; we find a supreme Brahminic dignity maintained with a supreme regard for Sanskrit. During this age Sanskrit metaphors and similes were largely imported into Bengali. Indeed the Vernacular of Bengal was so highly Sanskritised by the Renaissance Brahmins, and its metamorphosis so completely hid its original Prakrit form, that some of our people have been erroneously led to trace its orgin to Sanskrit and explain its construction by the rules of Panini and Mugdhabodha.

But when we come to these ballads we come to an altogether different atmosphere. The difference forcibly commands our attention showing the state of Hindu culture before the priestly Renaissance in an unmistakable manner.

A quite different standard of culture.

The high cultural level reached by the people of Eastern Mymensing is manifest in their folk-lore and ballads. In the style of composition and in spirit they show, as I have stated, a quite different standard from that inspired by the Brahmins. Here the girls select their own bride-grooms and they do not marry before attaining puberty. Mahua was sixteen years old when she fell in love with Naderchand. Mahua, Bhelua and Kamala were sixteen when they felt the "pangs of the five arrows" and got themselves married. If the choice of the girls ran counter to that of their guardians they did not yield to the decision of their elders, but followed the bent of their own minds. In doing so they remained pure and true to their vows and still behaved as modest women without showing that spirit of defiance and coquettish revolt which have characterised the heroines of some of our modern novels. On the other hand their spirit shows the holy flame of unflickering devotion with a graceful modesty and firmness of purpose which truly adorn the feminine nature. Mahua, though so meek and lovely, shows her quiet resolve and uncompromising preference when she says to her foster-father that Naderchand is like the sun while Shujan whom she is commanded to marry is like a glow-worm. The girl Sunai who has just attained her fourteenth year writes a love letter to Madhab. No girl of a Hindu family dominated over by modern Brahminic influence would dare write a love-epistle before her marriage. There is a frankness mingled with a spirit of freedom from all conventions and *sastric* canons which gives a sense of relief to our souls sickened by Brahminic rigidity in matrimony. Sunai escapes from her uncle and guardian Bhatuk, in order to follow her own choice in marriage, and Sakhina in spite of the opposition of her father, Omer Khan—the chief of Kella Tejpur—marries Firoj Khan of Jangalbari, nay, wages a war against her father to rescue her husband from prison. No girl would show such boldness in a Muhammadan home governed now by almost the same rules of discipline and obedience as are prevalent among the Hindus. Chandrávati after her disappointment in love takes the vow of maidenhood for life with her father's permission,—a course which is unheard of in Bengal during the several centuries since the days of the Buddhist Bhikkhunis. Kamala delivers her wonderful speech before the Raja of Raghupur, in which her pathetic appeal, no less than her modesty, moves the whole court to compassion, though like Desdemona she feels no shyness in describing the story of her love before her distinguished audience, presided over by no less a personage than the Raja himself. Lila is free as Mahua; no convention, no caste-prejudice, and no false modesty check her sentiments—pure and fragrant as the Indian lotus.

From this Eastern Mymensing were also recovered the five wonderful folk-stories called by Babu Dakshinarajan Mitra Majumdar, "The *Giti-kathas*" of which Malanchamala displays the very flower of Indian womanhood and its fully blossomed ideal.[1] Malancha, Mahua, Malua, Sakhina, Kajalrekha, Kamala, Lila and Chandrávati are all flowers from the same garden; the world's dust cannot soil them, and their inborn sweetness and purity assert themselves in all their severe trials. Kanchanmala of the *giti-kathas* is the twin sister of Malancha and should be placed in the front rank of our heroines. Like the treasures of Luxor these have been our latest and richest find. We knew only of one such woman—Behula in our old vernacular literature; but

[1] See "Folk Literature of Bengal" (Calcutta University), pp. 265-319.

we have here at least a dozen of the same type, showing the level of culture and force of character of quite a unique type.

Now if we take a bird's-eye view of the tract of land covered by Susunga and Garo hills on the north, run over by the rivers Someswari and the Kangsa, and gradually passing to the south-east, glance at the sub-divisions of Netrakona and Kishorganj, and then wend our course to the south-west up to the limits of Bhowal including Kapasia, Tangail and some portions of Savar and Manikganj, now forming the northern limits of the Dacca district, we have a well-defined boundary-line of a large country which had once formed a part of the old province of Assam under the sway of the Rajas of Pragjotispur, and which never bore any sign of the priestly influence, that has marked Bengal proper under the domination of Brahminic revival. The nick-name given to this part of the country by the Brahmins of the Renaissance is *baju* which is derived from the word *barjita* (prohibited). It is a prohibited area, because the Rajas who reigned there were found too formidable for the Sen Rajas to cope with, and the Brahminic canons with their 'Kaulinya' and stringent marriage rules could find no access into it. But this tract of land, ruled by a different society and a different standard of moral and communal life, is extremely interesting to us; as its culture is indigenous, and far more natural and fresh than that of the Renaissance. Where could a man be found like Garga amongst the Renaissance-Brahmins who had the courage to take a lad into his family and treat him like a son, though from his babyhood the boy was reared up and suckled by a Chandal-woman? Where could a Brahmin be found like Kanka who bowed down publicly to his foster-parent—the Chandal woman—and said that he considered her to be more sacred than all the shrines taken together? This society was not one of dogmas but of real life which flowed in its natural course. The characters painted in the ballads show great freedom and independence but are no propagandists. Being true offsprings of Nature, they never mislead us by settled and pre-conceived ideas but always elevate us by their direct inspiration and innate freshness. They do not depend on divinity but on their own action. They are full of tacts and resourcefulness. Mahua, when she felt a misgiving as to her chance of meeting Naderchand, resolved to commit suicide; but she instantly recollected that all possible recources had not yet been tried. So she proceeded on to make a further search for her lover without yielding to despair. She said that she would not end her life until she had tried her very best. Any of the characters in our Renaissance-literature under similar circumstances would sit down to weep and pray, depending entirely upon Providential help. This resourcefulness and self-dependence mark out the characters as essentially distinct from the Renaissance men and women. In the conception of the latter, devotion and faith have been emphasised and the ethical side completely ignored. The Hinduism prevalent in Eastern Mymensing followed the Buddhist maxim "As you will sow, so you will reap."

Localities connected with the ballads.

From Durgapur we are expecting every day "Raja Raghur Pálá." He was a descendant of Someswar Sing who usurped the throne of Susung from Vaisya Garo, the Koch Raja, in the 13th century. The devotion of the queen Kamala and her sacrifice form the essence of the plot of this ballad. The river Kangsa which streams out of Someswari is associated with Mahua and Naderchand. Here the unfortunate hero met his love after months of weary search, alas! to be cruelly assassinated by Homra's gang! The river Dhanu is mentioned in the ballad of Kenaram. It flows by Pergana Khaliajuri, which was in those days known as the 'Bhati.' The 'Bhati' in the 15th century fell into the hands of a Kshatriya chief named Lambodara.

Jahangir calls this *pergana* and its adjacent places by the common name of 'Bhati' in the *sanads* which he granted to the descendants of Lambodar. The line "ভাটী হইতে আইল বাঙ্গাল লম্বা লম্বা দাড়ী" in the Mainamati songs clearly refers to this portion of Mymensing. Close by the river Dhanu and bordering on the eastern boundaries of Pergana Khaliajuri lay the ancient villages of Bamun Kandi, Baman Thakurer bhiti, Badiar dighi and Ulnakandi, where the gayest of the singing birds in these ballads—Mahua—first listened to the flute of Naderchand and yielded herself to his embrace, and where her uncle Manik's eyes feasted on the sight of the rich *shali* crops that sprang in the fields of Uluakandi. Further down, about nine miles south of Khaliajuri lies Arulia, on the river Bahadair, a branch of the Dhanu, a village which will at once recall to the minds of the readers of Malua, the blind tank overgrown with weeds and water-plants and fenced on its four sides with hedges of the thorny *mándár* plants. It was here that Chand Binod had stood awhile witnessing the beautiful wood-land scene and the transparent water of the tank appearing like silver linings at intervals of weeds and plants with which it was covered. Here did his *Kora* send one of its wild shrieks which startled Malua and which made our hero who had fallen asleep on the landing steps to open his eyes and behold the loveliest flower that ever sprang up in such a lonely place—Malua, the heroine of the tale. Close to Arulia still flows the Sutia on the banks of which once stood the fine and artistic bungalows that Chand Binod had built with his own hands. The Dhalai *bil* abounding with purple-coloured lilies which offered a mild resistance to the pinnace of Dewan Jahangir as it proceeded on, led by Malua's directions, is about nine miles from Arulia and ten miles from Jahangirpur, the seat of the Dewan Sahib. There are more ballads which we expect from Chandankandi, Budhpasa and Raipur. The ballads secured from Jangalbari are full of a geographical interest, and though the subject relates to the adventures of the Muhammadan Dewans, they show a kindred element to the other ballads both in language and spirit, particularly in the character-sketches of the heroines.

Further down near Tangail was the old Chandrapur mentioned in the folk-tale of Malanchamálá; and the recent publications of Bengal folk-tales by Muhammadan writers have mostly issued from Tangail and Manikganj. The story of Malanchamálá itself was secured from a village near Tangail by Dakshinaranjan Mitra Majumdar.

Duftaries.

We find that Duftaries as a class are recruited in Calcutta from Eastern Mymensing and the neighbouring places. These people were called '*kagajis*' in Pre-English days. Hindus and Buddhists were at one time the founders of great libraries, especially the Buddhists who made immense collection of books in their monasteries. The '*kagajis*' (*lit.* makers of paper) did not give up their calling but continued in their hereditary avocation when they turned Muhammadan converts. The existence of a large community of Duftaries in this part of Bengal bear evidence to the extensive cultural progress which it had made in ancient times.

From what has been said above, it will be observed that this region of ballads and folk-tales possesses a special interest to the Bengalis, specially to the people of Eastern Bengal, for these songs of our rural poets are some of the best ever composed in our literature, though we have been late in discovering them. The Hindus and Muhammadans have made equal contributions to this literature; at times we find the composer to be a Muhammadan and the singers Hindus and at others *vice versá*, and the language is the common country dialect spoken by both the sections.

III

The School of Indigenous Songs and that of the Renaissance —a Comparison and a Contrast.

The Sanskritic style and spirit.

There is certainly a classical dignity in Kabikankan (16th century) and more especially in Bharat Chandra (b. 1712) who are the great land-marks of the two different epochs of the Renaissance literature. Kabikankan is a poet of the transition period and undoubtedly ranks high among Bengali poets of his age. His English translator, Mr. E. B. Cowell, justly compares him to Chaucer and Crabbe. But Kabikankan makes a hotch-potch of the classical and the indigenous elements in his poem. There is much of a rustic character in it though attempts have been made by the poet to refine the crude material by classical elements of the Renaissance School; while Bharatchandra, though he introduces scenes of vulgar and erotic humour in his poem of "Annada Mangal," is admittedly the high priest of the temple raised by the Renaissance Brahmins. His humour may be crude but there is no crudeness whatever in his language which is highly polished and dazzles us with its Sanskritic splendour.

But these ballads of Mymensing are pure Bengali and there is hardly any obtrusive Sanskritic element in them. They are all unadulterated metal of a high quality recovered from the purely Bengali mine. Most of the old Bengali poems, outside Vaisnava songs, struggle to express the classical ideas that had come with the new priests from Kanouj. The characters painted in them are seldom sustained or consistent. The poems are monotonous and they often embody an almost encyclopædic mass of traditions after the Sanskrit Purans whose foot-prints they seem to follow. In the enthusiasm of the poet, to say a thing in the literary style approved by Sanskrit Poetics, they often lose sight of their plots and characters. In fact, the attention of these poets seems to be devoted more to the style which they want to Sanskritise than to the subject-matter of their poems.

In fact, the Brahminic school, planted in the field of Bengali literature, suddenly coming in contact with the polished and artistic expressions of the Sanskrit language, lost sight of all other points and devoted itself entirely to embellishing the style and importing Sanskrit expressions and figures of speech. The Bengali language thus became bound up by an almost servile allegiance to Sanskrit Poetics. From rich figures of speech and high-sounding flowery expressions, down to the frivolous puns on words and the passion for alliteration that characterise the style of the latter-day Bengali poets, we owe all our elegance and flaws in the field of letters to the new school that had sprung up as the result of a conquest of our language by Sanskrit. In Kabikankan Chandi there is indeed a redeeming element in the genuine accounts of Bengali life, but they are often disturbed by accretions of exotic classical ideas which guided the taste of the Renaissance-poets. These classical ideas have been made so familiar to us within the last four hundred years that they appear almost natural ; but when we read the Renaissance poems side by side with the Mymensing ballads and other poems of the indigenous school, which bear on them the hall-mark of Bengali society before the Brahminic revival, we cannot help calling the classical element somewhat exotic and artificial.

The excellence of the ballads.

Indeed, these ballads and songs have come upon us with all the suddenness of a literary surprise. They are generally short and there is no repetition in most of them. The attention of the poets does not swerve a bit from the subject they treat of and the descriptions move with the utmost speed towards the end which often rises to great pathos and poetic excellence.

The heroines of these songs are not at all like those with whom we are familiar in the Renaissance literature. I have stated that in the previous order of society every bride used to select her own groom. This is quite contrary to the Brahminic canons which lay down that the most approved year when a girl should be married is the eighth. Married then she would rank with the goddess Gauri, the consort of Siva. Kabikankan evidently draws his inspiration from Brahminic jurisprudence when he refers to the duties of the parent, on this point. He is evidently struggling with the material found in the old poems of Chandi, which he is re-writing. He is trying to give a Brahminic tone to the traditional subject, which he does not dare change wholesale. The age of the girl has to be kept as he found it. Janardan Ojá, the family priest of Dhanapati the merchant, is made to admonish Lakshapati for allowing his daughter to remain unmarried, though she has stepped into her twelfth year. The indignant Brahmin explains the canons of the Renaissance school on this point :—

"It is an act of merit, O Lakshapati, to give a daughter in marriage at her seventh year. If a son be born to such a girl in due course he will indeed be the saviour of the whole family. At her eighth year, a bridegroom should be sought for with sweet words and the daughter's hand be offered him without charging him any *pan* (money). If in the ninth year you get a bridegroom for her—that is also good ; the son born of the pair will, by offering *pinda*, secure for you and your ancestors, a place in heaven.

"Alas! there was no one to instruct you in these most vital points of religion ; you remained stupidly indifferent when your daughter passed her tenth year. When she is in her eleventh year, she becomes seized with a woman's desire and you have not done rightly by allowing that year to pass also. In her twelfth year she attains her puberty[1] she may, any moment, take a fancy for a handsome youth, then the parents will be assuredly doomed to the pangs of hell."

["সপ্তম বৎসরে কন্যা, বিভা দিলে হবে ধন্যা, তার পুত্র কুলের পাবন। অষ্ট বর্ষে বর আনি, কহিয়া মধুর বাণী, পণ বিনা কর সম্প্রদান। তার পুত্র দিলে জল, সুরপুরে পায় স্থল, পিতৃলোক পায় বহু মান। কেহ না বুঝ্যাল তোমা, গত হৈল দশ সমা, তথাচ না কৈলা কন্যা দান। প্রবেশিলে একাদশে, মদন হৃদয়ে বৈসে, নব-রস হয় একস্থান। এগার বৎসর গেল, না করিলে কর্ম্ম ভাল, অপযশ করিলে সঞ্চয়। দ্বাদশ বৎসর বেলা, হয় কন্যা রজস্বলা, পুরুষেরে নাহি করে ভয়। নর দেখি অনুপাম, যদি কন্যা করে কাম, পায় পিতা নরক যন্ত্রনা "]

The women in these ballads marry after reaching their puberty and, as I have already said, nowhere in these poems is found an instance when the woman is not guided by her own personal sentiments when selecting her mate, and in no case does she blindly follow the selection of her guardian.

In the Renaissance literature this freedom and romance in sexual love would by no means be tolerated by the Brahmins. The idea of chastity in woman was fossilised by Brahminic canons. All freedom in woman was suppressed and she was reduced to a machine without life. In the Bengali poems written in the 17th and the 18th centuries, this artificiality reached its clinax. Jaynarayan, the East Bengal poet of the 18th century, puts the following piece of advice in the mouth of Chandra Bhan, the hero, in his address to his consort Sunetra on the eve of his starting on a sea-voyage. "During my absence, oh Sunetra, shun the shadows of all male persons as one would shun black snakes. If the voice of any male person reaches your ears, consider it as terrible as the sound of thundor." In an earlier age Krittibas had made Sita, when unjustly suspected by her husband,

[1] Puberty in the sense in which it is used here in this tropical elimate of ours is attained by girls rather early. So the poet is not very far from truth in his statement of the age of the girl in this respect.

say in defence of her character. "Even when I was a mere child I never came too close to a male play-fellow." If one compares these moral sicklings confined within the four walls of the zenana, afraid of light and air as if they were contamination, with the bold sketches of the heroines of these Mymensing songs, what a relief one would feel! The Vaisnava poetry indeed revolts against the orthodox society and spiritualises free love in the 'Sahajia' songs. But these rustic poems give us faithful pictures of devoted women in Bengali homes—the sisters of those who ascended the funeral pyres of their husbands and were true to them in life and death. They represent the ideal of a by-gone society and are not like the Sahajia women, the productions of a revolt.

Devoid of any priestly element, without any racial or sectarian propaganda, these songs have features in them which have a universal appeal. The air that we breathe in these songs is not like the storm that has come from the west in our modern literature, nor does it reach the dulness and the freezing point of the canonic artificiality of the Brahmnic Renaissance. But it is the air of Bengal blown on her fields and pastures, fresh and full of life. The homes described are Bengali homes. The landscapes, the rivulets, tanks, the landing steps are all of Bengal with a photographic accuracy. The characters speak the Bengali tongue and do not too scrupulously avoid the few Arabic and Persian words that have naturally crept into our popular dialect. They express Bengali sentiments without pretensions to metaphysical culture. They do not voice the ideas of Kalidas, Bhababhuti, Vyasa or Valmiki, but of the true Bengali men and women of the country-side. Chandravati's 'Ramayana' is as remote from the epic of Valmiki as a playful streamlet is from the whirl-pools of the Atlantic or of the Black Sea. A great stress is laid in these ballads on human passion, and seldom do the writers trouble themselves with the codes of the Hindu Jurisprudence. The Renaissance poet Kashidas says, "He who eats radish in the month of February (Magh) goes to the worst of hells." All such gibberish is out of question in this poetic literature. Seldom do the poets pour fourth reflections on the fleeting nature of worldly things and their transitoriness after the aphorisms of the apostles of the Brahminic cult. The characters solve their own destinies without seeking the aid of the gods. The poems are bright with sunny realistic descriptions. Yet human love reaches a height in them, which verges on the idealistic and is full of romance. Action is the motto and not spiritual devotion. And in these two words we have the entire key to the standards of the different schools of the Renaissance literature and of that which preceded it. Though the poems represent the old social order there is nothing in them of the queer theology of the Dharma cult, which inspired the Maynamati songs. Indeed they are entirely free from all mysticism and influence of Tantric miracles. The poems mirror life—the best ideas that permeated the Hindu society prior to Renaissance, and in which the simple but high life of the Bengalis is portrayed with fine poetic touches. Above all, the heroic element, the majesty, courage and wealth of feelings that characterise the Bengali women—their almost fanatical devotion to those whom they love, are brought forth with a force and vividness—the parallel of which it will be difficult to find elsewhere in the vast range of our literature.

The female characters in these poems and songs, I beg to repeat, possess a towering grandeur. They are resourceful, heedless of danger, and true as truth itself. But the environment of social bondage has an inevitable influence over them. Even the greatest of them find themselves helpless in fighting against the commandment of society which they know to be unalterable as the decree of fate and to which they submit without a protest. The ever-patient spirit of Indian women since the days of the exiled princess of Ayodhya has never shown a spirit of revolt but fallen a silent victim to the social altar. The Hindu wife is accustomed to accept the unjust brand of infamy on herself without a word of protest against her social tyrants. Even, Mahua—the entirely free bird in the sky of pure love—lifted her knife at the command of her father to kill her own Naderchand! Alas! the father's command which had made Ram leave the palace and turn an ascetic, and Parasuram kill his own mother! That inviolable conventional regard for the word of the elders and that age-long law of Hindu social life have entirely benumbed and enervated the people of India. Mahua, who sings like the lark and in whom we see the holy light of love ever-burning incensed with Nature's purity, yields to the weakness for a moment only. After this momentary frailty, her true nature asserts itself and she drops the knife that she lifted. For this conventional regard for the word of parents, innocent Lila could say nothing even by way of self-defence when she was groundlessly charged with infidelity. Social ostracism and tyranny these women accepted as the inexorable decree of fate. All their heroic energy and resourcefulness failed them here. Whatever wrongs they received from society, howsoever deep and unjustifiable, they bore with patience and had not the courage to utter a word against this hoary-headed wicked monster of human convention and prejudice.

IV

A General Survey of the Ballads.

In **Malua** we find a strange heroism and we know not whether to admire her sweet emotional nature or the ethical grandeur of her character the more. She is a spirit not at all influenced by a consideration of the things of the physical plane. In the hour of sore trial she could have gone back to her mother's arms and be happy for the rest of her life, still remaining true to her husband. Her fair name would not have been at all sullied by such an action. But she did not do so. Even when her husband took another wife and abandoned her, she remained near him, no matter, that she had not an access into the kitchen and to his bed-room. She obliged her husband to marry again. This she did not with the object of making a theatrical show or for a morbid sentimentalism. She felt that her husband's life would be miserable without a wife. When fatigued with the toil of the day, he would return home in the evening, who would give him meals, who would serve food to the poor old mother, grown unfit for work? The caste-rules would not allow them to take indiscriminate food in any place. She herself was made an outcast, and all those functions which it would have been the crowning joy of her life to discharge, she was rendered incapable of performing now. Loving her husband with all the might of her soul, she resolved to remove every thorn that would prick his feet in the walks of life, never caring for her own sentiments or comforts. Ultimately she gave up her life to remove the standing scandal that had hung on her husband's family and on his own fair name for *her* sakes. The grim Hindu society against which she vainly struck her head,—as unrelenting as the blind and impregnable Chinese walls,—as barbarous and cruel as her Muhammadan abductor,—as terrible as the life of chilling poverty which she voluntarily accepted and endured,—served only to accentuate her towering personality. And the last scene of her life—in which her white-crested virtue sparkles on the waves of the river like the crown of the goddess Lakshmi, sinking into the depths of the sea under the sage's curse—is one of superb tragic grandeur, and none will be able to read the touching and well-chosen refrains of the last page without having his eyes moist with tears.

Some of these characters—and we find it in the song of **Isha Khan** more than in others—are actuated by a spirit of retaliation. They sometimes look upon the misfortunes of their enemies with the complaisance of a savage warrior. Inspite of the genuine goodness of their nature they plot against the enemies like Machiavelei, though their primary object is to save themselves from some dangerous situation. These heroines show the deep feelings that actuate the womankind of the Orient, inspiring them with hatred and a spirit of revenge, when wronged, though they are otherwise the best specimens of their species. **Malua** of course is driven to such an extreme step by the exigencies of situation, but in the two daughters of **Kedar Roy** in the ballad of Isha Khan, the spirit of retribution shows itself in a monstrous light. Of course, self-defence is the plea everywhere, but when we see a soft thing growing terrible, we are involuntarily led to regret it to a little extent. Even **Kamala** whose power of endurance is martyr-like and who seems to be the abode of all womanly virtues, does not protest against the inhuman cruelty with which the Karkoon was slaughtered at the altar of Kali. In **Chandravati** we of course find deep wrongs only giving rise to a feeling of deep compassion and a spirit of self-dedication to the will of God. In **Lila** we find nothing but sweetness. She withered away with a smile on her face, and when her tender soul was torn by the wrongs done by her enemies, she died uncomplainingly, even as a flower fades, torn by wanton hands. But **Kajal-rekha**—the very soul of patience and sweet forbearance, has not a word to say protesting against the cruel murder of the Bracelet-Maid,—though certainly the latter is a demon of the grimmest type. I only say that it would be only more consistent with her own divine nature to intervene to lighten the cruel punishment.

The situations created in the wonderful ballad of **Mahua** are of a romantic plane, but nevertheless they do not cease to be dramatic. All prosaic details are skipped over. The author, Dwija Kanai, had a wonderful power of choosing situations which present to our imagination only poetic scenes, without encumbering them with too many realistic details. The first scene opens with a poetic picture and introduces the dawn of love in the hearts of the pair, half-hid in shyness, as if afraid fully to reveal itself, like the faint beams of the young moon on the ripples of a dark stream. Mahua is scaling the bamboo in order to reach the rope at the top. Hundreds of men are assembled to see the play. Nader Chand, the young and handsome lord of the place, sits among them. When the beautiful gypsy with the alacrity of a squirrel ascends the bamboo-top, Naderchand sees her for the first time. He is simply amazed at her beauty and stands up to observe her more closely, and when she plays her wonderful tricks and dances on the rope, he has no more the curiosity of a spectator. He already feels alarmed for her life and exclaims, "Ah me! she may fall and die."

This sweet compassion is the precursor of that vehement love which latterly made both of them stake everything near and dear to them for the sake of each other. In Malua too we find the same compassion gradually taking the shape of love. The situation is romantic. She is filling her pitcher in the stream. On the landing *ghat* sleeps Chand Binod. In the month of May, says the poet, the nights are short so that sleep sometimes lingers on the eye-lids even in daytime and one dozes and feels sleepy in the noon. The maiden felt that it was already a late hour of evening. If the handsome youth would go on sleeping and awake when the night was advanced, where would he go? He was a stranger there and did not know the village-paths. The clouds were roaring and the shadows of evening were already growing thick over the fair face of Nature. Where would he go and how could she make him awake? The scene becomes gradually more romantic. The water of the tank was dark-blue, on its sides was a thorny fence of the wild *mandar* plants. He lay under a *kadamba* tree covered with flowers, whose spike-like white petals adorned with the lovely yellow of their ball-like forms are inevitably associated with the rains of Bengal. Her feelings grew tender and when she retired to her bed chamber she could not sleep but thought, "The rains are falling and the night is dark. Ah me! Where does the stranger pass his night?"

Let us revert to **Mahua**, the second scene of the love-story brings us to the river *ghat*. The conversation of Mahua and Naderchand, full of pleasant humour and wit in that solitude, indicates the warmth of first love in Naderchand. But in Mahua it is not too apparent. True to her womanly instinct she is shy and forbears to use the language of sentiment. She even rudely reproves Naderchand when he hints at something like a proposal. All these only serve to show the feminine grace and reserve of her character. But she has already fallen in love, otherwise why should she come there in response to the request of the youth? Besides she tells Naderchand that her heart yearns for sympathy which she gets from no one. However covertly she hints at it, there is no doubt that she yearns to hear from the lips of Naderchand that in his heart sympathy is reserved for her. We should not be unsparingly hard upon Homra—the gypsy-chief. He knew it full well that though Naderchand would be an outcast in society, if he married Mahua, still there would be nothing to hinder him from enjoying his vast property. If Mahua would be given to him, the old chief would lose her forever. There is no doubt that he loved her with all the warmth of a father's heart. He very naturally wished that the beautiful gypsy girl should continue living with him to the last. She was by far the most attractive figure in the band of his players and if she left him he would not only be deprived of that affectionate attendance on him, which age wanted from youth, but his trade would materially suffer. Homra had already trained a young man named Sujan who would succeed him as the leader of the band. He had resolved to marry Mahua to him. Mahua, if she married him, would remain with the party for the rest of her foster-father's days and make him happy. This plan was now going to be frustrated ; hence his solicitude and efforts to keep her off from Naderchand ; when Homra said that Sujan was a handsome youth, Mahua retorted in his face that Sujan shone like a glow-worm by the side of her lord who was glorious as the sun. What wonder that the worst passions of a robber would be raised at this refractory conduct on the part of his daughter?

What strikes us in **Mahua** is an entire dearth of all superfluities. The very words are weighed without being deprived of their poetic grace. There is absolutely no place for convention here. Mahua and Naderchand do not talk of marriage or its sanctity. From the very first love sets its seal on the fate of the couple and this seal is never broken. What they want is to live like a pair of birds flying in the free illimitable sky. They owe no fealty to prejudices or custom, and always soar in an atmosphere of poetic emotion. Their happy life of a few days after their escape from the hands of the *sannyasi* is like a silver lining in their cloudy and ill-fated career of unremitting sorrows. This part of the story reminds us of the love of Haddi and Juan and charms us with its poetic spell. Curiously the old pirate of Don Juan bears also a family likeness to **Homra,** the gipsy chief. When faced by temptations Mahua does not make an indignant speech like Malua. In fact, the towering wrath of Malua when the Kazi sends her a proposal, rises to the majesty of a poetical outburst. But **Mahua** under similar circumstances scarcely thinks it worth her while to make a retort. She at once proceeds to take action. The entire situation becomes one of thrilling interest when after the glowing and long speech of the merchant, Mahua finishes the whole episode by her brilliant tactfulness in a few minutes and with a dramatic action which is as merciless as it is sudden.

In the last scene where **Palanka,** the true friend of the unfortunate gipsy-girl, with her sighs, songs and laments, sheds tears over her grave, as a solitary plant drops its gift of flowers over a burial-place, the pathos of the situation creates a tender impression on the mind which will follow the reader long after he has closed the pages of this remarkable poem. **Palanka,** was a true friend, true in life as in death. When she suspected the dawn of love in Mahua, she could foresee its fatal consequence and advised her to desist from the mad course. She gave the most practical advice by which a passion could be smothered in the beginning, *viz.*, not to see **Naderchand** for some days—but when she saw that her friend's case was a hopeless one she was full of sympathy for her. Before the last catastrophe she had signalled her to fly away. But this could not be done, and the last scene closing on the solitary figure of this maiden of a superb type, makes us bow down to her towering personality in silent admiration.

Miss Kramrisch has drawn attention to that romantic tale of medieval Europe Aucassin and Nicolete in connection with the ballad of Mahua. It is a happy coincidence that I had referred to that song of Europe while speaking of some of the Bengali ballads thirteen years ago in my History of Bengali Language and Literature (p. 164). My esteemed friend Mrs. M. M. Urquhart notices some points of similarity between the ballad of Mahua and " The Forest-lovers " by Maurice Hewlett. Indeed where Prosper and Isoult wander in the wilderness of East Morgraunt, there are situations which would remind one of the romantic life led by Mahua and Naderchand on the foresty banks of the hilly stream of Kangsa. But Hewlett's hero in the first stages of his career is a jolly good lad, innocent of all tender emotions and romance, and Isoult with her modesty and love finds herself like a ship stranded on a rock. Her love tinged with oriental idealism reaches the level of Christian ideal of self dedication and service. The pair illustrates Milton's maxim that man is born to rule and woman to yield to his sway. But the ballad of Mahua is absolutely free from all Hindu convention,

Despite their great social differences Naderchand and Mahua love each other at first sight and sacrifice everything at the altar of the blind god. "They have," says Kramrisch, "no other religion than that of the human heart in all its purity and strength."

The first part of the poem of **Kamala** does not show any peculiar excellence. The description of **Kamala's** beauty as that of **Lila** in **Lila and Kanka** is somewhat on the lines of the ornate style of the classical school. This is perhaps due to the fact that unlike most of the other writers of songs, the poet belonged to the Brahmanic caste. But, inspite of it and with occasional deviations, his spirit is akin to that of the rustic bards in whom the indigeneous element as a rule is found to predominate. Ishan's momentary sojourn in the artificial region of Poetics, however, shortly comes to an end, hardly leaving any impression, and the natural simplicity of the poet reasserts itself in the following cantos. The first few cantos are rather dull and even wearisome. The story grows tender and appealing from the time when **Kamala** all alone leaves her uncle's home and throws herself into the hands of fate without any other guide. Her short stay at the herdsman's cottage is of thrilling interest, and the pathos of the situation becomes irresistible from that point of time. The way in which **Kamala** rendered her whole hearted service to her protector is graphically described. From here the picture of the heroine becomes a living and vivid presentment of sorrows which deeply impresses the reader. Here in this cot the young falcon-hunter appears and here dawns on our youthful heroine those silver linings which give to her afflicted soul the romance of an altogether new character. Dilip Kumar pursues her as Gareth did Lynette, the difference being that **Kamala** was not inspired by contempt but by love from the very first. She kept her passion within herself as the bud does the fragrance and awaited the proper moment to disclose her sweetness to the world.

The poet **Ishan** very ingeniously makes her put her case before the Raja's Court. She frames no charge against the Karkoon. It would not be in keeping with the dignity and reserve of a high-caste Hindu woman to make even a bare statement of the facts of the case involving a breach of feminine modesty. She proves her case by documentary evidence alone and says nothing herself. From the beginning the poet carefully introduces documents in a quite unsuspected manner. They came quite naturally in the course of events; but when we find **Kamala** proving the case by dint of these alone with the help of other witnesses merely to corroborate them, we feel convinced of the motive and the art cleverly followed by the poet. The account of the twelve months—The '*baramashi*'—is full of pathos in the original and occasionally shows very lively poetic touches.

The description of **Nitai Kuttini** will remind one of the flower women Hira of Bharatchandra and of Bidu Brahmini and Lila Devi of Ramprasad and Mukunda Ram respectively. They seem to be of the same type. In the ballad, as in Kabi Kankan, stress is laid on these characters as sorceresses but the essential difference between the character of the ballad and that of Bharatchandra lies in the fact that while the ballad-maker builds his creation on materials all indigenous,—Bharatchandra assigns a classical refinement to his Hira. The ballad unmistakably proves that there were indigenous characters of this type in the old songs, one of which Bharatchandra took up and finished with his classical colouring, done to a fault.

These poems often scale great poetic heights by the use of refrains. These are to be met with in almost all of these ballads, though they do not come up to the excellence of those in the last passages of Malua.

The love tale of **Kanka and Lila** is one of the most charming things in our literature. They love each other with all the warmth of youthful love, yet curiously it is often like the affection between a brother and a sister. The holy flame of tender emotion in Lila burns pure like the lamp in a temple, yet all the intensity of womanly passion is there. Another interesting feature in this love—and what we find most remarkably in the story of **Malanchamala** of the old Bengali Folktales—is its complex character. The woman loves one and the same individual like a wife—like a sister and even like a mother. Our poets do not divide tender feelings and call them by separate names. I have dealt with these points at some length in my 'Folk-literature of Bengal.'

It is interesting to observe how little marriage laws had to do with the incidents of the love described in this poem. This is the more striking when we bear in mind that the story is one of a Brahmanic home. The end is tragic but there is another version of the poem in which the return of **Kanka** and his marriage with **Lila** have been drscribed.

That version I have not been able to secure yet. The more tender-hearted amongst the poets, opposed to pessimistic ideas, no doubt wanted to give a sunny view of life and thus alter the tragic tale into one ending happily. We find this to be also the case in respect of some Rajput ballads. There are two versions, one tragic and another with a happy sequel. And Sir George Grierson makes the following remarks on this point in his article on the "Popular Literature of Northern India" published in the "Bulletin of the School of Oriental Studies; Vol. I, Pt. III."

"Love ended disastrously, as such love must end in India, in the death of both the hero and heroine, but it is an interesting commentary on the sympathy with which the lovers are regarded by the mass of the people, that a very popular continuation of the story by another hand carries them to the Isles of the Blessed and shows them living together in happiness and peace, carrying on their old avocations amid their flocks and herds." (p. 88.)

In the *baramashi* in the poem of **Lila** the interest of the story is often sacrificed at the altar of poetry. It is always the case with a conventional thing in a poem. The poets while handling with it forget the thread of the narrative and sit quietly for sometime weaving words into the framing of an artistic garland of poetry. Of this, however, we propose to speak at some length shortly after.

The tale of **Kanka and Lila**, more than any other amongst the ballads collected, shows the Brahmin of the old school prior to Renaissance in a pronounced manner. In the account of Garga, who was not without his flaws and foibles, we find the older type of a Brahmin saint. He was not a slave of dogmas and kept his mind fairly open to conviction and sought divine grace by fast and vigil, when placed on the horns of a dilemma; whereas the Renaissance-Brahmin in such cases would certainly look for texts of Manu-Sambita and Raghunandan for guidance rather than try to solve his problem by the help of his conscience, his own intelligence or even by seeking divine grace. The wrongs that **Garga** did to poor **Lila** and **Kanka** were *boná fide* and though nobody would doubt for a moment that he acted madly, we feel that his wrath was a holy wrath, and howsoever we may condemn it, our sympathy is not altogether alienated from him. His great piety in taking care of a helpless orphan known as a *Chandal* by caste,—unclaimed by any and about to be starved on the cremation ground,—the pains he took to educate him and the generous treatment that the lad got at his home, his efforts to restore him to the Brahmanic caste in the teeth of opposition of the orthodox community,—show that he was a saintly character full of genuinely good and noble instincts though not exactly the model for the Renaissance Brahmins of the orthodox school. His great wrath produced by concocted evidences of the hostile camp, his mad resolve to kill his own daughter and **Kanka** and then to commit suicide,—his actually mixing poison with the food to be served to the innocent lad, show that he was a towering personality great in piety, and great in anger—of noble magnanimity and generous impulse—but of an uncompromising character, unable to stand what he considered a heinous crime. His subesequent repentance and great sorrows show that he was open to conviction and would not hesitate for a moment in admitting his faults when he understood them as such. With all his faults therefore he stands in this literature of ballads as an embodiment of all that is noble and high in a man. This was the type of the pre-Renaissance Brahmin of the old school.

Kanka, the hero of the tale, is a historical figure, as certainly all the rest of the characters of the poem are. In the preliminary verses of the 'Vidyasundar' written by him he sings praises of his *Chandal* parents. The woman of the *Chandal* caste who brought him up with all the affection of a mother, says our poet, "is pure as the Ganges." What Brahmin of the Renaissance would dare compare her with the holy Ganges and bow to her publicly, whatever her merits and his own personal obligations to her might be? This is a point to which I have already referred. All through these ballads we find a higher type of Brahmins than those familiar to us, held in the iron grip of caste-rules and superstitious beliefs. **Kabi Kanka** as described in this love tale is characterised by high qualities. The spirit of forbearance with which he looks upon the conduct of **Garga** who had tried to poison his innocent self is a remarkable feature showing his compassionate and forgiving nature. Even at that moment of a great wrong done to him, he retained the coolness of his head, nay an affectionate regard for the old Brahmin. He advised **Lila** not to lose her regard for her father whose head, **Kanka** said, was heated by the contrivances of the enemies. He assured her that he would surely repent his conduct when he would come to know them. In fact, accustomed as we are often to see the grim orthodoxy of the Brahmin community, we are struck with the contrast that the humane conduct and entire fearlessness of these Brahmins of the ballads offer to us in a striking manner.

It is curious and noteworthy that the ballads often deal lightly with the Brahminic faith about the efficacy of *jagnas* and prognostications of astrologers. In **Chandravati** and **Jaychandra,** the Brahmin astrologers after considering the horoscopes of the bride and the bridegroom declared that there could not be two horoscopes indicative of a greater happiness in nuptial life. Yet the events actually shewed that the pair were the most unfortunate of mortals. In **Rupavati** the astrologers are mercilessly caricatured. In the **Vidya Sundar,** by Kanka, Raja Malayaban performs the '*putresti*' and other *jagnas* which produce no fruit whatsoever. No writer of the Renaissance would have attributed failures to the prognostications of the astrologers or to the *jagna* ceremonies held infallible by the Hindus. The pet birds in a Brahmin's home, as we find in the **Lila,** do not recite the names of gods but call aloud the names of those who trained them. This is also what is opposed to the custom familiar to us.

V

The Baramashi Songs.

The earliest poetic tradition of the country was that a Bengali poem could not be complete without a *baramashi* or an account of the twelve months. Each of the twelve months of the year presents, as it were, a bioscopic scene on the landscape of this tropical climate of ours. There are flowers and fruits allocated to each of those months and even the tinge of clouds in the sky that hangs overhead varies with the varying seasons. This distinct season-mark which is apparent on the face of each of these twelve months, is an unceassing source of inspiration to our poets. In fact some of our old poems are known as *baramashis* though they comprise many things more than the word literally implies—it being a traditional and common name for lyric songs characterised by pathos. The story of Lila is called '*Lilar baramashi*' and that of Kamala as '*Kamalar baramashi*.' We have found *baramashis* even from the days of the aphorisms of Dak and Khana, composed probably in the ninth century. In the poems generally called by the name of *baramashi*, the poets usually presented accounts of the twelve months associated with the joys and sorrows of the chief characters delineated in them along with other things. And often an exaggerated importance is given to the *baramashis* not quite consistent with the thread of the narrative. Bharat Chandra and Jay Narayan Sen (18th century) were the last great poets who described the months following the foot-prints of the earlier Bengali poets.

Baramashi in Mahua and other ballads.

Among the Mymensing Ballads, 'Mahua' is by far the most free from all conventional ideas, but the *baramashi* is still there, though not in a loudly pronounced form. The poet Dwija Kanai does not halt over this poetic convention giving it an undue importance, to the detriment of the natural progress of the story, but only takes a passing notice of the months which, compared with the lengthy classical descriptions of other poets on the subject, does not strike us as a deviation from the main topics. In Lila and Kanka, the poets freely yield to the fascination of the old convention and to a certain extent mar the simplicity and flow of the story by introduction of long accounts of the months. It became quiet a craze with our old poets to describe the *baramashi*, and the stories have often lost some of their compactness and unity owing to the breach caused by such deviations.

The *baramashi* in Dewana Madina is, however, an exception to the rule. The poet being a thoroughly illiterate man did not care for the literary conventions of his country. His descriptions of months are short but full of thrilling pathos and by far the best to be met with in this literature of ballads from the points of view of brevity and relevancy.

VI

The Different Schools of Ballads and Songs—their Kinship in Language and Spirit.

Though none of these songs have come down to us from a period earlier than the sixteenth century, and though the original language has considerably been modernised by generations of minstrels who have sung them, it is clear that the spirit of the poems indicates a social order and literary standard which preceded the Renaissance. I have fully discussed this point in the course of these lectures and shewn that the poems disclose a state of society which is very different from that organised by the Brahmins of the Renaissance. I have stated that Mymensing was beyond the pale of Kulinism introduced by Ballal Sen and that the Sen Kings who were the patrons of the Hindu revival had no jurisdiction in the lands watered by the Dhanu, the Ghora-utra, the Kangsa and the Someshwari. The old order of society therefore continued till comparatively modern times in these places which the new Brahmins branded as "*bajudesh*" or 'the forbidden tracts.' If one should like to make a search for the facts of the early history of Bengal it would be well for the scholar to select his field of work in Sylhet, Tipperah, Chittagong, Noakhali, Bhowal, Mymensing and even in some parts of the Rajshahi district where the Sen Kings could not make their power felt in an appreciable degree. In these parts of the country one is likely to find very valuable materials for writing the early history of Bengal.

The social condition of the Hindu community differing in many respects from that of the present day, as disclosed in these songs, is not the only evidence to show that it belonged to a different and older school of thought and culture. Though the language has no doubt been modernised, yet there are evidences enough to show the kinship of these poems with the songs of Mainamati, Goraksha Vijaya, Krisna Kirtan, Sunyapuran and other works which were originally written before the Brahmanic revival.

Mannerisms.

There are certain mannerisms in the style of these earlier poems which are unmistakable. We find them in one and all of these poems and miss them altogether in the Renaissance literature. In pre-Renaissance literature a new episode is generally introduced by the queer phrase "কোন্ কাম করিল" (" what did he do after that?"). These words we find in every one of the works mentioned above, chiefly in the Mainamati songs. In these songs of Mymensing they occur very frequently. We need not refer to the texts as they are too numerous.

Common element.

Sometimes there are strikingly similar lines to be found in the Mainamati songs recovered from North Bengal and in these ballads obtained from Mymensing. We wonder how between the two widely distant places, separated by time no less than space, such a similarity could exist in language and spirit; for instance read the lines " দুগ্ধ মিঠা, চিনি গিঠা আর মিঠা ননী ; সগাৎ অধিক মিঠা মা বড় জননী" (Gopichandra, Calcutta University; ll. 675-76) and then read the text of Maluá (pp. 104-112, Canto XIV). The only explanations for this similarity is that these ballads and the Mainamati songs both belong to the one and the same school of the pre-Renaissance literature and are linked together not only by common ideas but also by set-phrases current in the atmosphere of that school. It is also a surprise to us to find that some of the most beautiful lines in Vaisnava poetry had their origin in these rustic songs evidently proving their pre-Vaisnava origin. For instance, the line "হাটিতে মাটীতে ভাসে অঙ্গের লাবণী" occurs in the ballad of Dewan Isha Khan and shows its very surprising similarity with the famous line "ঢল ঢল ঢল অঙ্গের লাবনি অবণী বহিয়া যায়" of Jnanadas. The ballad-maker had evinently no knowledge of Vaisnava poetry and this would be apparent to the readers of both these schools of poetry. We are gladly conscious of a unity of the whole of Bengal, eastern and western, in ideas, thought and language that had existed at a time when the new Brahminism had not yet linked the two provinces by a common religion.

Two and a half letters.

There are many little things besides, to be met with in these country-ballads, that show their kinship with the Mainamati songs and other works of the Pre-Renaissance school. The dowager queen Mainamati refers to the *Mahajnān* or the great esoteric knowledge contained "in two and a half letters." These "two and a half letters," the আড়াই অক্ষর, is a familiar expression in some of these ballads also. Malua writes an epistle to her brothers in two and a half letters, and Joy Chandra in the song of Chandrávati similarly writes a love-note to her in two and a half letters on the petals of a flower.

Manapavana.

The boat of '*manapabana*' is another such word. We have often found it occurring in Malua; and in the extensive literature of the period prior to Remaissance, the boat of '*manapabana*' is frequently mentioned. Whether it is a word to denote the fabulous speed of a boat, which could only be compared to the flight of a man's mind or that of the winds, or whether as some have imagined, the '*manapabana*,' was a kind of wood which was very light and strong and hence specially fit for the construction of sea-going vessels, cannot be definitely stated. But in the earliest of our folk-stories, in the Gorakshavijaya and its contemporary poems, as in these ballads of Mymensing, we find frequent mention of the '*manapabana*.' The earliest reference to it is, however, to be found in a *sloka* of the

Mahabharat where it is used as a metaphorical expression to denote the speed of a vessel compared to the flight of the winds or of the mind's course.

Nilakshár char.

Another familiar expression we find in these indigenous poems, is '*Nilakshár char*' which probably implies a dreary waste-land far beyond the habitation of man. We find Chand Binod carried to '*Nilakshár char*' for being buried alive. The word frequently occurs in our folk-lore where it sometimes takes the form of '*Tepántarer máth.*'

Months held auspicious for the marriage-ceremony.

We find in these poems customs and conventions contrary to those to which we have been accustomed in our present society, based on the canons introduced by the Renaissance. We all know that the month of Kartik is not auspicious for celebrating marriage ceremonies. No Hindu now would consent to perform a marriage in that month. Curiously, however, we find in the story of Malua a statement that Kartik was held specially auspicious by the people of Mymensing for marriage ceremonies at the time when the ballad was composed. "Hiradhar" (father of Malua), writes the poet, "expected that in the month of Kartik he would find a groom for his daughter, handsome as the god Kartikeya." Sravan (mid-July to mid-August) was held specially inauspicious by the people of the district at the time. It is said that Behula became a widow having married in that month. Though according to the convention that prevails now this month is not inexceptionable, yet hundreds of marriage ceremonies are celebrated during this month. It is not so specially inauspicious as indicated in the ballad. Asvin now, on the other hand, is branded as inauspicious. In the poem of Malua not a word is said against this month; the only bar to marriage ceremonies in Asvin, on which some stress is laid, is the fact that people busy themselves with the Pujas at the time and have scarcely leisure or the mood of mind to think of marrying their children. Thus we see that the social conventions that guided the affairs of men in this district a few centuries ago, are very different from those which obtain in Bengal at the present day, introduced, no doubt, by the Brahmanic revival and canonised by the jurisprudence of Raghunandan in the 16th century; but which were given a currency in Mymensing at a much later period.

Bengali taught in a Sanskrit *tol.*

It seems to us to be an important point that in the *tol* of Garga, along with the Samhitas and Purans in Sanskrit, *ferosai* songs, or those composed in Bengali and sung to order and the *baramashis* were taught to young pupils. In the literature born of Brahmanic Renaissance this would be quite impossible. Bengali crept into a corner, supported by rustic favour only, during the ascendancy of the Brahmin scholars and literally pined in the cold shade of priestly disdain. It could never have aspired to be a subject of studies in a *tol.*

The Prakrit elements as contrasted with those classical.

In fact, the Bengali of these songs is the pure country dialect. Sanskrit has no sway over it. Those who still labour under the misapprehension that the origin of Bengali is to be traced to Sanskrit, observing a preponderance of Sanskritic words in some of the Renaissance-poems, should read these ballads in order to be fully disillusioned. There are no Sanskritic dead-blocks to obstruct the natural simplicity of poetry in these. The Prakrit words, simple, sweet, and full of force and elegance, appeal straight to the heart and the verses in their limpid course move with the speed of a rivulet. I have had, more than once, occasions to mention that the whole of the Renaissance literature is permeated by Sanskrit metaphors and similes. The poets of this school never cared to observe things with their own eyes. They committed to memory certain passages from Sanskrit Poetics or from classical poems of that language, and whenever a description of a man or a woman was to be given they reproduced them from memory. The same stereotyped and hackneyed comparison without one word of original observation is to be met with everywhere. The face was to be like a lotus, the ears like those of a vulture, the neck of the form of a conch; the gait of a lady was compared to the grace of an elephant's movement; the lips were always like the *bimba* fruit in the delicacies of their colour, the eye-brows like the bow of Cupid or the rainbow and so forth. In the case of a man, his arms must reach the knee, the eyes should be so large as to stretch up to the ears, the nose to be like the beak of Gaḍura—the King of birds, etc. What one poet writes, the other poets repeat. The elegant poets tell all this in an attractive language; those who are not so gifted use a commonplace and stale language; but the same thing recurs in the descriptions; and so stereotyped the accounts are that the readers might altogether omit many passages without the risk of losing any poetical treat, however great the poet whose work they might be reading. This is the characteristic of all poets of the Renaissance School. But in these ballads, as in folk-tales and other works of the earlier period, we find the case to be completely different. The eyes of a lovely girl are compared in 'Kamala' to the beautiful *aparajita* flower. This flower grows abundantly in the countryside and offers a striking likeness to the dark eyes of the Begali women. It is certainly curious that the Bengali poets have so often stumbled over the huge blocks of Sanskritic figures, when there was such a simple path open to them near their own village-homes. The freshness of a *mahua* flower, the emblem of health and undecayed charm, which is a familiar sight here, never struck a Renaissance-poet who seemed to see everything through the eye-glass of classical culture. In these songs the face of a woman is often compared to the *mahua* flower with a great effect. Jaydeva, the Sanskrit poet, who had a greater knowledge of his rural country than the poets who followed him, once referred to this flower and called it *madhuka*,. and in the 'Krisnna-kirtan' of Chandidas, which is full of rural charm, we find references to it. The blind poet Fakir Faizu, who wrote one of these ballads—'Adhua Sundari and Surat-Jamal' beautifully describes the eyes of the heroine without caring for the classical metaphors. "He who has seen the dark eyes of the maiden, will never care to glance at the dark clouds of the sky or the dark waters of the river." This at once brings the whole wealth of dark colour of the oriental woman's eyes vividly before the mind.

There are many expressions in the songs which will at once recall their parallels found in Mainamati songs and other poems of the same school. The '*aver pankha*' or the fan of mica is a familiar and common article of luxury in all these works. In Malua we find the line "পাটের শাড়ী পইরা কন্যা সুখ নাহি পায়" (The girl does not even like to wear a *saḍi* of silk), and in the Mainamati song its parallel will be found in the line, "ঘিনে বাঁদী নাহি পিঁধে পাটের পাছুড়ি"

In fact, though the ballads are not certainly very old,—the chronological datum is of no importance here ; they owe little to Sanskritic influence—yet there are abundant characteristics in them to show that they belong to the pre-Renaissance school. As already noticed, they bear a striking likeness to the poems of Mainamati, Gorakshavijaya, Sunya puran, the folk-tales, the Bratakathas and other writings of the same school. In points of rural charm and true poetry, however, these ballads are by far the best of all other poems, excepting some four or five folk-tales of old Bengal, known as the *gitikathas*, of which the brightest gem is the story of Malanchamala. [1]

[1] An English translation of this story is to be found in my "Folk-literature of Bengal" (pp. 266-322).

VII

The Linguistic Peculiarities of the Songs.

Genuine Bengali words, which are Prakrit.

The songs of Mymensing possess a unique philological interest. They have been taken down by Chandrakumar as they are sung. In most cases the language is what the purists would sneeringly call *patois*. I will give here some of the words of the popular dialect found in the ballad, which will be interesting; they have not been Sanskritised when reduced to the written form, as such words are generally done in our literature; and it must be said to the credit of the compiler of the songs that he altogether abstained from giving to the words the usual classical shape which is familiar. In some cases the Prakrit forms of Mymensing are different from those in use in western Bengal as will be seen from our list. We find in Malua বচ্ছরের for বৎসরের, যদ্‌দূর for যতদূর, আইশ্‌না, for আশ্বিনা, পুতে for পুত্রে, হালি for শালি, (rice), শিগার for শিকার, জষ্ঠি for জৈ্যষ্ঠ, আঁধুয়া for অন্ধকার, গেরাম for গ্রাম, পাড়াপর্শির for পাড়াপড়শীর, আদিগুরি for আগাগোড়া, সাইসরসী for সাথী ও সখা, শায়ন for শ্রাবণ, আগন for অগ্রহায়ণ, বেবস্থা for ব্যবস্থা, গিরি for গৃহ, যৈবন for যৌবন, বৈদেশ for বিদেশ, ভাটুয়া for ভাট, তাপ্পা for তপ্ত, রইদ্র for রৌদ্র, সাউদ for সাধু, পর্‌তিশোধ for প্রতিশোধ; অপর্‌কাশ for অপ্রকাশ, উবাস for উপাশ, স্বীকুরি for স্বীকৃত, আশারি for আশান্বিত, বৈমুখ for বিমুখ, মাইন্‌সের for মানুষের, পাছুড়ি for পশ্চাৎ, পতিষ্ঠা for প্রতিষ্ঠা, পরাচিত্ত, for প্রায়শ্চিত্ত, দুপুরিয়া for দুপ্রহরিয়া, হাজি for সাজি, হেওলা for সেওলা, তিরি for স্ত্রী, etc.

It is a noteworthy point that in this literature which is full of the words of the popular dialect, none of the writers use so many words of indigenous origin, current in the popular speech, as does Fakir Faizu who was blind from birth. He could not read any written literature and dictated his poem in the very language that he spoke. This accounts for the spoken forms of words being retained in his composition in such a considerable degree. In his 'Adhua Sundari and Surat Jamal' which is a remarkable ballad from many points of view, we find words retaining the naked forms of Prakrit on almost every page. For instance, we find such words as হাচা for সাচ্চা (সত্য), চান্ for চাঁদ, ছোক, for শোক, রাজত্বি for রাজত্ব, সুরুয for সূর্য্য, আন্ধাইর for আঁধার, etc. We ought to mention here that some of the other ballad-makers, who were absolutely illiterate (such as Mansur Baiyiti), have shewn themselves almost as good as Shekh Faizu in this respect, owing to the simple reason that those who could not read were no better than the blind in the field of letters.

A large number of Prakrit words lies strewn all over these songs. I give here some words of this kind from other works at random. পদুম for পদ্ম, এনকালে for হেনকালে, বিয়ান for প্রভাত ('বিয়ানে' is current in Eastern Bengal. In Chandidas we find the word in the couplet, "শুনহে নিলাজ বন্ধু লাজ নাহি বাস। বিয়ানে পরের বাড়ী কোন্ কাজে আস" ॥) বেহুরা for বিরহী, আশ্রা for আশ্রয়, আইঞ্চল for অঞ্চল, চান্নি for চান্দিনী (moon-beams) ; ঠাডা for ঠাটা = বজ্র, কাডি for কাঠি, শুক্কুরবার for শুক্রবার, যৈবন for যৌবন, গহিন for গভীর, মুরথেক for মুহূর্ত্তেক, সন্দে for সন্দেহ, পরবুধ for প্রবোধ, পরখাই for পরীক্ষা, সাওরে for সাগরে, রাইত for রাত্রি, হাজি for সাজি, (basket) ছুটু for ছোট, ইয়ার for ইহার, জেঠ for জ্যৈষ্ঠ, হউরি for শ্বাশুরী, হেজা for সেজা (সজারু—porcupine).

The case-endings.

The case-endings are different from what obtain in other parts of this Province. The nominative singular is generally denoted by the word গোটা,—a word which formerly supplied the place of suffix generally implying the singular number. This word is largely to be found in the Ramayana of Krittibasha. It has been reduced to 'টা' in modern Bengali, a point which will be established by observing the use of the word in the following line, "লড়াই করিতে আছে পাঁচ গোটা ষাঁড়" in Malua. The locative is denoted by the suffix তনে, as ঘরতনে = from the house. The suffix is akin to and may have been derived from the

Sanskrit স্থানাৎ, a theory which will no doubt find a confirmation from another use of it in a slightly altered form as "কোথায় তনাৎ" (from where). In the dative for কে we sometimes find 'গড়া' as "বউগরা (বউকে) লইল মাও," etc. (Malua).

The use of participle here is what we still find in the spoken dialect of Eastern Bengal. The forms ঘুচ্যা for ঘুচিয়া, বান্‌ধ্যা for বান্ধিয়া; পাইক্যা for পাকিয়া, বইয়া for বসিয়া, বাইয়া for বাহিয়া and the like are numerous. The verbs in various tenses assume forms, some of which are still in use in Mymensing, Sylhet and other districts of Eastern Bengal. The forms দিবাম for দিব, যাইবাম for যাব are common, and শুনখাইন for শুনুন, আইছুন for এসেছেন shew the peculiarities of that dialect and prove its greater affinity to Prakit. As some of the texts have been published in this volume, my readers will have a direct access to the original; so I need not give further examples.

The affirmative sense of 'না.'

One thing that I cannot help mentioning here is the profuse use of the word 'না' with a meaning quite different from the negative. It is often used to assert a thing and to put emphasis on a statement rather than to negative it. The first line of Malua, "মন্দ্যানা আইশনার পানি" shews such use of 'না,' and there are many more in almost all of these poems; they are almost as thick as leaves of Vallombrosa, so we need scarcely allude to the texts. In the preliminary hymn attached to Kamala we have the first line "কানা মেঘারে তুইন আমার ভাই," here তুইন means তুই না and the 'না' here is affirmative and not negative. This use of 'না' is peculiar, it may have been an abbreviated form of the expression "is it not?"—which has an affirmative sense. Gradually the other parts of the sentence were dropped off and only the 'না' retained with an affirmative meaning. Even in our current dialect this 'না' sometimes occurs in the same sense, as in the query "তুমি না ভাত খাবে বলেছিলে?" Here the 'না,' though retaining the form of a query, has practically an affirmative meaning.

Arabic and Persian words.

In the old and modern literature of Bengal which bears the mark of Sanskritic influence on it in a striking manner we find Muhammadan words, *i.e.*, words of Persian or Arabic origin, scrupulously avoided. The writers avoid these exotic words even as an orthodox Brahmin avoids the touch of a Muhammadan after his bath. This grim orthodoxy is extremely to be deplored. The Muhammadans form a very considerable portion of the population of this province, and the majority by far of this population belongs to Eastern Bengal. These people are bound by sacred ties of religion with the people of Persia and Arabia and have to study their literature, theology, law and philosophy. The Muhammadans of Bengal are obliged to read their scriptures written in these classical languages and in this way they get themselves familiar with Arabic and Persian words. Though as children of Bengal, Bengali is certainly their mother-tongue, they have as much right to import Arabic and Persian words to it as the Brahmins have to introduce Sanskrit words. The classical languages of Arabia and Persia, no less than Sanskrit, have words of peculiar force and appropriateness which may be imported to our vocabulary with advantage, and this is the most natural course also. Though we try to avoid Arabic and Persian words in written Bengali, which we have made as exclusive as a Hindu temple, we have not been able to exclude such words from our current speech. Dame nature cares neither for theology nor for orthodoxy and has always her unrestrained course. In our current speech even the women of orthodox Brahmin families, whom we take to be the most fastidious types of intolerance, use these words of exotic origin in their every-day conversation, yet curiously we avoid them scrupulously in our written literature, and thus give offence to our Muhammadan brethren who by way of revenge sometimes try to alienate themselves from all interest in the literature of Bengal which they brand as essentially Hindu in character. I must always say that such orthodoxy is suicidal to the interests of both the sections of our population.

With what a sense of relief do we find in the ballads of Mymensing the current Persian and Arabic words admitted without any ado. They were admitted because they had an admission already, and no passport was therefore necessary to justify this admission. We find in the poems a profuse use of such words as রোসনাই, গোলাম, শল্লা, রুমাল, ছুরৎ, দরিয়া, আসমান, লড়াই, খিড়কী, অন্দর, তসবীর, পয়দা, আসল, খুসী, বেইজ্জত, etc. Some of these words are used by orthodox Hindus in their conversation every day.

While there are such words in these songs, there is, however, no sign of propagandism in the writers to give an undue importance to them, as some Muhammedan writers are trying to do now-a-days. The Battala works by Muhammadan writers, written in what is called the '*Musalmani Bangla*,' are so full of Urdu words that the literature created by them has become as exclusive as the Sanskritic Bengali of the Pundits of Fort William College. The songs of Mymensing are written in plain Bengali with only a small sprinkling of Urdu words which, without giving them an artificial air, only serve to accentuate their sense and render force to the ideas. These poems therefore will prove better than any logic that Bengali is the language of the Muhammadans and the Hindus alike and is as remote from Sanskrit as it is from Persian or Arabic, but always ready to enrich her vocabulary by importations of words from all of these three classical languages in a guarded way, so that she may not be overloaded or vitiated by them.

Moderation to be used.

VIII

The Political Condition of the Country.

The state of society disclosed by these poems is such as to make one shudder at the political features revealed. The condition of the country under the Muhammadan rule, at particular periods in our annals, especially towards the beginning of the 18th century, practically verged on anarchy. The Muhammadan chiefs often employed people called the *sindhukis* to give them information about beautiful Hindu girls. They could at any moment call for a surrender of the fair ones from their natural custodians. The *najar marecha* or the tax levied on marriage often proved so heavy that it practically ruined many a family. Chandrakumar says that it was introduced in Mymensing by the Dewan Sahibs of Jangalbari. That is however not true. This tax is still prevalent in many districts of India. In Murshidabad in Bengal, the ryots still pay the *najar marecha*; it may be called by a different name. In some countries of Europe the sub-lords under the feudal system, practically claimed the right over the person of a damsel who was married, and a tax had to be paid by the bride-groom in order to release his bride from such obligation. The seigniur had a right over all brides in his seigniory on the nuptial nights and the tax was called "Droit de Seiginiur." A reference to this will be found in Frazer's 'Folk-lore in the Testament.' *Najar marecha* was analogous to this tax. It appears from the poem 'Malua,' that the Muhammadan chiefs had the power of raising this tax to any amount at their sweet will. Chandrakumar mentions an historical

The nazar marecha.

instance in which a whole Brahmin family was about to be ruined by the impossible demand of the Muhammadan Governor in whose jurisdiction he lived, and they saved themselves by the most dishonourable and humiliating condition of offering the fair bride to the harem of the chief. It is reported to me that the harems of the Muhammadan Governors were sometimes filled with fair-looking Hindu women recruited in this process, and the children born of these women were called "*najarmarechar chhéle*"—or children of "*najar marecha.*" They were allowed to inherit properties and to assume the title of 'Dewan' by courtesy. The informers enjoyed great favours under some of the Muhammadan Chiefs, and Chandrakumar writes that the descendants of some of the *sindhukis*, as they were called, still enjoy rent-free lands granted to their ancestors in this manner.

Liking for Hindu girls.

There seems to be some special reason why some of the Dewan Sahibs seemed to be zealous in their hunt after fair Hindu women. The family was originally more Hindu than Muhammadan by blood. Its founder Kalidas Gajdani became a Muhammadan convert by the contrivances of a princess who loved him. His son Isha Khan married Subhadra (she is also known by her other name of Shona), sister of Kedar Roy of Sripur, one of the reputed twelve sub-lords of Bengal known as the "*bara bhuyans.*" Subhadra had two sons named Adam and Biram who in their turn married their cousins, daughters of Kedar Roy. So the history of this family is an account of love-romance from the very beginning. Many of the Dewans, both on their father's side and on their mother's, had Hindu blood running in their veins. It is not therefore unnatural that they should have a predilection for Hindu women. Of course I write all this from the evidence found in the ballads themselves, which, though they have certainly a historical basis, may not always stand the test of a scrutinizing enquiry.

Forcible abduction of a woman in a Rajput ballad.

The persecution of Malua by the Muhammadan Kaji and latterly by Dewan Jahangir has many a parallel in the history of India and specially in that of Rajputana. I crave the indulgence of my readers in quoting a short Rajput ballad, first brought to light by Sir George Grierson, K.C.I.E., and rendered into English verse by the illustrious poet Sir Edwin Arnold. I find this in an article called, 'The Popular Literature of Northern India' by Sir George Grierson and published in the Bulletin of the School of Oriental Studies, Vol. I, Part III. It will be interesting to note that much of the trouble which befell fair-looking Hindu women in those days had their origin in the bathing *ghat*, which is the only place where an outsider gets an opportunity of seeing them. This we find in some of the Bengali poems such as Kamala and Malua as well as in the Rajput ballad. Sir George Grierson collected the original ballad from Bihar. It runs thus:—

"Of eight great beams the boat was wrought,
With four red row-pins;—*Hu-ri-jee*!
When Mirja Sahib spied at the Ghaut
Bhagabati bathing:—*Hu-ri-jee*!

"Oh, girl! that hither the chatties bring,
Who is this bathing?'—*Hu-ri-jee*!
'The head of our village is Horil Singh;
"'Tis the Raja's sister!'—*Hu-ri-jee*!

"'Run thou, Barber! and, Peon! run thou.
Bring hither that Rajput!'—*Hu-ri-jee*!
'Oh, girls! who carry the chatties, now,
Which is his dwelling?'—*Hu-ri jee*!

"The dwelling of Horil Singh looks north,
And north of the door is a sandal tree,
With arms fast-bound they brought him forth;
'Salaam to the Mirza!'—*Hu-ri-jee*!

"'Take, Horil Singh, this basket of gold,
And give me thy sister, sweet Bhagabati.'
'Fire burn thy basket!' he answered bold—
My sister's a Rajput!'—*Hu-ri-jee*!

"Horail's wife came down from her house.
She weeps in the court-yard: 'cursed be,
Oh, sister-in-law, thy beautiful brows!
My husband is chained for them!'—*Hu-ri-jee*!

"Now, sister-in-law! of the house keep charge,
And the duties therein:' quoth Bhagabati;
'For Horil Singh shall be set at large,
I go to release him!'—*Hu-ri-jee.*

"When Bhagabati came to the Mirja's hall,
Low she salaamed to him:—*Hu-ri-jee*!
'The fetters of Horil Singh let fall,
If Mirja,' she said, 'thou desirest me.'

'If Mirja,' she said, 'thou wouldst have my love
Dye me a bride-cloth'—*Hu-ri-jee*!
'Saffron beneath and vermilion above
Fit for a Rajput!'—*Hu-ri-jee*!

"'If Mirja,' she said, 'I am fair in thine eyes
And mine is thy heart, now'—*Hu-ri-jee*!
'Command me jewels of rich device,
Fit for a Rajput'—*Hu-ri-jee*!

"'If Mirja,' she said, 'I must do this thing,
Quitting my people'—*Hu-ri-jee*!
'The palanquin and bearer bring,
That I go not afoot from them!'—*Hu-ri-jee*!

"'Smiling, he bade the dyers haste
To dye her a bride-cloth;—*Hu-ri-jee*!

Weeping, weeping—around her waist
Bhagabati bound it ;—*Hu-ri-jee* !

"Smiling, he bought from goldsmith's best
Jewels unparalleled ;—*Hu-ri-jee* !
Weeping, weeping on neck and breast
Bhagabati clasped them ;—*Hu-ri-jee* !

"Joyously smiling, 'Bring forth,' he cried,
'My gilded palanquin !'—*Hu-ri-jee* !
Bitterly sorrowing, entered the bride,
Beautiful Bhagabati.—*Hu-ri-jee* !

"A koss and half a koss went they
And another koss after ;—*Hu-ri-jee* !
Then Bhagabati thirsted : 'Bearers stay !
I would drink at the tank here !'—*Hu-ri-jee* !

"'Take from my cup,' the Mirza said,
'Oh, not to-day will I take !' quoth she
'For this was my father's tank, who is dead
And it will soon be distant !'—*Hu-ri-jee* !

"She quaffed one draught from her hollowed palm.
And again she dipped it ;—*Hu-ri-jee* !
Then leaped in the water—dark and calm
And sank from the sight of them ;—*Hu-ri-jee* !

"Sorely the Mirja bewailed, and hid
His face in his cloth, for rage to be
So mocked : 'See, now, in all she did
Bhagabati fooled me !'—*Hu-ri-jee* !

"Grieving the Mirja cast a net.
Dragging the water,—*Hu-ri-jee* !
Only shells and weeds did he get
Shells and bladder-weeds ;—*Hu-ri-jee* !

"Laughing, a net cast Horil Singh
Dragging the water ;—*Hu-ri-jee* !
Lo ! at the first sweep, up they bring
Dead, cold Bhagabati—fair to see !

"Laughing homeward the Rajput wends,
Chewing his betel : 'For now,'—quoth he,
'In honour this leap of Bhagabati ends
Three generations ! '—*Hu-ri-jee* !"[1]

[1] আটহি কাট কেরি নৈয়া রে নৈয়া।
ইগুঁরে ঠরাবল চারু ভঁগিয়া হুরেজী ॥১
তৈহি ঘাটে উতরৈলা মিরজা সইরবা।
জৈহি ঘাটে ভগবতী নহালে হুরেজী ॥২

পনিয়া ভরতি পনি ভরনি বিটিয়া।
কেকর বহিনি করে অসননিয়া হুরেজী।৩
গাঁবকের গৌঅাঁ হোরিল সিঙ্গ রজবা।
উম্হকর বহিনি করে অসননিয়া হুরেজী ॥৪

ধাব তুহ নৌআ ধাব চপরসিয়া।
হোরিল সিঙ্গ পকড়ি লে আবহু হুরেজী ॥
পনিয়া ভরতি পনিহারিনি বিটিয়!।
হোরিল সিঙ্গ মকনিয়া কহঁা বাড়ে হুরেজী।৫
উত্তর মুঁহে উত্তরাহুত উনকা।
দুয়ারে চননবা গচ্ছিয়া হুরেজী ॥৬

হোরিল সিঙ্গ মুসক চড়াব হুরেজী।
(জব রে) হোরিল সিঙ্গ গইলে মিরিজা পাসবা।
নই নই কৰৈলা সলমিয়া হুরেজী।৭
লৈউ না হোরিল সিঙ্গ ডাল ভর সৌনবা।৮
ভগবতী বহিনিয়া মোহি বকসহু হুরেজী ॥৯

আগি লগহু মিরিজা ডাল ভর সৌনবা
মোরা কুলে ভগবতী না জামলৈ হুরেজী ॥১০
ঘর মেঁ সেঁ নিকসি অঁগনা ঠাড়ি ভইলি।
অঁগনা ঠাড়িয় ভৌজী রোবৈলি হুরেজী ॥১১

We need not comment on the inaccurate renderings of some lines of the text, though otherwise it is a very happy translation. Evidently this ballad has many points of similarity with that of "Dewan Bhabna."

আগি লগহু ভগবতী তোহরি সুরতিয়া ।
তোহরা কারণ সামী বান্হল হুরেজী ॥১২
লৈউ না ভৌজী ঘর গিহিথানবা ।
হোরিল ছোড়াবন হন জাইব হুরেজী ॥১৩

জব (না) ভগবতি গইলি মিরিজাকা পাসবা ।
নৈ নৈ কৈরেলি সলমিয়া হুরেজী ॥১৪
জৌ তুহুঁ মিরিজা হমরা সেঁ লোভিয়া ।
হোরিল সিঙ্গ কৈ মুস্থক ছোড়াবঁহ হুরেজী ॥১৫

জোঁ তুহুঁ মিরিজা হমরা সে লোভিয়া ।
হমরা জোগে চুনরি রঁগাবহু হুরেজী ॥১৬
জোঁ তুঁহু মিরিজা হমরা সেঁ লোভিয়া ।
হমরা জোগে গহনা গড়াবহ হুরেজী ॥১৭

জোঁ তুহুঁ মিরিজা হমরা সেঁ লোভিয়া ।
হমরা জোগে ডঁরিয়া ফনাবহ হুরেজী ॥১৮
হঁসি হঁসি মিরিজা গহণা গড়োলে ।
রোই রোই পেহ্নে বেটী ভগবতী হুরেজী ॥১৯

হঁসি হঁসি মিরিজা চুনরী রংগোলে ।
রোই রোই পেহ্নে বেটী ভগবতী হুরেজী ॥২০
হঁসি হঁসি মিরিজা ডঁরিয়া ফনৌলে ।
রোই রোই ফানে বেটী ভগবতী হুরেজী ॥২১

এক কোস গইলি দুসর কোস গইলি ।
লাগি গৈল মধুরি পিয়সিয়া হুরেজী ॥২২
গোড় তোর লাগিলা অগিলা কহরবা ।
বুন এক পনিয়া পিয়াবহু হুরেজী ॥২৩

মিরিজা গড়ুঅবে পনিয়া পিয়হু হুরেজী ॥২৪
তোরা গড়ুএ মিরিজা নিতি উটি পিয়বোঁ ।
বাবা কৈ সগর বা দুরলভ ভইলে হুরেজী ॥২৫

Oppressions autocratic rather than racial.

It is usual to give a racial character to the oppressions mentioned in some of the ballads. But I think the oppressions were indiscriminate and autocratic, rather than peculiar to Muhammadan bigotry. In Malua we find the Muhammadan Kaji sentenced to death by impalement at the orders of Dewan Jahangir. There is no difference, from the point of view of justice, between this order and that of death passed on Chandbinod by the Kaji. The Hindu *karkoon's* treatment of Kamala in the ballad named after her is by no means less heinous than that of the Muhammadan Kaji to Malua. In those days much depended on the will of the autocrat; it was not safe to provoke him, and in this the Muhammedan and Hindu subjects laboured under the same disadvantage. One should be reminded of the Hindu Dewan of Bhati, described in the Mainamati songs,—of the treatment received by Raja Gopichandra at the hands of Hira, the harlot,—of the atrocities committed by Chand Roy of Gourdwar as narrated in the Prembilas, of the manner in which the Raja of Simhal is said to have punished Dhanapati, described by Mukundaram, and of many instances of perfidious villainy committed by the Hindu chiefs-in power, described in the Dharmamangal poems,—in order to come to the conclusion that the Hindu and Muhammadan autocrats used to oppress

এক চিরুআ পিয়লি হুসর চিরুয়া পিঅলি
তিসরে গইলি তরবৌরবা হুরেজী ॥২৬
রোবৌলা মিরিজবা মুঁহ দে রুমলিয়া ।
মৌরি বুধি ছরে বেটী ভগবতী হুরেজী ॥২৭

রোই রোই মিরিজবা রে জলিয়া লগাবৈলি ।
বাঝি গইল ঘোঘঁবা সৈববরা হুরেজী ॥২৮

হঁসি হোরিল সিঙ্গ জলিয়া লগাবৈলে ।
বাঝি গইলি ভগবতী বহিনিয়া হুরেজী ॥২৯
হবৈলা হোরিল সিঙ্গ মুঁহে খাই পনবা ।
তিন কুল রাখে বহিনিয়া ভগবতী হুরেজী ॥৩০

people alike and that all such oppressions had no bearing on religious or racial considerations. Of course, as the Muhammadan power became gradually established in the country, they represented the autocratic element in a numerically larger proportion. It was the fault of the administrative system of those days. The Dewans of Jangalbari were sometimes very friendly to the Hindus who elected them as judges and arbitrators even in their own social matters. Dewan Ibrahim Khan who died about a century ago, spent Rs. 50,000 at Mymensing for getting the whole of the Mahabharata read and explained before the public by competent Hindu pundits. This will show the catholic views of the illustrious family even in religious matters. The poets of Mymensing have faithfully narrated the story of love between the youthful men and women of both the communities and they found nothing objectionable in it. The love between Mamina Khatun and Kalidas, between Subhadra and Isha Khan and that between the daughters of Kedar Roy and the princes, Adam and Biram, have been described by the Muhammadan poet who wrote the ballad of Isha Khan. The blind poet Fakir Faiju describes the love of Adhua Sundari, the daughter of the Brahmin Raja Dubaraj for the youthful Dewan of Baniachang. These stories are in the form of songs which were sung by professional rhapsodists before the Hindus and Muhammadans of the localities where the events actually happened. The poets wrote the narratives without being influenced by bigotry, hence no one took objection to what they wrote. In modern times the minds of both the communities have been embittered to a certain extent. We find that some of the Muhammadan writers delight in giving pictures of Hindu women in love with Muhammadans, as a retaliation for Bankim Chatterji's delineation of the character of Ayesha. When the story is written by a member of one community in an unbiased mind, and not got-up with a motive to humiliate the other, it

Love between young men and women of the two communities.

can give no offence, as we find the case in these ballads of Mymensing. But malice, spite or bigotry should not inspire a writer whether a Hindu or a Muhammadan. We should try to bring amity and good feelings to both the sections of our population—a state of things which, I am glad to find, existed in this country in the days gone by.

Punishments.

The sorts of punishments given in those days were crude, not to say that they were sometimes cruel and inhumane to the extreme. People were then buried alive, and the treatment given to the prisoners was often harrowing. These were, of course, not peculiar to Bengal alone in the 17th and 18th centuries. In that age crude and cruel systems of punishment were prevalent in all countries. We find in the songs under review that the Muhammadan and Hindu chiefs used to keep a prison in their capitals called, '*Khoon-shala*' or the murder-house. There the prisoners were taken bound in chains, and stones of crushing weight were placed upon their breasts. One of the usual punishments given by a Hindu Raja to a Muhammadan was to pluck his beard by force in that cruel predicament. Ants were let lose to bite the unhappy man, and often his nose and ears were cut off. A fire was made in the cell giving rise to volumes of smoke which nearly suffocated the prisoner. Chillies were burnt there which tormented him all the while. From the beginning of the 18th century the country presented a universal scene of flagrant injustice which gradually developed into what has been called in a copper-plate inscription "the *matsyanaya*." The oppressions on Zemindars by Mursidkuli Khan reached a climax. The "*Baikuntha*" into which the Zemindars were thrown was a horrible place very naturally dreaded by the princely people of the country. In 1725 Krishnaprasad Nag, an officer of the Zemindar of Daskhahania (Sherpur) was arrested for non-payment of revenue and this was followed by the arrest of his master, Surya Narayan Choudhury who was stripped of his clothes, till made entirely naked and cruelly flogged. In fact, the cruelties inflicted on him were so severe that he gave up all claims to his Zemindary and thus made a miserable escape. The Zemindar of Kagmari, Indra Narayan Choudhury, unable to bear such oppressions, gave up Hinduism and became a Muhammadan under the name of Inatulla Choudhuri. The two Rajas of Susang, mere children, were arrested for non-payment of revenue and ordered to have twenty stripes of whip on their back every day till they cleared their arrears. Their old servant Bama Charan Nandi volunteered to bear this punishment on himself and submitted to twenty stripes daily for a long time till he was on the verge of death. But as the dues could not be still paid, it was ordered that the young children (the Rajas) should be placed in the mouth of a cannon and blown off.[1] On the day fixed for the merciless massacre of the lads, the cannons of the British Raj were heard on the Buriganga, roaring out their promise to save the country from anarchy. "During the period (1765-1772)," writes Mr. Marshman in his 'History of Bengal,' "there could scarcely be said to have been any government at all."

The favours of men in power were often as great as their punishments. The Kaji or the Magistrate could give redemption to a favoured individual from all punishments for all offences up to seven murders. The privileged person could do almost whatever he liked in a particular locality.

Loyal feelings.

But good rulers were not unknown, and the loyalty evoked by their kind and just administration is feelingly described in these ballads, and in the Dharmamangal and other old Bengali poems. We find in the Sanskrit work Sriharsha Charit written by Bán, that when the Raja died many of his nobles gave up their lives in sorrow. Some flung themselves from the tops of buildings and expired. Others took poison or drowned

[1] Kedarnath Majumdar's History of Mymensingh, pp. 81-82.

themselves. This reminds us of the general grief leading to suicides in Japan on the death of a Mikado. The loyal feelings evinced in this way are peculiarly oriental, shewing that the kings and chiefs of the country, true to the traditions of a Ramchandra and an Asoka sometimes possessed the talisman by which they could conquer the hearts of the people as they could conquer enemies by their weapons. In the Mainamati songs the general grief of the people described at the adoption of the vows of a *sannyas* by Gopichandra, though exaggerated, shows how a good Raja was loved by his subjects. In these ballads we have such accounts again and again. In the song of Surat Jamal and Adhua, the grief of the people at the desertion of Baniachang by Dewan Alal Khan and at the departure of young Jamal for meeting a tragic death at Delhi, recall the very language of the Gopichandra ballad. The Raja sometimes loved their subjects as their own chtldren and the subjects did not fail to reciprocate this love with all the warmth of their souls. The grief not only pervaded the men and women of the whole country but it is said, "even the birds stopped their songs, the rivulets ceased running their course and the beasts would be refraining from grazing in the fields." There is no doubt much poetic exaggeration in all this, but the extreme sentimentality of our people oftentimes inspires poetic fancy. During the Russo-Japanese war the Mikado was for some reason or other sad for a day or two. The report of this sadness of the king was received by the city with the utmost concern, and one lady is said to have actually committed suicide. In our country too, such loyal feelings are quite possible as we find from the accounts given by Bán.

Democratic ideas and patriotism.

That there was a limit to the people's power of suffering oppressions by autocrats is evidenced by numerous episodes described in the ballads. Here in Bengal the people elected Gopal as their king in the 9th century at a time when the country was groaning under anarchy. The *abhichar* performed by the subjects of Manik Chandra, when his minister began to maltreat them, was the result of a combined action on the part of the people, showing a spirit of revolt against oppression. That is, of course, a fable. But these fables oftentime faithfully reflect actual politics. When Gopi Chandra took his *sannyas*, he wished that during his absence for twelve years, Khetu, his half-brother, should reign in his stead. But Khetu knew the popular mind and said to the Raja that unless he announced his regency by a general proclamation the people might not accept him as their ruler. Raja Gopi Chandra did this ; but yet the subjects would not agree to accept Khetu as their Raja. They said that he was a low-born fellow and did menial service in the palace. How could they submit to the rule of such a man ? One of the principal ryots tauntingly said that he would keep the payment of government revenue in abeyance for the twelve years and pay it to Gopi Chand on his return, but not to the slave Khetu by any means. Though in the ballads of Mymensing we find instances of great oppression by the chiefs, in most cases the people being quite powerless to resist them, there are occasional descriptions of popular unity and well-concerted plans to defeat the objects of the oppressors. When young Jamal led the army of Dakshinbhag against his uncle Dewan Dulal of Baniachong which was being terribly oppressed by the latter, the people of the city deserted their chief and joined the young prince.

In Malua we find some ryots so daring as to save their relation from capital sentence by attacking the police force of the Kazi employed in carrying out his orders. In the same ballad we find Malua's kinsmen attacking Dewan Jahangir himself in his boat and carrying her away by assaulting the Dewan and his people. These kinsmen belonged to the caste of *Hele Kaivartas*, who are still powerful in Mymensing and known for their combined action to resist oppressions from outside.

In fact, the spirit of revolt was in the air of Bengal. The historical annals of this country have recorded the valorous deeds of Pratapaditya and Sitaram as rebels of the first rank. Daud Khan, the eldest son of Kalidas Gajdáni, true to the Kshatriya spirit of his father, died fighting for independence in 1575 A. D. Kalidas's second son Isha Khan also showed extraordinary courage and martial skill in fighting with Akbar though he was eventually won over by the Emperor by gentle ways of love and friendship. But the descendants of Kalidas Gajdáni kept up the fiery spirit of revolt for a long time and nowhere do we find this so powerfully expressed as in the ballad of Firoj Khan. This ambitious young man was ever alive to the glories of his ancestors and thought of nothing else in the first years of his rule except as how to make himself independent from the control of Delhi. He stopped paying revenues to the Emperor and fought against the force of Delhi that cooperated with Omar Khan, the Dewan of Tajpur.

Relation with Delhi.

The ballads show it very clearly that the Emperors of Delhi had good many tough fights with not only the Rulers of Bengal, but with her smaller chiefs such as Kedar Roy and Firoz Khan. There was always a demand made on the resources of Bengal if the Emperor required help from outside in the warfare that constantly engaged him. We find such a demand on Dewan Alal Khan for ten thousand soldiers made by an urgent Imperial mandate from Delhi.

Rulers of Bengal often went to the Court of Delhi to lodge their complaints for just or imagined causes. Kachu Ray of Jessore, we know, wanted such help from Jahangir. Omar Khan went to Delhi and brought a force from there to fight against Firoz Khan of Jangalbari.

Fighting women so often form the subject in Bengali poems that I am inclined te believe that there was a real and historical tradition in the country, of females fighting in the battle. In some of the old manuscripts of the Bengali Mahabharat we find Draupadi fighting in the field of Kurukshetra. In the Bengali Ramayana not only do we find the queen of Mahiravan engaged in a hand-to-hand fight with Hanuman, but in some of the Ramayanic songs Sita fights with the hydra-headed Ravan of Svetadwip and overcomes him. These are, however, purely mythological stories but we cannot say the same thing of the fight waged by Kalingá, a daughter of Haripal, against Lau Sen and of that of the Dom woman Lakshyá against the army of Gour, sent to take the fort of Mainagarh by force,—described in the Dharmamangal poems: that both Kalingá and Lakshyá fought in the field seems to be historical facts though the details of the narrative are no doubt poetical inventions. Here in the ballads we find Sakhiná fighting against the Delhi army, sent in aid of Kella Tajpur, and the two daughters of Kedar Roy taking up arms in their hands and killing men in order to save Adam and Biram. These incidents refer to historical facts which happened in comparatively recent times.

Fighting women.

IX

Society—Arts, Culture and Sports.

The state of society revealed in this literature of ballads, shows some of the excellent features of the rural people of Bengal. The women especially are endowed with power of endurance, devotion to truth and a spirit of renunciation which excites our admiration. It is also noteworthy that though the characters are mostly of agricultural and trading classes, women are always shown

Education of women.

as having received some degree of education. Women in the Brahmin families used to read scriptures in Sanskrit, and Chandrávati, whose learning and power as writer are historical facts, was, I believe no exceptional case. Malua, though a woman of the Hélé Kaivarta caste, knew how to write letters, and Kamalá and her aunt were fairly literate. From the instance of Khullana, the merchant's wife in the Chandi Kavya, and similar characters in other poems we find it established that the Hindus never neglected to give an average education to their girls in those days. Mr. Long in his 'Descriptive Catalogue of Bengali books' wrote that from 1700 to 1850, the arithmetical formulæ of Subhankar, the Bengali Cocker, were taught in forty thousand vernacular schools. There was a system as comprehensive in its scope, as conducive to culture, in which both women and men had opportunities of receiving a workable knowledge of letters in their childhood; and the testimonies of these ballads confirm this fact. In Kajalrekha we have a graphic account of the training which the young women of noble families received in the culinary art and in painting. (Canto XV.)

Art and Industry.

The Bengalis are now in the background in the matter of art and industry. The old history is forgotten and there is no means left to us to have a full account of our culture in these things. We once dazzled the world by our fine workmanship in cotton fabrics and in silver and gold wares. Streamed with a hundred rivers, Eastern Bengal is not the proper soil for the undertaking of artistic masonry works on any large scale. Her rivers would not allow her to build a Tajmahal. If any rich man ever attempted to build a city of palaces on the treacherous banks of the Padma, the Brahmaputra or Dhaleswari, they would assume the form of a Kirtinasha or "Destroyer of fame" and make the rich man's dream in marble vanish by their ever aggressive attacks. But with a less ambitious project the Bengali artist sat to build his

Bungalows.

unmatched *bungalows* with curvilinear roofings, which, according to Fergusson, have been imitated from Bengal all over the world. There are graphic descriptions of some of these *bungalows* in the songs under review. The ballad of Isha Khan particularly gives a very attractive account. The pillars, we understand, were made of crystals. The interiors of the roofs were covered with the feathers of the king-fishers, the cranes or the pea-cocks. The doors were cased with gold in rich men's houses. There was fine workmanship of gold on the roofs. The windows and shutters were protected and beautified with glass and mica of various designs. The walls, sometimes made of thatch wrought into fine decorative designs made of cane, were covered by artistic mats of various colour. The cane *sundi*, was particularly good for this purpose and employed for all fine works. Great labour and cost were required for the completion of these *bungalows* which sometimes looked like fairies touching the earth with their coloured wings, represented by the curvilinear roofs made of gay feathers of the pea-cock and other birds. In the countryside this dream of a *bungalow*, which the old artists of Bengal dreamt and actually built with subtle art, has now vanished, but we may still find in the interior of our country the descendants of those artists still sitting all day long and cutting and embellishing the cane and bamboo-sticks for construction of their *bungalows* which, when completed, look far more beautiful than the crude and unshaped mass of the corrugated-iron structures which have nearly driven the old traditional art of Bengal from her field. The descriptions of ships in the ballad of Bhelua are magnificent and give a fair idea of the artistic talent of our people.

Sports and pastimes.

The sports and pastimes of the Hindu society have ever been associated with religion. That the people were passionately fond of festivities can no better be illustrated than by the fact that they sometimes gave their babies as security to the money-lenders for loans in order to perform the Durga Puja in the house. (Malua, Canto I. L 8.) Boat-races were a favourite sport, and men who could afford it, kept the long canoe-shaped boats for racing in the rivers on which their houses stood. (Malua, Canto VIII, ll. 49-50.) A reference to fighting bulls, as a favourite pastime, is also found in one of the poems (Malua, Canto VIII, l. 50).

Korá-hunting.

Korá-hunting was by far the most favoured sport and also an avocation with many for earning their livelihood. The hunting of *Korá* was greatly encouraged by the artistocracy, and there are even now many people in the district of Mymensing, who enjoy rent-free lands earned by their ancestors for their skill in hunting with these birds. We find in Malua that the hero, who was an expert *Korá*-hunter, obtained a grant of considerable rent-free lands from the Dewan Sahib of Jahangirpur for his proficiency in the art. Trained *Korás* were also the carriers of letters. At a time when one village was separated from another by forests infested with venomous snakes and ferocious animals, no less than with robbers, a trained *Korá* was very valuable as a carrier of messages.

As *Korá*-hunting forms an interesting subject in some of the ballads, I give a summary of the articles recently published in two of the leading Bengali journals on the subject, by writers who evidently speak from their own observation of the game as prevalent in Eastern Bengal.[1]

Korá-hunting was at one time the craze of the Mymensing people. This curious bird has many points in common with the gallinule, though it does not belong to that species. It is generally of a large size, being one foot and a half in height. From the back to the tail the bird measures fifteen inches. Its leg is strong and thick as a two-anna silver piece.

[1] *Kora-pakhi*—an article in the "Monthly Vasumati," Pt. II, Magh, 1320 B E., and *Pakhshi Tatwa* in the "Pratibha," Kartic, Agrahayan and Pous (12th year) by Jatindranath Majumdar, B.L., and Purna Chandra Bhattacharyya, respectively.

From knee-joint to foot, the leg measures three to four inches and above the joint five to six. It has four claws in each foot. These are crooked, strong and sharp.

The beak is one and a half inches long and above it, stretching to the forehead, is its fine crest—a thin piece of protruding flesh of deep red which adorns the head. This crest is more beautiful than that of a cock. The eyes of the bird are bright and playful. It has a long neck, resembling a crane's, though not so thin. The feathers near the breast are black and on the sides ash-coloured. They grow bright and glossy after winter. These birds are very ferocious. The adage in the countryside is "Two *Korás* can not live together in the same swamp." If the boys are pugnacious, the old men call them "bully *Korás*." If a *Korá* hears the sound of another it gets angry and starts to fight. The sound of the *Korá* is deep and solemn; it is like the roaring of a cloud. At the advent of the rains, it fills the air, with its solemn cries which gradually get louder. The sound is not at all shrill. It rather resembles the croaking of a raven. The raven's sound is not pleasant to the ear, but while the *Korá's* sound rises to a far higher point, it has a majesty and sweep which bears no comparison with the raven's; it produces a solemn impression. The roaring of thunder is inspiring to the bird, and makes it send up those wild cries which are sometimes heard from a distance of two miles, filling the hunter's soul with strange excitement. From April to July, the *Korá* is in the hey-day of its health and spirit. From August it begins to lose strength; its feathers fall off and the crest loses its deep red and dwindles away leaving a faint trace like a yellow ribbon.

The cage of a trained *Korá* is kept covered with a blue cloth. *Korá*-hunting has been a favourite sport in many countries. The bird is trained by the hunters to decoy its fellows and pursue game. The *Korá*-hunting is a most exciting spectacle. Here is an account by an eye-witness. "It was August, our canals and marshes were all flooded over by the rains; on the north of our house was a road of the District Board and close to this road was a beautiful swamp. Its area was about one square mile. In the middle of the swamp were to be seen water-lilies of all kinds in full bloom and surrounding it lay extensive rice-fields. The swamp was a resort of the geese, the gallinule and various other water-fowls. As I walked over the road-side with some friends, I saw a Muhammadan hunter enter the swamp with cautious steps with a trained *Korá* in his hand. This raised our curiosity and we stopped there to observe his doings. The huntsman entered deep down the swamp till its water came up to his neck and then placed the cage of the bird on the weeds and plants with which the surface of the water was overgrown. Here he let his trained *Korá* fly up in the air. With the weeds and water-plants he thoroughly covered his head and remained unseen for some time in that posture. The hunter always hides himself in this way and remains close to his own bird. The wild *Korá* is far more powerful than the trained one. So if help is not received in time, it runs the risk of being torn to pieces by its adversary.

"Being free from the cage the trained *Korá* sent its deep and far-reaching cry '*Gurur-dhop-dhop*' in the air. It was a challenge and like lightning flew a wild *Korá* from the other side of the swamp and attacked the trained bird. I remember distinctly the figure of the wild *Korá* as it came roaring in great rage, with its head and neck bent to the right side. And in a moment the teribble fight began. They held each other in close grip, causing wounds on each other's body by their sharp and long claws and wounding each other with their beaks. They whirled like fly-shuttles on the surface of the water in close contact, throwing up spray on all sides. Just at that moment the hunter came out of the water-plants—and held both the birds fast in his hands. Then he brought them to the bank and extricated one from the other with great difficulty. We found that both the *Koras* were more or less wounded during the short fight and the hunter's body also bore signs of the contact with the sharp claws of the birds. I saw him covered with big leeches and blood gushing forth from his body. But indifferent to all physical pain, he looked triumphant over the game he had secured."

It is very difficult to secure the young of *Kora*. The hunter steals eggs from the nest of the birds and hatches them in a curious manner. He places four or five eggs in a cocoanut shell, after having filled it with cotton. This shell with eggs inside it, he tightly fits with a piece of cloth to his abdomen and keeps it in close contact. The eggs are hatched in this way for twenty or twenty-five days, and the great hardships which the hunter suffers may be easily conceived. He seldom takes bath during all this time only washing his head now and then when he feels giddy. Night and day, sleeping or awake, the bandage is kept tight and often the hunter is attacked with dysentery and other diseases. The hunting by means of a *kora* is a dangerous game exposing one to serpent-bite as the birds make their nests in jungly places near water full of weeds, infested by venomous snakes. We have an instance of snake-bite in the case of Chand Binod engaged in *kora*-hunting, mentioned in the ballad of Malua (Canto XVIII), and the writers of the articles here refer to many points besides which are substantiated by the accounts in the ballads.

In the 16th and 17th centuries *koras* were frequently engaged as carriers of messages. The trained *koras* were once in great demand in the countryside. An ordinary *kora* is now sold for twenty to twenty-five rupees. But in olden times, when a passion for hunting by these birds was the prevailing fashion and when difficulties of sending messages to a distant place were great, these birds sometimes used to be sold at enormous prices. One of the Dewans of Itna lately made the gift of a rent-free property to a hunter as the price of a trained *kora*; another Zemindar offered an elephant to a hunter as the price of the bird.

In Malua, the *kora* comes frequently on the scene showing itself as a trusted messenger in times of emergency, and at others, with its shrieks and cries from near the flowering Kadamba plants, bringing in the inevitable poetic associations of the rainy season.

Sports with the pigeons.

Another important and fashionable pastime with the higher classes of people in the 16th century was sporting with pigeons. Graphic and vivid accounts of these occur in the second part of the Chandi Kavya, where the merchant Dhanapati appears as the leader of the sportsmen. His party consists of about two dozens of young lads, his friends, who all go, carried on *dolás* or silver-palanquins borne on the shoulders of men. They all get down on a plain and, keeping the female pigeons in their hands, let loose the male ones, and the lads make a deafening noise by clapping their hands. The loud noise frightens the male pigeons and though their consorts are left behind they cannot return for fright. But sometimes love proves a more powerful factor, and that pigeon, which, inspite of the clappings and the noise comes back to the female bird first of all is declared victor of the field, and its owner wins the prize. Sometimes a trained pigeon is pursued by vultures, and in that case the owner, inspite of the thorns and briers of the forest path, goes running in great speed heedless of all danger making signs to the bird to light on the earth. The poet Mukundaram describes fifty-four birds engaged in these sports of Dhanapati, each called by a different name, to which the birds are trained to answer.

X

The Poetical and Ethical Value of the Songs.

When a Bengali poet, versed in Sanskrit lore, strives to excel in his description of Nature, we know too well from our Renaissance-literature what to expect from him; long and monotonous accounts of mornings and evenings with a catalogue of flower-plants, not omitting the butter-flies and the bees sucking honey from them—stereotyped and hackneyed figures of speech, copied from the earlier writers or what is worse, from Sanskrit classics—exhausting all resources of culture and obstructing the course of the narrative by wearisome diversions—these tax the patience of the readers to the utmost and create an apprehension at the outset, as if the description was never coming to an end.

Nature described in the ballads.

But when we come to these ballad-mongers, we are convinced that commonsense is by no means the monopoly of the learned; in fact we sometimes find the exact contrary to be the case. The rural bards do not sit down with the resolve to describe Nature and say something fine; they never write anything for the sake of display. In the course of a narrative of human action, Nature serves the purpose of a background, never made obtrusively prominent, but she often captures us being revealed by fine touches, all suddenly, as if by lightning-flash,—presenting a gay panorama of landscape views taken at snapshot. So we see the sky of a summer day with streaks of sun's rays coming out of the clouds diffusing an intensified heat, a phenomenon so common in our tropical climes,—the falcon[1] by its wild cries breaking the mid-day sleep of a fatigued wayfarer under the flowering Kadamba tree—the village tanks with its transparent water, surrounded by fences of thorny plants,—the bamboo-groves with sprouts shooting forth from them and boughs of mango-trees bending under ripe fruits and giving a resting place to the ravens and cuckoos whose croakings and cooings offer their contrast alternately like the voice of old men singing in chorus with young lads.

[1] In our translation of the text we have for the sake of convenience used the word alcon for *Kora*, though the *Kora* differs from the falcon in some points.

When a village-girl bathes in the river-ghat, the poet is amazed at seeing her black eyes and he knows not whether to admire the black waters of the river, the black clouds of the sky or the glance of her black eyes most.

Take for instance, the line in 'Kanka and Lila,' in the description of the rains : "হাতেতে সোনার ঝাড়ি বর্ষা নেমে আসে," picturing the season as a fair damsel with a golden vessel in her hand ; the lightning is the gold that sparkles from her pitcher of water. Nothing could be more indicative of the force of September rains in this country than the line which says that the flood of *Sravan* forcibly carries onwards the huge blocks of stone in its way (পাথর ভাসাইয়া যায় শ্রাবণের ধারা). There is a bird in this country called the "Bou-katha-kao" or "Oh-bride-speak." The poet says, "Heedless of the thunder-bolt overhead and wet with September-rain does the grief-stricken bird wander about the way-side, crying 'Oh bride speak' to appease her wrath." (শাওনিয়া ধারা শিরে বজ্র ধরি মাথে। বউ কথা কও বলি কান্দে পথে পথে) When speaking of a lady in anger, the poet says, "it seems that a garden of flowers was on fire." It brings the whole glow of purple on the brows and cheeks of a fair damsel vividly to the mind's eye. When a woman dies of her love, the poet compares her to a lily killed by November frost ; the line "মরণ বসিল আসি নয়নের কোলে" has all the elegance of modern style (Lila and Kanka, Canto 22, p. 240.) The sweet and gentle glance of a girl showed her innermost thought as "the moon-beams of October show the very bottom of a river" ("ভাদ্র মাসের চান্নি যেমন দেখায় নদীর তলা") is an exquisite instance of sparkling poetry. And the following passage in Malua, written about 300 years ago, is as fresh as a composition of to-day.

"Sweet is sugar-candy and the sweet-meat, sweet is also the water of the Ganges,—sweeter than these is the milk in the cocoanut. Sweetly comes the happy day after the hour of sorrow and sweeter than all these is the lost treasure found, and the coming of a baby to a lonely house. But sweeter than all and incomparably sweet is the union between lovers after parting." (Malua, Canto XIV, Ll. 106-112.) These poetic ideas were already in the air; for long before Malua was written, similar sentiments had been expressed in the Mainamati songs though in a crude and less elaborate style. (Gopichandra, Bujhán Khanda, p. 97, Calcutta University).

Through all these narratives, Bengal, with her vast rivers, her dead pools and her red *Sandhya-malati* and *Java* flowers, her white *Kunda* and yellow *Atashi*, with falcons hovering over her sky—with her evergreen shrubs and flow of rains—with her rustic women hailing their peasant lords with festive songs when the latter returned home at the close of the November day, with golden ears of new ripe crops hanging down from their heads,—the picturesque Bengal, seen a thousand times but never grown old, appears again and again with a new charm every time.

The female characters.

No flower in her garden is, however, so lovely as the figure of a Bengali woman. We find the woman of Bengal given to resigned grief and accepting the austere vows of an ascetic in Chandrávati; we find her dying in silent grief, shot by the flower-arrows of Cupid, without a word, in Lila; we find her again rising to a towering rage in Malua when tempted by a devilish man, a rage that express itself in poetic fire and unmatched wealth of language. We find her again in Kamala, taking a review of her life in a speech which, for pathos, elegance and guarded modesty is wonderful, addressed to an assembly of wise men who sat to give judgment over her. In the 'Dewan Bhabna' Sonai swallows her insult and unspeakable sorrows like the very poison which ends her life; and in Kajalrekha, she is like a statue, doomed to sufferings but commanding admiration by her incomparable modesty and feminine grace. Everywhere she is lovely, everywhere she is admirable by her martyr-like qualities and everywhere she is a strange

* * *

figure too, a poetic vision and wonder. The reader, I am afraid, will lose much of the beauty of the original in my poor English renderings. I will finish this discourse by quoting a passage from the ballads of Firoj Khan. Sakhina, the wife of Firoj Khan, expects her husband to return from the battlefield--a victor. She speaks her mind to Daria, who, however, has already heard bad news about him, but keeps silent :

Sakhina.

"Go Daria, go fast, bring *Champa* flowers and roses from our garden, I will weave a garland for my husband who is coming back as victor."

"Go Daria, go fast, and bring water for *aju*; I will reserve it in proper place for him when he returns home a victor."

"Go Daria, go fast and bring a fan of mica and place it on his bed ; I will sit by and fan him when he returns a victor."

"Go Daria, go fast, bring bottles full of *attar* and other scents made from rose for my husband. He will have need of them after the fatigue of war."

"Prepare, oh Daria, fine betels with spices, and fill a golden box with them for my husband."

"And go fast Daria, and bring dust from the mosques of five saints. I will mark his forehead with it as a token of their blessings, when he will return a victor."

"Go fast, oh Daria, go to the wives of the saints and convey my *salaam* to them."

* * * *

"Why, oh Daria, why is it that there is no smile on your lips to-day ?"

"But take heart, you will be happy, when you will see him a victor, come home again." [1]

The tragedy and the sequel of this enthusiasm can be better conceived than expressed.

১ দইরারে দেখিয়া বিবি কহিতে লাগিল।
" কালুকা বিয়ানে স্বামী রণ করিতে গেল ॥

Imagination loves to dwell upon the picture of Sakhina dying on horse-back,—killed not by a hundred bullets which fell powerless against the steel armour that protected her brave heart rendered invulnerable by its love,—not by a hundred swords directed against her that flashed like funeral fires around a *suttee*,—but by a cruel letter of divorce bearing the seal and signature of her own dear lord! Sakhina dying on horse-back is a symbol of nuptial love with all its old-world charm—a theme of epic grandeur worthy to be painted by a Raphael and sung by an Orpheus. She is a martyr to that love which is invulnerable against all physical forces, nay, triumphant over them, yet so sensitive and delicate that it cannot for a moment bear the loss of its supreme faith!

The field of *Kella* Tajpur, holier in our eyes than Karbala or Kurukshetra, is in the western limits of the sub-division of

শুন শুন দইরা আরে কহি যে তোমারে।
তুল্যা আন চাম্পা গোলাপ মালা গাথিবারে ॥
লড়াই জিত্যা আইলে স্বামী মালা দিবাম গলে।

"অজুর পানি তুল্যা রাখ সোণার গোছালে ॥
আবের পাঙ্কা আন্যা রাখ শয্যার উপরে।
রণ জিত্যা আইলে স্বামী বাতাস করবাম তারে ॥
ভাণ্ডে আছে আতর গোলাপ রাখত আনিয়া।
সোণার বাটায় সাজাও পান পতির লাগিয়া ॥

"পঞ্চপীরের দরগার মাটী আন্যা রাখ ঘরে।
রণে জিত্যা আইলে স্বামী দিতাম তার শিরে ॥"
পাচপীরেরে নারী সেলাম জানাইল।
হাসিমুখে বিবিজান কহিতে লাগিল ॥
"আইজ কেন দইরা তর হাসি নাইলো মুখে।
রণে জিত্যা আইব স্বামী দেখবা মনের সুখে ॥"

Netrokona in Bengal. There one may perchance still hear in the song of the cuckoo or lark the tale of Sakhina's wonderful love, and perchance the air may be still found charged with the fragrance of her last breath like that of a bud torn by a wanton hand; and to the imaginative mind day-light may still show the glitter of Sakhina's helmet over the heads of her wondering enemies, and midnight unveil the portrait of a divine woman, who fighting unwearied for three days on horse-back to rescue her husband from the hands of the enemies and baffling all their attempts, at the end turned the battlefield into a bower of sorrows, dying without uttering a word, of the shock at the proof of her husband's treachery, for he was reported to have bought peace with the enemy by signing the letter of divorce produced before her!

The ballad of Sakhina will be published in the next volume.

After going through these narratives descriptive of the sufferings of our women in their tenderest emotions, the reader will judge for himself whether the much abused *sattee* was the outcome of grim superstition as Ward and other missionaries attempted to prove early in the 19th century or that she offered herself of her own accord in many cases, as a mute sacrifice at the alter of love. It will be seen too from the ballads that the political atmosphere of the country before the British rule was such that many young and beautiful Hindu widows were drawn to this mad course to avoid a fate which they dreaded more than entering the funeral pyres of their husbands. The poems will at least clear up many points better than all the statistics collected by Mr. Ward could do.

India—the home of spirituality, mysticism, and tender emotions—should be approached with love and not with suspicion.

I know of no rustic song, so highly appealing, and so full of rugged and homely beauty as that of the *baramashi* in

Dewana Madina. (Canto VI). Here, the pathos of a poor Muhammadan girl's tale shows that true poetry sometimes grows like a lovely flower in the fields by the side of the plough and the scythe.

XI

The Singing of the Ballads.

The Gayans.

These ballads are sung in the district of Mymensing generally by Muhammadans and low-caste Hindus—those belonging to the Namasudra, the Háḍi, the Dom, the Jelé (fisherman), the Pátni (boatmen) and other depressed castes. As a rule, they are illiterate, their chief occupation is agriculture with other humble avocations in which they are engaged in the day-time. At night they assemble in some neighbour's house as invited guests to sing the songs. Most of them are amateur parties. There are some, however, who have made the singing of the ballads, their occupation.

The minstrel or the chief singer is called the Gayan. He is the main singer, adding interpretations and bringing out the hidden meaning of the poetical ideas, assisted by a chorus of eight or ten men who are called "Paile" (probably derived from the word *pálá-gayak*). They play on cymbals, tabors, and violins in course of singing. The harmonium is now and then seen amongst the musical instruments which is of course a modern innovation. Sometimes, young lads are introduced attired in picturesque dresses who sing and dance by way of diversion. The professional singers charge Rupees five to Rupees ten per night. Sometimes they do not fix any remuneration but depend on the gifts doled out by an appreciative audience. This is called '*pela*' in this part of Bengal and in Mymensing they call it '*fira*.' These gifts vary from As. 2 to As. 4 per head amongst the rural audience. The amateur parties, of course, do not charge anything, satisfied with betels and tobacco which are freely offered by the host.

The ballads are mostly poetical records of those events which had the greatest appeal for the people of the country-side. The poets acquired the art of versification, in most cases, without any knowledge of letters, and when their noble indignation or sympathy was roused at the report of some act of atrocity or renunciation they did not lack the power to describe it in the tongue which they had acquired from their mothers. The vivid pictures of actual scenes witnessed by them, or related to them first-hand by some eye-witness, created impressions which they reproduced as vividly as they were imaged in their minds without the least haziness about them, because these poets did not labour under some of the disadvantages from which the cultured historian of to-day can hardly expect to free himself, *viz.*, the restrictions of a conscious art and the biassed zeal of the propagandist. The rustic poet laboured under no such limitations; hence his accounts are sometimes truer than the prejudiced writings of many a historian. The rustic worshippers of Parnassus, however, sometimes yielded to the convention of the rural doggerel-mongers. The *bāramāsis* often made the narrative weak and historically untrue, though now and then they were aglow with excellent poetry. Secondly, an element of folk-tales was often mixed up with their songs, checking the easy flow of their poetry and weakening the truth of the narrative. Barring these, the ballads may be accepted as historical records of great value.

The '*Bhāts*' in our country, like the '*Chārans*' of Rajputana kept up the memory of stirring historical events in metrical ballads at a time when newspaper was unknown. Sylhet was the recognised seat of these '*Bhāts*' in Bengal in later times. And no place in that district was as famous for the ballads as Bāniachong, and no *Bhāt* achieved there higher laurels than Makaranda, the prince of the ballad-makers of the age gone by.

But the authors of the present ballads have scarcely concerned themselves with great historical episodes or other political revolutions, unless there was also some act of renunciation or great domestic virtue, shedding lustre upon such events. This will be seen in the historical ballads to be published in my second volume. The noble sacrifices which men and women made at the altar of love and devotion in the adjacent localities, proved to be a never-ceasing fountain of inspiration to the rural bards, innocent of all political culture and acquired ideas of nationality. The themes they chose were not of high ambition or valour, but pertained to the quieter virtues of home-life, which, with the intense human interest they carry, have a universal appeal.

Among those who distinguished themselves as singers of these ballads in the past in the district of Mymensing, the following names are the most noteworthy. Most of them are dead now.

(1) Jigir Gayan of the village Jigatala in Pergana Susang.

(2) Sula Gayan of the village Kabichandrapur.

(3) Sibu Gayan (a Patni or boatman by caste) of Pergana Asujia. His ancestors were all good singers. Names of some of them are to be found in the preface to 'Kanka and Lila.'

(4) Ramsankar Gayan (a washerman by caste) of Mashua in the Sub-division of Kishoreganj.

(5) Ravan Gayan (a jola or a low-caste weaver) of Sanchail in the Sub-division of Kishoreganj.

(6) Hari Gayan of Pathuria in Netrakona.

Amongst the modern singers we may name Hiraman Gayan (máli or sweeper by caste) of Jahangirpur, Bipin Gayan (a Kayastha) of Kalika and Abdul Gayan of Basati.

The ballads are out of fashion now.

Chandra Kumar says that these songs are losing public favour every day. Even a hundredth part of what was seen twenty years ago does not exist to-day. In every village, there were singers, and in fact, Mymensing was a veritable nest of singing birds in those days. "It is difficult," writes Chandra Kumar, "to get one singer in ten or fifteen villages now-a-days, and if by chance you meet one he will sing five or six songs and then stop, saying that he does not remember the rest. His memory needs be rusty, when his songs have run out of fashion and his services are not required even once a year. Yet the old peasants bemoan the loss of this treasure with tears in their eyes."

The future historian of Bengal may profitably use this vast material as Tod did the ballads of Rajputana and Kalhan those of Kasmir.

The Bhatial.

The songs are generally sung in that indigenous mode of music which is called the '*bhatial.*' It is the favourite mode of the rustics, especially the boatmen. Its plaintive appeal has a peculiar power of creating indescribable pathos. In the vast expanse of the East Bengal rivers, in the foaming Padma, the white-crested Dhaleswari, in the blue-tinted Brahmaputra and in the marshes and mires run over by the flood, the boatmen, as they ply their boats keeping time with the sound of the oars that strike the waves, yield to the irresistible fascination of their favourite '*bhatial rag*' which fills, so to speak, the whole region of the sky, and in its sweet and prolonged sound seems to be in harmony with the vast expanse, above and below, forming a fitting and congenial environment and background of the songs. The words are simple but the tune is lengthened to an almost endless, though somewhat monotonous, span of sound, moving the rustic heart with intense pathos and sweetness.

XII

Supplementary Notes, Acknowledgments and Concluding Remarks.

In my preface to Malua, I identified Dhalikona *bil* with the Dhalai *bil* mentioned in the ballad. One of the reasons that led me to do it was that I could not find any *bil* in the adjacent locality of the name of Dhalai. 'Dhalai,' the name of the *bil* into which Dewan Jahangir was led by the stratagem of Malua, I thought to be the abbreviated from of 'Dhalai-kona.' But while preparing a map of Eastern Mymensing for this book, I found, on a closer examination, of the Survey of India map a fairly large *bil* named Dhalai lying about eleven miles to the north-east of Jahangirpur and nine miles to the north of Arulia. It had escaped me at first. As we find the name of the *bil* exactly as mentioned in the ballad, situated in a locality easily approachable both from Arulia and Jahangirpur by following the courses of the river Dhanu, there seems to be no reason to doubt that this Dhalai *bil* is the one spoken of in the ballad. In the preface to the ballad of Kamalá, with some hesitancy I identified the village Hulia with Huliara, as I had always a doubt in my mind, that from the phonetic point of view the sounds of the two names might not quite justify this identification. But as Hulia was not to be found in the map I hit on Huliara as the nearest approach to the name, the proximity of this place to Raghupur (Raghurampur) lending support to my conjecture. But since the printing of the preface Mr. Kaliprasad Mallick of the Bengal Police, who lived in Mymensing for twenty years, has informed me that the village Hulia of the ballad appears to him to be the same as Haluaghat in the Sadar Subdivision, not only because the names are nearly the same,—the word *ghat* being a mere suffix and not a part of the name,—but also because close to this village are to be seen at a place called Raghupur the ruins of a palace. This seems to have been once a fortified town. The last owner of this place was one Keshar Rai, whose widow, about two centuries ago, drowned herself in a large tank, after having thrown all the treasures of the house into it, in order to escape from the hands of a gang of robbers who had attacked the place. Mr. Mallick writes, "There is a village about three or four miles from the Haluaghat Police Station in the district of Mymensing in the Sadar Subdivision, where there is a big tank with remains of *pucca ghats*, temples and big houses. The villagers reported that the house and tank belonged to one Keshar Rai who was a very wealthy man, and that after his death some dacoits came to attack the house. While they were attempting to enter the house by breaking open the main entrance, the widow of Keshar Rai threw all the valuables into the tank and committed suicide by drowning herself in it. Another rumour was also current that some property lay hidden near the tank under some huge pieces of stone. Mr. G. R. Macdowel, Additional Superintendent of Police, visited the place during the course of his *thana* inspection in 1909." The existence of a village named Raghupur with the ruins of palatial buildings in the vicinity of Halua or Haluaghat, seems to suggest that Keshar Rai might have been a descendant of Raja Dayal mentioned in the ballad as the lord of the place. The name of the village where Chand Binod lived (Malua) is not clearly indicated in the ballad; but the poet mentions the village as being on the banks of the Sutia. Accordingly in my preface to Malua, I suggested three villages on the Sutia, one of which, I said, might have been the home of the hero. There is, however, a word in the ballad (in L. 86, Canto XVIII) which may be taken to be the name of the village. The word is 'Bangshaia.' It may mean "in the clan or community" and I have given it this meaning in my translation (p. 16, l. 24). But more probably the word would imply the name of a village. I sought for a village 'Bangshaia' in the neighbourhood of the Sutia but found none. There is, however, a village named Bakshaia in that locality. Mistakes in scripts in regard to proper names are very common, and it will be no wonder if Bakshaia has been changed into Bangshaia—a more familiar word which the scribe is likely to have adopted by mistake.

The difference lies only in one or two letters *viz.*, '*ng*' for '*k.*' There is an old *kancha* road as indicated in the map from Bakshaia to Arulia. I could not find any trace of the villages Kanchannagar on the Dhanu (Mahua), and Dighalhati (Malua and Dewan Bhabna), though their geographical position is clearly indicated in the ballads. These villages must have totally disappeared and been reduced to mere mounds. It is not improbable also that some of the villages latterly adopted other names than those mentioned in the ballads. The maps issued by the Survey of India professing to give the names of all the villages are found defective in certain instances. Not only are the names of *haors* and small rivers omitted but even the names of villages are not infrequently missed. The names of the well-known rivers like the Fuleswari and Raji are not given. Unless, therefore, one is satisfied by a local enquiry, one cannot be sure on these points.

In conclusion I beg to acknowledge my deep gratitude to my esteemed friends Mrs. M. M Urquhart, the wife of Dr. Urquhart, Principal, Scottish Churches College, Captain Petavel, our University's widely known Poverty Problem Lecturer, and Mr. C. S. Paterson, the Secretary of the Y. M. C. A., for carefully going through the proofs of some of the ballads. The urgency of the press required them often to do this work for me in great haste and at a considerable sacrifice of their own valuable time. Still I cannot say that the book is free from errors. I had often to read the proofs myself without having the opportunity of help from outside, and I am not at all a good proof reader. Mr. A. C. Ghatak, Superintendent of the University Press, took a lively interest in the ballads as they are the poetry of his own native district, and the completion of the present volume in two parts within less than three months is entirely due to the great energy with which he expedited the work through the press. I am glad to note that almost all my friends, European and Indian, who read these ballads, have expressed their keen appreciation of their literary and poetical value. Mrs. Urquhart, a gifted lady of high refinement and culture, was specially struck with the beauty of these rural songs. I quote her remarks about Dewana Madina. "It is a very charming story, full of right feeling and with a very just appreciation of human motive, Shakespearian in its directness and simplicity. I like the restraint of the action. You have the possibilities of a great stage in India with your insight into human motive and natural dramatic gifts."

I had to labour very hard in connection with these ballads for more than three years. Apart from the pains involved in doing the literary portion of the work,—such as collating the MSS., improving the arrangement of the original composition, which in a few cases consisted of stray songs without much order or sequence, writing commentary on the texts, and historical and linguistic notes for the Introduction and translating the ballads into English—I had to keep up a steady and lengthy correspondence with Chandra Kumar for all these years defining his work and directing the course he was to follow at every stage of his research. Though he was actually in the field collecting the ballads, my anxious eyes have always followed him with the utmost solicitude in the performance of his task. I noted regularly in my diary the names of the persons he approached, and of the villages he visited in course of his tour, and suggested to him other villages which I knew of by my private enquiries. With his valuable help, and with a score of large Survey of India maps of Eastern Mymensing I had to work hard in identifying the places mentioned in the ballads, and the present map, hereto annexed, is the result of this labour.

Our University funds, as everybody knows, are far from satisfactory. I have spent some money from my own pocket in performing this arduous task. Dr. Abanindra Nath Tagore, C.I.E., has contributed Rs. 100 towards the cost of the map. Rai Bahadur G. C. Ghosh, the founder of Stephanos

Nirmalendu Ghosh Chair of our University, on receipt of a present of one of my latest publications, sent *me* Rupees hundred as a token of his appreciation. This amount and the small sum of about fifty rupees received from Babu Kiran Chandra Dutta, Secretary, the Bani Sevaka Samiti of Calcutta, I have used for the purposes of the illustrations given in this book. The University has supplemented this money by a grant of fifty rupees. My friend Mr. Satish Chandra Sinha, the well-known painter and artist, has drawn the pen-and-ink sketches. I should acknowledge with thanks that Mr. Sinha, Mr. D. N. Dhar, who has prepared litho impressions of the map and Mr. N. Chakravarty, who has made blocks of the illustrations, have all done their work at a reduced rate out of a patriotic motive.

I had sent advance copies of a few printed ballads to two illustrious men requesting them to favour me with an expression of their opinion in two or three brief sentences, so that, if they were favourable, I might use them as mottos on the title page. One was sent to the Earl of Ronaldshay, our late Governor, and another to Sir George Grierson, the recognised authority on Indian Vernaculars. Sir George Grierson wrote many complimentary things about the ballads and felt greatly interested in their collection. I am indebted to him for the suggestion of the famous words of Andrew Fletcher which I have put in as motto on the title page. Lord Ronaldshay wrote to me as follows :—" I have read Mahua with the greatest interest. After reading Mahua I sat down to write a few words about the ballads. I had intended merely to write two or three sentences of appreciation. But when I thought over the special interest and value of such a collection as the one which you have in hand, I found that what I wanted to say, could not be said in a few words only." He has favoured me with an appreciation which I have taken the liberty of using as foreword for this book. I felt gratified like one who wanted a penny but got a gold coin. Lord Ronaldshay is one of the greatest statesmen that ever came to this province as its ruler. The glare of his high administrative qualities and exalted rank has cast his fame as a scholar into comparative shade. But those who have read his book on the Eastern Himalayas and heard his addresses on Indian topics, especially Buddhism, know well that he has studied Indian history not only with the diligence of a student but with the enthusiasm of a lover.

In conclusion I offer my hearty gratitude to Sir Asutosh Mookerjee. Fifteen years ago I had already established some reputation as a writer in the field of Bengali letters. It was Sir Asutosh who drew me then from the seclusion of my narrow scope of work to the cause of our *Alma Mater* by engaging me to write a History of Bengali Language and Literature in English. The numerous works I have since written in English, which have elicited praise from the Press and Orientalists all over Europe, are solely due to the never-failing encouragement given me by that great Bengali.

We earnestly look forward to better days dawning on our University in near future when all the difficulties that beset her will have passed away, and we feel confident that under our present Chancellor, the scion of a family with claims on undying and universal fame in the world of letters, she will flourish and steadily advance in the cause of enlightenment and culture. I sincerely believe that His Excellency will be true to the great reputation of his noble ancestry. My own regret is, that with my shattered health, in fact with death in sight, I see no prospects of living to behold the glories of our University in the coming years. I have worked hard all my life to interpret my country to the world of learning. The true history of our people in comparatively modern times is not contained in the copper plate and rock inscriptions or in the accounts left by the foreign travellers. Neither are they to be found in the administrative accounts of the Moslem period or even in the Sanskrit classics. The real history of our people lies buried in the Vernacular works of each province, but which have not received the attention they deserve from scholars. I have tried all these years to draw attention to this important find by my numerous publications, English and Bengali. I feel myself entitled to the wages of a poor day-labourer engaged in collecting materials for a great purpose. The architect who is to build the future Taj mahal of Bengal in the region of her annals, consecrated to the recording of the tales of her illustrious heroes of the past—the historian who will give shape to all this material and construct a glorious account of our national life, is coming, and is not far off. This I foresee and I am so sure of it that I almost hear the sound of his foot-steps. But I may not live to see this achievement of my long-cherished hope. Meantime as a reward for the unremitting labours I have taken all my life I only wish to hear the words "well done," at the close of my career, if indeed it is to close now, from Sir Asutosh, His Excellency the Chancellor, and the Vice-Chancellor of our University, under whom I have been working.

I am afraid that some scholars may consider my estimate of the literary merits of the ballads to be higher than they really deserve. All that I can say is that I have written from my strong conviction. A European critic while speaking lately of one of my recent publications in terms of eulogy, charged me with over-estimating every good thing of Bengal, "which," he said, "is probably the outcome of ultra-modern nationalist enthusiasm." Even my kind friend Dr. Sylvain Levi referred good-humouredly to my "fanatic love" for Bengal in his foreword to my work "Chaitanya and his Age." If I have really loved Bengal overmuch, I have no reason to be ashamed of it. This love has been a great asset to me. But for this love no one could work as hard as I have done for a period of more than a quarter of a century in the hitherto unexplored field of old Bengali Literature which, only a little above a decade ago, was treated with contempt by my own countrymen. All honour to Sir Asutosh who has redeemed our past literature in the estimation of our countrymen by recognising it in the Post-Graduate Studies of the Calcutta University.

I will deal with the ballads bearing on the political history of Bengal in the second volume.

DINESH CHANDRA SEN.

7, Bishwakosh Lane,
Bagbazar, Calcutta.
The 30th September, 1923.

MAHUA THE GYPSY GIRL

PREFACE

This ballad is more in the form of a melodrama than a lyric poem and is complete in 755 lines; this odd number is due to the omission of certain lines which could not be traced by the compiler.

A tradition, prevalent throughout Eastern Mymensingh. ascribes the authorship of the drama to one Dvija Kanai, a priest of the Nama Sudra caste, who lived about 300 years ago. It is said that he organised a party of players and was the first to put the melodrama on the stage. Dvija Kanai is reputed to have fallen in love with a Nama Sudra woman of a social status inferior to his own. It is said that in the course of his devoted love, the poet himself experienced some of the sufferings ascribed to Naderchand. Tradition says that it is for this reason that he was able to portray the sentiments of the Brahmin lord in such a life-like and vivid way. But no details of this love-affair or indeed of any other events of his life are known to us.

The preliminary hymn of 16 lines, which I have not translated but which is to be found in the original text, was evidently composed by a Mahomedan *Gyen* or minstrel who sang it at a later period.

Mahua was at one time very popular in Eastern Mymensingh. But the freedom and romance of love in the melodrama could not, for obvious reasons, meet with the approval of the orthodox community which grew more and more rigid in later times as the Brahminic influence spread throughout the district. It has, therefore, naturally ceased to have any popularity amongst the Hindus, and this once favourite ballad is now almost forgotten. The peasants and other low-class people, specially the Mahomedans who do not share the scruples of the Hindus, occasionally sing some of its songs, and it was with great difficulty that Babu Chandra Kumar was able to recover the whole of it. Yet the shape in which it was at first compiled seemed to me to be faulty in many respects. Chandra Kumar tells me that owing to the opposition of the orthodox Brahmins who condemned the poem as corrupting the morals of young women, the song is scarcely sung now in Hindu houses. He had to take infinite trouble to gather scraps from peasants of different localities, none of whom (except Shek Ashakali) could give him more than one or two songs. As I have already said, the shape in which Chandra Kumar sent me his collection was far from satisfactory. In many places I found portions of some earlier cantos dovetailed into the end of the song. Naderchand's sorrows at parting with the gipsy-girl, before he had left his palace, were found incorporated with those he experienced in course of his search for her at a much later period. The romantic life of the pair in a far-off wilderness where they made a temporary residence is full of poetic situations and wonderfully happy imagery. The songs embodying these were found strewn at random over the whole collection in a quite unconnected way. I had to take great pains to rearrange the poem by a close and careful study of the text. The incongruities of the original compilation have, I hope, now been almost entirely removed. The compiler has informed me that the melodrama was interspersed with prose portions in the form of dialogues, which he could not collect. So the present text cannot be called perfect or faultless.

The subject of this ballad is a historical one. The places mentioned in it,—Kanchanpur, Baman Kandi, the river Dhanu (*lit.* bow), etc., are within the jurisdiction of the subdivision of Netrokona and under the police-station of Khaliajuri. Fifteen miles to the north of Rahamatpur lies the vast marsh known as "*Talar Hawor.*" To the east of this *Hawor* lie Baman Kandi, Baidar Dighi, Thakur Barir Bhita, Ulua Kandi and other places reduced to mounds,—once associated with the gipsies and the unfortunate hero of the tale—Naderchand. These places are now void of human habitation, but in the adjoining low lands one may see in their proper season, the rich crops of *shali* rice bending low with their gold-coloured ears—ready for the reaper's scythe.

The people relate many incidents of the life of Naderchand associated with the locality. The Baidar Dighi is the tank dug by the gipsy leader Homra in the part of the town, called Ulua Kandi, and the Thakur Barir Bhita represents the spot where once stood the palace of the Brahmin Raja.

People further north have, in recent years, advanced a claim on the incidents of the play as having taken place in their own locality. There is a Bamangaon in Susang Durgapur, near the Garo Hills. It is within 6 miles of Jigatala—the native village of the reputed song-master Azim Gayen. The nearness of this Bamangaon to the river Kangsha and to the Garo Hills has made some people imagine that the dwelling place of the Brahmin lord once stood here; and local tradition, probably of a much later origin, has tried to associate the incidents of the ballad with this place. This tradition may have got additional support from the desire of some of the singers of Jigatala to bring the scene of the melodrama nearer their own home.

But we find in the ballad itself that Homra the gipsy-chief was a native of the Jainta Hills which is but an eastern continuation of the ranges named the Garo and the Khasia Hills. It is stated in this song that the gipsies took one full month to reach Baman Kandi from their native hills. The Bamangaon of Durgapur is only 3 or 4 miles from the Jainta Hills whereas the Baman Kandi near *Talar Hawor* is about 60 miles to the north of those hills. Naderchand took some months to reach the Jainta Hills in quest of

Mahua. Of course neither the gipsies nor the Brahmin lord made one continuous journey, halting as they did at several stations,—the former in response to professional engagements and the latter in course of his search. Nor are the accounts given by the poet of time and space to be absolutely trusted, though the story is founded on facts. Yet from a perusal of the whole ballad it appears certain that the tradition which came down to the poet was that the home of the gipsies was far away from the village of Baman Kandi. It could by no means be only 2 or 3 miles. Besides the name of the village as mentioned in the ballad is Baman Kandi and not Bamangaon.

The ballad is written in the unadorned dialect of the rustics, but whether from the standpoint of supreme interest gathered round a complicated plot, or of the simple grandeur of the characters of the hero and the heroine, or from the points of view of freedom from all convention and a rapid succession of thrilling but romantic dramatic situations, it has a unique position in the whole range of Bengali Literature. And we hail Dvija Kanai for having vindicated the glory in the domain of poetry of the Nama Sudra community whom we have branded as a depressed caste and maltreated for centuries.

The drama evidently belongs to the romantic school, but its romance is toned down by a great many realistic incidents. Its brevity more than earns the compliment of the great poet who defines that quality "as the soul of wit" —by its striking contrast with the well-known verbosity of the classical school of Bengali poetry. The situations created often reach the level of idealism, but they move with a dramatic speed, scarcely giving the readers an opportunity to indulge in extravagant fancy. It will indeed be difficult to find another work in our literature which can approach the excellence of Mahua in respect of perfection of plot, romantic situations, richness of realistic incidents, brevity, force and literary grace. Its language is certainly crude, to which objection may be taken in some quarters. But for this crudeness, we would have got merely a string of glittering syllables, artificial and true to convention, and not the genuine expression of the people's heart as disclosed in this remarkable book. Couched in the coarse language of the people, sneeringly called the *patois*, this melodrama carries an intense poetic interest, shewing the fire that burns in the heart of our people, holy as the light of a temple on the banks of the sacred river.

In conclusion I take the liberty of quoting below a letter written to me in appreciation of Mahua by my esteemed friend Dr. Stella Kramrisch, Ph.D., our well-known critic of Indian Art.

23, THEATRE ROAD,
25th March. 1923.

DEAR SIR,

I wanted to write to you the very evening when I had the great privilege of listening to your reading of the translation of "Mahua." Unfortunately I was seized with fever on my return home. All the time Mahua, Naderchand, and the gipsies were round me and kept me in a world hitherto unknown to me, where emotions are deep and yet as simple as nursery rhymes, where nature echoes the voice of the human heart and man is spontaneous. Yet he fits into the plot as the seasons, which accompany his happiness and yearnings, fit into the course of the year.

The whole melodrama is welded together by a music of emotions and yet every character stands out by itself. Mahua's love and heroic death are not symbols of transcendental value. They have no other religion than that of the human heart in all its purity and strength. How dispassionately is Homra, the gipsy leader, Mahua's foster father, represented! His wrath and cruelty do not appear as such, they seem to be acts of subjective justice —that is to say even his figure has so much human appeal that we are bound to feel with him. And so it is with every one of them. Palanka, the maiden, Mahua's devoted friend, redeems the stern fervour of the action by a lyrical tenderness, natural and fresh like a flower and never sentimental.

Woman plays the leading part in our drama. Homra is nothing but setting and frame for Mahua's actions, and Naderchand, the youthful Brahmin lord, is the object which enables her to realise her devotion and greatness.

The play—but it is ballad—only it makes me wish to see it acted in all its dramatic conciseness—rushes on in one straight line from beginning to climax and there it breaks down. Characters and situations are sketched with utmost economy, that makes them so distinct and at the same time as closely interwoven as the variegated melodies of a song. Each person has a tune of his own; one need not know the name nor see the actor, yet one is bound to recognise him.

The simple intensity of composition and diction reminded me of that standard work of medieval European Literature—'Aucassin and Nicolette'; there too the narrow prejudices of society do not concern hero and heroine. And there up to now we knew of the connection and similarity of folk-literature in different countries and your 'Folk Literature of Bengal' furnished us with first-hand material. But we were unable to witness the affinity of people's poetry just on the verge where folklore and art become one. Also as far as my knowledge of Indian literature goes, I do not know of anything similarly fresh and immediate. Every sentence of the melo-drama Mahua can stand by itself and is final. It needs no ornament and no explanation. Bengal must be proud to have recovered such a treasure of her own—and you told me that it is only one of many. I sincerely hope your splendid discovery will find as much appreciation in Bengal itself as it is bound to get from all connoisseurs of literature in Europe and I am anxiously looking forward to the publication of all the ballads of Bengal.

Thanking you once more for the great pleasure of having come to know of these unique pieces of literature.

Yours sincerely,
STELLA KRAMRISCH.

Chandra Kumar collected this poem from several persons. For the major portion of it he is indebted to Umesh Chandra De and to Shek Asakali of Mashka, a village in Netrokana. The latter was already 80 years old when Chandra Kumar approached him for the song about two years ago. He also got great help from Nashu Shek of Ghorali. Both Maskha and Ghorali are near the postal town of Sandikona in Eastern Mymensingh. Some of the songs of the latter part of the ballad were taken down by the compiler in pencil as a ploughman was singing them while engaged in field-work. All these men are perfectly illiterate. It is said that there is still a party of professional singers at Mashka, who sing Mahua.

I received the poem of Mahua from Babu Chandra Kumar De on the 9th of March, 1921.

DINESH CHANDRA SEN.

7, BISHWAKOSH LANE, BAGBAZAR,
Calcutta, 28th February 1923.

MAHUA THE GIPSY GIRL

1. Homra—the Gipsy-Leader.

It takes six months to reach the Garo Hills by land. Beyond these hills are the snowy ranges of the Himalayas. And far on the other side of these ranges there are Seven Seas. The Sun and the Moon do not illuminate these regions. No human form moves there. The impenetrable forests are infested with tigers and bears.

Close to these forests, there was, however, at one time a small settlement of men. Their leader was Homra—a gipsy. O my friends, Hindus and Mahomedans, listen to the story of this gipsy-chief. He was a robber—the leader of a gang, and had a younger brother named Mainka. They wandered about in various places. I shall now relate to you at some length the wonderful story of this band of gipsies.

Once they travelled far and reached the banks of the Dhanu (*lit.*, the bow). There stood a village on its banks called Kanchanpur, in which dwelt an old Brahmin who had a beautiful baby-girl. The child was six months old. Towards the end of the night Homra, the leader of the gipsies, stole her and fled away.

The girl of six months grew to be one year old, and like a bird was thus caged and nurtured in the house of the gipsy—till she came to be a damsel of sixteen years—an expert player excelling chiefly in rope-dancing. Her beauty was so dazzling that she looked like a gem on a serpent's hood or a bright stone in a

[1] The writer belonged to the Sub-division of Netrokona in Mymensing. He implies the distance of the Garo Hills from his own district, though it is much exaggerated.

dark house. Whoever saw her was charmed. When she walked, her long-flowing tresses seemed to touch her very ankles. One could see the *champa* flower blooming, as it were, on her cheeks. Her large and bright eyes were as lovely as evening stars. No one who saw her for a moment ever forgot her. Even a saint would harbour thoughts of her in his mind, forgetting his ascetic vows.

With this girl Homra wandered about from place to place. Delighted with her handsome looks, Homra's wife gave her the name of 'Mahua' (after that of a wild flower that grows in hilly places). Ll. 1-36.

2. Scene : The Garo Hills.

Homra addressed his brother Máinka and said "Let us, O brother, go to some distant place to exhibit our feats."

Máinka said, "Very well, let us start on Friday next."

On the morning of Friday the gipsies packed up their things and got ready for the journey.

Homra, the leader of the party, went ahead of the others, followed by his brother Mainka, and behind them their numerous players, talking and shouting. They took with them camps, ropes and bamboos, besides trained parrots, jackdaws, gold-beaked '*dayals*' and other birds in cages. Horses and asses they had many in their train and took with them also the charmed bone of a Chandal—their talisman of success. There were many trained dogs with them for pursuing and seizing foxes and porcupines. Thus they travelled many a mile in jubilant spirits.

With them went Mahua—the beautiful one. Merrily did she go talking gaily with her companion Palanka. Many days passed on the way and at the end of the month they reached a village named Bamankanda. Ll. 1-19.

3. The Court of Naderchand.

The lord of the village was Naderchand—the Brahmin youth. Surrounded by his friends and courtiers he sat resplendent like the moon among the stars. The messenger Langra approached him and said, " Hear me, O lord, a new band of gipsies has arrived in our city. They want to show their feats of skill. With them is a young woman. She is very handsome. In fact I have never seen a maiden as beautiful as this gipsy-girl."

When Naderchand heard this, he rose up and went to the inner apartment, and saluting his mother, said," A new band of gipsies has come to our town. They want to give a show. If you have no objection, O mother, I wish to engage them."

Mother.

" What will be the cost ?"

Naderchand.

" A hundred rupees."

Mother.

" Yes, you may engage them, let them have their show in the outer court of our palace." Ll. 1-18.

4. The Gipsy Shows.

Homra called his brother Máinka and said " Take the bows and the quiver full of arrows. Let us go to the house of the young lord to exhibit our feats." Saying this Homra beat his drum. At the sound the people of the town began to run to the spot from all directions.

One man said to another, "There is going to be at the house of our lord an exhibition by the gipsies. Let us hurry on."

People sat on all sides and the young lord took his place in the midst of them and began to peep this way and that with curiosity.

As soon as the gipsy-girl appeared on the scene and gracefully shook the long bamboo, Naderchand, who had sat in the midst of his men, at once stood up steadily gazing at her. But when the girl ascended the top of the bamboo and began to show her skill, the young lord anxiously cried out, "Ah me, she may fall down from that height and die!"

She stood at the top of the bamboo and sang beating the tabor with her own hands, her bracelets making a jingling sound as she did so. Smiling she said from her place of eminence:—

"I have shown my tricks, now I must have some reward from our young lord." But within her heart she thought, "May I win his heart, that will be my best reward." Naderchand at once presented his shawl, worth a thousand rupees, to her, and besides gave her a great sum of money.

Homra prayed for a house to live in; the youth at once made him a grant of a good plot of land. The gift was made by a regular document. He also gave sufficient rice and other food-stuffs to the party to last for many months.

Naderchand said, "Now you have got lands from me and the documents are in your hands. Go to the part of my town called 'Uluakándi' where your land is and build a good house there."

A fine house was built on the plot of land. But Mahua, as she entered the house, began to weep.

Her foster-father planted brinjal-plants and said, "Do not weep, dear Mahua, I will sell brinjals and with the price buy a necklace for you."

In the new garden he produced quantities of bean and gently said to Mahua, "What good will there be with all these if you, my dear girl, do not stay with me? Say, that you will, or I will cut my own throat."

The edible roots grew plentifully in the garden and the old gipsy promised Mahua a pair of bracelets from the sale of these. From the proceeds of the sale of bananas he said he would buy her a beautiful chain.

The thatch-walls of the garden-house were decorated with glass doors and it was protected on all sides by a fence of plants.

One day he killed some pigeons, geese and parrots and said to the girl, "Cook a nice curry with these. Do not forget to put into it spices, specially the '*kalijira*' (cumin seed)."[1]

Thus did Homra, the gipsy, try to please Mahua and keep her engaged in the garden house. Ll. 1-38.

5. Naderchand and Mahua at the River-ghat.

One day Naderchand was passing that way. It was evening and the lamps were newly lighted in the houses by the way-side. Mahua was returning home having shown her dancing in the town. He met her all alone and said softly, "Will you wait a little to hear me, O maiden? When the moon-beams gently spread in the eastern horizon and the sun fades in the west, may I to-morrow at such an hour expect you at the river-ghat all alone? If the pitcher in your arms proves too heavy after it is filled with water, I will be there, dear maiden, to help you in lifting it up."

With the pitcher of water she went to the river-side in the evening. Naderchand was already there waiting for her.

[1] *Nigella Indica.*

Naderchand.

"You are so intent on filling your pitcher with water, do you recollect, dear maiden, what I told you yesterday ?"

Mahua.

"But, O Prince, O stranger, not a word do I recollect of what, you say, you have told me."

Naderchand.

"So young, so fresh, and yet so forgetful! It is only one night since that I told you."

Mahua.

"But you are a stranger, Prince, I feel greatly embarrassed in talking with you."

Naderchand.

"You have pushed the pitcher into the water, maiden, and gentle ripples have arisen. How beautiful you look! Smile on me, maiden, and speak to me. There is none here to see us. Who is your father and who your mother ? Where used you to be, maiden, before you came to our town ?"

Mahua.

"I have no parents, Prince, no, nor any brother to call mine own. I am like a weed turned adrift in the stream. Ill-starred am I, O Prince, I have become a gipsy living among the gipsies. With the fire in my heart I am inwardly consumed. There is none here to feel for me—to whom I may open my heart! You have a beautiful wife, O Prince, and happy are you at your home with her."

Naderchand.

"Hard is your heart like stone, O fair maiden, your words are untrue. I have no wife, I am still unmarried. Hard is your heart and hard is the heart of your parents! They have not yet given you a mate. You are allowing your youth to pass in vain."

Mahua,

"Hard is your heart, and hard the heart of your parents! No bride have they given you though you are a grown man, O stranger."

Naderchand.

"True, dear girl, my heart is hard and hard is the heart of my parents, but I assure you if I could win one like you, I would not remain hard but become a tender husband."

Mahua (affecting to be angry).

"You are a shameless youth to say so. Your words are insulting. Get a pitcher and tie it round your neck and drown yourself in the river."

Naderchand.

"Gladly do I take your sentence, fair maiden. Do you be the stream and I will drown myself therein." Ll. 1-44.

6. Palanka and Mahua.

Palanka.

"By my life hear me, O sister Mahua. Will you not tell me the secret of your heart? Why do you go to the river-ghat in the evening all alone? You spend the whole night weeping; I can detect the traces of your tears on your cheeks. Tell me in confidence the reason of all this. Why is it that you often sigh and gaze in the direction of the Brahmin lord's palace? The rumour here is that Naderchand has got a fancy for you and that he is charmed by your songs."

Softly did Mahua tell her story. "How can I, O dear Palanka, soothe the pain of my heart! Let us go away from this country. I have tried my best but it is not possible to change the mind's course. I cannot bring it to reason. It will not listen to good counsel." (She weeps.)

Palanka.

"You should follow my advice, dear sister; for seven days stop going to the river-ghat. If he comes here to enquire, I will tell him, 'Mahua, the beautiful one, died last night.'

Mahua (softly).

"If I do not see him for a day, that will itself kill me. The sun and the moon and you, my dear companion, be my witness. This Brahmin youth is the husband of my heart. I may go with the gipsies wherever they may lead me, but, believe me there is none amongst you who has now the power to bind me to this party. With him will I go, no matter where he leads me. Unless I can do this, I will either take poison or tie a rope round my neck and hang myself."

7. HOMRA AND MAINKA TALK BETWEEN THEMSELVES.

Homra.

"I tell you, brother Mainka, we must leave this place and go elsewhere. What shall I do with this goodly looking house and garden? Far better to live a-begging from door to door. Have you not heard, dear brother, that my daughter Mahua is crazed about the Brahmin lord!"

Mainka.

"What nonsense you talk, O brother? How can we leave this beautiful place? The landing steps of our tank are made of stone. This lovely tank of ours is full of water to the brim. Look there, our fields smile near the garden-house. The '*shali*' crops are ripe; they are gold-coloured. When we grind these we shall have good '*chira*' for our meal. Do not, for goodness sake, leave this country." Ll. 1-10.

8. The Still Hour of Night. Mahua and Naderchand meet.

The month of March is about to pass and the smile of April is already upon nature. From the boughs of the trees the gay note of the cuckoo is heard. It sings 'coo-oo.' The crops of '*shali*' rice with their flowering ears, full of ripe grain, have spread a charm over the fields. At midnight Naderchand rose from his sleep. He took up his flute and signalled to Mahua. In the sky the skylark was singing.

At the sound of the flute the beautiful one awoke. The houses were all newly built and the gipsies slept soundly in them. She was maddened by the flute and came out of the house. With slow steps the damsel advanced towards the landing-ghat of the river and there met Naderchand, who absorbed in his emotion, was still playing the flute. She ran to his embrace and he said tenderly, "I will leave my parents, my palace and my riches. With you I will go to a distant country."

The gipsy-girl wept and hung like a creeper on his neck and said, "I am helpless like a bird kept in a cage. Were you a flower, my love, I would hide you in my braids. I swear by you I will put an end to my life. Let us part. Go back to your palace and leave me. Do not, I pray you, for my sake trouble yourself."

She sobbed and ended here. Both were talking in this way, but a pair of piercing eyes pursued them all the while without their knowledge. He was on the track, following a little behind.

When the dawn peered through the east Naderchand returned to his palace. And with a pitcher in her arms Mahua came to the landing-ghat. Ll. 1-28.

9. Their Last Meeting in the Town.

Mahua.

"To-night we are going to leave this town of yours, my lord. I shall go with my foster-father and mother. This is the end, we shall meet no more. Never again shall we see each other. O how cruel! How can I live without seeing you? I am a helpless woman and must think of honour and caste. How can I go against the will of my elders? I leave my sweet garden-home and leave *you.* Alas, how shall I control my mad heart? No more shall I hear, my lord, your sweet flute calling me! No more shall I pass happy nights, all-wakeful and happy in your company! And no more shall I wake from sleep to see your sweet face again! No more shall I wander by the river-side in your company!

"Before I end, one word more. If ever you should feel a desire to meet me after this, come, some days hence, to the north (in the Garo Hills) and look for a house there fenced with long reeds and with doors open to the south. There shall we stay for some months before going on our wanderings again. If you come to that house of ours, you will find its hospitable doors open for you. How glad shall I be to spread a seat for you and serve you with '*chira*' of the '*shali*' rice, good bananas and curd made from buffalo milk.

"But perhaps this is the last meeting, and we shall never see each other again." Ll. 1-27,

Flight with the Treasure

"The gipsies all fled from the land of Naderchand, the Brahman lord."

Mahua, p. 11

10. The Gipsies Desert the Place.

Homra to Mainka.

"I am confirmed in my suspicion, I will not stay here a moment more. Let the garden and the house go to hell. No more do I care for the '*shali*' crops which are now ripe. By my life, O brother, we should not stay in this place for a day more."

They took their bamboos and ropes and all the rest of their possessions. In the dark night the gipsies all fled from the land of Naderchand—the Brahman lord.

They left the beautiful houses they had built, the crops in the field and their garden of fruit-trees. People were astonished at their sudden disappearance.

But when the young lord heard of it, he had just sat down to eat; the food he had lifted to his mouth dropped from his hand; his parents asked him many questions but he gave no reply. People said the young lord had lost his reason. Ll. 1-12.

11. Naderchand Resolves to Leave his Town.

Naderchand (alone).

"The house is falling down with the roof unrepaired. The bird is flown away, the cage remains. Here all alone she sat in the courtyard and wove garlands of flowers cleverly without a string.

"Days and months have passed and no more shall we see each other. I was a good Brahmin but my luck has ordained it otherwise."

Naderchand to his Mother.

"Make my rice ready, mother, for dinner. Do not stand in my way. I am bound for distant lands, to visit the far-off shrines. Give me permission, O mother.

The Mother.

" Dear as the apple of my eyes are you my son ! A moment parted from you, I feel pangs of age-long separation. You are my only son. There is none in this our palace for whom to light the evening lamp. With you I would happily share the fate of a beggar but not the pleasures of a palace without you. How many wintry nights, dear son, did I not spend waking and watching you as a baby ! What pains and anxieties I passed through, covering you with my *sadi*, when my own uncovered back lay exposed to the biting cold ! How can the pangs of a mother's heart be expressed ! If the son dies, far away in a foreign land, before any one has known it, the notice comes first to the mother's heart in a strange manner. No, I can never reconcile myself to parting from you. If you leave the palace, dear son, I will die of broken heart." Ll. 1-25.

12. NADERCHAND LEAVES HIS HOME.

It was the very depth of night. What did the hapless Naderchand do? He entered the room of his mother silently and bowed to her,—sleeping. He called the sun and the moon to witness and said, " To-day I leave this palace and everything that I have so long called my own. I am now bound for strange lands. I leave my parents and other inmates of the house. Though I had all that people wish for, I give up my all of my own accord."

He bowed to the sky which gets light from the sun, the moon and the stars. He bowed to his parents.

In that dark and silent hour of night Naderchand became homeless for the sake of the gipsy-girl. Ll. 1-10.

13. Naderchand searches Mahua.

He is not looking for the shrines—Benares, Gya and Brindaban. What does he care for these? It is the gipsy-girl whom he is seeking.

One month passed, then two months; three months passed and no clue did he get as to where Mahua had gone.

Where are the Jaiter hills about which she spoke? Like a madman did Naderchand wander about day and night. Travellers he saw going by the way; and of them he enquired, if they had seen a party of gipsies going. The cowboys ran in the field and played, and our young lord asked them, "Have you seen a girl of the name of Mahua? Her eyes are beautiful as a pair of stars and her hair like clouds. Has my sweet parrot flown to these skies? The beautiful one ascends the tall bamboos and dances on the rope. Her curling hair gracefully hangs about her face. If she sits in a dark room her dazzling colour shines like bright gold! With such an one does the gipsy-leader wander from place to place. In the garden the flowers bloom and on the hills bright stones sparkle; but none so beautiful as she; mad am I after her."

"How lovely the landing steps of the river here! Surely she filled her pitcher from these steps. Feign would I be drowned in this stream hallowed by the touch of my love!

"This is the path she trod. How happy I would have been to catch a sight of her from the distance if I had been here at the time!

"Alas, how am I to meet you, Mahua? Did we not vow to each other that separation even for a day would kill us!

"Ye birds that fly in the sky—ye see things from far. Can ye tell me what path the gipsies have taken?"

* * * * *

He could tell from the signs the place where Mahua had cooked her meal. He sat there and wept. He saw the signs of horses' hoofs and the grass with blades half-eaten by the goats of the gipsies. He understood that they had been there during March and April.

May and June passed in this way. The young wanderer trod the uneven paths of the waste-land, weeping.

Then came July and August in succession. The clouds passed from the eastern horizon to the western, roaring. And so also passed September and October. All these months Naderchand wandered about night and day seeking the gipsy-girl in every direction.

In the month of October the goddess Durga used to be worshipped at his home with great pomp. But this year the temple was without her image. The parents wept and the kinsmen lay plunged in deep sorrow.

And he, alternately burning in the rays of the sun and drenched in rain, passed his days and nights in agony all alone.

In November the mothers of Bengal worshipped the god Kartikeya praying for the welfare of their sons. But the eyes of his poor mother were blinded by tears.

In December, however, when the cold had not yet become severe on the banks of the Kangsha, he suddenly met Mahua. It was as though the parched lips had found a drop of water or the mad bee the scent of a full-blown lotus. Ll. 1-45.

14. The Guest.

A stranger is the guest at the house to-day.

Mahua with a pitcher in hand goes to the river for water.

The people of the party whisperingly say, "Ah, her youthful charms have grown pale and faded."

"She neither sleeps in the night nor takes her usual meals. She says there is pain in her head which maddens her and that her body aches continually and she spreads her own *sadi* on the floor and lies down there and weeps.

She seldom cooks, or plays with her comrades. Thus six months have passed—her life is despaired of.

"But what a strange change to-day! One, dead these six months, is won over to the fresh vigour of life."

She goes to the river-ghat and cooks her meal. The guest partakes of it giving up his caste.

Homra.

"Brother Mainka, I will examine to-day what sort of man this stranger is." (To the guest.) "Live with me, O lad. Our avocation is to give acrobatic exhibitions with bamboos and ropes. I shall get you trained in our art. Carefully learn it. All the year round we travel in the country-side showing our feats." Ll. 1-20.

15. Homra offers a Knife to Mahua.

It was a dark night and the stars sparkled in the sky. Homra, the gipsy leader, meditated long and resolved to do something.

On the banks of the Kangsha there was a *hijal* tree. Naderchand had made a bed of leaves under the tree and was sleeping.

Mahua was sleeping quietly in her bed. Homra went near her and called aloud, "Awake, O daughter. I have reared you up these sixteen summers. You must obey me to-day, that is the reward I ask for all my pains."

Mahua had been dreaming of her guest and the voice of her father passed by her ears like the roaring of clouds. She rose up from her bed, all startled. As she opened her eyes they met her foster-father's which burnt like flaming fires. He said, "Take this knife and go to the river-side. Naderchand is sleeping there. You are to kill him at once and then throw the blood-tinged knife into the river. What pains have I not taken to bring you up! Believe me, this stranger knows hypnotism. He is our enemy. You must plunge this knife into his heart straight."

There was no moon, and the stars that had been visible had disappeared. The lovely sky with the golden moon-beams was now overcast with clouds and looked like a sealed book.

She hesitated for a moment and then took the knife and went where the Brahmin lord was sleeping. Her long tresses, in their wavy dance, aspired to touch her very ankles, and tears were falling from her eyes. She turned like one insane and could not devise any means of escape. Ll. 1-28.

16. Mahua goes to the River-ghat and Weeps.

She tried to turn her heart into steel and sat near the bed of the sleeping Naderchand. O how handsome did he look! It was as though the moon had fallen from the sky down on the river-banks. She lifted the knife once, lifted it twice and then a third time. Each time she dropped it and then softly said, "How long will you sleep, O youth? Look and see your unfortunate Mahua weeping. My father's heart is made of stone; his order is that I should kill you. But how can I do so? Hard as stone is the heart of my father and hard as stone is my own heart. How can one think that I could be a monster like that and return home after killing you? Our lamp is lighted with butter; how can this light be blown out by the breath of my mouth? The order of my father is cruel as my death-sentence. But stop, I will obey my parents one way. Here see the knife. Its blade is smeared with poison. I will plunge it into my own heart."

He had been dreaming of her in his sleep. And now he saw her resolved to put an end to herself.

Mahua.

"My parents are cruel and my own heart no less. They have ordered me to kill you and I have come here for that purpose. But that cannot be. If I kill myself, all your trouble will cease. Go back home as fast as you can and return to the arms of your mother, whose treasure you are. Get a beautiful damsel for your bride, marry her and be happy. You are a noble man—a prince. I have been like death to your happy home. I lost my senses and obeyed an impulse without considering what was right and what was wrong and of the consequences."

(*She tries to thrust the knife into her heart. Naderchand catches hold of her hand and stops her.*)

Naderchand.

"Mahua, I have left my father and mother and the honour of my high caste, all for your sake. I am like a bee fascinated by a charming flower—Mahua. For your sake have I wandered all over the country like a madman. Were I to leave you now, no more would I return home. How could I do so? My caste is gone. Glad am I that I have given it up for your sake. If it is to be my cruel fate that I shall not win you, I pray, with thy tender hands lift up the knife again and kill me."

Mahua.

"No, my love, that cannot be. I will leave my parents and home to-day. I will have nothing more to do with them. I will go with you to a distant land if you will take me in your kindness. Where shall we go, you ask?—to where our eyes will lead. We shall enter the depths of the hilly lands, full of jungles, to hide ourselves. My father has fine steeds; there on yonder bank of the river is his stable; let us mount two of them and flee. My parents will not know nor any one else. We shall call the sun and the moon to witness and leave the place."

The thin clouds in the east showed the glamour of the dawn over the banks of the river and they rode together by the river-side—happy in the thought of escape. They looked glorious as the sun and the moon. They applied their whips, and the steeds flew like birds of the air—with the utmost speed.

Ll. 1-54.

17. A River Stream—they Stand facing it.

Mahua.

"O steeds of my father's stall, go back to his home—now far away. Say to my parents 'Your daughter Mahua has been killed by a tiger.'"

She unbridled the horses and then slapped them affectionately on their backs. They ran back swiftly by the way they had come.

"Look, O Prince," said Mahua, "at the furious waves of the hilly stream. How can we cross this?"

She prayed to the stream saying, "May there be some shoals in you for a little time, so that we may get over to the other side."

But they found no shoals underneath their feet. Instead the waves rose high as the wind was against the tide. Just at that moment they espied a boat approaching. "These are not white birds but the sails of a boat. By this boat shall we go whatever may befall us." They said and thanked their stars.

He called out to the master of the boat, "Your boat travels far and near. We two souls are here and do not know how to get to the other side of the river. If you will kindly help us to do so, we may be saved from perishing on this lonely bank."

The merchant looked at Mahua and felt the intoxicating influence of her beauty. He ordered the oarsmen to stay the boat there.

Mahua and Naderchand stepped in. And the boat flew with the speed of the wind. Ll. 1-22.

18. The Tragedy in the Merchant's Vessel.

The merchant wondered as to how he could secure Mahua, whose beauty had inflamed his mind. Secretly did he form a plot with the boatmen. The boat went against the tide.

And Naderchand was seen in the deep waters, struggling. The black whirlpools at the edge of the tide forcibly drowned whatever came in their way, and Naderchand fell into one of these. "Adieu, my parents, never more shall I see you again! Adieu, dear Mahua, remember me. We part for ever to-day."

"The waves that have carried my Naderchand will also carry me." Saying this she tried to jump into the water; but the boatmen forcibly stopped her. O how cruel is the wicked merchant!

The Merchant.

"Your eyes are large and dark, your hair long and glossy, fair maiden. Good luck has made me a gift of its choicest flower to-day.

"Do not, dear damsel, allow your precious youth to pass in vain. Return my great love for you and make me happy. Is it not strange, that though golden is the boat, there is none to steer it on. If youth passes away, the world will not hold you, maiden, in the same regard. Do not bud-like, O my little treasure, conceal your sweetness, but like the full-blown flower yield it to the air. Believe me, my life is in your hands. You may make it happy if you will.

"Golden ornaments I shall give you and a beautiful blue '*sadi*.' For your ears and nose golden flowerets will be ordered. Scented will be your long tresses with oil. Many servants and maids have I at home and they will vie with one another in carrying out your least desire. They will wash your feet, dear maiden, and make for you the softest bed. In winter I will get fine blankets of cotton and wrappers for you and maidservants will stand near you, awaiting orders.

"Elephants and horses have I in my stall and also men-at-arms. You will be the mistress of them all. Goodly tanks have I in my garden-house with landing steps of stone. There we shall bathe, swim and sport like two happy water-birds. Adjoining my home is a fine flower-garden. Evening and morning shall we walk there plucking flowers in full blossom.

"How pleasantly shall we pass our nights together! In winter, fair maiden, you will be warmed by my bosom and feel no cold. Should the bed seem hard for your tender body, on my soft breast will you sleep. I will myself prepare betels for you and sweetly offer them to your mouth. We will be always together, eat together and sleep entwined in each other's arms. And when I shall travel in distant countries for trade you will go with me visiting shores far and near. Diamonds and precious stones I will collect by trade; the treasure will be thine. I will give you a necklace worth a lakh of silver-coins. Many things more shall I present to you and you will see how I fulfil to the letter every word that I have said. Your shell-bracelets will be plated with gold, the costly *udayatara sadi*—its deep black, all inlaid with precious stones and pearls—shall I purchase for you for another lakh of silver coins. I will give you besides a waist-belt adorned with stones, and in your anklets golden pendants will make a merry jingling sound—"*runu runu, jhunu jhunu.*"

When she heard all his tempting words, what, think you, did Mahua do? Fine betels she prepared for the merchant who professed such love. With lime and catechu she mixed venom of adder secured from the hills, which she had kept concealed under her head-dress.[1] Smiling and playful she put one of these into the mouth of the merchant. He, charmed by her sweet smile, asked her to come to his arms. But she in the meantime had distributed her betels amongst the boatmen as well. They yawned and fell into a deep sleep as the venom spread swiftly through their veins. She had been smiling all the while, but now she laughed like a witch. The poisoned knife was with her. She cut to pieces the ropes of the anchors. The merchant lay unconscious in his boat. She took an axe in her hand and broke open the keel and the lower planks. And then before the boat sank, jumped into the waters. Swimming over the waves she saw the boat with its crew and cargo slowly sinking down. Ll. 1-64.

19. A Forest on the Other Side of the River.

Mahua looks around all alone.

Who takes notice of the flower that blooms and hides itself in a corner and of the diamond that sparkles in the mine? The maiden suffered her lot alone unheeded by any. "Where has he been carried by the waves?" She asks of the birds of the air and of the beasts in the wilderness. "O tigers and bears, feast upon my body and satisfy your hunger; but first let me have some tidings of him. I was the daughter of the gipsy-leader but loving a stranger I left my home."

The peacocks sat on the boughs of trees and she asks of them information about her lover like a madwoman. "Alas! the precious necklace of my breast is lost in deep waters—unhappy that I am. God has no mercy for me, to whom shall I appeal?" Ll. 1-14.

[1] The Indian gipsies generally carry poisonous drugs and venom of adders with them.

20. The Story of a Strange Sannyasi.

The trees yielded no fruit and the river lay at a distance. She became weak and unable to walk for hunger and thirst.

The big bears of the forest passed by but they did not kill the unfortunate Mahua though she longed for death. The big reptiles that swallowed goats and deer took another path as they espied the wretched girl.

" How can I forget him who made himself so miserable for me, giving up his vast riches and the comforts of home? All that a man would covet he had ; but he gave them up for me. He became a wanderer in the forests and on the river banks for my love.

" The wicked merchant threw him into the river and killed him. I shall either drown myself in the river or hang myself on a tree. Life is unbearable." "No," she reflected after a pause, " the search is not yet complete. I cannot think of dying until I have exhausted every possible means to find him out. But what is that feeble cry of agony in the forest ? "

It was twilight and she espied a broken temple—the abode of snakes. But she entered it fearless. In the dim light she saw a figure reduced to skeleton. There was no flesh—the bones were merely covered with skin. The figure was just like a dead body. She could not recognise that face, once so beautiful, but as she gazed on it, her doubts gradually gave way to a conviction that it was Naderchand and none other.

Just at this moment there came a hermit. His face looked grisly with moustache and beard and he had a long stick in his hand. The hermit was amazed at the sight of her beauty and said, " What part of the country, fair maiden, do you come from ? What palace of a king did you adorn and what crime have you committed to deserve an exile in this forest at this tender age? Your parents must be very hard-hearted, how can they live, parted from you?"

These words of compassion made her eyes tearful. She clasped the feet of the hermit and began to weep. His knotted hair was a mixture of yellow and gray and his beard and moustache looked faded brown. At the feet of the hermit she lay prostrate weeping. From beginning to end she related her whole story.

The hermit said, "In the deep waters there is a water-plant which I shall secure for you. Your husband will revive if it is applied. A deadly fever lies buried in the very bones of the youth, but he is living—not yet dead, I assure you. There lies the plant in the water, get it, fair damsel, and bring a little water also. I will restore him to life, you have my assurance."

The medicine was applied. One, two, three days passed away. On the fourth Naderchand opened his eyes.

The hermit said to Mahua, "Gather some flowers for me. You are to enter the jungle every day and pluck flowers all alone. These I will offer to the gods."

She did as she was bid. Alone she penetrated into the depths of the woods and gathered flowers for the hermit in a cane-basket. Meantime Naderchand became able to sit on his bed. He wanted rice. Mahua wept. Alas, where could she get rice in that forest? That day she did not go to gather flowers, but unable to get rice for Naderchand, she sat the whole day weeping all alone.

But the hermit, though a great sage he was, became enamoured of her beauty. In the cane-basket lay the flowers, gathered by Mahua, still fresh. And in the depth of the night he went to the temple and called her aloud, "Arise, fair damsel, if you want your husband to regain the full vigour of health, come with me and get some medicinal herbs." In all haste she followed the hermit and went to the river-bank. The place was lonely and the hermit said to her, "I implore you, sweet woman, surrender to me your youth. Your beauty is so great that though I struggled to control myself yet I find myself quite unable to do so. A flower you are to be adored and to be enjoyed. I must at all costs win you to satisfy my love. My mind has altogether lost its balance and there is nothing in it but your figure."

As she heard the words of the hermit, it seemed as if a sword had fallen on her head.

For a moment she meditated within herself and then said, "First restore my husband to full health and put him out of danger in every way. Then I shall do as you will bid."

The hermit turned pale at her words and said, "I grant you two days. Within this time you must poison your husband. This is my last word."

She was within the clutches of a demon. She began to devise some means of escape. She told all to Naderchand and discussed the matter fully with him. How could they flee ? This was their one thought. He was still very weak and ill with fever. He could not even stand. So how could he run away ?

After much thought she decided on her course. Slowly did she place Naderchand on her shoulders. It was midnight. She walked on, but glanced behind all the while to see if the fiend of a hermit was following them.

Ll. 1-88.

21. The Escape and Happy Union.

Time rolled on and six months passed. Naderchand was perfectly cured.

From the hill-stream Mahua brought sweet water. The trees of the forest yielded them plenty of fruits. Naderchand's strength returned.

He was one day bound for market. The gipsy-girl asked him to bring a nose-ornament for her.

Another day Naderchand was taking his meal. A fish-bone stuck in his throat. The gipsy-girl vowed that if her lord would be better again, she would offer two goats, one black and the other white, to the gods.

Once when Naderchand got fever and his head ached, the gipsy girl sat near him and gently touched his forehead with her soft hands.

* * * *

"We have got no house to live in, my love," she said, "but as we wander here and there, we retire to some spot like birds of the air."

With him she now crossed the hilly stream and with light-hearted steps they travelled together to a great distance. They met a large river on their way and swam across it and reached the other bank. There they found the cuckoo of the jungle singing its gayest note from the bough of a tree. He liked the place and said, "Here, fair maiden, shall we build our home." A rivulet gaily flowed there with its dancing waves. "Here," said Naderchand, "shall we stay and pass our days." He pointed to the landscape around and said, "There, see, Mahua, how flowers are laughing,—dressed in purple; and delicious fruits are hanging from the branches of the trees. The sweet water of yonder stream is pleasant to the eyes."

The two lived on the fruits the trees yielded in plenty. On a beautiful stone found there, they slept. The nights they spent happily in one another's arms. In the day-time they wandered hand in hand through the lonely forest enjoying the fruits they plucked here and there. They forgot their parents, they forgot their friends and dear kinsmen. It was a joyful life they passed oblivious to the rest of the world.

But all of a sudden a thunder-bolt was hurled on their heads by fate. Ll. 1-32.

22. They wander in the Forest—the Danger Signal.

One evening Naderchand accompanied by Mahua joyfully walked in the forest path. They entered into a deep jungle, Mahua entwining him with her creeper-like arms as they walked together. At a certain place they found a beautiful large stone and together sat on it gaily talking. At a little distance from that spot, the ripples of a small river were seen, but suddenly Mahua heard the sound of a flute and began to tremble in fear. He gently asked caressing her, "What is it, dear Mahua, that has made you start? Why do you look pale? To-day you must tell me the incidents of your life. Who are your parents? Why did you live with the gipsies? I have asked you this question times without number, but to-day you must tell me the whole story. Surely there is a mystery hanging about you; for as often as I asked you, you said nothing but only wept. There is some pain in your heart which you have concealed from me all the time. Last morning you told me a portion: Homra stole you when a baby from your father's house. But stop, the flute is sounding. Let us return to our house. Evening has passed away."

"If I live to-morrow, my dear lord," said the gipsy girl, "I will relate to you the whole story, but my head is full of pain."

As a creeper bends low blown by the wind, so did Mahua fall into Naderchand's arms.

"Is it a snake that has stung you, my love? Why are you so pale and sad in spirit? Tell me what trouble it is that you are suffering from?" asked Naderchand.

The dry leaves broke under the feet of the pair as they proceeded onward but suddenly she became seized, as it were, with a terrible fever, and she could not walk but fell down trembling. Naderchand in great fear made a bed of leaves for her there, and said, "Wait a moment, I will bring water for you, you are so thirsty." Mahua wept and said, "To-day is my last day on the earth. I am not bitten by a snake, but our happiness is at an end to-day. You heard the sound of the flute from that distant forest. The gipsies have come led by my foster-father. My friend, Palanka, the maiden, has by that flute signalled to me of their approach and given me the warning. He will kill us to-night, my lord, and only to-night shall we spend locked in each other's arms. To-morrow this happiness will end and we shall not see each other any more. Our sweet forest-life is going to be ended and we must be ready for entering the grim regions of death."

The night was over. The stars disappeared from the sky. They came to the door of their straw-hut and stepped outside.

Ll. 1-48.

23. Homra's Gang.

On all sides they saw hunting dogs. With their help Homra had at last traced them. The next moment they saw the dreaded figure of Homra standing like death itself. In his hand was a poisoned knife the blade of which sparkled. Living fire came out of his angry eyes and his heavy breath sounded like the roaring of a cloud.

Homra.

"If you want to live, Mahua, hear me. Kill our enemy with this knife. Sujan the player is my god-son; marry him and come with us.

Mahua.

"But how can I kill my husband? Stand, father, where you are and see how I die," said she in a soft faltering murmur.

Homra.

"But Sujan is young, healthy and handsome. Him will you get for your husband. Marry him and let us return home. I have sought you all the country over. Do not be obstinate."

Mahua.

"How can I kill my husband and return home, father? Believe me, I will not marry Sujan—the player. My husband's face shines like melted gold—like the moon and the sun, and Sujan's is like that of a glow-worm. He, my husband, is the handsomest youth—like a tree made of gold. Look at him once. And see him, father, with *my* eyes. Your eyes will be filled with his image."

The black cloud roared in furious rage and handed over the knife to Mahua.

Once only did she look at her friend Palanka—the maiden, who was standing by, and once only did she look at the face of her own dear Naderchand. She said, "O my husband, dearer than life, bid me farewell. Your own Mahua will no more be by your side. O my dear friend Palanka, you will surely understand my sufferings and feel for me. And you my father, I do not know whose little treasure you robbed, I do not remember ever having seen my own parents. Woe to me—to my stars. Now let me die—thus."

(*She plunges the knife in her own bosom and dies. The gipsies kill Naderchand at Homra's order.*) Ll. 1-86.

24. Homra's Laments and Palanka's Devotion.

" I took her when she was a baby of six months and reared her up all these years. Alas, who will adorn my house now—she is gone? Will you not, Mahua, open your eyes but once to see me, nor open your lips but once to speak to me? I cannot return home after this. (*Turning to his followers.*) You would do well to return home, I shall go to some forest and spend my days there."

Turning to Mainka he said, " No use my going home again. Make a grave for the child. This Brahmin lord gave up his home and riches for Mahua. They were madly attached to each other. Let them be buried in one grave."

They did as their leader bade them and then dispersed leaving the place lonely with its grave.

* * * *

The maiden Palanka did not go but remained there. She was the companion of Mahua's early years—the partner of her joys and sorrows. There she spent her days and nights weeping. She gathered wild flowers from the forest and placed them on the grave and made its dust wet with her tears. Sometimes she sang songs in that forest-region and their pathos filled the air. Sometimes like a mad woman she spoke thus to the grave "Awake, dear soul, how long will you sleep here? I am your friend, answer me. The gipsies have gone home. They will no longer come to disturb you. Awake and make once more this place your sweet home. No one will now stand in your way. The wicked gipsies have abandoned their pursuit of you. Bound in each others' embrace we spent our childhood and now both of us will weave fair garlands of flowers for your lord."

The tears of Palanka, the true friend, thus fell on the grave every day. Ll. 1-81.

MALUA

PREFACE.

'Malua' is a corruption of the name of a well-known flower—the '*mallika.*' In a certain passage of this poem the husband of the heroine endearingly calls her 'Mallu' (Canto XV, l. 66), which is nearer to the original word. No information, however, about the author of this remarkable ballad has yet been traced, though Babu Chandra Kumar tried his best to arrive at definite facts on the point. The preliminary hymn attached to the poem is found subscribed by Chandravati,—naturally leading to the conjecture that the gifted poetess herself composed the poem. One point in support of this theory is that in the poem of 'Kenaram,' she describes the country as groaning under the rule of the Mahomedan Kazis (magistrates), and in the tale of Malua also there is a practical illustration of the oppression of a Kazi. Beyond this, however, we do not find any reason to connect Chandravati with this poem. If she were its writer, it should have been composed sometime between 1575 and 1600; for her literary activities belonged to this period and probably she did not outlive the sixteenth century. It was at this period when Isha Khan Masnadali had just established his power in Eastern Bengal. There is, however, no evidence to show that any one of Isha Khan's immediate descendants, legitimate or otherwise, who took the title of 'Dewan,' ever made himself so notorious in the last decade of the sixteenth century, as to commit atrocities of the sort described in the ballad, though we know it for certain from Chandravati's poem of Kenaram that the Kazis very much oppressed the people even at that period. My own belief, however, is that the song was composed about a century later, when the children of

Nazar Morecha' [1] became plenty in the land, and made themselves notorious by their heinous oppressions. The reason why the name of the author is not found in the colophon is not far to seek. A public exposure of the atrocities committed by the Mahomedan aristocracy would make the life of the poet positively unsafe in the country, and he had therefore cogent reasons to hide his name. The hymn of Chandravati, found affixed to the poem, does not go a great way to establish her authorship. The hymn might have been picked up from elsewhere and joined to the poem by the rustic minstrels in order to heighten its importance, as Chandravati was already widely known as a poetess of high order. There is nothing in the ballad itself to establish its inevitable connection with her.

Chandra Kumar collected this ballad from several persons of the district of Mymensingh. The main portion was obtained from one Pashani Bewa, a professional singer, reputed for her wonderful memory. It is said that she can recite from memory whole episodes from the Ramayan, the Mahabharat and the Bhagavat, besides a very considerable number of the ballads of the nature of *bāramāsi* songs. She is a native of the village Padamasri, near Jahangirpur, the reputed seat of the Dewan Sahab of this ballad. Amongst others to whom the compiler is indebted for help in the collection of the ballad may be mentioned the names of Sekh Kancha of Rajibpur and Nidan Fakir of Mangalsiddhi, a village within a few miles of Padamasri. He completed his collection of the ballad on the 3rd of October, 1921.

The poem, as I have already stated, was probably written sometime in the 17th century, when some of the members of the Mahomedan aristocracy had made their names dreaded in the countryside by their forcible abduction of beautiful Hindu girls with the help of professional informers called the '*sindhukis*.'

There are some places mentioned in the ballad in connection with the locality of the incidents described. We find the

[1] See Introduction.

the name of the village of Arulia and that of an extensive mire called the "Dhalair *bil*," (Canto III, l. 2) described as abounding in water lilies (Canto XIV, l. 67). The dwelling place of Chand Binod, the hero of the tale, was, it is said, on the banks of the river Sutia (*lit.* a thread) which is a branch of the Dhanu, joining the Meghna near Ajmiralganj in the east. Jahangirpur was founded by Dewan Jahangir, who called the town after his own name. This town is in the subdivision of Netrakona, and is about nine miles to the north-west of Arulia. Jahangirpur stretches from north to south covering a wooded area of more than a square mile. The village Arulia, which our poet describes as possessed of a romantic woodland view, infested not only with venomous snakes but also with tigers and bears, is situated on the Bahadair, a branch of the Dhanu, in the subdivision of Kisoreganj and is 22 miles to the north-east of its head-quarters. The river Bahadair branching off from the Dhanu near Badla joins the original stream again four miles further east. Arulia is still surrounded by *bils* and marshes, and its position even now not only fully justifies Malua's fears that in the dark night it was not safe for a wayfarer to walk in that land, but also the anxieties of Chand Binod's mother expressed in the line, 'Who knows, my darling may fall a victim to snakes or tigers (Canto II, l. 21).' Chand Binod started from his home in the morning and reached Arulia in the afternoon, after having stayed for a couple of hours on the way in his sister's house where he also returned in the evening to spend the night. So his native village could not be very far from Arulia In the Surveyor-General's map Sutia meets the Dhanu at Dhanpur which is about six miles to the east of Arulia. There are also three small villages in the locality, *viz.*, Gopalnagar, Katar and Indua,—all on the banks of the Sutia, and within a mile of Dhanpur. One of these must have been the native village of Chand Binod. The village must have been of some importance as it was the seat of a Kazi (Mahomedan magistrate) in charge of the administration of the locality, who was an officer of Dewan Jahangir.

There is some difficulty in identifying the 'Dhalair *bil.*' Dhalai is a well-known river in the Netrakona sub-division. The natural assumption would be that the '*bil*' of that name was formed by a portion of that river separated from the main channel. But the Surveyor-General's map giving the names of all the villages does not show any trace of this '*bil.*' It is not, however, unlikely that a '*bil*' of that name had existed somewhere near the river Dhalai and in course of the last two centuries it was transformed into a dry field covered with green crops.

But there is actually a '*bil*' named the 'Dhalaikona *bil*' only half a mile south of Arulia. It is quite natural that Dhalaikona should be abbreviated into Dhalai in popular dialect. We are inclined to believe that it was this '*bil*' into which the Dewan was led to enter by the wily stratagem of Malua. The text shows that the '*bil*' was extensive in area; the word 'বিস্তর' means large. The 'Dhalaikona *bil*' is about a mile in length from south to north and the widest part of its breadth is about half a mile towards the middle. There is one weighty reason to suppose that this 'Dhalaikona *bil*' was the place from which Malua was rescued by her brothers. It is so close to Arulia that she must have found it most suitable for her purpose to mislead the Dewan and bring him there in order to get him within easy reach of her brothers, —at a distance from his own people. The Dhalaikona '*bil*' is about ten miles to the south-east of Jahangirpur, the town of Dewan Jahangir, who must have come down to the '*bil*' by following one of the numerous courses of the Dhanu.

There is another village named Arulia in the sub-division of Netrakona, six miles to the north-west of Kendua. But this Arulia is positively not the one with which Chand Binod was concerned; for Arulia, where our hero met Malua, was only a few miles from his own village on the Sutia. This will be apparent from the incidents described in the poem. The Arulia on the Bhadair exactly answers this purpose, being only five or six miles from the Sutia; whereas the Arulia to the north-west of Kendua is about thirty miles from Sutia. It would be impossible for Chand Binod to have travelled this distance within three or four hours as mentioned in this poem.

There is also another Jahangirpur about four miles to the west of Kisoreganj—twenty-eight miles from Arulia. We do not believe that this Jahangirpur is referred to in the ballad. The Jahangirpur, near the postal town of Sukhari which we have already mentioned, seems to be the one mentioned in the ballad. It is only nine miles to the north-west of Arulia, where the chief incidents of the scene were enacted. A line of the Dewans, bereft of all past glory, is still living in the place, and the neighbouring villages still resound with the song of Malua.

The song of Malua, though it does not bring us face to face with romantic scenery and dramatic situations as in 'Mahua,' and though it does not show much ingenuity in the weaving of the plot like the other ballad, is nevertheless possessed of a very high order of lyric beauty, and it rises to an almost epic grandeur in the last scene when Malua sacrifices her life. Malua's character does not indeed possess the simple charm and frank candour of the gipsy girl, but it rises to a dignity verging on the majestic in great moments of life. She appears like a queen in her flaming rage, and like the statue of a queen in her silent sufferings.

The ballad does not, however, form an organic whole. It breaks off after the marriage of Chand Binod with Malua. This portion may indeed be regarded as a prologue to the main story which commences from the advent of the Kazi on the scene. The episodes of this latter portion have given the story a homogeneous character being woven round a plot of high dramatic interest.

Malua is complete in 1,247 lines and is divided into 19 cantos. Besides, there are thirty lines of the preliminary song-tribute in it, composed by Chandravati.

DINESH CHANDRA SEN.

7, Biswakosh Lane, Bagbazar,

Calcutta, 5th March, 1923.

MALUA.

The Preliminary Hymn.

First of all I should sing a hymn in praise of the one God who is without a beginning. Among the Devas I offer a hymn to Siva, the great ascetic. Among the Devis I sing praises of Durga and her two daughters Lakshmi and Saraswati. By worshipping Lakshmi, one becomes master of riches and by singing a hymn in honour of Saraswati, one gets access to the treasure of learning. I hereby offer hymns to the sky above, to the winds and to Gaḍura—the Lord of birds. Praises do I offer also to Seven Nether regions and to Basuki—the great snake. My humble tribute of respect is due to Manasa Devi, the mother of Astika and the goddess of snakes, whose poison is dreaded by Brahma himself. Amongst her devotees, praises do I offer to the merchant king Chandradhar and to his son Lakshindara and his daughter-in-law Beula (Behula). Amongst the rivers allow me to sing a hymn in honour of the Ganges, brought down from heaven by Bhagiratha. Amongst the woman-kind, all honour to Sita—the chaste wife. Amongst shrines I make my obeisance to Kashi (Benares) and Gaya. Most esteemed amongst the mortals of the world are my parents by whose grace this wretched one has seen the light. Amongst the sages, my respects are due to Balmiki—the great saint. I also sing praises of all that moves and breathes in the world—the waters, the lands, the upper and the nether worlds. On the matted locks of Siva are Kála and Mahákála and I bow down to both. I do hereby pay my respects to the *guru* who initiated me into the secrets of spiritual life, and last of all, I bow down to the square-shaped earth.

Thus does Chandravati finish her offering of song-tribute.

Ll. 1-30.

1. The Flood and the Famine.

Slowly did the flood subside in October in the low lands. The mother of Chand Binod called aloud 'Arise, my son, from the bed, wash your face bright as the moon and go to the fields. There the ridges should be well made between the furrows to preserve rain water. Remember that the harvest time is November when we expect our *shali* crops. Hear the rumblings of the clouds, they seem like a call to the rain-water to pour in. Go to the fields early. The black clouds have covered the sky and they roar at intervals. How long will you remain idle, sleeping in the house?'

The rain came pouring and completely overflowed the fields. All agricultural operations were stopped as the land lay under the flood—to the intense disappointment of the peasants who lost all their resources. It was the season for the Durga Puja. The rustic-folk in their enthusiasm to perform the Puja at their houses, collected money by giving away their children as security to the money-lenders. In November all the fine crops of the season perished under water,—to the entire ruin of all the prospects of the peasants. The dews of November brought an obstinate fever on Chand Binod. His mother wept to see his condition and vowed to Durga that she would offer to the goddess a pair of buffaloes as sacrifice if Chand Binod recovered. So serious became his condition that she apprehended his death and wept day and night. By the grace of Providence, Chand Binod passed the crisis. It was now the middle of November, the mother protected her son from the shivering cold by her tattered rags.

Chand Binod now became completely cured by the grace of the Goddess of Fortune—Lakshmi, but there was not a grain of rice left in the house wherewith to worship the deity. On the day of worship the mother brought a scythe for reaping the crops and handed it to Chand Binod asking him to go to the field. He took five shoots of the plant *bátá* (a sort of cane) [1] in his hand and went towards the field singing a *baramashi* song. But to his utter dismay he found that the rain of October had totally destroyed the crop. In deep despair he returned home and informed his mother of the catastrophe. The mother and son were plunged in deep sorrow. The loss of this crop meant starvation for the whole year. There was already famine in the country and rice was selling at one-and-half *aras* [2] per rupee. In the month of January when black mist covered the land, the mother and the son anxiously thought over the matter but could not devise any means for their sustenance. The bulls were released from the yoke and sold. Five plots of land he made over to the money-lender as security. Now he had no lands—no bulls. How could he grow rice, pulses or mustard? January, February and a considerable part of March he spent idly at home, failing to secure any work. In the month of April he took a cage in his hand and said to his mother with a sweet smile, 'Permit me, dear mother, to go to hunt falcons.' With the help of burning fuel he prepared a *silim* and filling his *hooka* with water smoked a while. There was no cooked rice left of the night before; nor was there even any rice-dust for a meal in the house. Chand Binod was hungry and looked pale. He was going away to hunt but there was nothing for his breakfast in the house. The

[1] Some sheafs of grain are tied with the tops of these shoots which are marked with vermilion, and dedicated to the harvest goddess on the first day when crops are reaped in autumn by the peasants.

[2] One *árá* is equal to 4 mds. So 1½ *aras* means 6 mds. This was called famine-price in those days. The tradition of Eastern Mymensingh at one time was that when rice sold at 2 mds. per rupee the rigour of famine was so severe that parents were compelled to sell their children. Alas, the good old days!

mother's tears flowed down without check while bidding him farewell. She was maddened by grief, when her famished son left the house with the burning rays of April sun over his bare head in the paths where no cool wind blew to soothe his body, scorched by the heat of the season.

Ll. 1-60

2. On the Way.

There as he went he saw in the fields the crimson-coloured ears of the *shali* crop drooping low in the ground. He thought of paying a flying visit to his sister's house that lay on the way. He asked his sister to come out and said, 'Dear sister, I am starting on a hunting excursion and I have come to take leave of you.'

She prepared nice *shachi* betels with lime and catechu and filled a bag with fried *shali* rice and sweet banana fruits. Besides this she offered him a quantity of tobacoo. Taking leave of his sister Chand Binod started again. His sister strained her eyes and stood gazing at him as far as she could see him. With the trained falcon in his cage, Chand Binod proceeded on in his journey.

It was June and the falcon screamed at short intervals, glad at the prospect of rain. The sky was overcast with clouds whose shadow darkened the land. They roared and the flash of lightning dazzled the eyes. At home the poor mother wept for her son. The screams of the falcon indicated the advent of a full monsoon. The mother and sister passed their days in great anxiety for Chand Binod. 'Alas, where has he gone in the forest lands in pursuit of falcons!' The mother feared that her dear son might be bitten by snake or devoured by a tiger. In her lonely cottage she had not a wink of sleep and wept all night.

Ll. 1-22.

3. The Dawn of Love.

Now hear, O my audience, the tale of Chand Binod's journey. It was the village of Arulia which he reached at noon. At the extreme end of the village there was a blind pond covered with weeds. The place was full of shrubs, and on the four sides of the pond there were banana trees protected by a fence of thorny *mandar* plants. Arriving at that place, the weary passenger pleasantly looked at the beauty of the pond and its adjoining scenery. Near the landing *ghat* there was a *kadamba* tree covered with flowers in full bloom ; he took his seat under the tree. The July nights are short and sleep often lingers on one's eyes in the day-time. As Chand Binod sat under the *kadamba* tree during the hours of noon, he dozed for a while till he fell fast asleep. It was a sound sleep; evening came and he still slept in that lonely place.

Malua, the maiden who had gone to fetch water from the pond, wondered as to who could be the youth that slept on the landing *ghat*. She placed her pitcher on the ground and quickly came down to the last step of the *ghat*. As she did so, she stopped now and then to see the youth. How handsome was he and how soundly did he sleep ! The sun had already sunk on the western horizon and the evening was ready to yield her place to night. Yet how long would he sleep all alone in this place ! If in the depth of night he awakes, where will he go for shelter, a stranger as he is in this land ? 'O my traveller, you have no home, no parents here. Who will give you a place to spend the night in this lonely forest ?' Whence has he come ? Where is his home ? A maiden am I, how can I learn all this ? 'Awake, my traveller,' was the inaudible voice of the shy maiden's soul, 'Will he not,' thought she, 'respond to this silent call of my mind ? How can I stay here long near a stranger in this evening all alone ? If I had the power I would rouse him from his sleep and show him the way to my father's home. In the dark night where will you go, O traveller, unless some one shows you the path ? How strange that at this hour such a sound sleep has come upon you! Awake, O traveller, hasten to meet that one whose treasure of heart you are.' She pushed the water with her pitcher and created thereby small ripples and then thought again 'How can I rouse him from his sleep ? I have no one else with me. If one of my sisters-in-law were with me, somehow both of us might contrive to break his sleep. If my mother had come with me, I would have asked her to request the traveller to be a guest at our house. I am a helpless maiden and am all alone. For modesty's sake how can I talk to a stranger ? But still my heart is sad for him. He has apparently lost his way.' The pitcher of bell-metal she drew close to her breast and said 'O my pitcher ! break his sleep by your sound,' saying this she slowly filled it with water.

The sound awakened Chand Binod. It also made the falcon send one of its shrill cries to the sky.[1] Now fully awake Chand Binod espied that beautiful maiden returning home with her pitcher of water. Her dishevelled hair, black as clouds, almost touched her feet—this hair alone was worth a lakh of rupees ! She looked like a fresh *mahua* flower in a deserted garden. What a pair of large eyes ! Their glance was enough to madden even a saint's heart. 'I never saw a maiden so beautiful ! Alas whose house do you lighten, O lamp of beauty ?' murmured he to himself. 'Is it really a dream that I am dreaming—though wide awake ? Whose treasure of heart art thou, O maiden ? You look like a water-lily that has bloomed in the land,—like a star of the sky that has come down to the earth to gladden it by its light. O my falcon, fly on your wings and bring me the message. Where does

[1] It mistook the sound to be that of the clouds.

An Untimely Slumber

" How strange that at this hour such a sound sleep has come upon you ! "

Malua, p. 44

the girl live? Who are her parents and whose wife is she?' Turning to the maiden he said within himself, 'Look behind, dear maiden, so that I may once more have a sight of your moon-like face. Alas! I have lost my heart on this landing *ghat*! Are you married? If you are, how can I covet another man's wife? If you are still a maiden, even then where is the chance for me?' Troubled in his mind with these queries which he could not solve, he whispered again to his falcon 'Fly away homeward, dear one, and tell my mother that Chand Binod has been killed by a tiger. Tell her that her dear son will not visit his home again, and fly away, O falcon, and give the same message to my dear sister; and last, fly away and meet this maiden on her way and convey to her my innermost thoughts.'

The sight of the stranger, bright as the moon, brought the crimson glow of shyness to the maiden on whom youth had just dawned. She did not stop there a moment, but returned home. And Chand Binod with the falcon in his hand started for the house of his sister.

Ll. 1-90.

4. The Maiden taken to task and her Explanation.

The five sisters-in-law asked Malua 'How is it, sister, that you went to the bathing *ghat* yesterday all alone? And will you tell us why your disordered clothes fluttered in the wind and your hair hung round your face—all dishevelled? Half of your pitcher is filled with water and the other half empty. Surely we notice a change in you. But yesterday you looked like a mere bud and to-day you are a full-blown flower. Do not deceive us, sister, do not conceal anything. Come to-day with us to the bathing *ghat*. Take your pitcher, a haircomb of mica and a bottle of scented oil. We will comb your curling hair loosened in the night and scent it. And there all alone you will open your mind and hide nothing from us. It is just the time, dear sister, when maidens seek the company of their husbands. Pity it is, though you are so fair a girl, you have still to live at your father's home all alone! So beautiful are you that your charms have the power to captivate our mind, though women we are.

Malua.

'I cannot guess why you prevent my going to the bathing *ghat* alone.'

The sisters-in-law.

'You are like the moon, we fear lest the demon (*rahu*) gets hold of you in solitude.'

Malua.

'I had fever last night and there is pain in my limbs. You all go to the bathing *ghat* to-day. I am not going to accompany you.'

The sisters-in-law passed some remarks in inaudible whispers and started for the bathing *ghat*. Malua entered her sleeping room.

Ll. 1-28,

5. ALL ABOUT MALUA AND HER FATHER'S FAMILY.

Hiradhar, the father of Malua, was a *Hélé das* (ploughman) by caste. He was the head-man of the village. His five sons were well-off. Their granaries were filled with fine crops. There were ten milch-cows in the cowshed and a good number of bulls for ploughing. The Hélé das family was far above want. God had granted Hiradhar the boon of half-a-dozen excellent children and worldly riches besides. He possessed 22 *aras*[1] of agricultural land which yielded *shali* and *aman* crops only. The ceremonies of Durga Puja and

[1] Sixteen *kathas* make an *árá*—22 *árás* would make about 18 *bighas*.

Dol Utshava and other religious festivities were performed at his house and the Brahmins were fed well during the *sradh* ceremony of his ancestors. His only daughter Malua had passed her twelfth year and stepped into her first youth. The father became anxious to get her married. Hiradhar wished that as she was the only daughter in the house she should be married to a youth of the status of a prince. Many a bridegroom sought the hands of Malua, but Hiradhar did not find any one suitable amongst them. So he felt uneasy about the prospects of her marriage.

Ll. 1-16.

6. On the Bathing Ghat again.

Lying on her bed Malua yielded herself to thoughts like these :

'Whence did the youth come, glorious as the moon? Oh the indescribable moment when I saw him in the bathing *ghat*! He is surely a wanderer in these forest-regions—a-hunting falcons. Where did he spend the last night and where did he keep his falcon? Oh were I that falcon myself I would have stayed with him and wandered with him from forest to forest. Ye clouds, whom do you call aloud from the sky above? There the rains of July are falling in a hundred streams. The rivers are swollen with flood, their banks are under water. Not a plot of dry land is to be seen all around. Where did the hapless youth spend such a night as this? If he would come to our house as a guest I would, with the permission of my father, give him a seat to rest a while. A fine mat would I spread for him and offer him a box of betels.' And then she thought, 'If such a welcome guest would indeed come to our home and wish it, feign would I offer him myself.'

The noon she spent vexed with her own thoughts.

The after-noon she spent idly lying on her bed.

But when the evening came, with the pitcher of bell-metal in her hand she started towards the bathing *ghat*. She did not inform her five sisters-in-law of her intention.

The oblique rays of the setting sun of July peeping through the clouds produced an unbearable heat in the body and is it for this that Malua went there all alone to take her evening bath !

But do not dissemble, Oh girl. Filling the pitcher with water is really not your object; it is a pretext. Neither is bathing your object; it is also a pretext. The truth is that two hearts have been drawn to each other and this is the course of love.

She came to the bathing *ghat* and she saw, as on the day before, the youth asleep under the *kadamba* tree. The falcon screamed from the cage, and Chand Binod opened his eyes at the sound of his pet bird. He glanced at the landing steps and there saw the beautiful girl filling her pitcher with water.

Chand Binod.

'Hear me, O maiden, I wander from forest to forest, hunting falcons. There is none here to listen to the tale of my sorrows. My name is Chand Binod. My profession is falcon-hunting. Who are you, O beautiful girl ? Every day you come to fill your pitcher with water here. Whose daughter are you ? Are you married ? If you are another man's wife, tell it, fair maiden, I will in that case behold your sweet face for the last time and then go back home. I will not in future come to this land for hunting falcons. I was near you a little time yesterday but to-day I am waiting with an object. Kindly give an account of yourself.

Malua.

'My father's name is Hiradhar and mother's name is Ashama.

"I saw you yesterday also sleeping under the flower-tree.

"A stranger you are and it ill becomes me to hold a conversation here. Come to my father's home and be a guest there.

"With the falcon in your hand you wander about the forest. How do you pass your nights in this wilderness? Tigers and bears infest the place. Are you not afraid of losing your life? This pond is covered with weeds and has deep holes in its banks—the homes of black snakes. If one of them bites you it will end your young life. My father and mother are known for their saintly life all over the country. I have five brothers in our home, and there are many relations and kinsmen besides. We all live together. Come to our home and spend the night with us. You had better not follow the path by which I will go. Yonder lies the village path haunted by men and women. As you will proceed by it you will find there a big outer house, the doors are seen from the path. At the front there is a pond, its landing steps are built of stone. The house faces the east and has glass-doors. At its front and at the back you will find gardens full of flowers and fruits. If you ask the neighbours, they will say, 'It is the house of the head-man of the village.' Why should you spend the night in this wilderness? If you come over to our house, we shall spread a cool mat for you; my five sisters-in-law will prepare a rich variety of curries for your dinner. Stay, good youth, stay with us this night."

So saying Malua with the pitcher of water went away and Chand Binod with the cage in his hand took a different path.

Ll. 1-76.

7. The Welcome Guest.

A youth came to the house in the evening. Hiradhar called his five sons and asked them to attend to the guest. They brought him cool water to wash his hands and feet with.

Their five wives cooked a good meal for his entertainment. The esculent roots, the *man kachu*, were cut to pieces and fried; good sauce was prepared by *chalita* fruits. Stew was made of the *kai* fish with spice—the *jira*. Thirty-six different curries were cooked one by one, and dried fish was fried with rice-paste. With the five brothers Chand Binod sat down to dine. He relished the meal very much; in fact he had never eaten one so agreeable to the palate. The *sukta* and the curries he enjoyed well. The fried things had an excellent taste. Sweet cakes with thickened milk put inside them—of every variety—the *puly*, the *pati*, the *chandrapuli* and the *pou* put in liquid sugar and flavoured—were served to Chand Binod one after another and greatly relished by him.

When the repast was over he was shown a room in the outer apartment. The five wives had prepared *shachi* betels with cloves and cardamom. On a fine mat a good bed was spread and a fan decorated with mica was placed on one side of the bed.

He had a sound sleep in the night, and in the morning he took farewell of his host. He bowed to Hiradhar and to his five sons and then started from the place.

The beautiful Malua lay in her room all alone.

Ll. 1-28.

8. The Proposal.

Chand Binod paid a visit to his sister and related to her all that had taken place. But he naturally felt a delicacy in expressing his desire to marry Malua. A sister's heart could, however, read the innermost thought of a brother without his telling all.

He then came back home, but felt a great shyness in letting his mother know of his feelings. July and August passed and it was September. He could no longer bear the pain of his heart but told the whole story to his comrades.

Thus slowly the matter reached the ears of the mother. She sent a match-maker to Hiraḍhar with a proposal.

When the eleventh year had passed and the maiden had stepped into her twelfth, even from that time the parents were looking for a suitable groom for her.

The clothes she had worn all these days now became too short, and in vain did she struggle to cover her growing charms with her *saḍi*.

The neighbours whisperingly cut many a pleasant joke. Some of them said, "Behold there the bud of youth is blooming."

In the month of July, Hiradhar could not settle the marriage anywhere. August was held inauspicious. Behula, the devoted bride, had become a widow having been married in that month. In September no religious function could be performed according to the custom of the country. So her marriage had to be put off again. In the month of October people became busy with the Pujas; so no attention could be given to the question of her marriage. In the month of November (Kartik) Hiradhar had expected for his daughter a bridegroom handsome as the warrior-god Kartikeya. But none of the proposals that had come was found equal to his expectations. In December the fields looked glorious with golden harvest. Hiradhar thought that in such a month a bridegroom would be secured for his daughter, who would look as glorious as the rich crops of the field. But none was found of that description. In the month of January, the country lay under thick mist, and the custom of the country would not allow any marriage to take place in that month. In February the match-makers came up with a list of likely parties, and the father began to consider the proposals. The merchant Sonadhar of Champatala had an only son handsome as the god Kartikeya. He was the master of two-and-a-half *puras* of land. But Hiradhar said, "The family has no social status." From Dighalbati another proposal had come, and this was discussed. "The family is rich; there are many members in it. Their cowshed is full of cattle and their fields grow fine rice of all variety, which they weigh in big scales and gather in their granaries." Hiradhar, however, could not give his assent to this proposal either. There was the same difficulty. Their social status was not sufficiently high and there was besides some scandal about the family. From Susung in the north there had come a proposal. They were quite well off and their arrangement of the household was perfect. The father traded in rice and his four sons were handsome as angels. They had many fashionable boats for racing—anchored at the landing *ghat* of the river, and kept four fighting bulls besides. The food grain in the house was so profuse that they cared not if much was wasted. But Hiradhar knit his brows and said, "One of their ancestors was a leper—my daughter cannot be married into that family." When the list was thus considered and discussed, there came the proposal from Chand Binod's mother. Hiradhar learnt all particulars about the parentage of the lad and his home from the match-maker. The lad was accomplished and handsome. His social status was high. None amongst the *Hele Kaibartas* ranked higher in social esteem. His father was a big man in the country and there is no scandal against any one of the family. "But," Hiradhar shrugged his shoulders and thought, "how can I offer my daughter to such a home? Not even an acre of land has he to spread the rice for drying. There is only one room of which the straw roof is rotten. How will my daughter live in that room during the rains? She is the darling of her parents, and her five brothers hold her dear as life. How will she bear this extreme poverty? If a handful of rice be required for worshipping the harvest-goddess, they cannot supply it from their own store. My daughter is not satisfied even with her silk *saḍi*; how will she be able to wear rags? No no, this cannot be, I cannot agree to this proposal."

The match-maker returned and told all to Chand Binod's mother. She became sorry. "Providence," she thought, "will not fulfil my son's desire. What can be done?" Chand Binod came to know of it from his friends. He now resolved to go to some foreign land to try his fortune.

Ll. 1-82.

9. The Turning of the Wheels of Fortune.

One morning he rose up and said to his mother, "It does not become me, a healthy youth, to sit idly at home. We have no rice to eat and there is nothing earned. How can we preserve the honour of our family in this way? Allow me, good mother, to go abroad to seek money. I am determined."

There was some cooked rice of the night before. With some green chilly he ate this meal. He touched the feet of his mother to take leave of her and then started for home. The trained falcon he took with him in a cage. He went by the path leading to the guest house. The unfortunate mother stood at the gate pursuing his figure with her eyes through the bamboo groves and the leafy branches of trees which gently touched his back, as he proceeded on his path; she wiped her eyes after he had gone out of sight and returned home with slow steps.

Months passed after his departure and one complete year was now over.

* * *

"Your anxieties, O Chand Binod's mother, are now over. Come out and behold, your dear son has come back." As she heard these words of a neighbour, she was maddened with joy and forthwith came out and stood in the path. As she saw him back after a long full year, tears began to fall from her eyes. Falcon-hunting had proved a very profitable business this time. He had acquired large plots of land and some houses, besides prizes and rewards in plenty. The Dewan Saheb who was the lord of the surrounding country had favoured him and made a grant of twenty *aras* of land as reward for his skill. Chand Binod was a good architect himself; he now built with his own hands a nice house on the banks of the *Shutia* (*lit*, the thread). He built several houses, some with four and others with eight pitched roofs. The outer house was built with particular care. He covered the thatched walls with very fine mats, and the roofs with the straw called the *ulu*. He employed his artistic talents in the door-ways which with decorations looked bright as the moon. He decorated the walls with the wings of the king-fishers (*machhua ranga*). He now employed men to dig a pond. Its transparent water became a delight to the eyes. People said to one another, "Behold, the only son of his mother, how rich has he become! There is an elephant in his stall. The smile of Lakshmi is on his house."

Ll. 1-44.

10. The Proposal accepted—the Marriage.

Now the news of his turning rich spread in the country and Hiradhar himself sent a match-maker this time with the proposal (once rejected by him). The match-maker insisted on having the marriage ceremony performed in March. The details were settled and an astrologer was called to fix the auspicious day. He consulted the almanac and discussed the position of the planets and settled a date. The marriage was to take place in the father-in-law's house. Chand Binod started for the marriage with due pomp. He rode a horse. Before and behind him sounded the tabor, the trumpet and other musical instruments. The young lads of the village accompanied him. The sky became lit up with bonfires of various kinds such as rockets, bombs and other fire-works. They all came to Hiradhar's place. The womenfolk advanced to receive the bridegroom with due honour. They offered their blessings and sounded conch shells, and sang and played on musical instruments.

The mother of the bride with some elderly women went from house to house begging *shohag*, or blessings from their good neighbours upon the bride so that she might be loved at her husband's home. The mother besides carried a flat-shaped plate dedicated to the Goddess of Fortune on her head and kept it covered with the edge of her *sadi*. In that plate there were these articles,—the paste of first class rice of *shali* species, three pinches of dust picked up from the compound of the house, pieces of turmeric and some oil and vermilion. With these on the plate carried on the head she went from house to house. Behind her went the maidens of the village singing festive songs. Then she filled a cup with *chora pani* [1] and reserved it for the bride who was made to touch some coins; she did so with a prayer for her future fortune; she also touched the sacred wood called the *mana*, the prayer of the mother being that her daughter might win her husband's heart. The *nandi-mukha* (the sradh) and other sacred rites were performed and thus the marriage came to an end.

The bride and the bridegroom now played at dice. Curiously Chand Binod was defeated in the play because his mind was not in it. He prepared a bed of flowers for the bride but by the time the night was already over, and Chand Binod became anxious to return to his home. The next night was the *kalratri* or the 'black night' when the husband and wife should not meet. Then came *shuva ratri* or the auspicious night. Binod went to the nuptial chamber. One small lamp, like one solitary star, spread its dim light and what a surprise to the husband when just as his eyelids were closing under the

[1] The '*chora pani*' is water reserved on the night of marriage by the mother of the bride, in which are concealed some coins and a ring to be found out by the bride the next morning. It is called '*chora pani*' (*lit.* stealing water) because the water hides the articles.

spell of sleep, he saw the new bride standing before him! The sight of Malua took away sleep from his eyes and charmed them. He caught her by her arm and spoke endearingly. He removed the veil from her face. Oh what a wonder! How beautiful the face and how beautiful the curve of her eye-brows! What a happiness! It appeared that in a dark room one had suddenly come into the possession of pure gold. He was maddened by her beauty. Her long hair touched her very ankles. With the unbraided locks of her luxuriant hair Chand Binod played *meghuri* (a kind of sport). She said in whispers, "What are you doing, my heart's lord? The wives of my five brothers have known no sleep in their curiosity and through the small openings of the thatched walls their dark eyes are intent on gazing at you. I will not move, lest my ornaments make a sound. They will make the whole house ring with their laughter and jokes to-morrow morning and deal with me as if I were a culprit. Wait, dear lord, come not too close."

The light was put out and they slept apart. And thus the '*shubha ratri*' or the auspicious night passed.

Ll. 1.80.

11. Return Home.

In the morning Malua arose from her bed and Chand Binod sat in the courtyard and washed his hands and feet with the cool water reserved on the previous night for the purpose.

He was to start for his home that evening with the new bride. Her mother, aunt and other relations wept at parting with her. The mother lamented saying, "I took care to bring you up all these years. It was to prepare you for this hour. You are to leave us to-day and go to another family to become theirs." The father wept lamenting in the same strain. The neighbours came up and said, "Do not waste time in vain lamentings. Pack up the articles which should go with the pair. Many boxes and caskets were filled with things. Small bags were filled with spices; fine fried rice of the *binni* species, oil and vermilion were placed in vessels. When the final hour of departure came the mother wiped her eyes and said, "We could not give you any comfort in this house. Much have you suffered here. Now for good I come to bid you farewell. Behave well in your father-in-law's home. Let the neighbours have no opportunity to blame you."

As an auspicious thing curd was served to Chand Binod who partook of a portion. He bowed to his father-in-law and mother-in-law and paid his respects to other elderly relations of his wife and then started for his home with her.

"What are you doing, O Chand Binod's mother? Bestir yourself and behold your son coming with his bride. And you, Binod's aunt, unfurl the golden umbrella and hold it over the heads of the couple."

The mother approached in all haste. And with rice and fresh tufts of grass she hailed the new bride whose face shone like the moon. Chand Binod touched the feet of his mother with respect and she tenderly said, "Your beautiful face, my son, has grown pale owing to the fatigue of the journey." And then she hastened to welcome the new-comer, whom she took to be the Goddess of Fortune herself. The ladies of the house assembled there and sang songs of welcome. A cup of sacred water of the Ganges was placed near the couple and the women folk made presents of gold and silver to the bride.

Thus all the rites were performed and the mother's heart was filled with joy. Truly is it said, "The beauty of a house is the flower garden facing it. The beauty of the family is the new bride." She filled the gap in the mother's heart and made it overflow with joy.

The arrangements of the household were made anew and there was now perfect happiness in the little family.

Ll. 1-44.

12. The Oppression.

Now, my readers, you must be prepared for another epoch of Chand Binod's life which is full of suffering.

The Kazi of that town was a very wicked and licentious man. His powers were almost unlimited. He made friends with thieves and assassins and punished good men. There was no justice in the land. Things good and bad were inextricably confused in his mind. Chaste women living with their husbands were forcibly carried off by him.

One day the Kazi was riding that way when Malua happened to go to the pond to fetch water. The beauty of the damsel bewildered the Kazi's mind, who gazed with insatiate eyes on her from horseback. The long hair of Malua fell behind her back aspiring to touch the ground. Her face had a charm which reminded one of the *mahua* flower that grew on the hills. Her glances reminded one of the dance of the bird *khanjan*. The Kazi thenceforth daily came and went by that path. Daily he saw her and daily his desire to secure her increased till he grew mad after her. Like a bird that go away from the hand, his mind ran out of his control.

After much thinking he paid a visit to a woman named Netai who always offered help to those who wanted to seduce other men's wives. She was a corrupt woman when young, always delighting in new conquests. Now after the passing of her youth, she has lost all occupation and scarcely goes out. Though she has lost her youth she has not lost her habit. By her bad counsel many women are led astray. Her hair has grown grey and her teeth have fallen out. It is by this wicked profession (of seducing women) that she earns her livelihood. When the Kazi paid a visit to her house, she offered him a seat made of jackwood. She very humbly addressed him saying, "What is the business that has brought Your Honour to my house? I do not know how I acquired such virtue as to deserve this piece of good fortune." The Kazi said,

Cupid aims at the Devil

" The beauty of the damsel bewildered the Kazi's mind, who gazed with insatiate eyes on her from horseback."

Malua, p. 58

"Dear woman, you will have enough gold from me as reward, if you can help me to the attainment of my object. If I succeed through your help, take my assurance that I will give you full redemption from all punishments up to seven murders. It will be a turning-point of your luck. I will make you as free as the wild horse in the forest. You will be at liberty to do as you will wish. Your roof I shall build anew with straw. Whatever money you may require will be supplied from my treasury. Now to tell you my business, the other day I was going to a village near by. Near the landing steps of a pond I saw a beautiful damsel. She is the wife of Chand Binod—a man whom I consider my foe. Is there no bee in the country that a dung-worm sits on the lotus! Now on some pretext or other go to their house. When you will find her all alone tell her my message. Whatever money she may want I will gladly offer her. I will adorn her neck with a golden necklace of star pattern. I am really mad after her—tell her this. If she agrees to marry me according to the '*nika*' system, I will make all other wives of mine slaves to her wishes. Up to seven murders I have the power to grant redemption from all punishments, and this I will grant her. I will cover her whole person with gold. She will sleep on a golden couch on a right royal bed. She will wear on her breast a string of gold coins. Her nose ornament will sparkle with diamonds, and the pitcher that she carries for water will be plated with gold."

Saying this the Kazi went to his house. Now this witch of an old woman began to devise some means to accomplish her object. After much thinking Netai went to the house of Chand Binod. The wicked hag said to Binod's mother, "What is it, sister, that you are doing at this moment? I have come to see you after a long time. I hear that Binod's wife is marvellously beautiful. I have neither had an opportunity of seeing her nor of talking with her. Will you kindly bring her here and introduce her to me?"

In this way she called there frequently. One day she found Malua all alone on the bathing *ghat*. She communicated to her all that the Kazi had said. "You are a good wife, bright to look at as a genuine piece of gold, you do not know your own worth. The Kazi is the great judge of the country and is foremost in rank. I will tell you all about him and hide nothing. Your beauty has maddened him. He will cover your body with golden ornaments. If you agree to marry him according to the '*nika*' system, he will make all other wives of his, slaves to your wishes. He will present you with a string of gold coins to adorn your breast. And diamonds will sparkle from your nose ornament. Your pitcher of water will be plated with gold. On a royal bed spread upon a golden couch you will sleep."

As she filled her pitcher with water she evidently got frightened. She at once returned to her home. Netai followed her. Her mother-in-law was not at home at the time. For some moments she hid her feelings and did not say anything. But when the old woman resumed her speech tempting her, she could no longer remain silent but in great anger said, "Hear me, you old woman, my husband is not here. What should I say? If he were here I would break my broom on your white head. Your youth is gone and death is knocking at your door. In your youth you lived a corrupt life. You take all the women of the town to be like you. Tell your Kazi that I do not care for him. My husband is to me the prince of princes. He is to me glorious as the summit of a mountain and precious as a war-horse that wins the race. He is to me like the moon that rises in glory in the sky. The wicked Kazi has not the worth of my husband's toe. Now take this insult from me and go to your Kazi and tell him all. I take him to be my foe and hold him as a dog. If he had dared approach me directly I would have heaped upon him insults with this broom of mine. May my husband live a hundred years, and I will crush the string of gold coins offered by the Kazi under my feet. My husband is dearer far to me than any gold. The Kazi's gold is false and bears no comparison. He speaks of marriage by '*nika*' system; we are Hindus and unused to such things. Let Kazi's wives, if they have such longings, satisfy themselves by marrying seven times, which would be perfectly in accord with Muhammadan customs. As that wicked man has dared hold me in such a light I do hit his face with a broom from here. You are an old woman, older than my mother. Out of respect for your age I do not insult you. But go and never tread my threshold again."

Thus insulted Netai, the old woman, went to the Kazi and related all. He burnt with rage at this insult and plotted to take revenge. He served a warrant on Chand Binod commanding him to pay his '*najar moracha*' within seven days. The order ran thus: "You married six months ago and up to now have not paid the '*najar*' to the Dewan, due on your marriage. This is my command that if you do not pay the same to the Dewan within a week, your house and property will be confiscated to the State." The notice was duly served on Chand Binod and he knew not what to do at the crisis. It was rupees five hundred that was demanded. "How can I pay such a big amount? Where can I get it?" he thought. He could not secure the amount from anywhere and was maddened with despair. In the meantime the week passed away. Another warrant was then served. The Kazi's flag was planted on the homestead which along with other lands and property of Chand Binod was confiscated to the State.

He had lived happily for all these months, and now it was as if a thunderbolt had fallen on his bare head. His granaries were emptied of their store and immense sufferings were caused to the family. He first sold his bullocks with which he used to drive his plough. Then he sold his milch cows. Chand Binod's mother began to beat her breast in grief and lament. The beautiful eight-roofed bungalow that he had built so artistically was next disposed of. Only one room remained. That too he thought of selling. Chand Binod began to reflect thus, "Now are we to live under some tree. But how can my Malua dearer than life, live there? Where shall I keep her? My mother has grown old. Alas, how greatly does she suffer! By fastings and other sufferings her face has grown pale."

One day Chand Binod said to Malua, "Go to your father's place, Malua, with my mother. You are the only sister of five brothers who dearly love you. Even if some one hits you with a flower your tender body cannot bear it. Always accustomed to live in comfort you have not the experiences of poverty. How can you bear all this? Your parents are alive and your brothers hold you so dear. You will live there in happiness. As for me, I am a beggar and accustomed to a hard life. I will live here. But you, dear Malua, cannot share my pain." Softly did Malua reply, "All the happiness of my father's home has ended since the day of my marriage. Whether you live in a forest, or under a straw roof, or under the shade of a tree, you are my stay and none other. Even if I fast for seven days, the very sight of your face assuages all my pain. If I drink your *charanamrita* [1]—the water touched by your feet—it is to me like the elixir of life. Malua does not like the life of a princess in her father's home. If fasting the whole day I have only one meal in the evening, consisting of mere rice and vegetables boiled in water, I forget all my sufferings seeing your face. I cannot picture to myself any happiness greater than the privilege of touching your feet. Leaving you here I can by no means go to my father's place."

[1] The devout Hindus, men and women, every day drink a few drops of water with which the feet of their tutelary deity is washed every day and which is scented by flowers and sacred leaves used in worship. This is called the '*charnnamrita*' or "nectar of feet." A pious Hindu woman would not take any food before drinking a few drops of water touched by her husband's toe. This is also called '*charanamrita*.' The custom is fast disappearing.

Chand Binod now planned to go out to foreign lands to earn money. Malua became greatly depressed in spirit when she heard this and opposed him saying, " No, that cannot be, I cannot allow you to go. If you leave me and go, I will starve myself to death. Under the shade of a tree, with a part of my *saḍi* spread like a bed, I will sleep well, and will travel with you in forests seeking fruits for you. This I will do and share your sorrows."[1]

Ll. 1.78.

13. Distressing Poverty.

They managed to live during the month of July on the price of her *nath* (nose ornament) which Malua had sold. Even her pearl necklace she sold and they lived for some time on it. In the month of August she sold her anklets. Oh, what ill luck! The family spent somehow the month of September, getting a loan on the security of Malua's bracelets. Her silken robes she sold in October, and in the month of November she sold her earrings which she specially liked. The rest of her gold ornaments were all in the creditor's house as security for loan. Now her clothes were all tattered and full of patches and repairs. A pair of amulets was all that was left, and her clothes, all tattered and rent, hardly covered her shame. One full day she passed fasting, this was a severe trial. There was not a handful of rice in the house to offer to the harvest goddess for daily worship.

The interest of the creditors went on increasing from day to day. For two days they lived upon half-boiled grass and plants. But when Malua saw the pale face of her husband, her heart burst in sorrow. She herself went without her meals and did not tell it to others; but she could not bear the sight of her famished husband and mother-in-law when she could not serve them a meal. She could no more preserve the honour of the family and thought of begging from door to door.

[1] She opposes his plan of his going abroad, for fear of the Kazi, though she does not say so.

And when Chand Binod perceived this, he did not divulge his intention to his wife, neither said anything to his mother, but in December he secretly left his home with the purpose of earning money.

Ll. 1-24.

14. The Freaks of Fortune.

At this crisis the wicked Kazi sent the old woman Netai again to her. The old woman said, "O you, daughter of a big man, why should you suffer so much for others? If you go to the Kazi's house, you will eat your meal off golden plates. Why do you starve yourself here? There is not a handful of rice in your house. How long will your body bear all these privations? The Kazi has sent me again to you. Now take good counsel and consent to be his wife. Does it become you, daughter of a rich man, to husk rice and prepare yarns in hand-looms? Your beautiful body is ill-covered by the rags you wear. There is no ornament in your nose, and your ears have not their rings of flower pattern. Your body is dusty like the white petals of the *Dhutura* flower. We will cover your delicate body with golden ornaments. Marry the Kazi and go to his house."

Her eyes wore the flaming colour of the *java* flower. It was like putting salt in a sore. She could not bear the insult. "My husband has gone abroad," she said; "remembering his face I will bear all my sufferings. Better that I should husk rice for others or go a-begging from door to door than seek fortune from the Kazi's hands. I have five brothers who are a terror to wicked men. They are like so many lords of death. They will cut your nose and the ears of the wicked Kazi. They will kill you by smashing your head on a stone. Wait and let me send a letter to them."

Disappointed the old witch returned to her home.

Alone she lived in the house after her husband's departure and this raised whispers amongst the neighbours,

When the mother of Malua got a report of the distress that she was in, she sent her five sons without delay.

They dressed themselves in all haste and paid a visit to Malua's home and requested her to accompany them to theirs. When she saw them she began to weep. The brothers also wept to see her condition. They lamented saying, "The only sister among five brothers, you have been dear to us, Malua, as life. We got for you a husband who seemed worthy in every respect. Now all this trouble is surely due to bad luck. Our wives have gold ornaments more than they need, and, what a pity that our dear sister is without any. The cloth that you have worn is tattered and full of patches and repairs. Your bright colour is pale with dirt. Alas, you sleep here on the bare ground! Mother has kept in her store-room beautiful mats for you. Such a place as this is full of gnats. How can you sleep here in the night? In our house there is a room reserved for you. Beautiful fans of mica and a curtain adorned with beautiful laces are ready there for you. Plenty of food is wasted there and you starve here; what an irony of fate is this! At noon and in the evening strangers come to our house and are served with meals, and you, our dear sister, go without a meal. How cruel is the thought! For full twelve years, sister, you were at your father's home and lived there a free life; no one had ever asked you to do the least work in the house.

"Sweetmeats and other delicacies of rare sort have been prepared and no one has touched them,—mother has kept them all for you. She has not touched any food for these three days on getting the report of your condition, and for three days no fire has been kindled in the hearth and no evening lamps have been lighted at our house. We will send a palanquin for you to-morrow morning. If you do not go, mother will die of a broken heart. Three nights our mother has spent weeping, and now waits for you with all a mother's longings."

Softly did Malua say to her brothers, weeping all the time :—

"How can I tell you my grief? my heart breaks. You chose for me this house, and my good husband was after your own hearts in all respects. What fault is yours? Who can avoid fate? I am, however, resolved to live in this house. To me, I tell you, dear brothers, this house is the best of all the shrines. It is my Benares,—my Brindaban. Go back and look to the comforts of our dear parents. For me, my primary duty is to minister to my distressed mother-in-law. Tell mother that I cannot leave my old mother-in-law here all alone. Tell her I cannot go there now. Your wives are there; mother will be comforted in their company. If she heaves a sigh recollecting me, the five wives will console her. But my mother-in-law has none here. Her son has gone to a distant place. How can she be comforted in this distress if even I leave her and go?"

The brothers returned home and told all about her resolve to their parents.

She prepared yarns on the spinning wheel and husked rice with her old mother-in-law and in this way passed her days. The months of January and February she spent, constantly thinking of what she should do next. During March and April she looked forward to receiving some tidings of her husband. In the month of May the mangoes ripened and crows and ravens croaked from the boughs of the trees all day long. Alas, not a word from her husband to tell her where he was staying. In the month of June when showers fell on all sides like tears, the clouds roared and the lightnings flashed, she sweetly recollected her husband's face, and waited with deep longings to meet him. In July people worshipped Manasha Devi. When the whole country was astir on the festive occasion, he will come, he will come—she still hoped. But July passed also, and August came and went. It was now the month of September. People talked of the Pujas drawing near and of nothing else. Her hopes, however, were not fulfilled; he did not return even during the Pujas. How miserable was the house at the time of this general festivity, that did not ring with the voices of home-comers!

But when the month of October came he returned with his earnings of the year. He stood near the room of his mother and called her aloud. She hastened to meet him. Night and day she had wept. "At last, oh, dear one, hast thou come to comfort thy wretched mother!" He placed his purse containing all that he had earned before her, and sending the outstanding '*najar*' to the Dewan, released the property that had been confiscated.

He again built a Bungalow with eight pitched roofs.[1] Now he was once more restored to his Malua. In the night she told him all that she had suffered during his absence.

Sweet are sweetmeats and sugar, and sweet is the water of the Holy River! Sweeter than these is the water inside a cocoanut, cool and refreshing. Sweeter still are bright days coming after the evil ones. But when a baby comes to the mother's arms, the sweetness of it surpasses that of the smile of fortune. Sweeter perhaps than this is the lost one found. But the sweetest of all is the meeting of the lovers after separation!

Ll. 1-112.

15. The Great Trial.

Thus through these vicissitudes of fortune Chand Binod went on. His sky, that had been cloudy, for a little while brightened again.

But the inexorable, the terrible Kazi again plotted against him and threw him into a fresh trouble.

A warrant was served on Chand Binod to the following effect:

[1] Joined to one another slantingly to give it the look of an octagonal tower.

"His Highness the Dewan Saheb has learnt through a secret messenger that you have in your house a damsel of exceeding beauty. She is reported to be as handsome as a fairy. I serve this warrant by his order. Within seven days from to-day you must send your wife to the palace of His Highness. If you do not do so your life will be at stake. If you allow a week to pass without complying with the order of this warrant, know that your death will be sure."

His head sank to his knees as Chand Binod read this warrant. He looked like a deer fallen within the claws of a tiger. Death, and men terrible as death, were pulling him from two sides. What a fate, alas, was reserved for poor Chand Binod!

The week passed. Mridha, the police-officer of the Kazi, came to the house of Chand Binod in due course, bound him hand and foot, and dragged him through the public road by a rope tied round his neck, and brought him to the presence of the Kazi.

The Kazi said:

"You rogue, you have not complied with my order. You have still kept the handsome woman in your house."

Turning to the office peons he ordered them: "Take Chand Binod to the waste land known as the *nilakshar char* [1] and bury him alive there. You should also seize his wife and carry her to the palace of His Highness the Dewan Jahangir of Jahangirpur."

The Mridhas and the peons did as they were bid. Binod was taken by them to the *nilakshar char*. His mother lamented saying, "O my dear son, if death would have carried you away in the usual course I would have bowed to the inscrutable decree of Providence, how can I bear the thought that you are going to be killed by men in this

[1] "*Nilakshar char*" is a word which we find frequently in folk-tales—another name for it is "tepantarer māth." The words mean a vast moor or waste land without any habitation of men.

way? You are dearer than my life. Oh my pet-bird of the cage, a rib, it seems, has been taken out of my breast."

Malua shed tears as she sat near her mother-in-law trying to console her. But she stopped weeping a little while after, and wrote a short epistle in two-and-a-half letters[1] to her five brothers. In this short letter she wrote all about the doings of the Kazi and how Chand Binod was taken away for execution.

Having written the letter she trusted it to her trained falcon. A bare hint was sufficient for the falcon to understand its mission, and it flew at once to her father's home.

As soon as the brothers received the letter, they hurried to the *nilakshar char* armed with weapons. Just at the moment when they reached the vast waste, they found the men of the Kazi digging a grave for Chand Binod. The brothers at once fell upon the men and belaboured them with their long sticks. Chand Binod was thus released. Next they proceeded towards his home, seeking Malua.

When Chand Binod's mother saw them she began to weep bitterly. Alas, that home was now emptied of its chief treasure! The beautiful one was not there. Wicked Ravana had absconded with Sita—the true bride of Rama. Alas, the golden cage was there, but the sweet parrot was gone! The five brothers lay benumbed with grief and it was a heart-rending sight to see Chand Binod bewailing the loss of his wife. One's heart would break to hear his words.

Her pitcher was there but who would go to the river-*ghat* with it? The house once shone bright, but Malua who was like the lamp of it, was gone and it now looked dark. The home with its garden—the fine mat on which she slept—the doors and everything, were as they were before. It was she alone—the golden treasure of that house that was gone. Like a mad man Chand Binod went to his falcon and said, "Brother

[1] "Two and a half letters"—Here means a very short letter.

falcon, we have lived together for long years, now give me information about my Malua."

With the cage in hand and with his mother he left the house, and wandered about from place to place in that vast country.

Ll. 1-76.

16. Malua in Dewan Saheb's Harem.

Malua sat in the drawing room of the Dewan's palace and wept. There was a bed spread on a stately couch in the hall, but she sat on the bare floor. The attending maidens were ready with splendid dishes to serve her, and His Highness the Dewan Saheb himself stood near her, swearing by his life that she must partake of them. He said, "Upon my life, dear girl, do not deceive me in this way and make me the most wretched man amongst human beings. Partake of the meal and sit on the couch. I will give you all the pleasures one can expect in this world. From Delhi I will get for you a flame-coloured *sadi*. With gold of the purest quality I will make for you a nose ornament. There are numerous servants and maid-servants in the palace,—know them all to be thine. They will be ready to carry out your least wishes. On the couch you will enjoy rest, whilst myself, your humble slave, will await your pleasure, standing."

Just like a deer within the claws of a tiger Malua trembled in fear and weeping said to the Dewan Saheb:

"I have taken a vow of abstinence and worship for twelve months, of which nine months have passed. After three months my vow will be fulfilled. My humble prayer to you is that you should allow me to act according to these conditions of my vow, *viz.*, I will not during this period take any food touched by others, nor will I drink any water from this place. I will cook my own meal, and this will consist merely of rice boiled with potato in water. And I will take this without salt.[1] My bed will be but a portion of the *sadi* which I wear, spread on the floor. I will do penance and will not break any of these conditions. I will in no case look at the face of a man nor should any be allowed to come near me during the term of my vow. For these three months your Highness must not enter my compartment. On the expiry of the time I will consider your case.

"If you do otherwise I will consider you as my foe and destroy my life by poison."

The first, the second, and the third months passed. On the expiration of the third month His Highness the Dewan with scented betel in his mouth and a handkerchief lined with gold in hand entered Malua's apartment with slow steps.

She trembled in fear as doth a deer in the claws of a tiger. The Dewan said, "You have deceived me, fair one, all these three long months. But never mind, I have respected your vow. Now leave the floor and come up and sit on the couch. Accept me as your mate with a glad heart. Your presence is a delight to the eyes and now make me fully happy. I will not keep any cause of your complaint. I will release your husband."

Malua said, "Great sorrows, sir, I have had at the hands of the wicked Kazi. Unjustly he has killed my husband. How can you release one who was buried alive in the waste of *nilaksha*? How can you expect me to give you my heart so long as I am not avenged, and the Kazi is allowed to live in peace? How can I forget the unnumbered woes which the wicked Kazi has caused me?"

Then the Dewan was wroth. He ordered the Prefect of Police to start at once and see the Kazi executed. With constables and Mridhas the Kotwal went to carry out the order. And Malua after her long sufferings caused by the

[1] The reason of this restriction is that during the days of mourning, a Hindu does not take salt. There may be another reason also, *viz.*, according to the notions of Indians, it is a sacrilegious thing to go against a man whose salt one has taken.

Kazi was now glad to have this retaliation. Now she was pleased and said to the Dewan, "Only twelve days are remaining of the three months. Patiently wait for this short time. We shall go together to hunt falcons. So kindly order a pleasure-boat to be made ready. You are no doubt aware that my husband was an expert hunter. For long years I lived with him and learnt the art of hunting falcons myself. You will see that I shall secure a hundred falcons by a single trap."

The date of hunting, and the auspicious hour to start were settled, and Malua in the meantime wrote a letter to her five brothers with her own hand and she trusted it to her trained falcon.

The five brothers started from their home on the pretext of hunting. The Dewan Saheb too went one midday to the extensive swamp full of lilies and known as the *Dhalair bil.* With him went the beautiful Malua. The five brothers with their light pinnaces surrounded the Dewan's boat. The brothers and their kinsmen belaboured the oarsmen and the captain of the Dewan's boat with their long sticks and they fell into the swamp, with their heads downwards. The boat on which the five brothers were was beautiful to see and Malua stepped into it with a light and brisk leap. The kinsmen of the brothers rowed the pinnaces which flew like birds, crushing the lilies with which the bog abounded under their keels. With her husband did Malua come to her father's home. Thus was she rescued as was Sita by her husband Rama from the clutches of the enemy.

Ll. 1-78.

17. The Unrelenting Kinsmen.

Now the kinsmen of Malua created fresh trouble by their wickedness. One of them said, "Malua has lost her character.

She has, besides, lost her caste as she took food in a Muhammadan's house. How could she live there without doing so?"

The maternal uncle of Chand Binod was a man of high social status. He was the recognised head of the *hele kaibartas.* He said, "I, for myself, assure you, I see no way how I can take meals at the hands of Malua. Let Chand Binod do penance, and we will admit him to caste again."

Another kinsman who was Chand Binod's uncle on the father's side came up and repeated the same charge. "For three months," he said, "she was in the palace of the Dewan. How could she live there without food?"

Chand Binod thought over this matter for some days after this discussion and then applied to the Brahmins. Following their advice he did the necessary penance *and divorced his wife.* And the beautiful one hid herself in a dark corner of the house and wept.

"Alas!" she asked herself, "where am I to go and to whom can I tell this tale of my grief? As he has divorced me it is better that I should die." The five brothers said, "Do not weep, dear sister, we will take you with us. You will have no trouble about your food and raiments at our house. We assure you that you will be happy there." The father tried to soothe her and the brothers used all the force of their logic, but she was not convinced. She said weeping, "I shall be a maid-servant in this house, but still live near my husband. In the hours of the morning and evening will I do the washing of the house. I will do the work which devolves upon a servant of the outer compound." Looking at her husband she said, "I shall not be able to cook food for you or touch the water that you would drink. Take another wife and be happy."

By her life did she swear and request her five brothers to get a beautiful wife for Chand Binod. "How will my mother-in-law who has grown deaf and blind with age, live without help, if my husband does not marry again?"

The kinsmen insisted on the step and helped Chand Binod to marry again. But she, as maid-servant, worked in the outer courtyard and spent her days in unhappiness. She took great care of the new wife whom she sincerely loved. Still did she not go to her father's home. She served her husband and mother-in-law so far as lay in her power.

Ll. 1-42.

18. The Dead brought to Life Again.

The unfortunate mother was sleeping in her room and was dreaming a bad dream. Chand Binod roused her from sleep and wanted food. She regretted that the rice was not husked so early. But Chand Binod insisted on her giving him some meal as he was about to go a-hunting. He could not wait till rice was cooked. There was some cooked rice in the house of the night before mixed with water. He ate this and bowed to his mother and took leave. In his right hand was the cage and in his left was the falcon. It was noon-time when Chand Binod started from home. His sister's house stood on the way and he paid a visit to her. She wept over family matters whilst talking with her brother. Taking leave of his sister, he entered a deep forest with the falcon in his hand.

There were long reeds and grasses in a meadow where he set the falcon free. He kept the cage in his hand and sat under the shade of the *banchhobra* plants. Hidden under these plants was a black snake which bit the toe of Chand Binod. The poison at once became mixed with blood and rose up affecting the brain. Chand Binod could not keep his head steady, but reeled and fell on the ground.

" O, ye birds and beasts, carry the message to my mother that I die of snake-bite in this forest. Alas, who will inform my mother! Oh, what a pity! I shall not see my own beautiful Malua once before I die! My house and all I leave and I die here forlorn under the uncovered sky and not under a roof! Who are you, O traveller, carry the message to my mother."

In the evening a traveller brought the news to the poor mother. "Your son Binod, Madam, lies dead in the deep forest." With her hair all dishevelled, she at once ran to the spot where Binod lay. There was no breath in his nostrils and no word in his mouth. The mother fell down on the ground crying. The kinsmen all brought Chand Binod to his home, unconscious—like one dead. Malua's tears knew no stop. "O, my dear lord," she cried, "the whole treasure of a poor woman's heart—how can I live without thee? Why did not the snake bite me instead of you? Alas! the wretched life of a maid-servant whose lot is to work outside the house, is, perhaps, too contemptible even to serve as a meal for a tiger or a snake! They too avoid it! I live outside, I work outside, not having liberty to enter into the bed rooms and the kitchen, yet I forget all my woes seeing my husband day and night! Even this piece of luck will not cruel Providence vouchsafe unto me! I no longer covet life. I will burn myself on the funeral pyre of my husband or enter water and drown myself or I shall tie a rope on the yonder *hijal* tree and hang myself."

When she was lamenting in this way, her five brothers came up to this spot having heard the bad news. They sat near Chand Binod's body and found his eyes grown dim, saliva flowing from the corners of his lips. They too lamented saying, "How is it, dear brother, how could you cut the ties that have bound us to you all these long years? We gave you our dear sister. How will she live the hard life of a widow? Scandal has thrice cursed her life, but still she had one great comfort. How will she have the heart to break her shell-bracelets plated with gold? How shall we bear the sight of her sad face?"

MALUA.

" Do not weep, my dear brothers. But listen to what I am going to say. Examine well if there is still life in him. There on the landing *ghat* of the river lies anchored our boat made of the wood *man paban*. Carry this body swiftly to the house of the physician of snake-bite who lives afar.

The five brothers came up to the boat. They became themselves its oarsmen. Malua sat with her husband's body near her. It usually took seven days to reach the physician's place, but so swiftly did they ply their oars that they reached it in a day.

The physician examined the breath and studied the face with care. Then he slapped the head of Chand Binod with some force. The poison came down to the breast of the patient, then gradually it descended to his knees and last to his feet. The black snake was in the nether world, it sucked the poison from the feet. When the poison was thus sucked, the whole body of Chand Binod was soothed and he opened his eyes.

Thus having restored her husband to life, Malua triumphantly returned home. The whole town rang with her praise. Some said, " She is a second Behula. She has restored her husband to life as Behula did to Lakshmindra." Others said, " The chaste woman has achieved this by the direct grace of the gods. The whole community of the *hele dashes* has been sanctified by this chaste woman. Let us offer flower and betel to her and admit her back to caste. She has brought her dead husband back to life. Why should we still feel any hesitancy in admitting her to caste ? "

Ll. 1-91.

19. The Last Tragic Scene.

The maternal uncle of Chand Binod, who was one of the headmen of the community, said "He that will dare do this, will lose his caste." Another elderly kinsman gave the matter a full consideration and delivered his judgment: "We cannot give up our religion and caste for the sake of Malua. She must be where she is now."

The unfortunate woman passed her days in sorrow. Oh how unlucky was she! As a child she had lived happily with her parents for a short period. She was the star of her mother's eyes. If anybody would then hit her with a flower, it would be too much for her. The parents prized her more than they did her five brothers. Darling she was of the whole family. And behold her lot now!

She thought over her lot and could not decide what to do. Then she thought, "So long as I shall live my husband will be unhappy on my account. People will spread scandal and he will be the sufferer for it." Then she resolved to die.

The same boat made of *man paban* lay anchored at the landing *ghat* of the river. One day at the hour of noon she came up there and stepped into the boat with her light steps. The boat was already broken and as she sat in it, water came pouring from all sides. "I do not know how far down the nether world may be. I will go down and see the bottom. Let the water rise and rise to the awning over the boat." This was her resolve.

The sister of Chand Binod came swiftly to the *ghat*.

Sister.

"Listen to me, dear sister, leave that leaky boat, and come back."

Malua.

"No, sister, that cannot be, my heart breaks at the sight of you all. Let the water of the river rise and rise till the boat is sunk. Once for all look at Malua whom you loved so well and whom you will see no more."

The mother-in-law came running to the spot maddened with grief and careless of her attire, her hair all dishevelled.—

Mother-in-law.

"O my daughter, dearer than life, you are the Goddess Lakshmi of our house. Come back I pray. Of my tottering house you are the sole stay—you are the moonbeams of my torn straw-roof and the light of my house. Without you I cannot live for a moment."

Malua.

"Let the water rise and rise evermore till the leaky boat is sunk, mother; bless me, I bid you farewell, and for the last time bow to your feet."

The water came splashing into the boat, and one-half of it was already sunk. The mother-in-law stood on the bank and wept.

One after another the five brothers, came there. The kinsmen came one and all. The five brothers called aloud and said, "Come out of that leaky boat and return to your father's home. We will bring a golden pinnace for you to take you there and will protect you by our lives."

Malua bids farewell to her brothers, "Let the water rise and rise and the leaky boat be sunk. Leave your Malua here, O dear brothers, and return home."

The water now rose over the sides of the boat. "Run fast Chand Binod, if you want to see her for the last time."

Running did he come and stand on the banks of the river.

Chand Binod.

"Can it be that the light of my soul is to perish thus before my eyes? Let the sun and moon sink. I have nothing more to do with the world. I no longer want my kinsmen and friends. If indeed you are to die in this way I will accompany you. Tell me, dear Malua, but once, how I can remove your suffering. I will take you again into my home and if my community will outcaste me, I will not care for my caste. Do not, I pray you, do not drown yourself. By the gods of heaven I do pray unto you."

Malua.

"My days have just approached their close. What charm has this world for me and why should I live? So long as I shall live, there will be scandal and you will suffer for it. The kinsmen and friends will worry you by their talk. This life of sullied fame I will throw into the waters. O my dear husband, do not wait to see the end, but go from here. You have now a fair lady for your wife at home. Live with her and be happy. Let the waters rise and rise and the broken boat be sunk. Leave the unfortunate one here and go back."

At that moment the wind carried the boat away to the mid-river. She addressed the kinsmen, and said:--

"Even she whose crimes are great will not live to trouble you for ever.

"The faults are all mine, my sorrows were ordained by fate. How could I have avoided them? But do not, I pray you, blame my husband. He is blameless. O my mother-in-law! May you be my mother in hundreds of lives to come. From here in the mid stream, do I bow to your feet for the last time."

She addressed her co-wife and said, "Live with your husband, dear sister, happily; from to-day you will no more see my face. If you feel any pain remembering me, look at the face of our husband, that will remove all your pain."

In the eastern horizon a storm arose and the clouds roared. The sea that faced her had no banks, nor any boat to ferry a pilgrim across.

"Let the waters rise and rise and let the boat sink. The shores after all may not be far off. I will go down and see the bottom of the stream."

The clouds roared from the eastern sky. The storm swept clear everything in its mad course.

Alas! Where was the beautiful one gone with her boat made of *man paban*!

Ll. 1-76.

CHANDRAVATI

BY

NAYAN CHAND GHOSH

PREFACE

Narayan Deb, one of the earliest poets of the Manasa-cult was born in the old city of Magadha in the beginning of the 14th century. When still young the poet came down and settled in the small village of Baro[1] in the district of Mymensing. He wrote his famous 'Manasar Bhashan' about six hundred years ago. His descendants still live at Baro and the adult members of the family are the twenty-first generation in descent from the poet.

The next poet of the same cult in Mymensing, who nearly eclipsed the fame of Narayan Deb, was Bangshi Das, who, as I have stated elsewhere, belonged to the village of Patuari on the Phuleshwari, in the subdivision of Kishorgung. Bangshi Das's 'Bhashan' was finished in the year 1575 with the co-operation of his daughter Chandrávati. In the earlier manuscripts of the work, the name of Chandrávati often occurs in the colophons of stray passages composed by her and incorporated with the poem of Bangshi Das, her father. The Bat-tala Presses of Calcutta following the practice of the later manuscript-writers have dropped the names of the lesser poets, retaining the name of the most famous one in the colophon. We find this to be the case in regard to the poem of Bangshi Das also.

Bangshi Das's piety and faith are best illustrated in the anecdote of his life recounted by Chandrávati in her poem of Kenaram. He was not only saintly in his character but a learned Sanskrit scholar and wrote three erudite works

[1] Baro is a village on the river Phuleshwari, about 40 miles to the south-east of the town of Mymensing and 22 miles to the south of Netrakona in the same district.

besides the 'Manasa Mangal.' These are the 'Ram Gita,' the 'Chandi' and the 'Krisna Gunarnava.'

Bangshi Das received a sound training from his father Jadavananda, himself a scholar of some renown. Anjaná, the mother of the poet, was an accomplished woman known for her devotion and pure life. In the 'Padmápurana' Bangshi Das pays his tribute of respect to his predecessor in the field—Narayan Deb, in the preliminary verses.

Chandrávati, Bangshi Das's daughter, was the only issue of the poet. He had taken care to give her a sound education. Chandrá says "I bow down to my mother Sulochaná and father Bangshi Das who took great pains in teaching me the Puranas." With an exquisite grace and tenderness she offers her praises to the river Phuleshwari (lit. mistress of flowers) which, she says, supplied her with poetic inspiration.

The story of her ill-fated love is sung all over the country by professional minstrels even now. Chandrá was born in the middle of the sixteenth century. The date cannot be very far from 1550 A.D., as she participated in the labours of composing the 'Manasa Mangal' with her father—a work that was finished in 1575.

The present ballad was composed by the poet Nayan Chand Ghosh, whose name also occurs in a few colophons of the poem named 'Lila and Kanka.' The style of the present song is full of simple charm, and offers a contrast to the classical and somewhat pedantic language adopted by the poet in the other poem which he wrote in conjunction with Raghusuta and other poets who flourished in the beginning of the 17th century.

Chandrá is the typical Hindu girl of the old school,—spiritual almost to austerity. There is also a tender side to her character which, though based on the solid rock of her patience and resignation, reveals the gentler human graces. Inspite of the rigidity of her vow, we do not miss for a moment a feminine sweetness and tenderness of heart. This is very noticeable in the account of Sita given by her in the Ramayana which she wrote in compliance with her father's wishes. That work, though very popular amongst the women-folk of Eastern Mymensing who sing and recite it from memory, has not yet been published. I have, however, secured a manuscript of the poem for the Library of the University of Calcutta. Her account of Kenaram the Robber and her Ramayana are fountains of unceasing pathos which no doubt sprang from the grief-stricken recesses of her heart.

The village Patuari exists to the present day on the banks of the Phuleshwari—a branch of the river Narsunda, and it is said the relics of the old temple which Chandrá had dedicated to Siva are still to be seen there. Patuari is only a few miles to the north-east of Kishorganj. No trace, however, of the village Sundha, the home of Jaychandra, is to be found in the Surveyor General's map.

The present ballad is divided into 12 cantos and is complete in 354 lines of verse all in the *payar* metre.

DINESH CHANDRA SEN

7, Bishwakosh Lane,

Bagbazar, Calcutta. 12th March, 1923.

CHANDRÁVATI

1. The Plucking of Flowers.

Chandrá.

"There have bloomed the *champa* and *nageshvar* flowers on the four sides of the tank. Who are you, O youth, that break the branches of the plants and rob them of their flowers?"

Jaychandra.

"Yonder river separates my home from yours. Why do you, dear maiden, yourself pluck these *malati* flowers."

Chadrá.

"Here have I come this morning to gather flowers; my father will worship Siva in the temple with these."

They selected the freshest ones among the flowers. The scarlet *java*, the yellow *champa* and the *gandha* of various species,—white, yellow and red—were gathered by Jaychandra in his cane-basket. The blue *aparajita* and the crescent-shaped *atashi* were also gathered there. The choicest *mallika* and the soft and fragrant *malati* were not lost sight of. With gladsome hearts, did they finish their pleasant morning task.

Days passed by in this way. At morning and evening, the youth and the maiden plucked flowers from the sides of the tank, and always they were all alone there. None knew of their meetings.

When from the high branches of the sweet *malati* plants Chandrá wished to pluck flowers, Jaychandra caught hold of a branch and pulled it down so that his fair companion might have easy access to its floral treasure.

One day she gathered flowers at dawn, but these were not meant for her father. She strung them into a garland and hung it round the youth's neck.

Ll. 1-18.

2. The Love-epistle.

For the first time he wrote her a letter. It was an epistle in 'two and a half letters,'[1] written on the petals of a flower.

Into that letter, short though it was, he poured his whole soul. "Do you know, maiden, how every day in solitude I weep over the presents of garlands of flowers, plucked and strung by your tender hands! The smiling garden of flowers becomes dark to my eyes when you depart. It ill becomes me to tell you the whole story. I have no power to express it. Your father is a man of austere principles and holds you dear as life. For myself, I have no parents—they are dead. I live in my uncle's home. How can I say what I am feeling? From the day I saw your beautiful face I have been like a mad man. Anxious am I to know what your own feelings are for me. If there be a chance for me to get you for my bride, I will surrender everything I have to your lovely feet. If not, from to-day I will cease to gather flowers. I will go to strange lands, bidding you a last farewell. If good fortune smiles on me and I get a favourable reply, know, dear girl, that I will be a slave to your wishes for life."

Ll. 1-20.

[1] We find frequent mention of "$2\frac{1}{2}$ letters" of the Bengali alphabet used in a mystic sense in old Bengali literature. In the Maynamati Songs, some *mantras* are said to be complete in $2\frac{1}{2}$ letters, possessed of great occult virtue. In the literature of Mymensing-ballads the words merely mean "very brief."—See Malua, Canto 15, line 42.

How one helped the other

" Jaychandra caught hold of a branch and pulled it down so that his fair companion might have easy access to its floral treasure."

Chandravati, p. 88

3. The Lad hands the little Note to the Maiden.

The morning sun[1] appeared on the horizon robed in yellow. His rays, half-hid in the thin clouds, sparkled like gold in the firmament.

The night had departed; the maiden Chandrávati rose in the morning and went as usual with her basket to gather flowers.

First of all she gathered the scarlet *java* flowers with which her father would worship Siva. Next she plucked the small white *bakul* and *malati* flowers to weave them into a garland (for Jaychandra).

Just at that moment the youth approached her with the short letter written on flower-petals.

Jaychandra.

"Busy are you, Oh maiden, plucking flowers and breaking the branches of plants. Will you allow me a little time to speak to you. After I have finished, you may again busy yourself with your *champa* and *nageshvar* flowers."

Chandrá

"I have done now; I have no need for more flowers. Just look at the east. The sun shines high above the horizon. Give me leave now, I cannot tarry. My father is waiting for these flowers to worship Siva."

Jaychandra

"Yes maiden, I will give you leave and bid you farewell, it may be for life."

[1] The bride and bridegroom wear a yellow dress coloured by turmeric at the wedding time. The sun's yellow robes have a symbolical meaning here implying the prospect of marriage.

Then he handed her the flower-petals and left the place in all haste without another word.

Ll. 1-18,

4. Bangshi Das prays to Siva for a Bridegroom for Chandrá.

In the corner of her *sadi* she tied and hid the floral epistle.

To the temple she came and washed its floor with the water of the holy Ganges. Facing the god, she spread a seat for her father and then crushed the sandal on stone and produced a scented paste. In the flower vase—the *puspapatra*—carefully did she place the flowers.

Her father now came and took his seat and prepared for worship.

Bangshi Das worshipped Siva and prayed to the god for a boon for his daughter. She was now grown up but no suitable groom had yet been found for her.

"O, Ever-lasting One, O Siva," he prayed, "bless the child. Every day I will worship thee with flowers of the forest and with my piety and devotion which are .like the flowers of my mind, grant me this boon that Chandrá may be blessed with a husband after her own mind. I am a poor man and without means to present a good dowry. None is there in the world on whose help I can rely save thee.

He offered a flower to Siva praying that a match-maker might bring a good proposal that very day by the blessing of the god.

Another flower he offered praying that the bridegroom might be one of high family—"resplendent as the god Indra may he be amongst men."

Another flower he offered praying that the bridegroom's social status might be worthy of his own,—of the illustrious family of tqe Bhattacharyas of Patuari.

Then he prostrated himself on the ground before the god and prayed "May my daughter, O lord, be happy in marriage."

Ll. 1-20.

5. She reads the Letter.

Doing her duties in the temple and seeing her father engaged in worship Chandrá retired to her room all alone, and with tender care opened Jaychandra's floral epistle.

As she read it tears began to flow from both her eyes. She knew not what reply she should give.

Then she again read the letter and wept again. "Alas, why has my mind become like his?" she thought, "Am I not helpless as the bird *suka* in the cage? It was enough for me to see his face—to hear his voice and gather flowers together. Why wish for more?"

"I am now grown up, my father wants to give me to some one. How can I tell him what I feel? My father is the master. Yes, Jaychandra gathers flower for me and I love him. I have held him dear as my life even from infancy; but how can I say that?"

She wrote a short reply. "There is my father in the house. What do I know? How can I give a reply—I am but a helpless girl?"

She hid all her feelings and wrote the letter cautiously in reserved language.

But retiring to her chamber she called the sun and moon to bear witness to her feelings and prayed to the gods to grant Jaychandra to her as a husband. She bowed to Siva with folded hands with this prayer in her mind, and sent the letter to the youth.

But from that day she ceased to go to gather flowers. Thus did she pass her days, not altogether in sorrow, not altogether in joy.

Ll. 1-4.

6. Her silent Reciprocation.

In the court-yard of her own house there had bloomed the *champa* and *nageshwar* flowers. All alone she went thither to gather flowers, but her mind was not in them.

"I shall see you with my insatiate eyes, I shall yield myself unto your arms and call you my husband. These small and sweet smelling *bakul* and *malati* flowers have bloomed here. I shall pluck the choicest of these for weaving garlands for you. The scarlet *javas* are there. How I wish to offer these as my tribute of worship to your feet. The *mallika* and the *malati* are spreading their fragrance, and I swear by them that I wish you to be my husband not only for this life but for all my future lives to come. Yonder are those thorny *ketaki* plants. Are such thorns in my way too? Who knows?"

Thus did she reflect and shed tears all alone. Now let us revert to the topic of her marriage.

Ll. 1-14.

7. The Proposal and its Acceptance.

A match-maker saw Bangshi Das one day and said "You have a beautiful daughter. Bright as the moon are your fair reputation and social honour. No family is there in this part of the country claiming a higher status. Your daughter is now grown up. Why not get her married to a worthy groom?"

"Where is such an one to be had?" asked Banshi. "Ready am I to favour a really good proposal."

The match-maker said "In the village of Sundha is such an one. His family is held in high esteem. They are Chakrabarties and *kulins* of the first order. The name of the youth is Jaychandra. Handsome is he as the god Kartikeya. I truly think him to be worthy of your fair daughter in every way. A good scholar is he in various branches of study,—the darling of his kinsmen, he looks glorious as the sun. Happy will your daughter be in this marriage and for myself I would have no hesitation about it."

"The western wind now produces a shiver as it blows. There is an ebb-tide in the mid stream of the river which flows slowly. The tops of the mango groves are full of blossoms. The season is a good one. And if you wish, I see no reason why the marriage should not take place during this very month."

The horoscopes were consulted and the palms of the bride and the bride-groom were examined. "A happier match was never indicated by the planets," said the astrologer.

Bangshi Das.

"As the horoscopes have proved satisfactory, ready am I to offer my daughter to this youth."

Ll. 1-26.

8 Preparations.

The negotiations were complete and the day and hour of the marriage settled. It seemed to be a bright and auspicious day. The southern wind was blowing and the cuckoo's gay warblings were heard from far. The bees hummed round the mango-blossoms. Merrily did the trees, surrounded as they were by tender creepers, present an array of new leaves. Betels were distributed amongst the kinsmen and the women-folk sang marriage-songs and praises of the gods. The court-yards of the house showed floral paintings of various design drawn by women. Various rites were performed and the women sat to worship the gods.

First of all pujas and offerings were made to Siva—the Ever-lasting One—He that is uncreated and without a beginning.

Then they worshipped the other gods in succession,—the goddess Syama—the Dark-blue One—Ekachura 'Of One crown' and Bana Durga or the divine mother who presides over the forests.

The usual ceremony of *adhivas* on the day previous to marriage was observed by the bride. Pitchers were filled with '*chorapani*' (lit. stealing water).[1] They sang songs and praises and anon the father of Chandrá sat in the court-yard of the temple to perform the '*sradh*' of his ancestors. The '*yajnakunda*' or the sacrificial altar was dug by the women. By the earth obtained in this way, bricks were made and these were duly anointed with oil.

The mother of the bride went begging blessings for her from the good neighbours and relations. She took a plate filled with some auspicious things on her head and went ahead of her companions, while the aunt of the bride carried a pitcher and followed her, singing festive songs.

Ll. 1-38.

9. Jaychandra and the Mahomedan Girl.

They had first met on the banks of the Sundha. She had gone there to fill her pitcher with water. Her gait was pleasant as that of the bird *khanjan* and her words were sweet as the cooings of the cuckoo. As she approached the landing *ghat* of the river, the whole place became bright with her presence.

"Who are you, fair woman, going to the river-*ghat* with slow steps? Will you but once cast a sweet glance at me? I see you here every day and my eyes are still insatiate. Pray tell me what you feel. For myself I cannot express my heart, but dear to me you are already as life itself."

[1] For explanation of the word see the text of Malua, Canto 10, line 35.

These were the thoughts of the youth, for delicacy he could not speak them out.

Going to the landing steps he peeped through the branches of a *hijal* tree in all directions; and where its flowers hang down and looked all crimson, he placed a love-letter with care. "She is sure to glance in this direction and this will certainly attract her notice. Bear witness, O *hijal* tree—the dweller of these banks,—I have rightly put my thoughts in this letter. When the handsome maiden will come up here, show my letter to her. Thou sun, who brightenest the darkest spot of the world, kindly tell the fair one of the colour of the *champaka* flower, how greatly I am suffering on her account. She will surely come here and stand at the landing *ghat*. I will slowly retire from here and watch her hiding myself for a moment when, after her bath, she will return to the landing steps softly like a wave that goes onward to return to the bank."

He went away and next day he visited the flower-garden for a moment where the beautiful *tagara*, the gem-like *bela* and the white *shefalika* lined with red had all bloomed. The youth with the *tilak* mark on his forehead and the flower-basket in his hands stood there unmindful of his pleasant task. For his heart was pierced by a thorn-like pain.

Ll. 1-30.

10. The dire News.

The trumpet and the tabor sounded high, and sweetly were the festive songs sung; the women wove flowers into garlands and performed many a pleasant and auspicious rite.

At such an hour did the shadow of a great sin fall upon the house and cloud its fair fame. People whispered on all sides 'What is the matter ?' And they feared to believe the gossip that ran.

Then arose a sound of lament in the bridal house and Bangshi Das himself lost all control over his mind. Alas, his caste and family honour were going to be lost for ever.

"Why should Providence be blamed? Rather blame our own luck. The sages sometimes err, and such a steady animal as the elephant oftentimes slips. Even the merchant's ship that has crossed the seas from afar, sometimes sinks near the landing *ghat*."

Thus did the neighbours talk amongst themselves and addressing the Brahmin said "Sir, it is not a tale worth telling. A great danger has befallen us. The bridegroom elect has done a very heinous thing. He has married a Mahomedan girl and given up his caste."

A thunder-bolt, as it were, fell breaking the pinnacle of a temple. All joy, all music were suspended in the house.

Bangshi Das sat benumbed on the ground; there was no cloud, no storm in the sky, but suddenly lightning had fallen on his head.

Ll. 1-20.

11. What did Chandra do?

"What can you, O Chandrá, do now?" The attending maids questioned her in whispers.

They all lamented the lot of the unfortunate maiden. But she became stiff, wordless and tearless. She neither wept nor smiled, nor spoke to her maids. Soft as clay was the maiden, but now was she turned into an image of stone.

They all wept and abused the bridegroom. But she was severe and quiet, controlling herself with all her might. The first, the second and the third day passed. Daily she sat to eat her meal but not a morsel did she relish.

It was all a bed of thorns and arrows in the night when she was left quite alone. She could not sleep a moment, but wept all unseen. The pillow was wet with her silent tears. She recolleted how both of them used to gather flowers on the sides of the tank ; how they swam together and sported in the Phuleswari. His smile, his words constantly came to her mind and for the whole night there was no sleep for her eyes. In the morning the pallor of her cheeks showed the agony of her despair.

The father could read her thoughts better than any one else. He felt a deep affection for her. Many proposals of marriage came from different places, and he began to consider these.

At this stage Chandrá saw her father and told him that she was determined not to marry. "I have dedicated myself to Siva," she said, "I will worship Him all my life. O father, be gracious unto your poor daughter and grant her permission for this "

The father sadly granted her the permission she sought, and ordered :

"Dedicate your life to Siva, I will not stand in your way. I will give you a task. Write a Ramayana in Bengali."

ll. 1-24

12. The Tragedy of the Tale

A temple was erected and Siva in stone was established there. She exercised great control over her mind and worshipped the great God. During leisure hours she composed the Ramayana in Bengali. One's mind becomes sinless as one reads this Ramayana written by the saintly Chandrá.

Thus did she live the life of a celibate all her days. Devoted to Siva she surrendered to Him her life and all. If any one spoke to her she was indifferent and scarcely gave a reply; and no one ever saw her smile again. The bud had become a full blown flower for a single night only to fade and wither in the morning.

Another stirring event happened about this time.

Seated was she in the temple, concentrating her mind on Siva. She uttered the *mantras* and performed holy rites and was devout in her prayer.

It was the month of May. The Sun sent his burning rays from the zenith. The mango trees smiled with their treasures of ripe fruits that hung from the boughs in goodly number.

A man came at such a time with a letter from Jay Chandra who had begged in it an interview with Chandrá. In that letter the young man had written his sad tale. It ran thus:—

"O my Chandrá, dear as life, will you not bear with me a moment when I tell you my story? My whole mind and body are on fire. I took poison thinking it to be nectar. The garland of flowers on my breast has proved a poisonous snake. I have myself invited death to my doors. I eschewed the sacred *tulasi* plant favoured by the gods and have worshipped the vile *seora* haunted by witches. I have myself placed a load of sorrow on my own head and whom can I accuse now? I see poison around me, poison in air, poison in water and everywhere. How can I make my escape from it? Will you not, O Chandrá, forgive a wretch like me? I long to have a sight of you for the last time—a sight of your playful eyes and their side-long glances; I long to hear but once your ever sweet words; I long to wash but once your tender feet with my tears. I assure you, O maiden, O holy one, I will not touch you; I will not come too close; from a distance I will look at your face beaming with holiness, and soothe myself by the sight. Companion of my childhood and the adored one of my early youth, how eagerly do I long to be near you! For a moment I will behold your face, and after that precious moment, feign would I drown or hang myself or take poison. Too well do I feel that you cannot have any love for a wretch like me; but for the last time I beg permission to bow to your feet and bid you farewell. This interview will be the last one between us Eyes will meet eyes for the last time. There is no peace, no happiness for me in this world. After I have seen you I will march to meet death. For Providence has ordained it, and it is inevitable."

As she read the letter her cheeks were wet with tears and a whole train of past associations came to her mind. She read the letter once, she read it twice, she read it a third time. The letters were washed away by her tears.

Chandrá.

"Hear me, O dear father, hear my sad story. You alone will feel for me and be able to sympathise with my sufferings.

Jay Chandra has written me a letter. He requests an interview for a moment."

Bangshi Das.

"And how can you allow it now, fair daughter? With a single-hearted devotion should you now worship the great god Siva. Do not indulge in any other thought. How can you favour him again? Your life has been dreary as death for his sake. How can Siva be worshipped with a flower soiled by an infidel's touch, or with a fruit from which some one has already taken a portion. Even so your heart will not be a fit offering to Siva if you still give place in it to a thought of the unholy one. He was a good youth and I knew his mind was pure as the Ganges' stream in his early years; but he has defiled himself. Providence has ordained that you would be unhappy in this way. How can the inevitable be avoided? Pursue the path, my dear daughter, that you have adopted. Do not allow your mind to be disturbed by anything else."

Chandrá did write a reply, but the interview prayed for by Jay Chandra was refused.

With the offerings of flower and blades of grass she again entered the temple to worship Siva.

She sat in the attitude of *yoga* shutting her eyes. She made offerings of flower and sacred *bel* leaves to Siva with single-hearted devotion. Slowly did the tears dry up in her eyes and slowly did her mind become free from all worldly thoughts. With one soul, one mind, she yielded herself to Siva—the God uncreated and without a beginning. Then came a state of peace in her soul in which the thought of this world, her home or even of her parents had no place. Absorbed in the thought of Siva, she forgot the tale of her childhood that had caused her pain. Jay Chandra was nothing to her in her trance-like, all-absorbing devotion, but Siva was to her all and all. She prayed and prayed till her mind was restored to a state of complete tranquillity.

At this moment Jay Chandra came thither and called her.

"Open the door, O Chandrá, once for the last time I want to see your face. A last interview I ask and after that I shall not pray for it again. I long to hear from your lips but once that you have forgiven me."

He knocked at the door and then smote his own breast in a frantic manner.

But she was absorbed in *yoga*, lost in a mystic trance, no sound from outside entered her ears.

Then like one mad, he cast his glances round but saw no one there. The door was not opened, no sound came there word from within the temple.

His heart broke at this. Like a mad man Jay Chandra again called out:

"Open the door, Chandrá. Show thyself only once. You are like a flower dedicated to God, you are like the Ganges holy by nature. My touch will defile you; I know it very well; but for one moment I want to see your beautiful eyes, for one moment with insatiate gaze I want to have a sight of your face. From this distance I will see and not enter the temple. Once for life, dear Chandrá, give me a reply."

She did not speak a word, nor open the door; for there she lay in the temple lost in her mystic trance, her outward senses all shut.

Glancing on all sides the youth saw nothing. But near him he saw the red blossoms of the flower-plant, known as the 'Malati of the Evening.' Sadly did he pluck some flowers from these and with the red juice write the following inscription on the temple door:

"O Chandrá, playmate of my childhood and companion of early youth, forgive me—you did not allow me an interview as I am wicked. But here ends all. No more would I come to you with a request. Farewell."

Her trance was broken and she looked around and saw no one there. The place was lonely. She opened the door and came out. The lines written on the door met her eyes. With a pitcher she went to the river for water to wash the temple. Tears flowed from her eyes. Just then she saw the river swollen by the inflowing tide. There was none near and on the waves was floating the dead body of Jay Chandra.

How handsome did he look, though dead; it seemed as if moon-beams played on the waves. His eyes were half-closed and the mouth had lost for ever the power of speech.

Maddened with grief Chandrá saw this woeful sight.

"Our smiles and tears," says the poet Nayanchand, "are verily like dreams.

"Hard it is for a poet to convey the pathos of a story to others, over which he sheds tears himself."

Ll. 1-126.

KAMALÁ

BY

DVIJA ISHAN

PREFACE

The author of this ballad is Dvija Ishan; but beyond his name we have not been able to ascertain anything more about him. The first portion of the ballad is commonplace, almost frivolous, but gradually its interest increases and the pathos of the last scene is remarkable. It is complete in 1,320 lines, all in the *payar* metre, and divided into 17 cantos.

The society which the ballad reveals is scarcely found to conform to the rules of the orthodox Hindu community of to-day. A maiden could not only move the court of a Raja to compassion by her public address, but heroically make a confession of her love. The Bengali maidens in those days could open their lips when necessary, and show their innermost feelings without a blush, not because they were less shy or more forward than now, but because they were guileless and did not consider pure love to be a sin. The control shown by Kamalá over her feelings is striking. Even when she knew that her father and brother were going to be sacrificed at the altar of Kali, she did not rend the air by her lamentations as an ordinary woman would do. While her mind was torn by agony, she retained an outward calm, did her duties quietly and when the prince came and related who the victims were that were going to be sacrificed, she simply turned aside her face for a moment to hide a tear, and then talked with him without betraying any sign of emotion. Her calm and dignified, modest but heroic attitude invests her with a quiet beauty which leaves an impression on the mind not to be quickly effaced.

We find in this poem reference to the fact that the barbers of Navadwipa were at one time expert in their profession and had a fame all over Bengal and that the Kochas had the monopoly of beating drums during the Kali Puja.

When a prince fell in love with a woman, he never cared to know to what caste she belonged. The state of society indicates a stage when following the canon of a well-known *sloka*, one could marry a woman from a low caste, if he liked.

Unlike most of the ballads of this class, its end is happy.

It seems to us that the ballad had a historical origin, though the imagination of the poet has no doubt played an important part in shaping the material.

'Hulia' seems to be an abbreviation of 'Haliura.' If so, there is a village of that name about ten miles to the south-west of Nandail in Mymensing. Raghupur (Raghurampur) is seven miles to the north of a Haliura.

The song of Kamalá was like most of the other ballads of Mymensing, probably composed in the 17th Century. It was collected by Babu Chandra Kumar De from 3 or 4 women living near Kendua. He sent me the song on the 19th Ashar 1328 B.E.

DINESH CHANDRA SEN

7, Bishwakosh Lane,

Bagbazar, Calcutta, 12th March, 1923.

KAMALÁ

1. Manik Chakladar.

The village of Hulia was one of the most beautiful in the country-side. Every house had a flower garden surrounding it. Manik Chakladar lived in that village. He flourished in prosperity and enjoyed the affection of his kinsmen and followers. He had fine straw-built houses, some with four and others with eight pitched roofs. The walls looked gay with workmanship in fine *sundhi* cane and the roofs were of a species of straw called the *ulu.* There were five compartments and altogether twenty spacious rooms. His retinue consisted of a thousand soldiers who belonged to the *Gabhur* and *Dhangor* classes. Forty *puras* of land he had under the plough. There were ten elephants and thirty horses in his stables. The neighbouring pastures were filled with his cows. In his mews there were innumerable goats and buffaloes. His granaries were loaded with corn. Hundreds of men had their meals in his house every day, and if a guest came to his house he never went away disappointed. If a Fakir or a Vaishnav knocked at his doors for alms he received rice weighed in scales until he was quite satisfied, and if a cooked meal was ready at the time he was sumptuously fed; he besides received a present of new clothes. If the guest happened to be a Brahmin he got a fee for deigning to eat at his host's house. There were thirteen religious festivities performed with great pomp at his house every year, and by the favour of the gods the family flourished in every way.

He had a son named Sadhan, who was as handsome as Madan (the god of love)—the husband of Rati. A very handsome daughter had been previously born to him. It seemed that the Goddess Saraswati had descended from heaven and was born there as the daughter of Manik Chakladar. In her the astrologer could discover signs of great luck, and her gentle charms like moon-beams brightened the house.

Manik Chakladar had an officer named Nidan who looked after his estate, collected rents and had the charge of accounts.

Ll. 1-30.

2. Chikan—the Milk-woman.

In that village lived a milk-woman named Chikan. In her youth she was full of mirth and humour, and her pleasantries were as enjoyable to young men as the sugared banana fruit. Her profession was to sell milk. She mixed three parts of water with one part of milk and thus made up her *seer*. She was ever jolly, and smiled at the end of the little speech she made every time. In fact, her words were sweeter than the milk or curd that she sold, and she made a better bargain because of the former. In her younger days lovers gathered round her as the bees round a flower. Merrily did she pass her days in their company. The very name of Chikan—the milk-maid—was a sauce to conversation, and the villagers took a great interest in her.

Youth had faded away but she still dressed herself gaily. True, her hair had turned grey, but that was because she could not help it. Some of her teeth had already fallen out and others were about to fall. Though her husband had died long ago, she did not dispense with her shell-bracelets (the signs of a wife). Her house was haunted by licentious and dissolute fellows. For it was widely known that the milk-woman knew sorcery, and the charmed betels given by her had the power of seducing even the most faithful wife; they were held infallible. Her charmed oil was also an efficacious thing which made devoted wives give up their husbands.

A Peep

"The Karkoon hid himself behind a *Kadamba* tree to have a full view of her dazzling beauty."

Kamala, p. 109

She had another charm prepared from the ears of the vulture, the flesh of the owl and the *kalapana* fish. These three things she pressed together on a stone and then made very small pills with them. These she dried in the sun. Each of the pills she sold for five *thubis* of cowries. It had to be taken with cool water preserved from a day or two before; the inevitable result was that if any lover could make a woman swallow only one of them she would think no more of her husband, however chaste she might have been.

Ll. 1-23.

3. Kamala steps into her Youth.

The beauty of the Chakladar's daughter is a topic well worth a description in detail. Her voice was like the cooings of the cuckoo. Black as the clouds of August hung down her profuse hair sometimes in braids and at others in curling locks. The dark blue *aparajita* flower was no match for her two beautiful eyes. When she wore clothes of the colour of flaming fire, her beauty surpassed that of the heavenly stars.

One day she went to bathe accompanied with her maids. Seated on the landing steps she washed her hands and feet. There the Karkoon (her father's officer) happened to see her. And then when she plunged herself into the water, her face rested on it like a full-blown lily. Hiding himself behind the flowering branches of a *bakul* tree, the Karkoon gazed at her with insatiate eyes. Then when after her bath she returned home with slow steps, the Karkoon changed his position and hid himself behind a *kadamba* tree to have a full view of her dazzling beauty.

He did not, however, express his thoughts but suppressed the fire of his soul and planned as to how he could allay his burning desire.

Ll. 1-22.

4. The Karkoon and the Milkmaid.

The old milk-woman was a frequent visitor to the Chakladar's house. She sold thickened milk, butter and curd at that place and was intimately known to Kamalá. They spent many a sweet hour in talk when they met.

The Karkoon came to learn of this intimacy between the two and of the wonderful charms of the milk-woman. He heard of her magical powers. He had already put a betel into his mouth; but he forgot to take a little lime (without which the betel loses all taste). He went with slow steps to the milk-woman's cottage. She asked him the reason of his kind visit. "I took betel, but there was no lime at my house. I have come to you for a little lime"—said the Karkoon. "But," he added, "I have no money with me to offer you." She smiled and said, "I am not a dealer in betels or lime, and do not charge anything if I offer them to any one—provided, of course, I find *that one* after my mind." The Karkoon good-humouredly replied, "You have grown old now. What a fine stock of humour did your milkman give you—it is not exhausted though your hair has turned grey!" She retorted, "The chilly grows the more tasty and hot the riper it becomes. One's jollity need not go because one has grown old. People like me for my words. But have you not in sooth heard of my magic powers? I can get the moon down from the sky by my spell. Now tell me, Karkoon, what is it in reality that has brought you here?" She offered him a seat. She prepared a betel with catechu of the *keya* (screw) plant with her own hands. She then brought a *hooka* and offered him a smoke. He pleasantly smoked and slowly spoke his mind. "You were once a young woman—one in whom the maidenly charms were full like the flow-tide. You know surely how the desires of youth torment the mind. I will tell you what I have come for. I have seen Kamalá—the Chakladar's daughter. Since seeing her I have been ill at ease. By my life, I pray you, dear milk-woman, secure for me the girl. If you do not do so, I will kill myself here. Strike me if you wish but do not forsake me." And saying this he entreatingly caught hold of the milk-woman's hands and looked at her imploringly.

The milk-woman assumed a grave air and said, "I warn you, do not say again what you have said. If the Chakladar hears it, your head will be blown off. What a mad idea? Why should you lose your life for nothing when you are so young in a foolish pursuit like this?"

The Karkoon at this stage bowed low at the milk-woman's feet and said, "I know the wonderful magical powers that you possess. Do not deprive me of your help in this way. If you be kind my life will be saved. Strike or even kill me if you like, but help me." Saying so he offered her a purse containing a hundred rupees.

Ll. 1-76.

5. The Reward of the Message-bearer.

And from that time forward the Karkoon called frequently on the milk-woman who often got some money for her advice. Then one day he wrote a letter to Kamalá to this effect.

"Dear maiden, you cannot imagine how greatly I, a stranger, feel for you. One kind glance from your eyes is enough to revive my drooping spirits. Is it too much for me to expect an offer of your youth! I hereby agree to give unto you all that I have. For you I am ready to give up my life itself. You are my religion, my life, my all. You are the flower-garland of my breast. If I do not see you for a day, my mind becomes restless. The weight of my grief presses my soul. Even the trees show their sympathy for me, when I weep, by dropping their leaves. Will you not be moved to compassion?"

The milk-woman went to Kamalá with the letter. She tied it in the corner of her *saḍi* and went straightway to the Chakladar's place.

Kamalá was seated on a golden couch. She was chewing a scented betel. She hid her growing charms under her blue *saḍi* as the lily plant hides its flower in September lest the bees should see it. When she smiled it seemed that the white *mallika* flowers bloomed on her lips. When she went to bathe at the landing *ghat* and threw the whole wealth of her unbraided hair all loose on her back, it touched her very ankles. The wind played with her red veil removing it from her face for a little time. Then would the bees leave the lily of the water for the more beautiful lily of the land.

A garland of the sweet *malati* flower adorned her breast. And as the milk-woman approached her, she said in feigned anger, "The curd you supply to our house, milk-woman, is sour. The butter is not fresh. I will tell my father all this. He will drive you from this village of ours."

Milk-woman.

"It is all the fault of my age and of my bad luck. When I was a young woman my curd and butter tasted sweet. Even if I had mixed seven seers of water with one seer of milk, people then praised me for supplying genuine curd. My butter and curd were in high demand. Like the bees humming round a hive, these people gathered at my house to sing my praise. My sour curd had then a sweet taste. But now my youth is gone; though I prepare my curd with nothing but pure milk they find fault with my preparation. What a great care do I now take in preparing my butter yet they have not one word to say in praise of my ways! I shall never, O maiden, henceforth sell curd and butter, whatever may befall me in this old age."

Ishan, the poet, regrets " O, what an evil day ! From now the milk-woman's cup will go empty."

THE MILK-WOMAN.

" Youth has dawned on you, fair damsel, but you live the stern life of a nun. When the flower blooms, the bees gather, but no bee visits a withered flower. Very sorry indeed am I for you. You weave a garland yourself to adorn your youth. Where is the pleasure ? (Some one else ought to do it for you.) Many are the bees that have been maddened by you, my adored flower ; why do you keep yourself concealed from them ? If you were married I would have given the groom the best curd that I can prepare and how overjoyed he would be to taste it ! "

As Kamalá heard her words she came close to the milk-woman and softly said, " I will tell you a wonderful story, O milk-woman, concerning my marriage.

" In this world, I assure you, there is none who is my peer. To whom, shall I offer my garland ? I will tell you the story of my previous life. In heaven I was Rati (the queen of Kama, the God of Love). My husband Kama and myself came down to share the world's woes under a curse. Behold my figure. Does it not shine brighter than the moon ? What mortal youth is there who can be a worthy groom for me ? But there is another reason too why I should not marry. If I elect some one else as my husband and perchance my lord Kama visits me some day, how shall I explain my conduct to him ? I have therefore taken the vow of remaining unmarried all my life. I will steer the boat of my youth slowly on this sea of life with the flag of Kama unfurled and remain true to the end."

The milk-woman was delighted with Kamalá's wit and jolly words. And she laughed till she grew nervous and her hair fell dishevelled round her face.

The Milk-woman.

"I will also tell you a true story, if you will only believe it. Some days ago I made a trip to heaven. Thither I went to sell curd. On the path I met your Kama. Separated from you he looked pale. He was overjoyed at seeing me there, He approached me and said, 'You have come from the earth. Your calling is to sell milk and curd, and you pay visits to the palaces of the Rajas. Did you, O milk-woman, meet my Rati there ? You must tell me the truth.' I told him as eagerly, 'Yes I know her, she is born in the house of a rich landlord and her beauty is like the lamp of that house. Her name on the earth is Kamalá.' And then I told him all about your parents.

"He was standing, but when he heard all that I told him he bent low and bowed down to me ; and then with great care he wrote a letter to you. I have brought it here for you. Just read the contents of the letter and you will see how intensely he is suffering from the pangs of separation."

"Imagine what a trouble I have taken for you. I went all the way from earth to heaven for your sake. I had to mount thousands of steps,—for the staircase to heaven is many miles long. O what a pain ! I got lumbago in my attempts to ascend the steps. It is only from a person of my resolute temper and devotion to you that you could expect such services."

The poet Ishan says, "Yes, milk-woman, you deserve a good reward for your pains. But first the letter should be read."

As she read the letter her whole frame burnt in rage. She looked like a flower-garden on fire. Blood rose to her head and her heart palpitated. But suppressing her feeling she said with a forced smile, "Yes, my dear milk-woman, you have suffered much for my sake ; you travelled all the way to heaven for me, and certainly you deserve a rich reward for your pains. Parted from my Kama, I pass my days in great sorrow But it seems, through your help a change will come over my life. How is the god—Kama—to look at? I have not seen him for many days."

The Milk-woman.

"He is handsome as the god Kartikeya. Surrounded is he by a halo like the moon-beams. He saw you when you were bathing. He was then standing under a *bakul* tree. When he tries to speak of you his emotions overpower him and the words 'Alas, alas!' come from his lips. His eyes, if you could but once see their glance, would charm you, as they have done many a woman. He is an officer under your father, Kamalá."

"What can I give you as reward for your pains? But take something," saying this Kamalá held up her necklace as if wishing to present it to the milk-woman. She approached her, and Kamalá suddenly caught her by her locks and gave her some slaps on her cheeks. The few teeth she had were already shaky and she was troubled with chronic tooth-ache. The slaps caused them to fall out. Some blows also fell on her back as additional reward

The milk-woman clasped the feet of Kamalá and piteously implored her to desist. She could not cry aloud lest people should know of her wickedness.

Kamalá.

"You, wicked woman, you have passed already through the three periods of life and are in the fourth or last stage. You have lived a life of vile lust and you want others also to do the same. I would have told all to my father and in that case your death would have been certain. But I desist from doing so; there is no credit in blackening one's hand by killing such a gnat as you are. But take the warning; do not come to my place any more. If you do so, your life will be at stake. Tell that rogue of the Karkoon all this. How audacious is he, being our servant! Like a frog aspiring to the lotus is he. A slave wants a place on the head. The sentence of death would be his just punishment. But if a mad dog bites, no sane man would bite it in return."

With slow steps did the milk-woman leave the room; blood was falling from her gums. When on the way some people asked her as to what was the matter with her, she said it was chronic tooth-ache that troubled her. If still some outsiders pressed for further details she grew angry and abused them. When she returned home she did not speak to anybody but wept all alone. Says Dvija Ishan, "it is better to swallow an insult without noise."

Ll. 1-264.

6. The Revenge.

The Karkoon had spent a restless day; and now when the day was coming to a close, he hurried to the house of the milk-woman. On the way he was feeling a great agitation in his heart thinking what the maiden would say in reply to his letter. But as soon as he crossed the threshold of the milk-woman's house and entered it, she came upon him with a ferocious look and before he could address her she poured forth a shower of abuse in a wild manner. "You rogue, if you come here again I will break my broom on your back. You will be punished with death if you attempt again what you have done once. Had I been a man instead of being the weak woman that I am, I would have cut off both your ears."

The Karkoon was greatly depressed in spirit, and without replying to the abuse of the milk-woman, returned home with a determination to avenge the wrong. "I will within seven days destroy all the property and all the wealth of this

Chakladar who is a mere sub-lord, holding a lease under the Zamindar. I will anyhow avenge myself of this insult."

He wrote a letter to the Zamindar. The Zamindar's name was Dayal and his town was called Raghupur. Manik Chakladar, under whom the Karkoon held his office, was but a sub-lord under the Zamindar. The letter of the Karkoon ran as follows:

"I bow to Your Highness as Justice Incarnate. Be pleased to read my humble petition. The Chakladar has got immense riches underground. He has got seven large jars full of gold coins. They rightfully belong to the Zamindar. But the Chakladar has appropriated them to his treasury."

Ll. 1-32.

7. Oppression.

As soon as the Zamindar got this letter he ordered the Chakladar to be brought to his presence at once. Thousands of men surrounded the Chakladar's house. He was bound hand and foot and brought before the Zamindar, who asked him "How much money have you got underground ? "

The Chakladar was surprised at this query and said, "Who told this lie to Your Highness ? I have not got a cowrie. Why should I be treated like a criminal for nothing ? "

The Zamindar was angry at this reply and ordered the Chakladar to be thrown into one of his prisons called the *khunshala* (the murder-house).

In the meantime the Karkoon's plans matured further. A thief crosses a fence to get into a house and then attempts the next one. "The first fence," thought the Karkoon, "has been crossed. Now the second one should be got over. It is the Chakladar's son, Sadhan, who should be removed now."

He came up before the youth and said, "It is a great pity that your father is in such a cruel predicament. We hear that he has been bound hand and foot and a heavy stone has been placed on his breast. On his bed thorny plants have been spread. Now it is no good spending your time in vain grief. You must at once go to save him from this danger. The Purans tell us that the princes Ram and Lakshmana went to the forests and lived like beggars for fourteen years for a pledge to their father. Parashuram killed his mother at the bidding of his father. And Srimanta went away to a great distance from home seeking his father. It is not becoming of you to stay at home at this critical moment. Try to get your father released. See the Zamindar and present him with some gold coins."

By such crafty words he made Sadhan leave the house and start for the Zamindar's city. Now when all obstructions were thus removed he paid a visit to the Chakladar's house.

Sadhan reached the Zamindar's place and made obeisance to him. He presented him with a purse of gold mohars.

The Zamindar asked Sadhan the reason of his visit. Sadhan referred to the unjust imprisonment of his father.

Zamindar.

"You must at once give me all the gold mohars that your father has got underground and misappropriated; and then only can I think of releasing him. The money that he has got is legally mine, but he has robbed me of it.

"It is a false charge," said Sadhan and pleaded his case with all humility.

The Zamindar did not argue but at once ordered Sadhan to be sent to the same prison where his father lay, and there a heavy stone was placed on his breast.

The order was "All the gold coins must be given me. And then, and then only can the father and son expect to be released."

Ll. 1-52.

8. The Karkoon steps into the Shoes of the Chakladar.

Meantime the Karkoon was right glad at all that had happened. He collected all the outstanding revenues from the *rayats* with great energy and submitted them to the Zamindar praying for the post of the Chakladar now vacant. The Zamindar was pleased with his promptitude and issued a Sanad appointing the Karkoon to the Chakladar's post.

When he thus obtained the Sanad he paid a visit to Kamalá and addressed her thus :—

"Oh beautiful one, I have got the Chakladarship to-day. If you would now agree to marry me, there would be perfect happiness on the part of both. I shall carry out your least wish like your loyal servant in that case. If you do not agree, your lot will be miserable. Even the trees will drop their leaves at your sorrow. Now consider the matter well. If you do not agree to my prayer, you must go out of this house which is no longer your father's, but mine by virtue of my office."

Indignantly did Kamalá reply, "Who has heard that one ever married a devil in human form! You have eaten the salt of my father all your life. For that your heart did not feel a throb in bringing about his ruin in this way. Dear as life is my brother whom you have treated so! It is a kick on the face that you deserve for all these. It is better for me to live in the wilderness infested with beasts rather than seek shelter under the roof of such a devil as you are. I would rather beg alms from door to door than stay a moment in this house. If my father and brother were present here to-day, you would be bound to a triangle and scourged to death."

There were two palanquin-bearers, Andhi and Sandhi, devoted to the family of Manik Chakladar. And Kamalá sent for them. They carried Kamalá and her mother by palanquin to the house of Kamalá's maternal uncle.

Ll. 1-40.

9. The Scandal.

The Karkoon, now raised to the position of Chakladar, got information as to the whereabouts of the mother and the daughter. He at once wrote a letter to the uncle of Kamalá who was then living in a foreign land. The letter ran thus:—

"Your niece, Dear Sir, has lost her character. If you permit her to remain at your village home, the Panchayet (village-judges) will surely outcaste your family. The barbers will not shave in your home and the priests will not perform any religious function there. You will be excommunicated, and there will be no escape from this. She is madly in love with a Chandal youth; for him she has given up all social ties. She has no place in her father's house and has gone to your house to damn it. You must give peremptory orders to drive her out of your home. Another point. The Zamindar has issued an order that whoever will give her a place in his house shall be punished with death."

The uncle, as already stated, was living in a foreign country. As soon as he received this letter he wrote to his wife at home. "From this distance I have learnt that Kamalá with her mother, my sister, is living at my house. She is yet a maiden and what a shame that there is such a scandal against her name! I am told that she is secretly in love with Bharai, the Chandal youth. You must at once drive her off. For if you allow her to remain at my house we shall be all outcasted. Do not let a moment pass on receiving this letter, but at once drive her from our home. If she attempts to stay, seize her by her locks and pull her out of the house by force."

The aunt was sad at heart at receiving this note from her husband and reflected, "Kamalá's mother is my husband's own sister and she is our niece. How can I drive her off? Where will Kamalá go and how preserve her honour? Oh what misery! When learning all this the mother and daughter will begin to cry, how shall I bear to see the sight? They are very tender-hearted. How can I give them pain?"

Ll. 1-44.

10. Kamala´ deserts her Uncle's House.

The aunt for a long time thought over the matter and then all alone went to Kamalá's room when she and her mother were not there, and placed her husband's letter on the bed.

Kamalá in the evening entered the room and found the letter lying on her bed. As she read it her face was suffused with tears. "What ill-luck is mine!" she said to herself. "My father and brother are prisoners and God knows what evil fate has brought me to my uncle's house! All the wealth that we had has been plundered by robbers." She remembered the cruel insult received from the Karkoon and then resolved "O what a terrible sky from above is staring me in the face! There is no sun no moon there. But no matter. Not a moment shall I stay here. If I am a true daughter of my parents, whether I drown myself or drink poison or cut my throat with a knife, whatever may befall me—not a moment shall I stay here. Let Bana Durga, the goddess, decide my fate any way."

Not once did the maiden wish an interview with her mother; nor did she stop a moment to bid farewell to her aunt; she hesitated not to think of the grief it would cause to her mother; nor how a solitary and youthful way-farer, she would save her honour in the hour of peril and get over the dangers that beset her way; she cared not to ask any one of the path she should follow, nor enquired but once as to where she should go seeking shelter. In that quiet hour when the stars were just beginning to twinkle in the sky and the sun sank in the furthest boundary of the horizon,—she offered her silent prayers to Bana Durga, the sylvan deity, and then left home all alone. She proceeded onward where her two eyes flooded with tears feebly espied the path. Again and again tears blinded her eyes and she could not see the path at all.

Ll. 1-32.

11. She meets a Herdsman.

She wiped her eyes again and again; her tender frame unused to walking trembled at every step; she walked a few paces and then took a little rest and again proceeded on. Just then a deep jungle called the *howar* appeared in sight. There was no habitation of men nor was any traveller seen who trod that region at that hour. Here perhaps the Almighty God heard that cry for help which came from her innermost soul. In that grim loneliness a worn-out old traveller, a herdsman, appeared with a buffalo. Kamalá approached him.

Kamalá.

"I take you, O herdsman, as the help of the helpless; allow me to call you 'father.' A great mishap has fallen upon me obliging me to leave my home. What ill-luck it is for me! But I pray you, O herdsman, that you may kindly give me a little shelter in a corner of your cowshed so that I may spend the night there. I will neither want food nor water; only permit me, O father, to spread a part of my *saḍi* that I may lie down in a corner of your cowshed."

The herdsman was taken by surprise at the dazzling beauty of Kamalá and thought that the Goddess of Fortune, Lakshmi, herself had appeared to him in disguise to try his devotion.

HERDSMAN.

"Deign to come to my house, O goddess, I assure you I will worship you by my soul. You must for ever stay with me at my humble cot and never leave me. And grant me this boon that my fortune may go on flourishing. Another boon that I seek is that through your grace no danger or mishap may cross my threshold, and may my buffaloes yield milk three times more."

Saying this he led her to his home. She lighted the evening lamp and did all the work of the house. For three days she stayed there After lighting the lamp in the evening, she made a fire in the shed of the animals to drive the gnats and insects away by the smoke. Spreading the straw with her delicate hands she made a bed for the old man every night, and cooked his meals three times every day. Thus she looked after the household in all matters. The herdsman returned every day from the pastures after his day's work and was greatly delighted to find his meals ready. Curd of excellent quality did she make with milk and fine fried rice of the *ula* species. This she served to her foster-father and waited standing near him when he took his meals. The old man felt the joy of a new life, and things at his house took altogether a new and a better turn.

Ll. 1-32.

12. SHE GOES WITH THE STRANGER.

One day a young man came to that part of the country to hunt falcons. Nobody knew from what place he came or what home he adorned, but accomplished and handsome he was like a god. His colour shone as bright gold, and he wore a golden dress. He looked like a prince in all respects. The herdsman returned home from the field in the evening and found the young man standing near his cottage, bright as the warrior god Kartikeya.

THE HUNTER.

"I am very weary. I passed through great trouble and worry in the forest and am thirsty. Will you give me a cup of water ?"

Kamalá offered him a cup of water and he felt his fatigue gone after the drink.

THE HUNTER.

"I am here, O old man, much fatigued and wearied. I cannot make out who this girl is at your house that offered me water. Quiet as the evening star and beautiful as the young moon in the blue sky is she. It seems the Goddess of Fortune Lakshmi, is no match for her in beauty. Who is she ? Who are her parents ? I take her to be a princess; or is it possible that by some special favour of the gods you, old man, have got this daughter born in your own house ? Is she married or is she still a maiden ? You must tell me the whole truth about her."

THE OLD MAN.

" O thou, Justice Incarnate, deign to listen to me. I myself do not know who her parents are, neither can I tell you where her house is. I know her to be the Goddess Lakshmi herself. She has, out of her great mercy for me, condescended to be a guest at my house. From the day she has been here my fortune has improved I have got unexpected sums of money by the sale of my milk and a buffalo, long given up as barren, has conceived. Better days, it seems, have dawned on me by her grace."

The Hunter.

"Now hear me, O herdsman, give this girl to me; I will take her to my home. I will weigh a basketful of pearls and gold and give it to you as reward. I will with the sanction of my father, make you a gift of fourteen *puras* of land besides."

The herdsman said weeping:—

"No, that cannot be, I do not want riches. I have already known her as my daughter, I cannot now live without her. I will worship her lotus-feet all my life. She is the Goddess Lakshmi herself, and can be no other. Within this short time she has grown dearer to me than everything. The world would seem dark and void to me without her."

All that the young man pleaded proved unavailing. The herdsman was deeply distressed by the proposal and would by no means be persuaded to consent.

One full day passed in discussion. And on the next day it was settled, the young hunter would take her with him to his home.

The herdsman said to Kamalá, "You were in great discomfort in my poor house, but forgive all the trouble and inconvenience you suffered here, and remember me with kindness. I do not want riches nor fourteen *puras* of land. May your lotus-feet shower their heavenly grace on me at the hour of my death."

The tears of the herdsman fell on the straw and grass that grew in his compound.

The prince in the meantime took her with him to his home.

Ll. 1-156.

13. Prince Pradip Kumar and Kamala.

As she lighted the lamp in her room in the evening she wept at the recollection of her mother. At that hour prince

Pradip Kumar slowly entered her room. Seated on a couch she was thinking of her mother, who was now far away and the prince approached her at the time.

The Prince.

"Not to-day but to-morrow" in this way, dear maiden, you have been deceiving me, ever since you have been a guest here. I want from you this information only. Where is your home and whose daughter are you? I am maddened by your beauty, but such is my lot that I see you always weeping. The more you wipe away your tears the more they increase. What is your pain? Will you not marry me and make me happy? From the day I saw you first in the house of the old herdsman, I have dedicated my life and all to you. I have lost my passion for hunting falcons from that day and you see that I seldom go out. I am now careless about everything else. The blooming flowers of my garden, all purple and white, have lost their charm for me. For your love, dear, I have become like one mad. You are to me more welcome than any gold, you are the precious diamond necklace of my breast. If you leave me I will never leave you. I will cling to your feet even like your sweet anklets, humming your praises all day long."

Ishan, the poet, says, "It is the shaft of the god of love that has surely pierced the hearts of both."

In the morning the prince goes to Kamalá's room and re-enters it in the evening; and thrice every day he asks imploringly "Tell me, O maiden, who you are?"

Kamala.

"I will tell you, O prince, who I am, when the proper time will come, but not now. Meantime bear in mind that you have given the word of honour to the herdsman that you will not apply anything like force to extort a reply from me. You will surely know everything about me and you ought to know it, but you should patiently wait for the right moment."

So did the prince call on the maiden many a time every day. But as often, returned to his own chamber, disappointed. Love secretly burnt his heart, but for shyness he could not speak much. Like a bee flying away unwillingly from the beloved flower that gives it a nod of refusal, and ever returning to it in hope,—did he come and go.

And thus passed three months.

Ll. 1-42.

14. The Human Sacrifice.

One day at the palace loud beatings of drums were heard.

"What is this noisy music of drums for in the palace?"

"The Raja will worship the goddess Raksha Kali by human sacrifice."

The maiden gradually came to learn who the persons were who were to be sacrificed before Kali and how the function was to be performed.

It was her father and brother who were to be sacrificed. She wept and at her tears even the trees dropped their flowers and leaves as a token of sympathy.

At this hour of her grief came to her room prince Pradip Kumar.

The Prince.

Have you heard, O dear maid, a strange story? My father will worship Kali by human sacrifices. Let us both go to the temple and see the wonderful sight.

She sadly asked, "Who are these wretched men who have been brought for sacrifice? At what price did your father get them?"

The prince thereupon related the story of these two victims, and as the maiden heard it, her heart burst in grief.

She wiped away her growing tears and hid her face from the prince and turning aside, said, "To-day, O prince, you will hear from me my whole story. I will no more hide it from you. Before your royal father's full court, the place of justice, shall I reveal the cause of my grief. But I have a request to make to you. In the village of Hulia there lives the Karkoon, now made the Chakladar of the place. You must send for him and bring him up here. There are besides the two palanquin-bearers Andhi and Sandhi in that village. They know a part of the story and they should be made to appear before your royal father's court. In that village there is also a milk-woman called Chikan. She is an important witness. Then she told the names of her uncle and aunt, without referring to her own relationship with them, and wanted that they also should be produced. She next said that the herdsman at whose house she had been found should not be forgotten. All these persons should be present before the court. And until this was done she would not tell her story.

The court sits. The parties appear. Prince Pradip Kumar takes his seat near his father. The maiden tells her story.

Ll. 1-36.

15. The Baramasi.

"It is the month of Baisakh, O wise men of the court, hear the sad tale of the unfortunate one.

"O sun and moon, bear witness! The gods of heaven, the trees and plants, I call on you all as my witnesses. Here the temple of the Divine Mother stands facing me. I pray unto her to be my witness. Fire, Water,—Indra, the god of the sky, and Yama, the god of death, all bear witness.

And thou, O mother earth, avow the truth of what I am going to say. In the forest I have worshipped the forest-deity, Bana Durga many years. And her I call upon as my witness. Ye that fly in the air and wander in the land, I appeal to you all for the verification of my tale.

"My first witnesses are my parents. And to their feet I bow a hundred times. High and esteemed are they to me as God Himself. My own dear brother is here; he will be my witness. Here is the Karkoon; he must speak the truth. And the milk-woman Chikan must confirm my tale. My uncle and aunt are my important witnesses. There is the evening star that shines in the sky. I call upon it to bear witness. And my own tears are the witnesses of my sorrows proving my sincerity. Here is a piece of evidence (she produces a letter). This letter my uncle wrote to my aunt. The herdsman who gave me shelter like a father and his kinsmen are all my witnesses. My last witness is the prince himself who saved me from the great distress I was in. He is the lord of my heart and I will hide nothing, Sirs, from you.

It was the month of May, black clouds darkened the sky; towards the end of the night this unfortunate one was born. My mother affectionately gave me the name of Kamala.[1] When three years had passed after my birth, a brother was born in our home. Bright as the moon I saw the baby in my mother's arms, and my heart was soothed at the sight. I took him in my arms, played with him and swung him in the cradle. Thus passed my childhood in play and joy. My brother was as the light of my eyes and the affection of my parent was the most prized thing in my life. When thirteen years of my life had passed, I heard father talking about my marriage. I will here tell you some private incidents of my life and I pray that Your Highness may justly deal with my case. Youth dawned on me

[1] A name of the Goddess of Fortune.

and brought on the crimson glow in my colour. Mother said, 'Do not go to the river-*ghat* alone.' I clothed myself richly and adorned my body with ornaments. My long braids I everyday bound with garlands of *champa* flower. My tresses were scented by my attendant maids at the time of the bath, and with hair-combs beautifully decorated with mica, they combed and arranged my dishevelled hair. I used to go to the bathing *ghat* every day with my maids, and no one dared come too near.

It was the month of December, when the day was the shortest. Of her eleven sisters she (December) was the youngest, and one saw the world already filled with light as one awoke from sleep. I rose up one morning and worshipped the forest-goddess Bana Durga. When the mid-day came I scented my body with oil and took off the big diamond necklace from my breast; then with a golden pitcher in hand I went to the river-*ghat* with my maids. They sang merrily, and some of them danced; and happily did we all walk to the landing steps. But as we started, my feet struck a brick, which was a bad omen. I trembled in fear as to what would happen. Had I known that a black snake lay in my path, never would I have thought of coming out!" She stopped in emotion and pointing to the Karkoon asked the court to enquire of him as to what he knew of the incident.

"Now passed January and February. It was biting cold. The poor suffered from want of clothes and the long nights tarried, and hesitated, as if, unwilling to depart. One day this milk-woman Chikan came to our house to sell curds. Here is the letter she brought to me." (She produces the letter and says.)

"I need not say what is written in it, I pray the court to read it through.

"Then came sweet April. The creepers and flower-plants displayed their wealth of colour. The God of Love lurked, it seemed, behind each plant with his flower-arrows; and those, parted from their dear ones, felt a pang. The humming of the bees made the gardens gay and the cuckoo sang all day long. In the compound of the house danced the playful *khanjans*. I heard that my parents whispered between themselves something about my marriage. Just at this time came a messenger from Your Highness ordering my father to pay you a visit. The elephants and the horses were made ready; and accompanied by his body-guards and retainers he left home to come to Your Highness's capital. At the hour of starting he came to me and said, 'I do not know, dear daughter, how many days I may have to stay abroad. Take proper care of yourself during my absence.' My eyes became tearful at parting with him. The whole house looked dark when my father went away.

"Then came June. People worshipped Bana Durga with pomp. The tabor sounded and the drums made a noisy din. In the courtyard of temples the cymbals and *kartals* sounded merrily. The temples were beautifully decorated, and children and women gaily dressed took part in the general festivity under roofs made of canopies. I and my mother wept in solitude fearing what evil might have happened to my father. At this time we received information from Your Highness's palace that my father had been imprisoned. Here is the letter conveying the cruel news." (She produces the letter and says.)

"Now Your Highness, O Justice Incarnate, may I ask you for what fault my father was punished?

"The Karkoon—our officer, explained to my brother that it was his duty to go and save our father from the danger. Thus my brother, an innocent lad who knew not the wicked ways of the world, was made to leave us; I and my mother sat down on the bare ground and cried. How could I take part in the worship of Bana Durga? Suspending the upper part of our *sadi* from the neck on both sides as a sign of humility, we offered one prayer of our heart to the goddess, and that was for the boon of the return of my father and brother to our home

"The month of June advanced. The mango blossoms ripened into green fruits on the branches of the mango trees. The merry swinging of men and women on floral cradles went on in the country. A letter came to us informing us that both my father and brother had been put into the prison. What could we, helpless as we were, do, but weep the whole day! Who is the god, we thought, whom we should propitiate to have them back? The black snake was in the office room. We could not cry aloud for fear.

"Towards the end of June the mangoes became ripe on the boughs of the trees. My mother went to the temple of Chandi and fasted praying for the return of the prisoners. She fasted and remained prostrate near the gateway of the temple. With one hand did I wipe my own tears, and with the other I caught my mother's arm and brought her home. She worshipped Shashthi (the goddess who preserves children) and night and day her tears did not cease. One day the wicked Karkoon came into the inner apartment and showed me the Sanad received from Your Highness. That Sanad he should produce now and it will be my evidence.

"In our own home we became like prisoners. Then I and my mother left the house. We had not a cowrie in hand. We went by palanquin to my maternal uncle's house. In the month of July rain fell day and night, and like rain too fell our tears in a room of my uncle's house where we lived. Our lives hung on one thread of hope. The rivers were now full. The oarsmen would row our pinnace, and my father and brother would return back some day during the rains.

"But all on a sudden a letter was received from my uncle who resided then in a distant country, It was like fresh. fuel added to the fire of our grief. What ill-luck overtook me! My poor mother does not yet know of the contents of the letter. I did not wait to say farewell to her, but straightway left my uncle's home. Here is the letter. This is my evidence." (She produces the letter and resumes.)

"I left my uncle's home. No more will I eat any food in that house, no more will I stay there a moment—was the one resolve of my heart; rather would I drown myself in the river,—rather drink poison.

"Alone did I come near a great forest. It was all dark. The poisonous snakes did not bite me, nor did the tigers in that forest end my days. What god was there in heaven, I asked, who could give me shelter? I called aloud with tears, 'Shew me a place, O gods, to hide myself.' My eyes rained tears; the more I wiped them, the more they increased. Through my tears I could not see the path. There was no sympathiser, no friend near me. It was at such an hour of despair that I met the herdsman. He must have been my friend for many a past life. He was my one friend in that distress, and treated me as my own father would have done. The affection he showed me, was even more than I received from my own parents. At his cottage I found a shelter for three nights. This herdsman is my chief witness. He saved my honour when I was helpless.

"I have mentioned all witnesses. Now I must mention him who is the lord of my heart. It was the month of August. In the marshy land, the falcons filled the air with their shrill cries. The prince came there to hunt. In the herdsman's place I met him. He asked me who I was. I said, 'Not now, I will tell you all about myself when the time will come.' I filled a cup with cold water as he was thirsty and handed it to him. But at the same time an emotion sprang up in my heart, tender and sweet as the water-lily in water. He looked bright as the god Kartikeya, and my eyes were charmed by the sight. He, the lord of my heart, took me with him. I suppressed all my feelings and wanted that I should live all alone. The boatmen rowed the golden pinnace which looked proud with its blue sail—favoured by the wind, and I came here and became the willing servant of the queen. She has treated me as my own mother would do; night and day I waited on her, ready to serve her least wishes. One day I heard the sound of drums; the dancers danced and the servants dressed in gay apparel appeared in the streets. 'What is the festivity,' I enquired. It was the last day of Sravana (about the 15th of September), they were worshipping the goddess Manasa Devi. As I heard this, I recollected my home, and my heart was as if pierced by a spear. The temple in my father's house was empty. Alas, where was the goddess gone, and where her devout worshippers? I remembered my mother also whom I had cruelly left one evening. Parted from me for a moment she would be mad with grief. In the month of September my mother used to prepare sweet cakes of *tal* fruits; I felt a pang in my heart recollecting those days gone by. Separated from her I felt myself plunged in great sorrow. The moon of September-nights so bright that one could even see the bottom of the river by her beams, looked dark to my eyes. Then in October they performed the *pujas* in every house. In the temple of my father's house no candle was lighted. In my heart of hearts I prayed to the divine mother Durga that by her grace my father and brother might return home. In November they lighted the lamps and kept up nights, illuminating the house-tops with an array of lights. Men and women knew no sleep and passed their time in songs and music. The maidens decked in richest attire enjoyed the festive nights. Then came December, when fields were covered with ripe crops. The sight of golden crops filled the souls of the peasants with joy. When they returned home in the evening with golden ears of grain hanging down from their heads, the wives with lamps in hand came to receive them singing festive songs and praying for good luck all the year round. The harvest goddess Lakshmi was worshipped in every house. With the new rice of the season the wives prepared cakes and *khichudi* to offer tc the goddess. When all the world worshipped the goddess of good luck, I asked myself :

'How could I get good luck?' My parents were gone, my brother was gone,—there was none in the world whom I might call my own. The whole night I passed weeping. Now at this stage, my witness is the queen herself. One day as I got scented oil for her bath and was ready to go to the *ghat* to bring water, I heard the sound of drums and saw people running in haste dressed in good attire. I asked what god was being worshipped in the temple. They said that Kali was going to be worshipped and added that human sacrifices were going to be made at the altar of the goddess. They began to talk in whispers, but as they named them, I knew that it was my father and brother who were going to be offered as sacrifice. I filled my pitcher with water in haste and helped the queen in her bath. The queen put on her best attire to go to the temple; but I returned to my chamber all alone! With the edge of my *sadi* I wiped my tears. No way could I mak out to avert the danger impending.

"At this time the prince came to my room and said, 'Marry me, dear maiden, and make me happy.' I asked him what the tumult in the palace was for and why such loud beatings of the drum? He said, 'My father worships Kali to-day with offering of human sacrifice.' I heard from him who the victims were, and was maddened with grief. But calmly I told the prince. 'To-day, O prince, the day has arrived when I will tell my story. Send me to the temple where the Koch musicians are beating the drum.' The prince came and I followed him. Here the goddess Kali herself is my witness. Here my story ends. I pray for justice to Your Royal Highness. First try the case and then offer human sacrifice as you will."

Ll. 1-104.

16. The Judgment.

The *baramasi* or the songs of twelve months is over here. Now listen to what judgment the king passed. All the friends of the Raja, the ministers and other courtiers were called and His Royal Highness sat to deliver judgment. In great rage he ordered the Karkoon to tell the truth—"You wicked man, you cannot plead for mercy." It was as if a thunder-bolt fell on his head from the sky. He was so much bewildered that he remained silent without being able to speak. The Raja read his letters before all his courtiers. He next asked Chikan—the milk-woman. "How did you lose your teeth, you witch?" First she tried to offer some excuses. Then suddenly she said in a firm voice, "Your Highness, I had long been suffering from swollen gums. It is owing to this disease that I lost my teeth." The Raja became angry, and at his order the Town-Inspector of Police caught hold of her by her locks. She, in great dilemma, began to abuse the Karkoon saying that it was he that had brought on her ruin. "It is his fault. I do not know what was written in the letter. I am innocent. Release me poor as I am." The two brothers Andhi and Sandhi gave evidence that they had carried Kamalá with her mother in a palanquin to her uncle's home. The uncle and aunt verified the portion of the story relating to them, and the herdsman told the plain truth. The prince said that he had met Kamalá in the herdsman's place when he had visited it on a hunting excursion.

One and all of the witnesses gave their evidence. Now came the judgment.

The Karkoon was bound hand and foot and brought to the Raja who said that death by impalement was no adequate punishment for him. That night towards its end, the worship of mother Kali would be finished and then the Karkoon should be sacrificed at her altar.

The poet Ishan says that the worship of Kali was performed duly as ordered and now let the readers cry "Peace to all" in honour of the Divine Mother

Ll. 1-36.

17. The Marriage.

We need not describe how the Karkoon was sacrificed. Let us refer to the topic of Kamalá's marriage.

The Brahmins and astrologers were called and they fixed the auspicious day. Letters of invitation were written in blazing ink. Seven marks of vermilion were put on each of these letters. These letters were sent to friends and relatives all over the country. The sound of the drums and tabors was heard day and night accompanied with the melody of the musical pipe *shanai*. In the courtyard dancing and songs went on. The palace became filled with men and women. Sweetmeats were prepared by four sets of trained confectioners; and thousands of milkmen supplied milk and fine curd. The palace was illuminated with thousands of lights and was splendidly decorated.

Kinsmen and relatives came from all quarters. The priests and Brahmin scholars paid their usual visits to the palace. In the inner compartments there was a regular market of fair women. All the gods were duly worshipped. The forest goddess Bana Durga was worshipped with songs, and Kali with a pair of goats and a buffalo for sacrifice. The *sradh* of the ancestors was performed in the courtyard of the temple and the whole sky was filled with music.[1]

There is a stray song of Kamalá appended to the story. It must have once formed a part of another version. Kamalá sings a song of love all alone in the palace, immediately after she had been brought there. I translate a few lines from the short song.

After this is a description of the rites performed by women on marriage occasions and that of the ornaments and robes with which the bride was decked. I omit these details. Anyone curious to read this portion may consult the original text published in a separate volume.

"I start at the sound of your foot-steps, my love, and when I awake from my sleep how restless do I feel! My heart breaks, but for shyness I cannot tell you what I feel. If you were a bird, my heart would be the cage for you. If you were a flower I would keep you on my breast. If you were the moon I would remain awake the whole night gazing at your face from this my solitude. I prepare sweet betels and fill the betel-box with them; but because of my shyness I cannot offer them to you and only shed tears as a sign of my incapacity" (abridged).

Ll. 1-90.

DEWAN BHÁBNÁ

PREFACE

Dewan Bháhná was sent to me by Chandra Kumar in September, 1922. He had collected parts of this ballad from one Kailas Chandra Das and the rest from some boatmen living in the vicinity of Kendua, in the sub-division of Netrakona. The latter sang it in chorus at boat-races. The poem contains 378 lines, all composed in the *payar* metre. I have divided it into 9 cantos. It is a short poem, but typical of this class of songs, and the verses are oftentimes exquisitely sweet and possessed of a simple rural charm. The ballad was at one time very popular amongst the peasants of Eastern Mymensing.

The peasants used to sing these ballads during the season when their hands were comparatively free—when the autumnal harvests were reaped and stored in their granaries, and their fields were yet unprepared for the sowing of new seed for the next season. The songs were composed and sung by illiterate people. Hence everything had to be committed to memory. In the good old days when our people were not pressed by so many wants, and were inspired by a passionate love for songs, it was a pleasant occupation on their part to commit them to memory and sing before an eager audience who periodically gathered to hear them. Many people in those days used therefore to get them by heart.

But the spirit of the times has now changed. The peasants have imbibed new tastes, and the ghost of modern civilisation which aims at creating perpetual wants and a feeling of unrest has, in some degree at least, also attacked the huts of these humble people and affected their simple lives. The ballads are scarcely sung now-a-days, and as no written copies of them are available, any one who wishes to collect them has to be contented with gathering scraps from individual singers, who, after reproducing one or two songs, are often found to be baffled in their efforts to recollect the others. Chandra Kumar had therefore to travel a good deal, visiting many people in order to collect a complete ballad.

The tragic death of Sunái was an event which caused a great sensation in the country at the time of its occurrence. In other countries such an event awakens a spirit of retribution and is followed by blood-shed and other drastic measures. But here in these lower Gangetic plains the ruled can suffer but are scarcely able to resist an evil. The political atmosphere of the country is what they call their 'fate.' It is like a nightmare that perpetually pursues and frightens them. It is oftentimes like a grim monster beyond all resistance and "unshunable as death." But that they nevertheless feel the wrongs as keenly as any other people is evidenced by the pathos created by the ballads. Their tears are never allowed to dry over such matters, and with a wonderful sense of their ideal of spiritual culture, they give permanence to their sentiments by showing in vivid life-like sketches the noble types of their people who suffer for love, sacrifice themselves for others and are perfectly selfless in their devotion. Even now when a ploughman, with a *tocá* on his head to protect it from the burning sun, drives the plough over his field, often does a tear start to his eyes at the recollection of the death of poor Sunái, as he hums the lines,—"Oh, tell my poor mother, my dear Shalla, that my pitcher floats in yonder stream and I am seized by Dewan Bhábná's men!" Grim Dewan Bhábná! Grim Bághrá the spy! and no less grim Bhatuk the uncle! all three conspired to ruin the life of a poor innocent girl.

The incidents of the episode, as also the style of composition show that the event occurred more than two hundred years ago. There is that freedom of love,—in electing the bridegroom by a youthful maiden,—which was prevalent in Eastern Mymensing as late as two hundred years ago, whereas in Bengal proper, swayed by the Sens and priests, such a thing is unheard of within the last four or five hundred years.

Sunái preferred death to dishonour. Alas, what else could she do? The soldier goes to the battle-field to die when the last hope of victory has faded away. Sunái went to the city of the Dewan very much in the same spirit! She cared for her honour above all! She could have saved her life and returned to her husband's home after having satisfied the fleeting and ever evanescent desire of a despot (not to be mistaken for love), which in such cases seldom lasted longer than a day. And Hindu society, however rigid, often showed a humane consideration in dealing with cases of compulsory abduction as will be seen from the chapters on "*Ághat*" in the genealogical works of the Brahmins.

Monna Vanna went to the enemy's camp to save the people of her country from destruction and Sunái did so to save her dear husband's life. Where lies the difference? It is only the angle of vision that is to be changed in order to estimate the merits of each case rightly. But Monna Vanna went to surrender the supreme sanctity of wifehood, whilst the other was all holiness. Is it good to surrender one's ideal of love and devotion for the sake of the public good?

There is no depth into which human nature will not sink if it is allowed to lose sight of its higher ideals of truth and loyalty and to give preference to utilitarian considerations. Maeterlinck, however, had not the courage to paint his heroine as fallen, proving that he really feared to follow to the end the theory he preached, lest such a course should blacken rather than glorify her.

Sunái's father-in-law is not indeed an ideal head of the family, but he is the ordinary type, ready to save his only son's life at the price of family honour. He is after all prudent from a practical point of view. The ballad-maker has indeed saved the hero of the tale from being shown as acting under a similar weakness by taking him off altogether from our sight. The drop-scene falls upon the tragic death of Sunái and there is no suggestion given by the poet of anything dishonourable on the part of the hero who is kept in the background.

The "*báromáshi*" in these ballads is often their weak point. When the poets know beforehand that the joys and sorrows of the twelve months must, as a matter of course, be described, the easy flow of their poetry meets with a check, and in their attempts to be superfine and to excel the predecessors in the field, their poetry becomes strained, stereotyped and conventional to a degree. Therefore although these '*baromashis*' are not occasionally without some lines of sparkling glamour, the general deterioration of the poetical element in such passages is obvious. In this short poem also we have to apologise for the weak '*baromashi.*' In the original it is not so bad, but when the conventional ideas of a particular people are to be clothed in the garb of a different language, the blemishes of such passages become glaringly apparent, creating a feeling of weariness, if not actual disgust.

The episode described took place in the sub-division of Netrakona, Mymensing. The great knave Bághrá has been immortalised in the name of a marsh called after him. The '*Bághrá rháor*' lies ten miles to the south-east of Netrakona. The popular tradition is that Bághrá was a '*sindhuki*'—a spy who used to supply the Dewans with information about beautiful Hindu girls. There were many such '*sindhukis*' in the employ of the Dewans whose descendants, as stated already in the introduction, still enjoy rent-free lands in Mymensing, granted to their ancestors in recognition of their expertness in that particular avocation. So the big marsh called the

'*Bághrár háor*' still reminds one of the crafty knave who ruined poor Sunái and got the ownership of that extensive area as reward for this and similar other venal services which he rendered to the unscrupulous autocrats of the land. I could not find Dighalháti in the maps of Eastern Mymensing. It must have been somewhere near the '*Bághrár háor*,' for, it was here that both Bághrá and Bhatuk lived. 'Bhábná,' whether the chief belonged to the more genuine line of the Dewans or to an illegitimate one, is evidently a pet name, and until his more dignified name is found, it will be difficult to trace him out from the genealogy of the Dewan family. There is a village named Dewanpara on the river Dholái close to *Bághrár háor*. This may not unlikely have been the place of Dewan Bhábná. There is no mention of the poet's name anywhere in the ballad. The reason is obvious. The poets have always observed a scrupulous silence in regard to themselves in those songs which deal with the atrocities of the Dewans. It was positively unsafe for one to disclose one's name after having exposed the misdeeds of the rulers of the country.

DINESH CH. SEN.

7, Bishwakosh Lane,
Calcutta, June 4, 1923.

DEWAN BHÁBNÁ

I

When she was barely six, Sunái sparkled like a small diamond or pearl as she playfully ran into the arms of her mother, laughing.

When seven, a sweet smile was always on her lips. She seemed to spread moonbeams around her, seated on the lap of her mother.

When eight, she learnt to bind her flowing tresses herself, and the blossom of a hundred lilies appeared on her cheeks.

At nine, she was the very lamp of the house; its whole court-yard was brightened by her presence as by heaven's light.

It was now her tenth year—the time when a zero is added to the arithmetical figure—1. God was against her and she fell into great sorrows.

Hear, oh my audience, the story of this unfortunate girl.

In her tenth year she lost her father. She had no brother; and now fatherless, she could count for help upon none except her widowed mother. Wretched she became from this tender age. There was no good neighbour to extend a helping hand to the two souls, or to share their sorrows by living with them. The unfortunate mother suffered her lot alone in her house. She was like a creeper that lies low on the dust, losing its support when the tree is uprooted; or like leaves and flowers which fade away when the creeper is no more. Sunái keenly felt the grief that rent her mother's heart and often did she shed tears, unseen by others, in deep sympathy.

Ill could the poor mother afford the food and raiment that the poor girl needed, and there was no end to their suffering.

Sunái's uncle lived at the village of Dighalháti; he was her mother's own brother. Sunái thought that it did not look well to live in their own home alone. The beautiful one constantly devised in her mind plans as to what should be done in their extremity. She had now stepped into her eleventh year. The mother's anxieties grew at the thought of her approaching youth. "She is beautiful and will soon attain her youth. Alas! who will secure for her a worthy bridegroom or means for maintenance?" She thus thought again and again and then decided to go to her brother's home (at Dighalháti).

Ll. 1-30.

II

Bhatuk Thakur was a Brahmin whose avocation was that of a priest in the village. Here I shall give an account of this Brahmin. He had no children; his wife (Sunái's aunt) lived alone in the house. Bhatuk Thakur's only source of income was his fees as a priest.

The widowed mother with Sunái reached her brother's home one evening in a destitute condition. She said, "How can I describe to you, oh dear brother, our sad condition! you are no doubt aware of my recent distresses; it is all due to my bad luck! Sunái is growing up quickly. There is none to look after us or secure a suitable bridegroom for her. I thought over the matter for long and then made up my mind to come to your house."

The Brahmin, I have already said, had no child. He was alone there with his wife and was therefore right glad to receive his relations into his home.

Thus Sunái lived there with her mother. Often did the brother and sister put their heads together to -devise means for getting a suitable bridegroom for the girl.

In her cheeks there was the glow of a hundred *champaka* flowers in full bloom. She was exceedingly handsome and her flowing hair was long and curly. Her uncle had given her a *nilámbari*—a blue-coloured *sari* with beautiful border-lines woven in the two ends and in the middle. Wearing this *sari* she used to go every day to the river to fill her pitcher. On the banks bloomed the flowers of the *kewa* (screw plants) in the groves that were in plenty there. The sweet smell attracted the bees that made the place resonant with their constant hummings. With the pitcher in her hand and with her fine blue-coloured *sari* she looked so beautiful that those who passed by that way often stopped to have a sight of her. It seemed that her charms radiated from her slender body and spread a halo all around illuminating the spot she trod upon. The twelfth year is complete and she now stands on the first step to youth. Like a fine pinnace—a sport of the winds—floating in the new floods of August, Sunái's youth was gay and playful.

The neighbours whispered, 'From what place has this beautiful one come to our village ? Like the golden streaks of lightning that play on the dark clouds, she dispels the gloom of a dismal and dark house by her beauty.'

Ll. 1-30.

III

" Go on, weaving your garland, fair girl, with the *malati* flower and do not forget the small *bakuls* which sparkle like gems in plenty dropped on the ground from yonder tree.[1]

[1] When a girl chooses her own bridegroom , it is the practice on her part to hang a garland of flowers woven by her own hands on his neck. Here the words of the neighbours indicate that the time has arrived when she should choose a husband.

"Do you know that a match-maker came to your house with a proposal last morning? What the bridegroom's qualifications are, has to be considered.

"What the Creator has written on your forehead, fair girl, is inevitable. The mother is puzzled and is not able to decide her course."

The match-maker is dismissed. The bridegroom is not after the mother's mind.

"My girl," she reflected, "is fair to look at as the moon, but of a dusky colour is this youth."

Another match-maker comes with an offer from a different quarter. But the mother could not give her consent here either. She shook her head saying, "This one too is not the fit groom for my beautiful daughter. My daughter's husband must have a fine Bungalow with twelve gate-ways. He must be handsome as the warrior-god Kartikeya. His colour must be bright as the moonbeams. His status in society must be unimpeachable and lineage high. He must have besides a large landed estate."

Each month match-makers came with new offers; but none was entertained by the mother of Sunái.

Ll. 1-16.

IV

Over the *ikari* plant rustles the wind making a pleasant murmur, and its boughs are interwoven with fine textures spun by the spiders. Here also is a tree on which flowers of the colour of gold bloomed all the twelve months of the year. On the boughs one can see these sparkling flowers, their colour variegated by the varying seasons.

With arrows made of long reeds and a cage in hand the youth comes to the river-side every evening; a trained falcon he brings with him as he walks, and he looks bright and glorious as the moon. Like the warrior-god Kartikeya he wanders about in that village-path carrying a bow and arrows in his hands. On the banks of the river he happened to see Sunái, the beautiful one. The *ketaki* had just bloomed and its sweet fragrance, carried by the wind, had spread a charm over the land, when near the groves of the screw plants they saw one another for the first time.

Her Random Thoughts.

"Who are you, oh beautiful youth, and where lies your home? To whom may I put the question and who will give me the right reply? Our four eyes met and exchanged glances; and then and there my heart was captured. Who art thou, oh gracious Providence, that hast brought before my eyes the youth of my heart!

"Oh my bee! Where lies your own garden? Where is that sweet flower that you seek!

Unweary the bee flies seeking its flower. It comes and goes and sometimes stops a little, casting a glance behind.

"Tell me, what flower thou seekest so anxiously! Fain would I catch you in the stillness of midnight hours, and hide you within the flowers that adorn my chignon. A seat would I reserve for you (in my heart) and offer a cup of honey; and then I would fly with you to distant lands.

"Were you a bird, my love, I would put you in a cage and keep you near me day and night; and were you the black paint *kajjal* (collyrium) I would hide you under my dark eyes; and were you a flower I would put you into my braids and cover you from others' view! Resolved am I to go with you wherever you may lead me—whatever that country may be, I do not care."

The Prince.

"Oh beautiful maiden! for whom are you weaving this garland to-day sitting all alone? I wrote you a letter on a lotus-leaf yesterday. Did you care to know who wrote it and what were its contents?"

The Letter.

The letter reached her. She read it. The name of the youth was Mádhab. She read the letter with a beating heart—once, twice, thrice did she glance over each line of it. Then, sad at heart, she sat to weep.

The youthful Mádhab writes that "he saw her for the first time all alone at her own home. Then, he makes the request, "On the banks of the river there is a *hijal* tree densely covered with small thin leaves. There if you come to spend a while under the tree I may open my heart and unreservedly tell you all that is in my thoughts. The banks of the river are overgrown with *ketaki* groves; there all alone we would sit together and have a pleasant love-talk. You are sweet to me as honey, and dear as a garland of flowers to adorn my breast. For you, oh dear maiden, I have turned as one mad. My father is a millionaire. He has besides, large landed properties. What shall I not do to please you, my love!

"I will give you a *saḍi* of the colour of flaming fire. In the front of our house there is a flower-garden in which blue and red flowers bloom in plenty. I will gather these every morning for you and you will weave garlands with them. On the opposite side of our spacious house is a beautiful tank with landing steps all made of stone. You will bathe there, my love, and I will be your companion. If with your tender arms it be hard for you to lift up your pitcher, I will help you to do so. We will swim together, pleased with ourselves in the blue waters of the tank, and on your arms will sparkle bracelets bright with pearls, while a diamond necklace will decorate your breast. At our home there is a pleasure-house erected in the midst of the tank. You will spend your evening there and shine as its very lamp. In our palace there is a great drawing-room. There we will spend the night playing at dice. Your necklace will sparkle as a string of glow-worms; and in the nuptial chamber I will teach you a hundred playful ways to make you happy. It will be my pleasure to gather the choicest flowers from our garden to adorn your hair, and flower-vases filled with sweet-smelling *malati* will be presented to you every morning as you open your eyes after the night's sleep. I will give you all my wealth, all my treasure and with them and above all, my heart which is already yours. Be pleased with me, dear maiden, and accept me as the companion of your life."

The Reply.

"Oh friend of my heart, listen to my story. I am but a maiden just stepped into youth. Not married yet am I. My mother and aunt are looking for a bridegroom for me. Alas! if I were one of these *ketaki* flowers springing on the river-side, I could meet you every day without a scandal. Were you my friend, the moon that shines above, I would open my eyes and fix my insatiate gaze on you for the whole night and people could say nothing! Were you the river my love, I would pour my thirsty soul into you freely and without reserve. But what am I? A woman in society, and but a captive within the four walls of my home! My sorrows are all my own. From the day I saw you first on the banks of yonder river, my heart like a mad thing has been wandering in pursuit of you in all directions. I cannot open my mind to my mother: a sense of shame stops my mouth, making me powerless.

"Trust to my friend Shalla your message. Tell me through her what prospects we have of union and when our wishes may be fulfilled. I write this letter looking forward to happy things that are still at a distance."

She handed over the letter perfumed with sandal and with it a garland of flowers woven by herself to Shalla, her maid, and sent her to Madhab. She left the room and Sunái struggled in her soul between expectation and doubt, with all the yearnings of first youth.

Ll. 1-88.

Bághrá was a knave; wicked was he to the back-bone. It was he who carried the report to Dewan Bhábná. In his big bungalow with twelve gateways, the Dewan was seated at ease, when Bághrá approached him and said:—

"Within your own jurisdiction, my lord, there is a girl in the house of one Bhatuk—a Brahmin. She is lovely as a fairy. She is in her thirteenth year. No girl that I know of in this country is her match. She is not yet married. If your Highness wishes, it is quite possible to secure her for your bride."

When Bhábná heard this account, so glad was he that he presented him with some gold beforehand, weighing it in scales.

"Now, hear me, oh Brahmin," Bághrá said to Bhatuk, "you have a beautiful girl at your house. Dewan Bhábná was beholding the boat-race from his pinnace the other day and he saw the girl on the landing steps. From that day he has turned mad after her.

"If you agree to give the girl in marriage to the Dewan, all the ladies that he has in his harem, married under the *nika* system, will be mere slaves to her wishes. He will order a tank to be dug for your use in front of your house and its landing steps will be all of stone. He will besides grant you 52 *puras* of rent-free land as reward. Now, it is the wish of the Dewan that you agree to his offer."

Naturally greedy he was, being a priest by profession. The temptations offered, especially the offer of the land proved too much for his sense of honour, and he gave his consent. The Brahmin planned to destroy the caste of the poor girl secretly. So he did not let the mother or the daughter know of it. But still whispers were heard in the village about this private arrangement.

Ll. 1-28.

V

Sunái.

"Oh my dear maid Shalla, go at once with this letter of mine to my friend. Tell him that he must at all costs take me away from here before evening to-day. If the evening star sets, and he does not come, I know not what will be my fate! My uncle is wicked and insincere. He has arranged everything to get me married to Bhábná this day. Go and tell all these to my friend and request him to have me removed from here this very day."

The maid hastened towards the city of Mádhab and reached it in a short time. She related all the circumstances to the youth and then gave him the letter. She took a reply from him and returned home quickly.

Sunái.

"I dreamt a bad dream last night. To-day my heart seems to say 'Do not go to the river-side;' without any cause a tear has sprung up in my left eye and a strange fear has seized my soul. I feel my tongue dry, and I have not the strength to-day to carry an empty pitcher in my arms. What is the matter with me I cannot say. My feet, it seems, are unwilling to tread the path towards the landing *ghat*. From the dry bough of yonder tree the raven croaks hoarsely and I hear the ticking of the house-lizard and sound of sneezing. These are ominous signs and seem to prevent me from going to the river-ghat to-day."

She sits quietly awhile and again reflects, "I will remain with my mother and must not go anywhere to-day. I do not know what evil is in store for me." After stopping a while, she addresses Shalla, "But listen to me, oh my dear maid, if I do not go to the river-side, I may lose this chance of seeing him for ever. The friend of my heart will go away disappointed, and it may be that he will never visit the river-side again."

Saying this, the maiden did not tarry, but resigning herself to her fate, she slowly walked her way to the river-side with the empty pitcher in her arms.

Shalla, her friend and confidante, went ahead and she with shy steps followed her.

As ill luck would have it, they espied a pinnace lying anchored near the groves of the screw plants. As soon as Sunái had reached the spot, the men of the Dewan carried her to the boat by force.

Sunái.

"Oh my friend Shalla, hasten back to our home to tell my mother that the men of Dewan Bhábná are carrying me by force. Tell her, oh my dear friend, that the pitcher I brought with me is left floating in the current near the landing steps, to tell my sad tale!

"Tell my uncle that he may now be happy with the 52 *puras* of land he has got as reward.

"Tell the dear lord of my heart that his own Sunái is within the clutches of the tiger-like Dewan Bhábná.

"Oh sun and moon, be my witness. Oh day and night, be my witness. If you ever see my loving friend, give him an account of my suffering.

"You birds that fly in the air; far-reaching is your ken. Tell my beloved, that his Sunái has been stolen by a thief.

"Thou *hijal* tree—that standest on the bank of the river and hast witnessed all that has taken place,—acquaint my love with all, if ever he comes to seek me here. The *ketaki* flowers are spreading their sweet fragrance on the lonely banks; I pray," she said, "Ye may report my sorrows to my love, if ever he comes to seek me here.

The Loot

"He carries me away for no fault; he carries me away because, they say, I am beautiful."

Dewan Bhabna, p. 157

"Rivers and canals, birds and beasts, all be my witness. Providence is against unfortunate Sunái. Oh winds, you have been blowing over this earth ever since creation : tell my love that his Sunái is now as dead to him.

"How wretched am I! why did I come to this place? A pariah is going to taste the sacred butter of the sacrificial fire. Had I known that things would come to such a pass, with a halter I would tie this pitcher to my neck and drown myself in these waters.

"He promised to come, why did he not keep his promise? Has any danger befallen him? No matter that he has not come, I will suffer my own lot; but how alarmed I feel to think that some danger may have overtaken him! The river is furious, the waves rise and fall whirling in a chaotic fury; his boat may have capsized! Alas! but let me hope still, that he is well. Oh birds, fly quickly with this message to my love. Your Sunái is being taken away to Dewan Bhábná's palace! He carries me away for no fault; he carries me away because, they say, I am beautiful."

* * * * *

"Who are you, men, that row the pinnace in such a hot haste. Whose youthful wife do you forcibly carry therein?"

From his boat Mádhab again called aloud, "Who are you damsel, why do you cry in this way in the pinnace?"

When she recognised the voice of her own Mádhab, she burst into loud laments.

A fierce battle ensued in the darkness of the night. The boatmen and others of the Dewan's pinnace were all beaten and drowned in the river.

Ll. 1-76.

VI

Why is the sound of trumpet heard aloud in the city? What festivity is it for which the citizens have stirred themselves to such excitement?

Gather flowers, oh friends, from all the gardens of the city to your heart's content. Mádhab will marry Sunái to-day. Listen, the ladies are singing festive songs praying for good luck! Some are busy decorating the nuptial room with flower-garlands; the women of the city have assembled on the landing *ghats* and are filling their pitchers to perform the sacred rites! They are so happy,—for, Mádhab will to-day marry Sunái.

Ll. 1-8.

VII

"Madhab, it does not become you to sit idly in the house when your father has been bound with chains at Dewan Bhábná's order and carried to his palace."

Mádhab rose up pale with fear in all haste at the report and ordered his boat to be ready. He went to the palace of the Dewan. Sunái remained in the house with her maid-servants. Here I shall sing to you, "The song of the twelve months."

In the month of July, Mádhab started on his pinnace to rescue his father from the Dewan's prison. She was all alone in her room with Shalla for her only friend and confidante! She passed the whole month in hopes and fears, distressed at his delay.

In August they worshiped Manasa Devi with pomp in the city. "But how can there be," she reflected, "any joy in this house? None has come to fulfil my hopes, wretched that I am."

"In September the *tal* fruits are plentiful and they made cakes with them. All are happy, it is our house and my youth that are under the shadow of a great grief."

In October Durga is worshipped in every house. People have returned to their homes, alas! he has not come to join the general festivity of the country!

"In November the rivers get shallower losing their liquid treasure. How anxiously have I not awaited his return! The servants of the house shed tears for him in silence and the mother laments her lot. Thus, the month has passed away in bitter grief!

"In December, misty vapours rise up in the sky; my love is away, what pleasure can there be for me?

"In January, the biting cold makes all shiver and mists obstruct the sight of men. In this cold season the mind yearns for one's beloved. Alone in my bed I pass my time while he is far away!

"December and January passed away and then came February and March. It is the spring season and every one is gay save Sunái, the unfortunate bride.

"In April, festivities are going on everywhere. He has not yet returned and I am maddened by grief. With this month the year ends. "This whole year I have not combed my hair a single day nor have I gathered flowers from our garden but once. Vain is my youth! I have grown thin and pale. Alas! where does my love linger all the while? In whose bower does my beloved beguile his weary hours?

"In May the ripe mangoes peep from leafy trees. The heat is unbearable and the maid-servants fan me with palm-leaves. But can they ever hope to cool my burning heart?

Ll. 1-42.

VIII

The father-in-law of Sunái has returned home. He meets his daughter-in-law and says with tears in his eyes.

"You are no doubt dear to us as life. I am going to speak to you freely. I have an only son—the solitary lamp of my house is he! Owing to ill luck, I am going to lose this only treasure of my heart.

"Dewan Bhábná has found fault with me for you. He got me bound in iron chains and took me to his city. When Mádhab went to help me, the Dewan set me free and imprisoned him. Oh my daughter-in-law, if you do not come to the rescue at this crisis, my son will be put to death. The Dewan is inexorable as a demon. He has resolved that he will release Mádhab, provided he obtains you. What should I say! He is my only son—the only scion of our family—and I have not another child; you know this. Losing you, however sad a thing it may be, we may yet hope to get my dear son back."

When she heard this, tears began to flow from her eyes. She adjusted her long flowing hair with one hand and with the other she wiped away her tears. She asked her father-in-law to make one of their big boats ready. She was resolved to go to the palace of the Dewan to rescue her husband. In a small casket she took with her pills of fatal poison and soon she reached the city of Bhábná. As soon as the Dewan heard the report of her arrival, he hastened to meet her in the boat. He was maddened with her beauty; it seemed to him that the full moon had fallen down from the sky to his city.

Sunái.

"Now, listen to me, oh Dewan, you have imprisoned my dear husband in your city. Please keep it a secret from him that I have come here. I swear to you by my life and ask this favour that you should order all your men and informants not to divulge the facts about me to him. And then you must release him at once. If you will do all these things, then only can I satisfy your desire."

In the prison lay Mádhab with a heavy stone placed on his breast. His hands and feet were bound with iron chains. He was now released. And the Dewan offered him the same pinnace on which Sunái had come to his city for his return home. Being thus set free, Mádhab sailed homewards. Now, hear what happened to Sunái.

It was the dead hour of night and no star was seen in the sky. In a spacious Bungalow which had twelve gate-ways lay Sunái alone—with guards and sentinels surrounding the house. From that distance, she bowed to the feet of her mother and prayed for her blessings.

Then she remembered the sweet face of Mádhab. Even the thought of the beloved cne gave her some happiness at this gloomy hour of sorrow. She bowed her head low a hundred times remembering his feet, and then she prayed to Durga, the Divine Mother, to give her strength.

The sky was black and the land was black all around, covered with darkness; the night looked black, standing face to face before her. At such an hour the unfortunate girl opened her small casket containing black poison.

To-day she recalled to her mind the figure of her father long dead. She had a faint memory of him but to-day the dread hour of his death came vividly before her mind.

In the depth of the night the Dewan entered the chamber wih slow steps. He found her lying unconscious on the couch. Poison had spread all over her body, making her fair skin discoloured and dark. She was in the agonies of death and her body burnt with poison as with fire.

Alas! that she could not see her dear mother at this last hour. Alas! that she could not behold her husband to bid him a last farewell. Alas! where is her father-in-law and where her mother-in-law who loved her so well! And where alas! is her friend and confidante, the maid Shalla? But cruellest sorrow of all that her husband should not be by her bed at this last moment!

The wicked Dewan could not gratify his devil's passion. To save the life of her husband, Sunái yielded up her own.

Ll. 1-60.

KENARAM THE ROBBER-CHIEF

BY

CHANDRÁVATI

PREFACE

In the whole range of the world's literary history there is perhaps hardly a more tender tale of woe silently suffered by a poetess than that of Chandrávati, born, 1550 A.D., the gifted daughter of Bangshi Das, who figures as one of the best exponents of the poetical literature of the Manasa-cult.

Bangshi Das, Chandrávati's father, was born in the village Patwari in the sub-division of Kishoreganj (District Mymensingh) in Eastern Bengal. The village stands on the river Phuleswari. He was a poor Brahmin, but he took pride in his poverty and would not stoop to anything mean to earn riches. I have briefly stated in my "Bengali Ramayanas" the circumstances which led to the reformation of the robber Kenaram by Bangshi Das. The story shows the wonderful power of faith and was written by Chandrávati herself in her characteristic style, full of appeal to the heart.

Those were very evil days for Bengal. The country was passing through a political revolution. The miseries of the transition-period were in evidence on all sides. The Pathans were losing their hold upon Bengal and the army of the Great Moghul was knocking at her gate. At the approach of the powerful enemy, the attention of the Emperor of Gour was wholly centred in defending the country against the foreign invasion that was imminent. The feudal system of Government which was in vogue in the country was not strong enough to unify its different parts under a common banner. It was martial power and terrorism that had kept the twelve chiefs of Bengal named "*Bara Bhuians*" in check. As soon, therefore, as the Emperor of

Gour grew weak or became engaged in warfare outside Bengal, the chiefs tried to assert their independence and alienate themselves from the suzerain. It was about this time that Chand Ray, the Raja of Gourdwar had become so powerful that the army of Kutlu Khan, the Pathan emperor, actually held him in dread. We read in the "Prem-bilash" by Nityananda that the generals of Kutlu Khan did not venture to make an expedition to Gourdwar to realise the outstanding arrears of revenue which Chand had refused to pay to the Gour Emperor. In Western Bengal Bir Hamvir had practically established his independence,—nay, planned to invade Gour and drive the Pathans from the country. When the central power was busy in an all-absorbing struggle to fight with the Moghuls, the twelve sub-lords of Bengal grew practically independent, and the Emperor did not consider it expedient or prudent to take any serious notice of the revolts. His object perhaps was to meet the Moghuls first and save the country from the impending danger, and then, when the political atmosphere would assume a quieter aspect, to deal with and subdue the refractory chiefs. Hence we find him almost indifferent to the attempts of the chiefs of Gourdwar and Banabishnupur to sever connection with the suzerain.

The political atmosphere presented a relaxation and an anarchical condition which became at this time a source of serious danger to the people of Bengal. Writes Chandrávati in her short story of Kenaram : "The Dacoits are the true masters of the country, and no one believes in the power of the Emperor." She also refers to the Thugs who strangled people to death with nooses of rope. It should be borne in mind that though the Thugs became a regular menace to public safety in later times, when they were suppressed by Bentinck in 1831, they had already been in existence in the country from very early times. Chandrá speaks of the great panic amongst the people which the chaotic condition of administration produced everywhere: "They kept," says she, "all their wealth buried under the earth for fear of plunder." Many villages presented a scene of total desertion, and no one's name amongst the dacoits was so greatly dreaded in Eastern Mymensingh as that of Kenaram, the leader of a powerful gang.

Chandrávati has given a full account of Kenaram and his conversion. It is a historical account given by one who knew it first-hand, so that the metrical form of the ballad does not affect its historical value.

Some of the places mentioned in the poem are still to be found in the district. The extensive mire and muddy lands full of long reeds, known as the *Jaliar hawor*, in which the main incident of the poem took place lies about 9 miles to the south-east of the Subdivisional town of Kishoreganj, and the village of Bakulia in which Kenaram was born is described as situated in close proximity to these marshy lands. Bangshi Das was travelling here with the musical party on his way to his native village Patwari—8 miles to the south of the *Jaliar hawor* where he was overtaken by Kenarám and his gang. The incidents of the poem took place sometime between 1575 and 1590.

There are altogether 1,054 lines of verse in the Bengali text. I have greatly abridged the story of Manasar Bhashan introduced in Canto V, in my English translation, giving the mere gist just to enable my readers to follow the incidents of Kenaram's reformation. I have also curtailed passages here and there, but have nowhere introduced any idea that is not to be found in the text.

DINESH CHANDRA SEN.

7, BISHWAKOSH LANE,
Bagbazar, Calcutta, 12 March 1923.

KENARAM THE ROBBER-CHIEF

(ABRIDGED FROM THE ORIGINAL)

1.

There is a wide waste-land called *Jaliar hawor* in close proximity to which lies the village of Bakulia. In this village lived a Brahmin named Khelaram with his wife Jashodhará. The couple were happy in all other respects but they had no child. This grieved them much. In the country-side a man without any issue is called by the hated name of '*Atkuriá*' They bemoaned their lot saying, "What is the good of our existence without any issue? We will starve ourselves to death and no more see our neighbours to hear only abuse from them. We will not light our evening lamp nor show ourselves to the sun in the day-time. With doors bolted, we will shut ourselves up in the house. Let eternal darkness cover our shame." The couple spent three days in fasting in this way, and on the night of the third day Jashodhará dreamed that she saw the goddess Manasa Devi calling her up and ordering her to dedicate a cup (*ghata*) in her honour on the last day of the month of Ashar (about the 15th of July). For the whole of the following thirty days she was required to lead an austere life of penance and devotion, and burn incense and make flower-offerings to the goddess in the evening. On the last day of Sravana (about 15th of August) the *puja* of Manasa Devi was to be completed by an observance of the proper rites.

The woman told the story of her dream to her husband and they did as they were bid.

Ll. 1-50 (abridged).

2. The Birth of Kenaram—the Vicissitudes of his Fortune.

Devout believer in Manasa Devi as Chandrá was, she ascribes the birth of a son to the couple to the mercy of the goddess.

The son born to the couple at a rather late hour of life was a healthy-looking baby of dusky colour. The overjoyed mother did not, however, live long to enjoy her good fortune. She died when the child was only seven months old. They called him Kenaram (*lit.* purchased by Ram,—entirely owned by Ram). The death of his loving wife gave such a rude shock to the Brahmin that he went away shortly after to visit the shrines, and three years passed,—he never returned home. His little son, only one year old, was left to the care of his maternal uncles who lived in the village of Devpur in Mymensingh. They fed the baby cow's milk and took special care of him. Thus in spite of the calamities suffered in his infancy, things fared comparatively well for him till he grew to be three years' old.

The district of Mymensingh at this time, however, was visited by one of the most cruel famines that had ever come upon Bengal. There was no rain during the rainy months, and as a result, the agricultural outlook became menacing. The homes of many families became scenes of terrible suffering, and men and women died by hundreds. First they lived on fruits, next they ate grasses and when these also were scorched by the rays of the sun, they sold their cattle and house-utensils. Next husbands sold wives and wives their children. All convention, all affection and feelings were gone and, men became like lower animals seeking the whole day long for something to live upon. The uncles of Kenaram sold him for five *cattahs* of rice

Ll. 1-52.

3. He joins a Gang of Robbers.

A man of the Kaivarta caste purchased the boy and was delighted with his bargain owing to the robust physique of the child.

Seven sons of this Kaivarta were the leaders of seven gangs. From the Garo Hills to the sea coast in the south, the extensive tract of country was without any habitation of men in those days. The land was overgrown with a dense jungle of long reeds, which afforded shelter to the robbers. The people buried their wealth under the earth for fear of plunder. The robbers strangled the wayfarers with nooses of rope. The Dacoits became in fact the masters of the country and no one believed in the power of the king. Many villages presented a scene of total desertion under the rule of the Kajis.

Brought up amongst the robber from childhood, Kenaram became expert in the art of robbing people and killing them. The Kaivarta brothers had grown immensely rich by their wicked trade, yet they did not give up their calling, but continued to store the wealth they acquired by robbery under the earth in that extensive jungle of reeds.

Says Chandrá, the poetess, "Kenaram became a man of gigantic physique. If he stood up, it seemed that his head touched the skies, while the earth looked like his foot-stool. He appeared like a small hillock, all dusky, strong in his limbs like a second Ravana."

Though a Brahmin by birth, no one had instructed him in the ways of religion. He had never learnt to distinguish between virtue and vice. He never cared to hear the tales of the gods; he had not the faintest idea as to what sin was. His need was small as he had no wife, no children. Yet he delighted in robbing and killing men. He murdered men for the sake of murder, he stole money merely for the sake of burying it under the earth. Just as a tiger kills animals for the sake of sport, even so did Kenaram kill men.

He seldom went to his uncles' house. Like an uncouth-looking boar he slept on the bare ground in the depth of the jungles, heedless of the bites of gnats or insects. He had no thought of luxury, nor cared to spend money for his own comfort. Daily he plundered and daily he buried his booty under the earth.

The straggling herds of buffaloes and cows in the neighbouring meadows exceeded all calculation, and Kenaram and his men drank milk abundantly and became robust and strong beyond all measure. From the hilly land of Susang to the great tract of the jungly land called the "*Jalia hawor*" Kenaram and his band wandered about in ferocious quest of wealthy wayfarers and pilgrims. Frequently some poor merchant passing by the river with his cargo was killed, and his boat was sunk in the river after having been looted of its merchandise. His name thus became a dread in the country; mothers in half-audible words uttered his name to the little lads, and more than a lullaby the name made the young eye-lids close instantly and brought sleep to them. "The very leaves of the trees," says Chandrá, "shivered as if in fright, when the robbers of Kenaram's gang shouted their war-cry. None dared to light a lamp in the evening lest it would attract notice to the house, nor dared to come outside after dusk."

Ll. 1-64.

4. Kenaram meets Bangshidas.

It was on one occasion when Bangshi Das the poet and devotee, who rejoiced ever in Manasa Devi's name happened to pass through the dismal tract of "*Jalia hawor*" with his band of singers. He had gone on a professional call to a distant part of the country and was on his way back home. His mind was filled with devotion so that as he travelled he sang the praises of Manasa Devi to the music of his one-stringed lyre. And the band played on tabors and cymbals. They were so lost in devotional fervour that they not only sang and played on their musical instruments, but danced as they went their way. " Bangshi Das," says Chandrá, " had a cloth round his body on which the names of his god were inscribed. Such clothes were called '*námábalis.*' He was dressed as an ascetic, his hair was knotted, and on his forehead was the long *tilak*-mark showing the creed that he professed." The whole band was, so to speak, lost in spiritual reveries. They did not care to look at the way through the thick jungle, nor at the sky, nor at the landscape around. It was an all-absorbing joy to them that they sang the Mother's name. They now suddenly felt their path obstructed by the long reeds and knew that they had reached the " *Jalia hawor* "—a tract which would require them a full day to cross. Just at that time they heard a cry " Victory to Káli " which chilled the very life-blood of the musical party led by Bangshi Das; and before a moment had passed, stood before them the stalwart dark figure of Kenaram, the redoubted robber-chief. His clothes were wound up round the waist in the fashion of North-Western people; he looked like a menacing cloud charged with lightning. Like the very god of death Kenaram with his party stood near them demanding the surrender of their money and life. Kenaram said with a loud laugh, " Do you know who I am ? " Bangshi smiled and replied, " You are an Evil One, who is there that does not know such a man ? But what have we with us to deserve your notice ? Here, look "—and saying this he opened and emptied his bag before Kenaram. " Some torn clothes and a few seers of rice are all my property. What would you do with these ? Of course you are quite welcome to have them if you like.—It is a sad thing to reflect that you do not care for real treasure, which is devotion to Manasa Devi, but commit heinous crimes for temporal riches which will not last."

"No, I am not going to be tutored by you in such matters; murder has been my occupation for many years, and it is hopeless for you to try to convert me by a sermon," said the robber-chief smiling, and then added, "I will kill you and all your men. Whether you have anything or not does not matter. Killing is my profession and I delight in killing. I have no other object. Where I get money I rob, but where I do not get, I kill."

"What do you do with the money? Do you distribute it among the poor as some robbers do?"

"No, I bury it under the earth. Why should I give this money to the poor? If I would do that, they would grow rich and run after vile pleasures, and become like some of us; for possession of money puts all kinds of wrong things into the head."

Amused a little, in spite of the critical condition in which Bangshi stood, with the queer reply of the robber, he asked him to tell him his name. Kenaram smiled and softly said, "Yea, my name is Kenaram." Then a shudder passed through the nerves of the singers; their blood, it seemed, became icy-cold in horror. But Bangshi stood calm as ever, facing the robber as if nothing had happened. On his lips played the serene smile which had already puzzled the robber-chief a little. "Take heed, Kenaram, you have been spending this life in vice, but the end is coming. Don't you see that? Is it not high time that you should reform your ways?"

Never before this had any other man ventured to preach to Kenaram the philosophy of religion, when once placed within his clutches. He wondered at the courage of the man and said, "No more talk, be ready to meet death."

Bangshi said, "That I would be presently. But will you tell me one thing. Do you spend a part of your money for your own comforts?" "Not a bit, that would be nourishing greed and weakening myself, for I would hopelessly throw myself into the snare of desire if I indulged in luxuries, and cease to be the free man that I am."

Still more amazed at the curious words of the robber-chief Bangshi said, " If you do not give money to the poor, nor indulge in luxury, what good do you derive from burying it under the earth and killing men for no purpose ? "

Kenaram replied indifferently, " Do all the rich men of your country give their money to the poor ? Not a bit. So you see I do not do less than they do. Most of them do not spend money for their own comforts either. They are satisfied by merely storing it away. Whereas I return all my wealth to its real owner."

" Who is that owner ? " asked Bangshi.

' Why ?—mother earth," said Kenaram. " All coins, gold and silver come from the earth and will be reduced to earth. So I bury them under earth. Is it not the right thing that I do ? I kill men because I have been accustomed to do so and I delight in doing this out of long habit." " But," he hastily added, " I cannot waste time in this way. What is your name ? I ask this because I see you are a very bold fellow to speak to me in this way."

" I am Bangshi Das," said the poet coolly. At this Kenaram was startled. He said, " Are you that celebrated man whose songs are said to melt even a stone ? " Bangshi said, " Yes, they may melt a stone but not the stony heart of a robber."

Then the robber-chief told him that in spite of everything he would not spare him or his band. There was no other alternative and they must make themselves ready.

Ll. 1-160 (abridged).

5. The Song of Manasa Devi.[1]

Bangshi said, "Behold, O robber-chief, the evening has come and we are going to start for the new shores ; standing, however, here on this old soil from which we are to depart for ever I want to sing once for all those songs about Manasa Devi which have given my soul joys of the other world all my life."

Kenaram hesitated for a moment and then decided to comply with the request. The singers with eyes full of tears, resigned children of Manasa Devi, began those songs which had stirred the hearts of men and women of the vast district for many years. Kenaram said, "Listen to me, here do I sheathe my sword. I give you permission to sing the songs so long that I do not unsheathe it again."

In the dismal regions, the sky served as canopy, and a few robbers were their silent audience. On the green grass sat Kenaram in the midst of his crew with the hilt of his sword in his right hand. And Bangshi Das began to sing assisted by a well-trained chorus, full of devotion intensified by the thought of his approaching end. Bangshi sang sweetly and every word that he sang had added pathos from his tears. The whole music breathed a tender wail of devotion which became irresistible. The very birds that flew in the air came near and sat on the boughs of trees close by, attracted by the melody and pathos of Bangshi's voice. Twilight was succeeded by an impenetrable darkness in that forest land. But Kenaram gave orders to his crew for a general illumination, and the whole tract was illumined by

[1] The song of Manasa Devi is complete in 728 lines of verse and bears the names of 4 poets in the colophons, *viz.*, Bangshi Das, Narayan Deb, Kotishwar Das and Ravan Pundit. It gives the story of Durga's quarrel with Siva, the birth of Manasa Devi, her quarrel with Chand, the death of his six sons, and ends in the account of the widowhood of Behula and her starting with her husband's corpse on a raft. I give here very shortly the gist of this story as it is altogether a different subject and not relevant to the present topic.

hundreds of torch-lights so that the night lost all grimness and looked smiling and bright as day.

Kenaram, as he sat still with the sword by his side, became the more and more moved as the song went on and his emotion became visible in his face. The story of Behula, the faithful bride, was the subject of the song. In the bridal chamber her husband had died by snake-bite. They saw her seated quietly like a statue. The women of the house called her 'the unlucky one'—a witch; on the bridal night her husband had died. "It is not the snake but your ill luck—your evil eye,—that has killed him." This was the cruel remark of the maids in attendance. Heedless of sympathy and abuse alike, she sat still and suppressed the tears that were ready to spring to her eyes. She was thinking of the request which her husband had made to her to come to a closer embrace, but which, out of her shyness, the new bride had not complied with.

Then the corpse was about to be taken for cremation. Here she stepped forward and said that she would carry it on a raft, till she reached those shores from which she could win him back to life. Without him she could not—she would not live. She would visit the regions of death, and of deathless pangs, if necessary, to restore her husband to life.

The pathos reached the highest point where against the remonstrances of thousands of people who had assembled on the banks of the Gangoor, she, a girl of fourteen, stood heroic in her determination—griefless amongst many who were grieving, tearless amongst hundreds of tearful men and women. Emaciated by fasting and the secret pain of her heart, she looked like the very angel of love—prepared for all martyrdom, for all risks and sacrifices. "O our dear Savitri!" they all cried out, as they importuned her to return to home-life; for Savitri is the adored name of one of our mythological heroines whose sacrifice for love remains unparalleled in world's history to this day. Ll. 1-728.

6. The Reformation.

At this stage of the song Kenaram threw away his sword and began to cry aloud like a woman. The stone had actually melted at last. He said, "Sing, O Brahmin, sing again what you have sung." He stopped for a time only to clear his voice choked with tears and said to Bangshi: "I surrender myself to you, O Brahmin; I have amassed enough wealth for a family to live upon in comfort for generations. All this I offer to you, you will have no need to beg from door to door; be gracious unto me and tell me as to how I may be saved from sin." Bangshi said in reply, "I sing praises of Manasa Devi and live upon the small alms that my honest audience give me. I am a seeker of that wealth, compared to which your riches are but as lead before the diamond. I wish to live and die as an honest Brahmin. What shall I do with temporal riches? No, I will not defile my hand by taking what you have got by killing innocent men."

Then did Kenaram helplessly look around and saw everything dark before him. He reflected on his past life and the memory of his childhood caused him great pain. "I do not remember to have seen my parents. There was none to instruct me in the ways of truth. Losing my parents, I took shelter in my uncle's house who sold me for 5 *cattas* of rice during famine time. I mixed with bad men and have since been living as a robber in this forest. The merchants do not ply their boats in these regions for fear of me—Alas! my riches will be of no avail, when I shall die. I will throw all my wealth—my whole life's accumulation—into yonder river and I will drown myself therein." Kenaram's emotions were now roused to the highest pitch. He ordered his men to bring him the hoards that he had buried under the earth. These were brought before him in pitchers. Kenaram looked at the river that flowed by[1] and flung the pitchers into the waters one

[1] It was the Phueleshwari into which Kenaram had thrown all his wealth.

The Cobra under the Spell of a Song

" At this stage of the song Kenaram threw away his sword and began to cry aloud like a woman."

Kenaram, p. 178

after another, till none was left. The strong man was all tears and in burning remorse he bit his body and tore his own hair. He unsheathed his sword and said to Banghsi, "O my master behold, I will kill myself before you to atone for my sins."

Bangshi Das took compassion on him and as the man was really and sincerely repentant gave him sound advice for reforming his character. Kenaram had a sweet voice and in course of time became an earnest disciple of Bangshi and lived by singing songs on Manasa Devi. Chandrávati says that his great renunciation and pure life were much appreciated by the people soon after. "When singing, tears often came to his eyes, and he sang and danced like a man lost to this world —absorbed in reveries. Those to whom he had been once a terror, now approached him with requests to sing the beautiful songs of Manasa Devi and they often burst into tears at the pathos created by the singer who had once been a ruffian." "Thus did the influence of a saintly life turn a stone into a soft-hearted man. When he sang, it seemed that the very trees became spell-bound and shed tears in the shape of dew," says Chandrá, the daughter of Bangshi in the *payar* metre.

Ll. 1-89.

RUPAVATI

PREFACE

This ballad was collected by Chandra Kumar Dey from different sources, and sent to me on the 30th of March, 1920.

For some reasons which I am not allowed to disclose, I will not mention the names of the persons who helped Chandra Kumar in recovering the song. They purposely omitted some portions in which further particulars about the principal characters of the song were given; and following Chandra Kumar's advice I had to change the names of the hero, heroine and of their native place as originally found in the ballad.

The incidents of the ballad took place about the latter part of the 17th Century; and there is no doubt that it is the popular version of an event which caused a considerable commotion in the locality where it occurred. The memory of it is still fresh in some quarters. But I need not lay any further stress on the historical side of this interesting poem.

It will be seen that one version of the story ends on page 193, where the marriage of the hero with the daughter of the Raja is described as having taken place with his permission. (Canto III, Ll. 80-90.) The episode of the concluding chapter of this version is far from being authentic. What good could the Raja derive by giving his daughter in marriage to the first man whose face he would see one particular morning? He could as well have married the girl to a man whose status in society was equal to his own. It would have made no difference in the situation; whereas it would have saved the family from a great dishonour. The course, he is described to have followed in the first version, seems therefore to be an a solutely whimsical one.

The Raja at a late hour sanctioned the marriage. This was a fact. The poet who gave this version of the story was evidently not cognisant of the details.

Now, in some of the folk-tales current in the country, we have met with a similar incident of an autocrat's vow to give away his daughter to the first man he would see one particular morning. It therefore seems to me that this quite familiar episode that we find in our folk-tales was dovetailed into the story by the rural bard, who did not know fully well the circumstances which had led the Raja to sanction the marriage of his daughter with Madan. Up to the Raja's return home in a highly distracted state of mind, the poet gave a true and well authenticated story. No doubt that the events happened exactly as they are found described in the ballad. But, as I have already mentioned elsewhere, the ballad-mongers had a great tendency to mix up facts with folk-tales, in order to capture the imagination of the rural people most effectively. The last episode in the first version is introduced with the object of heightening the charm of the narrative by means of a familiar folk-tale which had already an appeal for the people.

But, the second version, which begins from Canto IV, is an obvious exposition of the real facts of the case.

The situation of the Raja was briefly this. He was bound to carry out the orders of the Nawab, as a feudatory chief under him; but his risk either way was great, bringing in a complication of puzzling circumstances. If he disobeyed the Sultan it would mean the loss of his life and property. On the other hand, for a Hindu to give away his daughter to the harem of a Muhammadan is even worse than death. By doing so he would forfeit all claims to remain a Hindu. His own kith and kin would give him up altogether, however great he might be in wealth and power.

What was he to do under the circumstances? It would not at all save the situation if he gave away his daughter to a suitable bride-groom; it would complicate it the more. The Nawab's wrath would not only fall on him but on the bride-groom also, and they would both be treated like the worst of criminals.

At this juncture, the queen came to the rescue with a shrewd plan which showed the woman's keener common sense.

In the mid-night she called to her presence one of the young servants of the palace named Madan. This lad was not only exceedingly handsome in appearance but a talented youth of tried integrity of character. The queen at her great crisis offered him the hands of her daughter privately without caring for his low status in society.

No one knew it, not even the boatman Káná-Chaitá on whom her strict order was to land the couple at the first place he would reach at day-break, after having rowed the boat as fast as he could with his oarsmen during the hours of the night. He was not to question as to who they were, nor have any chance of seeing their face as he was to leave them before it was dawn and row his boat back homewards.

The disappearance of the princess with a young servant from the palace naturally gave rise to a great scandal, but all the same, it saved the Raja from a great danger. Possibly, he knew nothing of it as the whole thing was planned and carried out by the queen very privately. The anger, chagrin and disappointment he felt at this abduction of his daughter were all *bona fide*, and the Nawab instead of getting angry with him probably felt a sympathy in his distress. Thus a great crisis was averted by this cunning device of the queen.

Now the pursuit of the unhappy pair by the Raja's people continued for a long time after their flight. For the Raja naturally felt a desire to punish the culprit. After some time the young man Madan was arrested one day, and the news of his arrest reached Rupavati who hastened to the palace to rescue her husband from the hands of the infuriated Raja. In the meantime, it may be easily surmised, the Nawab's anger was abated. For the fancy of an autocrat for a fair girl and the measures adopted for securing her for his harem, never continued long. It was always a passing whim with these men.

When thus the Nawab had ceased taking any interest in the affair, our hero's case came up for trial before the

Raja. It was at this time that he was apprised of the real circumstances and for the first time learnt that his own queen had given Rupavati in marriage to Madan.

Then he himself formally sanctioned the marriage, and by raising his son-in-law to the rank of a Zaminder, did his best to remove the stigma which had attached to his family owing to the alleged abduction of the girl. But as that son-in-law belonged to a lower caste, the tongue of scandal has not yet been silenced after the lapse of more than two centuries.

What we have had occasion to notice in similar ballads again and again, forms also the most prominent and noteworthy point in this one, *viz.*, the womanly virtues and devotion of the heroine. Unfailingly these women always stand out as the very personifications of all that is lovely and noble in the softer sex. The character of Madan is brought out in bold lines. He is not a weakling as sometimes we find the heroes in the other ballads to be. Listen to his first words to Rupavati. He never forgets the difference between his position and that of his wife,—given him by a mere chance. How tenderly and tremulously does he approach her with sweet words of consolation, yet all the time alluding to his own low social status in terms of extreme humility! The pathos which Rupavati's parting with him gives rise to has a tender appeal and the whole thing is very poetically put. Her determined attitude to rescue her husband in the hour of danger invests her character with a grandeur, in which we find an instance of sweetness mingled with nobility, and devotedness intensified by the most humiliating distresses. The poem which I have divided into seven cantos contains 493 lines. The reason why the author appears incognito is obvious.

DINESH CHANDRA SEN.

7, Biswakosh Lane,
Bagbazar, Calcutta, the 20th May, 1923.

RUPAVATI

I

In the town of Rampur reigned a prince named Rajchandra on the banks of the Phuleshwari; he had built there a spacious bungalow with twelve gate-ways. The income from his estates was several lakh a year, and he had stables full of elephants and horses. He had countless soldiers, besides a good many officers employed to collect rents. The drummers and tabor-players dwelt in his town in plenty, and the Nahabat orchestra played their music every morning rousing the Raja from his sleep.

One day he held his *durbar* as usual; his officers were all present and he expressed to them his wish to pay his respects to the Nawab of Bengal who was his feudal lord. He ordered the court-astrologer to find out an auspicious day. The latter settled the day and hour which would come eight days after; and the Raja made preparations to start at the auspicious hour. Káná Chaitá and Ubhutiá, two brothers, took charge of the Raja's pinnace. There were sixteen oarsmen and besides a splendid sail to increase the speed of the boat. The Raja filled it with many valuable goods. He took with him hair-combs and fans made of mica and many other indigenous articles such as mats made of ivory called the *sital-páti*, strings of large pearls, etc.—all to be presented to the Nawab. Besides he took Rupees Ten Thousand to be paid as his Nazar. A band of musicians and singers accompanied him.

The Raja, on the eve of his departure, bade farewell to his queen leaving his only daughter in her charge with many a word of good advice. He said good-bye to the citizens assembled, and performing some acts of religious merit such as giving away sums in charity and for religious purposes, started in his boat, which ran against the tide swiftly, aided by the favourable wind. He was delighted with the sight of the villages on both sides of the river, and having travelled the course of the Phuleshwari came to the mouth of the Narsunda. He passed through that river and entered another which was called the Ghoráutrá. Having passed along this river also, he reached the noble stream of the Meghná. The waves there were in a state of chaotic dance, foaming, as it were, in great fury, the banks at intervals breaking down dashed by the waves with a crash. Three months did the Raja pass in the bed of waters and in the fourth he arrived at the Nawab's city.

His men took the presents to the Durbar. The artistic hair-combs of mica and the ivory mats which the Raja had brought with him, were unknown in the city and the Nawab prized them very much. He was also pleased to receive the sum of Rupees Ten Thousand from the Raja and ordered fine quarters for his stay in his city. There the Raja lived happily for some time. Ll. 1-44.

II

Thus passed one—two—three months and more, till one full year rolled on. Another year passed and the Raja still did not return home. But when the third year also passed away, the queen got alarmed. She dreamt many bad dreams. By this time her daughter had grown up and completed her fourteenth year. She was yet unmarried. The neighbours shook their heads and whispered amongst themselves disapproving this delay, and it well-nigh became a matter of their grave and serious talk. The queen heard all this. The girl had reached her youth and yet there was no near prospect of her marriage. The queen was distracted with anxiety on the score of her daughter and passed her nights and days unhappily.

Then after much thought she sent a letter to the Raja. In this she first paid her respects to him and then informed him of the affairs of his State as they stood, and finished her letter with these concluding words:—" Three years you have lived away from us. All this time you have not cared to know how your daughter is faring. She has just stepped into her youth, and the neighbours whisper a lot of things. How can I, being her mother, bear all these? If a daughter is kept unmarried when she attains her puberty, all the religious merits of her parents go for naught. When this letter will reach you, tarry not a moment but come home at once."

After having written this letter, she trusted it to a servant and sent him to Murshidabad.

An astrologer came with his old books and took great pains to calculate the luck of the young maiden. He expressed his wisdom in these words " She is beautiful as a fairy or a nymph. Words fall short in my attempts to give an idea of the great fortune in store for her. She is sure to be married to a prince and become his chief queen." Another astrologer delivered himself thus, " Her manners are pleasing to the eyes. This is indeed a good sign. Her fine eye-brows are distinct, and her hair long and flowing, her forehead broad and her teeth are like a string of pearls. I do predict that a merchant from the south will marry her, and her feet will be washed by a hundred slaves."

Another astrologer said, " She has all the signs of a lucky girl. Her feet are like lotus-buds. When she walks, her foot-steps leave distinct marks on the ground and there is no hollow in the sole of her feet. Her bride-groom will come from the north. Her signs are all very favourable and I predict that her status will be nothing short of a queen's."

Yet another who predicted after closely examining her palms, " Sure as I live, this girl will be married to a prince. How beautiful is her face! it is more beautiful than a water-lily; her eyes are playful as Khanjan's; there is a glow of red on her cheeks, and her colour is like that of the moon-beams.

There is no bad sign about her—none that I can detect. I do predict that she will live to be the mother of seven sons and that she will be a queen."

Then last came a prophet who predicted, "The eyes of the girl are dark and pleasing. She will be a fortunate lady. Indeed, she will be a queen. But there is a slight flaw in her luck, this is the *gara dosh.* It can however, be easily rectified now. Bring a pair of silken clothes and some banana fruits. Fill a plate with thickened milk, butter and rice. With these feed twelve Brahmins. The little flaw in her luck will be removed. She will have to take a bath in the holy waters brought from the shrines. This should be done in my presence. I assure you if I perform this ceremony to-day, all evil influences of the planets will pass away, and she is sure to be married to-morrow."

The queen did all this in a devout spirit of faith.

Ll. 1-66.

III

The Raja has come back to his city after his rather long stay abroad, avowedly with the object of getting his daughter married.

He looks pale and care-worn. He does not perform the usual duties of his State and he is indifferent to his exalted rank. He lies down in his couch the live-long day but scarcely shuts his eyes to sleep. On his bed he is restless; he often rises from it and paces the floor with slow steps. He is sometimes heard to say in a low voice. "Alas, alas!"

The queen marks this and asks of him, "What is the matter with you, my lord? The fine betels prepared with my own hands and scented with *chuá* lie untouched in the betel-box and I find you sleepless in your bed. Rice and curry are served in the plate but you do not touch them. Indeed, you do not seem to relish any food. Your daughter was dear to you as life, but what is the matter that you never greet her with sweet words? It appears that for some unknown reason this palace has grown bitter to you as poison. Myself and our darling child have, for some unknown offence, lost your favour. You seem to be indifferent even to the all-engrossing question of her marriage. I feel so aggrieved at your conduct that at times I wish to commit suicide."

The-Raja—"Bear out with me, dear queen, for a little while, as I disclose matters to you. I am as if fallen into a sea. My ribs seem to be eaten up by crocodiles. I am in a jungle where a hundred tigers are tearing my body to pieces. It seems that an arrow has pierced deep into my heart.

"What did you do, oh queen! In an evil hour did you write the letter to me! I took the letter to the Nawab to let him know how urgently I was required at home and sought permission to return. He read the letter containing the news that my daughter has stepped into youth. He said, 'I have heard, oh Raja, that your daughter is very beautiful. Why not marry her to me and enjoy all the honour of this high connection! I will shower titles on you and in the *durbar* you will receive salutes from me as my esteemed relation. In all haste therefore, go to your city. Meantime, I shall be making preparations here for the marriage.'

"Oh queen my caste, my religion are thus all going to be destroyed! What is the good of dragging this miserable life? I care not for my State now. Let us, dear queen, go together, away—far away to a forest. Now hear what I have resolved to do. The first man whom I shall see rising from my bed to-morrow morning, to him will I give away my daughter. A pariah, a Dom or even one of a lower caste, if there be any, whoever he may be I shall make no distinction between caste and caste. Let him only be a Hindu and I shall offer my daughter to him. But to a Muhammadan, it is impossible—never! You see, dear queen, this Raj is now my gall and wormwood. Sometimes I feel inclined to drown myself into the river tying a pitcher to my neck with a rope. You speak of poison—the poison that is consuming me cannot be removed even by Dhanwantari—the physician of the gods."

The First Version.

The queen, as she heard this, became sorely troubled in her heart and thus reflected with sorrow, "If this night passes away it will be ruin to us. I pray to God that this night may last for ever and that the sun may never rise to expose us to lasting shame and infamy."

There was a young lad in the palace who held the position of *Baksi*. His name was Madan and he belonged not to a quite high family. He used to make small purchases from the market for the palace and was always ready at call. He had a handsome appearance; he looked quiet and lovely like the morning star. The lad had a free access into the inner apartments of the palace. His colour was bright like molten gold. The queen sent for him and when he appeared near her, she said, "Do not be frightened, dear child, I take you as my son and shall frankly tell you all." And here she related to him the whole story of the Raja's cruel resolve and ended her short speech thus. "Now listen to me Madan. At the dawn of the day to-morrow, stay near the door-way of our sleeping chamber. Wait there with a *silim* of tobacco for the Raja. Let that be your pretext. Remain standing at the gate-way and do not fail."

He did not pause for a moment over this worderful request. He did not care to know whether it was east, west or north to which he was going, but at once agreed to the queen's command.

The queen retired to her bed-room, and Madan came at the dawn of day near the gateway as directed.

Dark clouds lay scattered all over the sky and the red sun was just peeping through the eastern horizon. The Nahabat orchestra had just begun to play at the music-hall. The Raja left his couch and the queen opened the door for him. He came out of his room and glancing behind saw the lad waiting with a *hooká* in his hand. The Raja sat on a wooden seat carved on all sides with floral designs. Before it lay a golden cup of cold water. He washed his hands and face with it and felt refreshed. He then asked Madan, "What makes you come here near my sleeping-room at such an hour?" He saluted and replied, "I am your Highness' slave and am always ready to carry out your orders. I have free access to the inner appartments; for twelve years I have been at this palace, my lord, carrying out your commands. I am perfectly pleased with the kindness and indulgence with which I am treated here."

The Rajá asked him many a question as to who his parents were and what country he came from; when he got all information, the Raja gave orders for the marriage. An auspicious day was fixed and at an auspicious moment his daughter was given in marriage to Madan. A very rich dowry was given together with the grant of a whole village as a present to Rupavati. Ll. 1-90.

A Second Version.

IV

The Raja said, "Dear queen, let us decide our course, if we do not send our daughter to the Nawab, our *ráj* will be lost; that is sure. Take my word, oh queen, I will destroy my city with my own hands and its ruins I will throw into the river. The Pathan soldiers will come and take me to Murshidábád bound hand and foot. For this daughter's sake, we are in this sorry plight to day. She is like a dagger pierced through my heart. Alas, my caste and religion are all going to be destroyed, and I am approaching fast a miserable end. The time has been fixed within which she must be sent and what am I to do now? Shall I poison her or burn her alive? To what country can I go to escape this dire mishap? Make preparations, oh queen, to send her away at once, wherever you like. For myself, I have resolved to drown myself into the river."

When the queen heard what the Raja said, she at once decided her course.

She had a page named Madan—a very handsome young man. His duty was to gather flowers for the temple and carry out her wishes in small matters. A quiet submissive boy he was, always ready at call. He looked like the morning star, pleasing to the eyes. The queen did not care to consider the question of caste or family status. She resolved to abandon all affection for her dear daughter. Rupavati knew nothing of what had happened. In the hours of midnight the queen paid a visit to her chamber privately. There she slept radiant like the moon. Her beautiful form caused to-day only a deep pain in the mother's heart. "Ah! she is my pet bird, dear as a rib of my heart! How can I think of sending her away from this golden cage of affection in which I have reared her up?"—she thought. And then she called out, "Now arise, my darling, and see your unfortunate mother standing near your bed. Awake, dear one, and see; the whole city is, as it were, on fire and burning for your sake. For you, your dear father has resolved to drown himself in the river. For you, we are going away to some forests to live like exiles."

Rupavati was dreaming at the time as if the whole city was in mourning. She awoke with a start and saw her mother wiping away her tears with the edge of her *sadi*. She said, "What is it, mother, that you are crying for? I cannot bear this sight. What have I done to hurt your feelings thus?"

" No offence, dear daughter, have you committed "—said the unfortunate mother. " Providence has been hostile to us and cut off all our hopes ; oh cruel Providence, how couldst thou cut off the tree under whose shadow I came seeking shade ! Alas, never more shall I have the fortune, oh dear girl, of seeing your moon-like face. Never more shall I be allowed to hear that sweet address 'mama' from your lips ! Oh my pet bird, you are going to fly away cutting off for ever the chain of affection which binds you here." Ll. 1-48.

V

No bridal song was sung, no ceremony took place. The ladies of the house did not cry 'Victory and Joy' at the auspicious moment, nor uttered their blessings. No one came to anoint the bride with turmeric and sweet scents. The mother did not go to the good neighbours, seeking blessings for the child, and the ladies of the house did not assemble together by the side of the tank to fill pitchers for the sacred ceremony, singing in chorus as customary.

The mother's heart secretly bled. The night was dark and still and from the sky sparkled a few stars. Madan came at that hour and waited at the gate-way. In deep shame Rupavati had not the power to arrange her long flowing hair which fell in curls round her face. In all hurry she donned a bridal dress. No priest came to perform the usual rites. In that solemn hour of night the mother offered her child to the hands of Madan. She took the girl's hands and placed them on Madan's and there was none to witness it. The hall did not resound with the glee voices of women wishing good for the couple. Silent grief surged in the mother's heart in the place of festive songs in the great hall of the Raja.

The sun and the moon she called to witness as she offered Rupavati to the youth Madan.

The queen—" Now, Madan, a word have I to say to you. I have now offered you my darling daughter, she is the one solitary lamp of the house—my only child—I am giving her to you and what words are there which can adequately express my feelings at this hour ! I have taken out, it seems to me, a rib from my side to offer you. I have broken the golden cage with my own hands to offer you the pet bird I have adored and loved all these years ! Whether it be your lot to live in a city or wander in woods, bear one word of mine in mind. Do not give any pain to the heart of this girl. As you are now her lord, it is fully in your power to make her happy or miserable. None is there in this world to look after this unfortunate girl except you."

The mother and the daughter wept. On the boughs of trees sat the mute birds, as if struck dumb by grief, and the wind rustled through leaves with a moaning sound.

In that depth of night the queen had brought the boatman to the palace, and no one amongst the citizens had known of this. The boatman Chaitā was blind of one eye but he was an adept in his profession. The queen presented him a purse. Madan came to the boat with his new bride Rupavati. The queen bade them farewell and retired to her chamber.

The boat went like a shooting star, rowed by expert hands and with her sails all unfurled. She passed through thirteen *báks* (bends) of the river, and when the fourteenth *bák* was half-completed, they saw the sun rising in the east. The boatman Chaitā stopped there and said, " Passengers, whoever you may be, it is the order of the queen that as soon as the night will be over you are to leave my boat."

There was no village or town in the neighbourhood. The turbulent waves danced furiously in the river. The growls of tigers and bears were heard from the jungles on the bank, and in the waters the crocodiles roamed in quest of prey. There Chaitá left the couple as exiles in the forest, and rowed his boat homewards.

"Oh the pleasure-boat of my father's palace," said the girl to herself, "you too are going to leave me! Tell my mother, I pray you, the news of her unfortunate daughter, she has been left in the forest as an exile by the boatmen. By my life, tell my father that I am left in this jungle without any means of preserving life."

Swiftly did the boat go out of sight. Like a wild deer Rupavati wandered about in the forest. "Hear me, oh woodland," she said weeping, "carry the message to my mother that her daughter is going to be devoured by hungry tigers."

Madan—"Do not cry, oh maiden, what does it avail to sorrow over your lot? It is God's decree, who can alter his dispensation? A serpent has bitten on the head. The poison is already in the brain. What will the physician do at such a stage? For some evil we did in our past life, are we here exiled to the forest!

"You are, oh maiden, like a sacred offering to the gods,—a dog am I who have ventured to touch it. Is it for this that you are crying? I am hateful as a Pariah, and you are holy as the stream of the Ganges. But, by my life, I assure you, I will not come too near nor dare touch your feet. Here am I to gather fruits from the forest for you when you will be hungry, and I will serve you with water when you will suffer from thirst. The tender leaves of trees will I spread here, to make a bed for you. The darling of the Raja are you, oh maiden, unaccustomed to hardships! How alas! will you pass the term of your exile in the forest all alone? What a pity, that for your companion you have one who is no better than a slave to you!"

When she heard this she wept and said, "I will tell you frankly, dear lord of my heart, my mother has offered me unto you. Though I may live in these woods, I know that I am in the custody of my husband. There is none else for whom I would care in this world. Ah me! Ill luck has brought on us all these misfortunes. How grieved am I that it is for me that you too are an exile in this forest." Ll. 1-76.

VI

Kángáliá and Jangaliá are two brothers. Their trade is to catch fish with nets. That is their only employment and source of income. They carry baskets tied to their waists and with nets in hands wander about in mornings and afternoons in quest of fish by the river-side.

While journeying in this way they happened to meet Rupavati. The two brothers had three wives. But not one of them had borne them a child. The eldest of them was Punái by name. She was Kángáliá's wife.

Kángáliá returning home, called aloud, "Come out Punái and see." Punai came out and looked around.

She saw a stranger and a maiden beautiful as a nymph. She looked like the Goddess of Fortune herself.

Kángália said, "I dragged my net through the waters from morn to eve but not even a lobster could I catch in the river. But curiously this little Goddess of Fortune I picked up from the wayside. Take her to the house with care and look after her comforts."

Punái had neither son nor daughter as already stated. She was always unhappy for this. She was right glad to have the fair maiden for her daughter.

"Whose daughter are you, child? Where is your home and who is this young man with you?" And a hundred questions more she asked affectionately.

"No mother—no father have I, nor a brother even. Like a weed drifted by current I wander about as luck would lead me. My evil stars have sent me here as an exile. I was passing my day in great sorrow and helplessness. It is a good chance that we have met you; you are a mother unto me. I crave a little shelter at your feet."

Without children in the house, the world was a void to Punai. But by the grace of God she got a son and a daughter now, and she considered it as her greatest fortune on the earth. Ll. 1-32.

The Fishermen's Prize

" While journeying in this way they happened to meet Rupavati."

Rupavati, p. 198

VII

Madan

"Oh my dearest! I beg leave of you for a fortnight. I lived at your father's palace continually for six years last time and did not take any notice of my parents all this period. I do not know if they are alive or dead. I intend to pay a visit to my home for seeing them once. For a short time I wish to be absent from here with your permission."

* * * * *

Rupavati

"Oh my little bee! The night passes away and the dawn approaches fast! Black is your colour, but your eyes gleam like silver! Who is the god that has made you, my little fly, to hover about in the woods! Will you, oh dear one, do me one favour? Fly where my love is and get some tidings of him. He went away promising a speedy return, taking leave for a fortnight from me. The moon had faded away at the time but now, look to the sky, she has appeared again with her round form and yet he has not come back to me! The fortnight is gone and another is drawing to its end;—has he forgotten me, unfortunate as I am? I cast my eager glances towards the path morn and eve in vain hope! A mist of tears, like cobweb, covers both my eyes in the dark. Many a garland of flowers did I weave for you, my love, and they have all faded away! Alas my love! Why are you absent leaving my expectant youth to pine from day to day! My night I pass in alternate hopes and despairs and the day lingers on and passes too, keeping me in vain expectations. Here do I sit the live-long day looking to the path with unweary eyes which grow dim with dust."

Thus did the girl mourn in solitude. Now listen to what came next.

The Raja, meantime, announced thus by a beat of drum in the city and in the markets :—

"Whoever will find out my enemy who has brought on this disgrace to my family and exposed it to scandal, lowering my caste, will be suitably rewarded ; and the miscreant will be sacrificed at the altar of Kali."

Some one whispered this message to Rupavati.

"Your husband has been arrested. No way there is for him to escape death."

A thunder-bolt, as it were, fell on Rupavati's head and her heart got pierced through as if by a shaft.

"Oh my foster-mother Punai ! allow me to depart hence.

"What have I heard—Oh what a dire news ? Allow me to depart hence.

"I was born in a palace. My ill luck however has brought on all these ills. Alas ! whom shall I accuse ? Allow me to depart hence, oh my dear foster-mother !

"In the depth of night did my mother offer me to him. Undecided as to my course and distressed with thoughts did I leave the house in that dark hour of the night ! Allow me, oh my foster-mother, to depart hence.

"The noble mansion of my father I left and left my hundred servants and maids. With my love as my sole companion I turned an exile in this forest. Allow me, oh my foster-mother, to depart hence.

"By the grace of God I met one who became my foster-father, and for a short time there appeared a silver lining in my life of sorrow. Allow me to depart.

"I forgot my father, my mother and all. It was written in my forehead that I would give up all who are near and dear to me. Alas ! how could I avoid doing so ! Allow me to depart.

"Oh pity ! not once did I with my own hands prepare scented betels to offer my love ! Nor by lamp light fed with butter, did I but once fix my gaze on his moon-like face. Allow me to depart.

"With ivory mats spread on the floor not once did I rest by his side, pleased with his company. Allow me to depart.

"Not for a short while did we together live as husband and wife in the house. Ill luck pursues us and blasts away all hopes that we plan. Allow me to depart.

"For shame I did not once hang a garland of flowers on his neck nor did cook for him meals of sweet *sali* rice and sit by his side to see him eat! Allow me to depart, oh my dear foster-mother."

Punái tried her utmost to console her, but all in vain.

Rupavati.—"Here do I fall at your feet, good mother, and make this earnest request. Kindly take me where he may be now. Where he is, thither will I go. I will be his companion in death. Without him I shall not—I cannot live.

"How unfortunate am I that we were not spared even for a few days to live happily as husband and wife. My father is now my enemy—it is he that has caused me all this pain. My parents are behaving as if they are nobody to me! Here will I poison myself, if you do not take me to my husband. I will drown myself or cut my own throat with a knife. None, I tell you, will be able to stop me."

Punai tried her utmost to soothe her unquiet mind, but it was so difficult! With sweet words of hope and consolation, however, she kept the sorrowing one in the house for that night.

Early next morning Punai ordered Jangáliá to make his boat ready. He brought it to the *ghat.* Punai with the crying maiden started for the city of the Raja.

He was then holding the Durbar. Punai entered the Audience Hall and stood a supplicant The two brothers Kángáliá and Jangáliá stood behind her.

Punai with folded hands saluted the God Dharma and next paid respects to the Raja and addressed him thus :

"I have a complaint to make to Your Highness. Where is it that you have kept my son-in-lâw as prisoner? And why is it so? For what fault, may I ask Your Highness, have you punished him thus?"

The courtiers ordered her to stop and asked her who that son-in-law was about whom she was speaking.

Punai could not resist her tears but began to cry helplessly. Then with tears in her voice she said:

"She is a very unfortunate girl, my heart breaks in giving an account of my daughter.

"Oh esteemed Raja, where was it heard, that one ever shot his pet bird with his own hands or one set fire to the house he had himself built, or cut the plants he had himself planted with care? Where was it ever heard that one kicked and broke the sacred cup preserved in the temple of gods.

"The dark midnight hours witnessed it, when your queen offered the hands of her girl to some one. That one is your son-in-law. Is he not deserving of an affectionate tenderness? Like a son he is to you. What fault can there be on the part of your daughter and the son-in-law in the matter?

"Losing her husband she is frantic with grief. She has resolved to die, she was going to drown herself; oh, how difficult has it been for us to prevent your mad daughter from committing suicide!

"Listen to me, oh my lord, go to the prison yourself and release him at once with your own hands. Why did you allow this marriage if you would sentence him to death afterwards? She was exiled to the forests and lived with poor people, not her kith or kin. Alas, humble though we are, we cannot conceive, how has it been possible for Your Highness to treat your own children in this way!"

Punai abused the Raja in an outspoken way, while tears still flowed down her cheeks; and the courtiers all heard her words silently. The Raja remembered the sweet face of his daughter and his heart melted into a hundred pities—tears began to fall from his eyes. The courtiers took the liberty of explaining the matter to His Highness. And the Raja was persuaded to give orders for their formal marriage.

Madan was released from the prison. Horses, elephants, landed estates and palatial buildings were given him as dowry. The Raja elected the pair as heirs to his own palace and property. A large building was raised with twelve gate-ways for their temporary residence in his city.

After a while Madan started for his own home with Rupavati as his bride.

Ll. 1-137.

KANKA AND LILA

PREFACE

Kanka and Lila, as the colophons in the present text will shew, was written by four poets, *viz.*, Raghusut, Damodar, Nayan Chand Ghosh and Srinath Baniya. Raghusut lived about 250 years ago. One of his descendants, Shibu Gayen, whose memory was a storehouse of this class of songs, died recently. Raghusut seems to me to be the best of the four poets. It is he who wrote many a picturesque and exquisite line in the *baramashi*, such as "হাতেতে সোণার ঝারি বর্ষা নেমে আসে" and "শাউনিয়া ধারা শিরে বজ্র ধরি মাথে। 'বউ কথা কও' বলি কাঁদে পথে পথে" (Canto 18, Ll. 47, 77, 78). The poet was an inhabitant of the village Āwazia under the Police station of Kendua and four miles to the south-east of Biprapur (Bipra barga), where the hero of the poem Kanka was born. Raghusut's descendants were formerly professional singers of *baramashi* songs, and for their proficiency in this calling, received from time to time grants of rent-free lands from the well-known zemindars of Gauripur. Shibu Gayen, son of Rammohan Gayen and a remote descendant of Raghusut, was a singer of high order, and Chandra Kumar says that many of the *bar mashi* songs, unmatched for poetry and pathos, were lost to Mymensing, on the day when he was cremated in the outskirts of the village Awazia about 20 years ago. They are *patnis* or boatmen by caste, the title 'Gayen' suffixed to their names means 'singer' whose profession they have adopted.

By far the greatest portion of this ballad was written by Raghusut and Damodar. The names of Nayan Chand and Srinath Baniya occur only in a few colophons.

This ballad has been influenced by Sanskrit more than many others of this class of songs. The poet Nayan Chand particularly introduces Sanskrit similes in the description of a beauty and proceeds in many passages on the lines of classic writers. It is, however, curious to note that in the poem of Jay Chandra and Chandravati, written by this poet, the style seems to be quite free from all Sanskritic influence and bears a flavour of rural sweetness and simplicity. The poet Srinath Baniya is guilty of a little sensuousness which we would not have noticed at all, but for the fact that almost all the rest of these ballads elevate us by their severely pure moral tone and high ethical dignity. We do not mean to say that this ballad is strikingly erotic or repelling to our æsthetic taste, but contrasted with the stiff air and dignified style of the other love-tales of this kind, this one seems to have occasionally been written in a somewhat light vein, and the subtleties of metaphysical expressions indulged in by Nayan Ghosh, have ill suited the atmosphere of these popular tales, the essential and characteristic beauty of which is simplicity and a plain unadorned language.

The story is told with lively enthusiasm and the characters are all well-conceived and developed. In most of the other ballads collected from Mymensing, the heroine is by far the most striking character. All other figures appear like cliffs and summits of a lesser height and contribute chiefly to forming a background from which she is shown with advantage. But here though Lila the maid, Lila the lover and Lila the heroine is the most charming of the lot, the character of Garga and that of Kanka are no negligible factors.

The pathos, as in the other ballads, centres towards the end upon the heroine who reminds us of F. D. Hemans' line "A rose's brief but life of joy, such unto *her* was given." The description of the months, the *baramashi*, is full of noble poetry, the beauty of which, I must confess, has been ill-preserved in my poor translation.

It is a historical ballad ; the characters were all living men and women. Kanka is a well-known name in the literary history of Mymensing. His "Malayar *Baramashi*" is still sung by the peasants of the eastern part of the District. I have been able to recover scraps only from this song. But Chandra Kumar assures me that he will ere long secure the entire poem for me. We have, however, secured the whole of Kanka's Vidya Sundara—the first of its kind in Bengali. Kanka was born, as I have already stated, at Bipragram (Bipra barga) on the Raji. There is some trace of the village now. But the Ráji (Rájeshwari) which used to flow down the village has slightly altered her course. It now runs along the outskirts of Kendua.

From a reference given in the poem itself and from the tradition current in the locality we surmise that Kanka was a contemporary of Chaitanya. In one place of the song we find the couplet (Canto 20, Ll. 65-66) "বিদায় হইয়া কঙ্ক আমাদের স্থানে। সংসার ত্যজিয়া যায় গৌর অন্বেষণে।" and in another place (Canto 20, Ll. 19-20) we have "যে দেশে বাজিছে গৌরের চরণ নুপূর। সেই পথ ধরি তোমরা যাও তত দূর।" Of course we do not urge that although the ballad as a whole is based on historical facts, the details are to be accepted as true in every case. But here lies the evidence for what it is worth, and the tradition current in the country substantiates it. If Kanka was a contemporary of Chaitanya, he flourished in the sixteenth century and lived a little before the time when Bangshi Das and his gifted daughter Chandravati wrote the Manasar Bhasan and other poems.

I believe that a ballad describing the love of Kanka and Lila was composed immediately after the tragic incidents had taken place. The present one is, it seems to me, a revised version of the old story partly embellished by later writers on a classical model. The *tripadi* metre which we find in the poem seems to be an innovation, for in very few cases of these indigenous songs of Mymensing do we come across this metre. The rustic poets generally preferred the *payár* and it was the scholarly poets only who occasionally took recourse to *tripadi* in order to introduce pathetic incidents.

We have found instances of *tripadi* occurring in Bangshi Das's Manashar Bhasan. Bangshi was a great Sanskrit scholar.

There are some other versions of the poem of Lila and Kanka extant in Mymensing, in which the last scene in the life of the unfortunate heroine is differently put. One poet describes Lila as having hung herself on the bough of a *hizal* tree, unable to bear her grief. Another version says that Lila did not actually die though she was on the point of death, but lived to be once more restored to Kanka. Tragic ends became out of fashion with the poets of Brahminic Renaissance, and hence some of the later poets have yielded to the taste of the age by altering the situation described in the last canto. We have found similar manipulations taken recourse to in regard to some Rajput ballads.

Before I conclude I must say a word more about Kanka the poet, who figures in the present poem, as the hero of a love-tale. Most of the facts of his early life as found in this ballad are given in an outline in the Introduction, written by himself, to his famous poem the Vidya Sundara. This work is called "Satya Pirer Kathá" just as Bharat Chandra's poem is called "Annada Mangal." We find reference to this poem of "Satya Pirer Katha" in the present ballad and learn from it that it was written at the command of a Pir who had made a mosque at Bipragram and lived there for some time. Thanks to the unflagging zeal of Chanda Kumar, the whole of this poem on Satyapir "By Kanka, the poet" has been recovered. Close to Bipragram, there is a small marsh called Dhaleshwari. On one of its sides is a pastoral field named Panch Pirer Kánda; the mosque of the Pir was evidently built on this plot of land. A stone held sacred by the local people still exists there and is called as "The Pir's stone."

For satisfying the curiosity of those readers who may be willing to know what the subject-matter of Kanka's Vidya Sundara is, I beg to subjoin herewith a short summary of the poem.

SATYA PIRER KATHA OR VIDYA-SUNDARA

By

KAVI KANKA.

Malyaban, the Raja of Eastern Districts of Bengal, considered himself very unfortunate for not having got an issue, inspite of his great wealth and power. He performed the Vedic sacrifice of Putreshti, but it proved of no avail. Then he sought the help of the great sages who dwelt in the Naga hills and in the Udaygiri hills of Orissa. They performed many *jagnas*, and much *ghee* and wood were burnt, but no good came out of the vaunts of the sages. The Raja could not get any child by their help. Then the Raja, in order to while away his mind by diversion, went a-hunting in the forest and met there a Mohamedan Pir who was no other than Satya Pir himself. By his blessings he chanced to see a wonderfully handsome baby lying in a helpless condition in the forest. He brought it home and offered it to the chief queen. She was pleased with the baby, but said that she could not accept it, as there was no knowing how grieved its parents were having lost their little treasure. The Raja said that the baby was a gift from a great Pir, so she should feel no hesitancy in accepting it. But as the Queen would not listen to the Raja's words but insisted on her refusal, it was announced throughout the whole land that a little baby was found in a forest; if any one claimed it and could prove his claim, the baby would be made over to him. For many a day the drum beat announcing the notice, but none came forward to claim the little thing. The Queen was satisfied that she could now accept the baby without a sting of conscience.

The baby grew in time to be the handsomest and the most accomplished prince on earth. But the Raja, who had promised to offer his Puja to the Pir on arriving at the city, forgot his promise, and as a consequence the Prince who had gone to hunt in the forest lost his way and got himself separated from his companions and his army. He did not return to the Palace to the great despair of his parents.

The Prince, parted from his people, slept under a tree, greatly fatigued, when some thieves ran away with his horse which was one of the noblest of its kind. The Pir appeared to him and gave direction as to the place where he could get the horse back. He accordingly travelled a good deal and at last reached the city of Champaka, mentioned by the Pir.

The name of the Prince was Sundara, and the Raja of Champaka had a daughter named Vidya. Sundara entered the garden of the Princess without knowing it to be so. He was very much fatigued by his worry and journey, and slept under a tree there. The mistress of the garden came there in the meantime and fell in love at first sight.

Though Sundara said that he was a mere gardener and that his caste was low, Vidya would by no means believe it and offered herself to him. Through the help of a flower-woman a meeting between them was brought about soon after, and Vidya and Sundara were married according to the Gandharva system. Since then they met every day. Sundara disguised himself as a woman and gave out that he was a niece of the flower-woman. In the meantime whispers were heard in the palace about this affair, and matters took a serious aspect. The Raja and his Queen came to know of it. At last the whole police force was engaged in searching out the youth who had hidden himself in a private place as soon as he had got news about the search. But he was caught at last and brought before the Raja, bound in chains. By the grace of the Pir and the testimony borne by several witnesses, Sundara however, established his innocence, and was released. His horse, which the thieves had sold to the Royal stable, was produced and it at once recognised its old master. Sundara's real account was now made known to the Raja, and the marriage of the prince and the princess took place again publicly. They spent some days in the city of Champaka, after which the Prince returned with his bride to his father's palace.

The Puja of the Pir became widely current in the country after this happy end.

From the above summary of the poem by Kanka, one may suppose that it is a piece of folk-lore pure and simple. But the details have been rendered so beautifully that the tale has transcended the limits of folk-lore and reached the domain of true poetry. It is writen in a simple and elegant style, and no indelicacy or bad taste mars the charm of the love-tale though the very names of the hero and the heroine inevitably bring in such associations, on account of the erotic treatment of the subject by some of the later poets.

The Satya Pir cult, which originated during the reign of Husen Saha in Bengal in the early part of the sixteenth century, was not accepted by the Hindus without some opposition. Here in this ballad itself we find that when the relation between the Hindus and Mahomedans in a particular locality became estranged, the former sometimes burnt the poems in honour of Satya Pir. Kanka was one of the earliest exponents of the Satya Pir-cult and composed the poem when he was scarcely above his teens.

I have surveyed the characters of the ballad in my introductory chapter. The feelings of Lila, I have therein stated, are complicated like those of Malancha-málá of the folk-lore. In the beginning Lila regarded Kanka as Anne did Enoch Arden; then Lila's feeling became sisterly and both felt the same filial affection for Garga, and as the intensity of this feeling increased it developed into a romantic passion without the least element of sensuousness. She was never ashamed of it, as in the white heat of her self-less devotion there was no fire of earthly passion. Her feelings are absolutely pure and innocent which are shown in contrast with the wiliness of the Brahmins, to which she, the child of Nature, eventually succumbed.

I have had to notice more than once one feature in connection with the language of these rural songs. In many places the rhyming is perfect though on account of a difference between the spoken forms of words and their recognised written forms the rhyming sometimes appears faulty. The word রোল for instance is pronounced as রুল in the current dialect of Mymensing. It has been therefore aptly used to rhyme with ফুল and মুকুল. The word চোর is pronounced as চুর, hence it is made to rhyme with words like সুর and দূর. Those who are unacquainted with these features of the spoken dialect of Eastern Bengal, may find fault with the rhyming of some of the verses. But it will not be fair to do so.

In conclusion I beg to add that there are three preliminary hymns attached to the text, *viz.*, by Damodar Das, Nayan Chand Ghosh, and by Shibu Gayen respectively. The hymns are more or less on the lines of that of Chandravati given in the beginning of "Malua." I have not translated them into English as they do not possess any poetical or historical value. Lila and Kanka is complete in 1,122 lines, divided into 23 cantos; there are besides 54 lines of the preliminary hymns in the beginning of the poem and 12 lines of verse containing a prayer of the minstrel for reward and blessings from his audience, given at the end of the ballad.

DINESH CHANDRA SEN.

7, BISHWAKOSH LANE,
Bagbazar, Calcutta, 31st August, 1923.

KANKA AND LILA

1. Birth of Kanka and Death of his Parents.

Chorus.—"Human life is a rare blessing, it may be that we may not have this human form in our next life."

At the village of Biprapur there was a poor Brahmin named Gunaraj who lived by begging. He begged from door to door and brought home in the evening what he got during the day. His wife Basumati was a virtuous woman devoted to him and known for her chaste and pure life. In course of time a son was born to the pair, and the mother gave him the name of Kanka. They were so poor that they found no means to bring the child up. The poet laments "Some have a son, but have no means to rear him up, while others cannot get one (who have plenty)." On an auspicious day a palm leaf was brought and the mother gave the baby the name of Kanka and duly recorded it on that leaf. When the baby was only six months old, its mother Basumati died. Gunaraj was in great distress. There was none to look after the baby when he went to beg. The Brahmin could not long bear his bereavement and worry. He too died a short while after. "Such is the cruel decree of fate," says the poet Nayan Chand.

Chorus.—"O mother! where hast thou gone leaving the child helpless in the ocean of life." Ll. 1-24.

2. He is taken care of by a Chandal.

No one amongst the Brahmins came forward to take the charge of the baby, as he was declared to be an ill-starred one. But a *Chandal* (the lowest caste amongst the Hindus) was moved with compassion and took the unclaimed child to his house. The name of this man was Murari and his wife was called Kaushalya. They became father and mother to the child who remembered no other. He was quite happy with his new parents. The poet Raghusut says "See the freaks of fate, a Brahmin's son thus becomes a *Chandal.*"

When Kanka grew to be a lad of five years, the Chandal, his foster-father, died of '*tirakha jar*' (fever of the nature of typhoid). The chaste wife abstained from all food and would not shut her eyes for grief for some nights. Within a short time she too left this world. Says the poet, "Wherever the lad found a temporary shelter, the ground proved slippery under his feet. How would he live now?"

There on the cremation ground of his deceased foster-father and mother, the lad lay like one dead, crying in utter helplessness. None was there to take him to a house, or feed him in that forlorn state. For two days he lay on the *shmashan* without food or drink. "But," says the poet, "who can kill one whom God will preserve?" Ll. 1-30.

3. Kanka gets a Shelter in the House of the Brahmin Garga.

Chorus.—"Alas! death will not come as a relief to me! It seems my life is a string of tears."

There was a great Brahmin scholar in the country, versed in the Vedas and known for his piety and spotless character. He was called Garga—the sage. One day he was returning home from the house of a disciple when he chanced to see the child rolling in the mud on the cremation ground, half-dead with hunger and fear. He instantly took him up by the hand, and with his sacred *namabalee* (*lit.*, a string of names—an outer garment in which the names of gods are inscribed) he wiped the dust and mud from the child's face and brought him to his home. His wife Gayatri Devi was right glad to have the child for she had no son. The orphan found a mother in her and the childless mother found a child in him. She fed him with butter and milk. She affectionately gave him the name 'Gopal' and showed great affection. The lad was appointed to tend a cow that belonged to the house. In the morning Kanka went to the field with the cow and when late in the afternoon he returned, Gayatri brought ripe bananas and thickened milk that she had kept stored for him and fed the lad with her own hands. His amiable nature and good manners pleased everybody. "His memory was so sharp," says the poet, "that though so young, he had already learnt many Sanskrit *slokes* from Garga."

The Brahmin Garga finding the lad exceptionally intelligent began to teach him Sanskrit when he reached his tenth year. In the mornings and nights the boy thus received his lessons from Garga, and in the noon time he tended the cow in the pastures of Bipragram. Ll. 1-24.

4. Disaster after Disaster.

But again happened a dire mishap to the lad. Gayatri Devi, Garga's wife, suddenly died of small-pox. Says the poet Raghusut, "The lord preserved his life only to afflict it with miseries one after another." Tigers and wild buffaloes would not kill him, even the witches of the forest did not end his days as they did of so many people. Like a weed carried by the tide, he wandered about helpless, having lost a mother, this third time. Now Garga had a daughter named Lila. She was only eight years old. She was in deep grief having lost her mother. But all the more she could now sympathise with the orphan Kanka. Says the poet, "Because of her own affliction, she could now truly feel the grief of Kanka." The two lived in the house like brother and sister. If the one wept, the other consoled. Lila would never touch her meal until Kanka had eaten. They wandered about the fields, pleased with each other's company. Lila did not like that Kanka should go to the fields in the sun for tending the cow. She could not bear to part with him even for a few hours. So long as the lad did not return she spent anxious hours in great restlessness. Sometimes tears would be seen flowing down her cheeks and at others she would wait at the gate wistfully looking towards the field. She had no mind in her household-work, which was often left unfinished. But when Kanka returned home with the cow, her face brightened with a smile and taking a fan adorned with mica in her hand there she would sit near him offering her kind services. Ll. 1-26.

5. Lila steps into her Youth.

Playing, laughing and talking all day long, thus did they pass their childhood. And now she stepped into the golden period of her youth. Like when the flood comes to a river in August, the banks cannot keep the rising water in check, the growing charms of Lila now overflowed, as it were, all physical bounds. Her glowing beauty was like the moonbeams of October, that penetrate into the depths of a river and shows its bottom. When she stood under a tree her beauty brightened the spreading shades below. If she touched the ripples of a river, it appeared as if moonbeams played on them. The merchants stopped their boats to have a sight of her face; and the silent wayfarer as he passed by, stopped to look at her and for a moment became transfixed to the spot. The curling hair sometimes hid and sometimes showed her face, like the clouds of a rainy night alternately covering and disclosing the moon. The flowers hid themselves under the leaves, smitten with shame at the sight of this glorious human flower. But unmindful of her beauty she cared not to bind her tresses nor did she care for her dress. "Whence has this mad overflow of youth come upon her?" asks the poet. Her motion was graceful like that of the water of a full pitcher, which waving to and fro in the carrier's arms, yet keeps to the brim and does not overflow. She was a thing of joy like a star that appears from the evening cloud, or a pomegranate flower gently touched by the wind.

Like a solitary flower in the forest did she bloom in this region. "It is youth," says Nayan Chand the poet, "which never comes before its time, nor can be stopped when it passes away." On the banks of the Rajeswari often did the maiden stand to look at the dark waves, but as often she saw herself mirrored in the transparent water, her new charms took her by surprise each time and she returned home with her pitcher abruptly lest they should take others also by surprise.

In the house of Garga Kanka was happy. The scholarly Brahmin had now given him a sound education. He was now versed in the Puranas and the Samhitas and had mastered rhetoric and several other branches of study. He had besides learnt a hundred ballads and songs known as *baramashis*. He sang them and played on his flute. The songs were mostly sung in the *bhatial* mode. The very leaves of the trees seemed to feel a thrill in response to his sweet voice and the waves of the river flowed in a contrary course to listen to it.

Often did the youth return from the meadows with his cow, and Lila stood gazing at the path to see him coming. She did not like that he would go to the meadows every day. She wiped the dust from his face and fanned him. She wept over the cruel signs of thorns in his feet. When he delayed in the fields she would murmur to herself, "How cruel is it to make your Lila wait alone in the house and weep!"

Behold, Suravi, the cow, is returning from the field. From far the music of his flute comes floating in the air. "You have come back fatigued, your hair has grown wet by the sweat." As she said this she entered her room to bring a fan. And Kanka spread a part of his cloth and lay down in the compound to rest. Ll. 1-88.

6. The Preacher of the Satya Pir Cult.

At this time there came a Mahomedan *pir* in that village. He built a mosque in its outskirts, and for the whole day sat under a fig tree. The whole space he cleared with care so that there was not one tuft of grass left. His fame soon spread far and wide. Everybody talked of the occult powers that he possessed. If a sick man called on him he would cure him at once by dust or some trifle touched by him. He read and spoke the innermost thoughts of a man before he opened his mouth. He took a little dust in his hand and out of it prepared sugar balls to the astonishment of the boys and girls who gathered round him. They greatly relished these presents from him. Hundreds of men and women came every day to pay him their respects. Whatever they wanted they miraculously got from this saint. Presents of rice, fruits and other delicious food, goats, chickens and fowls came in large quantities to his doors. Of these offerings, the *pir* did not touch a bit but freely destributed all amongst the poor.

Ll. 1-20.

7. Kanka meets the Pir.

The cow grazed at a distance and Kanka was playing on his flute sitting under a tree. The sound was so sweet that men and boys crowded there to hear his songs. The birds silently sat on the boughs of the near trees and would not move, charmed with them. The cuckoo ceased to sing listening to the flute, and youth seemed to return to old men at the sound. Women, who went to fetch water from the river, left their pitchers floating in the stream, and forgetful of them, stopped to hear the flute.

From where he played on the flute, the mosque of the *pir* was not far away. Every day the saint heard the sweet songs played on the flute by the young man, and he felt a great desire to see the singer. He sent a man and called Kanka to him one day. At his request Kanka played on his flute. The subject was Malayar *baramashi* of the lad's own composition.

The saintly person was so greatly moved by the flute-player's songs, that he shed tears over them. Both of them liked one another; the young man was drawn by the sermons of the *pir* and the latter by the youth's sweet songs. So every day the cow was left to graze in the pastures, and Kanka sat at the feet of the *pir* for hours together. The old man was pleased with the affability, intelligence and the accomplishments of the youth. His nature was so amiable that no one could help loving him. The *pir* wanted the youth to be near him always, and Kanka who was already attracted by the gracious words of the wise man, ere long became his disciple and was initiated into the esoteric creed of the fakir. He found the boy to be indeed a remarkable one; "Properly guided he would soon be able to arrive at the true knowledge of life and death." Says Damodar Das, the poet, "This boy is not an ordinary one. He is like a lily sprung from the mud. He will throw a lustre on the family in which he was born by his noble qualities." Ll. 1-40.

8. Kanka observes Strict Privacy.

The jeweller knows his stone and the goldsmith his gold. The saintly men can easily detect good qualities in others. The *pir* performed some miracles by his occult powers and Kanka's mind became filled with wonder. His admiration and love for him grew from day to day and at noon time he made it a point every day to sit at his feet to receive instructions. He touched his feet at the time of coming and going and showed him respects in other ways which a disciple only pays to his Guru.

But more than that, Kanka forgot the tenets of his own religion and violated the rules of caste. He ate at the plate from which the *pir* had taken his food. He submitted to initiation and elected the *pir* his *Guru*. This dire news nobody gave to Garga, for Kanka's connection with his Guru was so long kept strictly private. He took the *pir's* creed and dedicated his life to him. Says the poet Damodar Das, "It is a sign of growing spirituality in a man to place implicit confidence on the Guru."

9. Kanka, the Poet.

The *pir* pleased with Kanka ordered him to write a poem on *Satya Pir*[1] and went away from that land. He wrote the poem which soon enjoyed a great celebrity. Following the instructions of the *pir*, copies of it he circulated to places far and near. There were hundreds of men and women who now admired the poetical style of Kanka, and the youth was no longer called a cowherd but became known all over the country as "Kanka the poet." Hindus and Mahomedans equally appreciated the poem and there were enthusiasts who spread his fame in distant countries by their ardent praises.

One might now suppose, that Kanka's future was brightening and that better days were in store for him. The poet Raghusut says, "No, one who is born in sorrows is destined to be happy ever after in his life." Ll. 1-16.

10. The Question of restoring him to the Brahmin's Status.

Now no one was more pleased with Kanka's literary fame than Garga himself, though he knew nothing about the youth's connection with the *pir*.

One day Garga called all the Brahmins of the locality to his house and said, "This Kanka of ours is the son of a Brahmin, as every one knows. His only fault is that when he was a mere baby and did not know how to distinguish between good and bad, he was reared up in the house of a *chandal*. This may be forgotten and forgiven and we may once more take him to caste."

[1] This *pir* happened to be a propagandist of the *Satya Pir* cult which now counts followers amongst Hindus and Mahomedans alike. It is one of those cults in Bengal which offer a common ground to the two sections of the Bengali population to meet in the religious domain.

The Brahmin[1] Nandu and other orthodox members of his community shook their heads and said in a firm tone, "We do not agree. But, Sir, as you love the boy, you may give us up and live with him."

The orthodox Brahmins offered a strong opposition and argued, "One, who though born of Brahmin parents, takes food at the house of a *chandal*, loses all claims on the Brahmanic status. If we tolerate a breach of rules on this point, we shall thereby break our whole social fabric. If a flower falls on the ground, does anybody pick it up for offering it to the gods?"

Such was the view of a party. But there were others who feared Garga. They knew the great piety of the man and his influence over society. Outwardly they gave their assent to Garga's proposal, but behind his back conspired to frustrate his intention. Garga tried his utmost to convince the Brahmins of the fairness of his proposal and argued his case well. But the Brahmins could not be unanimous in their opinions. And the verdict of the assembly was not generally in Kanka's favour. Some said, "Late us take him back," others shook their head and would not agree. There were great discussions even outside the society of Brahmins, some standing for and others against Kanka. The cry went, "Look, how the *chandal* becomes a Brahmin." And Garga's house was on the brink of being burnt down by the fire of animosity which was roused. Garga the saintly Brahmin and Kanka had to pay the penalty. The Brahmins now deliberately tried to ruin Kanka. Ll. 1-30.

11. The Conspiracy against Kanka.

The hostile Brahmins contrived all means, fair and foul, to do harm to Garga. They spread scandal everywhere.

[1] It should be understood that he was so long living in the house of Garga as a menial and outcaste and not as a member, however greatly he might have been treated with affection there.

"Kanka," said they, "was not only adopted as a son by a *chandal*, but has been initiated into the Mahomedan faith by the *pir*."

The popular sentiment grew strong every day by the persistent efforts of the scandal-mongers. The people in fury tore the poem of Satya Pir that Kanka had written. Some threw the book into fire. "It is a book which propounds the Mahomedan creed," said every one. "A touch of the book is profane" and the Hindus at whose house the book was found, were compelled to pass through a regular penance. But the worst was yet to come. They spread the most cruel scandal about Lila saying that she had surrendered her youth to Kanka. Those of the Brahmins who knew nothing of the scriptures, nor observed *sandhya* and other Brahmanical rites, who ate meat and drank wine and were depraved in every way, became the most forward in branding poor Lila with the grossest infamy, and they established their charge with lies and false evidences in such a manner that even Garga, the pious Brahmin, could not help believing in what they said. Thus did the father doubt the character of his innocent child who knew not the wily ways of the world.

When the suspicion of the old Brahmin was confirmed by false evidences they had got up, his naturally upright nature burnt with indignation. "It is by milk then that I have nurtured a venomous snake," he thought. "If I drive him from the house it will not be enough. I must kill him with my own hand." Says the poet Raghusut, "In his great rage he could not discriminate between a friend and a foe, but determined to take violent and drastic steps."

12. Attempts to kill Kanka and Lila.

"First I will kill Kanka and next Lila," he said to himself, "and then as a penance for my sins, I will throw myself into fire and put an end to my life."

The shame of the family-scandal and great anger thus maddened Garga. He wandered about for a time in the fields and near the river in an unsettled state of mind. He called Lila to his presence and said, "Take the pitcher and fetch water from the river without delay. The temple has been defiled. I dreamt a dream that my god is going to leave the temple greatly disgusted with us. Bring water instantly, so that with my own hands I may wash the temple-floor. For the last time I will sit to worship there."

Lila perceived a harshness in the voice of her father which frightened her. Tears sprang to her eyes. In her great fear she could not ask her father as to what it was that had given rise to such a temper in him. She went forthwith to the river-side as her father had bidden her do. "Why is my father so angry to-day? Never before this did he speak to me so rudely." This was her thought, and her eyes were full of tears and quite blinded by them so that she could scarcely see the path.

Then as she walked on, she heard the voice of her father from behind. He said, "Stop, keep the pitcher here and go back, I will bring the water myself. The offerings reserved for my god have been defiled by a dog which ate from them." [1]

With the pitcher in his hand the Brahmin went to the river-*ghat* and brought water himself. He cleared the temple and washed the floor with care. Then he became satisfied that everything was made holy again. He threw away the flowers gathered by Lila as unholy. He washed the stone *Salgram* (the emblem of the god Viṣnu) and the throne on which it was placed. And then he sat to worship. After finishing his *puja* he went to the dining room. On other days when he sat down to breakfast he used to call Lila to him affectionately. She fanned him while he ate and attended him

[1] The reason of the Brahmin's forbidding Lila to fetch water was that at a second thought he felt it would not be right to wash the temple-floor with the water brought by one whom he considered to be a fallen woman.

with the utmost care. "Why does not my father call me to-day to his presence?" She said to herself with tearful eyes. The meals prepared for Kanka, rice and curry, were kept carefully by Lila in a neat place. Garga entered the room and looked around. He was all alone there. He opened a small box and taking some black pills of poison from it mixed them with the meal kept for Kanka. Unseen by her father, however, had Lila observed all that he had done.

Her very soul, as it were, ran out of her, so frightened was she to see her father's act which was inhuman and cruel as cruelty itself.

From the meadows Kanka now returned with the cow Suravi, accompanied by its frolicsome and gay calf Patuli. He took his bath as usual and came to the dining room. To his utter amazement and sorrow he found Lila weeping. He said, "Why is it, Lila, why dost thou shed tears? What is it that has happened to the house? As I was returning home I met some inauspicious signs. Suravi the cow looked unhappy and she scarcely showed a desire to eat the grass or drink water. On other days father used to receive me with a smile, but to-day what have I done to annoy him? He did not talk with me, and why do I see tears in your eyes?"

He asked her once, he asked her twice, but she did not give any reply—and continued weeping. Kanka did not press for a reply but stood silent like a statue. His heart was being rent in twain at the sight of Lila weeping. Then he timidly said again: "If knowingly or unknowingly, sleeping or awake, I have given you the least cause of annoyance, forgive me Lila. I never saw you cry before this. I do not remember what I have done to cause you pain; pray tell me what it is."

Then did Lila speak. Tears choked her voice all the time. But anyhow she delivered herself and said:—

"Hear me, O Kanka. Fly away from this place. Go where there are no father, no mother, no friend and no

An astounding Revelation

"Then did Lila speak."

Kanka and Lila, p. 226

habitation of men. Go there where people do not profess friendship." Here she sobbed and stopped for a time. Then with words that came from the depths of her heart, she related the story of the scandal and of her father's act. She spoke with the utmost sympathy and affection for Kanka and ended with these words. "Here look at this witch appointed to minister food to you, hungry and fatigued with the day's work. Here is the food that will kill you. Am I a human being? I am certainly so in form, what monster is so cruel as I am —ready to poison an innocent person who has come to ask food from my hands? Go away instantly, leave this house. This poisoned food I will myself take. But wait, dear Kanka, do not leave this house just now, see me dead before you leave this house."

Had a thunderbolt fallen on his head, Kanka would not have been more astonished. He stood for a time as if stunned by a blow, but gradually recovering himself he said:

"The sun and the moon and the gods of heaven be my witness. I have not acted any way against our father Garga. He has been duped by false scandal spread by wicked men. This feeling of his will not last. He is a wise man and a profound scholar; sooner or later he will be convinced that we are innocent. My advice is, O Lila, we should act with a cool head. For some time I shall be off from here and wander in distant places, visiting the shrines. I will come back, when father's wrong notion is dispelled. Do not lose respect for him. He has been deceived. Take every care of him and I warn you he will come back to his senses ere long. For as sure as I am of our innocence so sure am I of his power of judgment. His reason will not long remain clouded. Now, farewell, O Lila. We shall meet again if we live. Do not be sorry at my departure. Shuravi and her calf Patuli will remain here, make friends with them. And our dear bird, Hiraman, will sing its gay notes. Call it by my name, call it Kanka, and this will give you some consolation.

For myself no father, no mother, no friend have I. My luck has repeatedly brought such turns to my life of which I could not have the barest idea beforehand. Just like a straw in the waves carried adrift by the tide over which it has no control, am I. My last prayer, O dear Lila, is, do not forget me—the companion of your childhood." He stopped a moment to wipe away a tear and then said sweetly in a sad tone again, "There, Lila, are the birds Hiraman and Shuka, do not forget to feed them with milk and butter. There Lila are the flower-plants, water them every evening as I have done. The *malati* creeper laden with buds and flowers is there. We made garlands with their floral treasure together even yesterday, perhaps for the last time! Shuravi and Patuli are in the house. If they look wistfully towards the meadows remembering me, gently pat their back and soothe them. The *Shalgram* stone remains in the house; offer worship to Vishnu, for in our distress He is our sole refuge. Inspite of everything lose not your regard for our father, for to us he is God Himself in mortal guise. Even if by mistake he be cruel to you for a time, accept his punishments and bear them with patience. And all the while, dear Lila, resign yourself to the will of God. For without Him there is no other stay of the helpless. Do not sorrow over my lot, if we live we shall meet again." Saying this Kanka began to think within himself, "How am I to take leave of father Garga? Will it be good to leave the house without bidding him farewell?" Ll. 1-150.

13. SURAVI, THE COW, DIES FROM THE EFFECT OF POISON.

At this time Garga, who had left his house and been wandering about, yielded himself to wild thoughts: "My home has been defiled,—witches are haunting the temples. The blot in the moon has spread and covered her entirely. Monkeys have defiled with their vile touch the offerings to gods. No, this should not be borne, I will not return home but set fire to it and destroy everything that is in it. Ah Lila!

Beautiful and loving are you! I was about to leave home and turn a *sannyasi* when your mother died. It was for you, Lila, that I abandoned the idea and stayed at this home of ours! Even the enemies stop to have a sight of your face and the stone melts in sympathy, so lovely you are! And now, Garga is turned to a stone; not a drop of affection is in him for you. With the blood of Kanka will he make his offerings to God."

Kanka thought of leaving the house. He resolved to go to a place where there was no habitation of men. Nobody would come to him to make enquiries and torment him. Puzzled and worried he could not yet decide his course, when Lila came to him running. Her hair was all dishevelled and she faltered in her speech as she said, "Come along, Kanka, do not lose a moment. See what a dire calamity has happened in our house. Shuravi, our dear cow, is lying on the ground quite senseless and struggling for life. Some venomous snake has bitten her. Go, run in quest of a physician."

Kanka and Lila hurried on to see the cow. There she lay on the ground in the agonies of death. Kanka asked "Where did you throw the meal that was poisoned?" She trembled like the tendril of a creeper as she pointed to the spot where the poisoned rice was thrown. Kanka said, "Had I died myself it would not have mattered much. What a great disaster! A cow is poisoned in the compound of the temple house!" He had scarcely finished his words when the cow breathed her last, before any medical aid could be called.[1]

Lila, as she saw the heart-rending sight, retired to the kitchen, and there spreading a part of her *sadi*, lay down, covered with shame, repentance and grief.

Kanka sat like a statue till night was far advanced and then rose up and went outside the house and slept under a *kadamba* tree which had just flowered. He dreamt wild

[1] The death of a cow in a Hindu house is considered a great calamity.

dreams. His sleep was broken and he often screamed out. Towards the end of the night he dreamt a strange dream. It appeared that he had died and that they had taken him to the cremation ground. A great fire was made and his body was slowly burning. Ghosts were dancing around in wild ecstasy. At that moment of excruciating torture; he prayed to some one whom he did not know, saying, "Save me, save me from this torture."

All on a sudden he saw a tall and handsome man coming to him. His fair colour was aglow with red. He looked bright as an image of burning gold. He took Kanka by the hand and helped him to make his escape. When he was going to thank him, the god-like man told him to go in quest of him and disappeared. In the morning, Kanka left the place, seeking Chaitanya as he was bid. For it was him that he had seen in his dream. Ll. 1-68.

14. Lila's Search for Kanka.

Lila rose from her bed all shrinking in fear. She also had no quiet sleep. Her tresses were all unloose. She entered the sleeping room of Kanka, and did not find him there. She went to the cowshed, there also she did not find him. With eyes that had known no sleep in the night, pale with grief and fast, she searched every spot of the village but could not find Kanka.

It was the end of winter, in the river the ebb-tide had set in. On her banks the grief-stricken maiden wandered about seeking Kanka. To the *malati* and *bakul* flowers she went, and like a foolish one, enquired of them if they had seen Kanka going by that path. The same spot she searched over again and cried out 'Kanka, Kanka.' Alas! there was no reply. She wept and spoke to her pet birds in the cage, "Can you tell me, dear ones, where he has gone?" The bees hummed on *malati* flowers and there she stood listening like a mad soul as if they could give her some clue.

She took no care of her flowing tresses. Her clothes streamed forth in the air all loose and disordered. She wept and said to herself, "Alas! He has turned a *sannyasi.* What a sorrow that he did not even wait to bid me farewell! Alas! even such a cruel stroke of misery was in store for me!

Ll. 1-24.

15. Garga's Vow of Fast and Penance and the Oracle from the Temple.

Now let us return to Garga. For the whole day and night he wandered like a mad man sometimes by the lonely path, sometimes by the river-side. Fatigued and totally distracted he returned home in the morning. Many inauspicious signs did he meet on the way. In the air he thought, he heard the light footsteps of ghosts and evil spirits. The crows and the vultures by their wild cries in the broad daylight struck terror to his heart. A jackal passed by and crossed his path and did not look behind. He heard strange shrieks in the air. Coming home he saw the doors of his house shut from within. The flowers lay all withered in the garden, nor did the bees hum there as usual—"Yesterday," he thought within himself, "none was perhaps at this house to light the evening lamp in the temple." What a pity! The pet birds sat mute and did not call Kanka and Lila by their names, as usual with them. But the most heart-rending sight followed. In the compound of the house lay the dead body of the dear cow Suravi, almost blue with poison, the unhappy calf Patuli piteously moaning near her. His heart melted in deep pity at the sight. He found the young one bellowing and going times without number to its dead mother and trying, as it were, to rouse her by its cries, and when she did not give any response, it ran towards Garga and helplessly laid its head down at his feet.

The strong man now thoroughly broke down. He wept like a child and gradually collecting himself he became firm in his resolve to propitiate the gods by fast and vigil. He entered the temple and bolted the door from within. He sat to worship, his eyes incessantly shedding tears.

"He was resolved to give his life up. He would give no other offerings to his god than his tears." Says the poet Damodar. The gossip ran in the village that the Brahmin Garga had taken the vow of consecrating his life to the gods. If they were propitiated by his fast and vigil, well and good, if not, he would not move an inch from his seat but die in the self-same position.

He did not touch any food for two days, neither did he open the door of the temple. His pupils came every morning and evening to make enquiries, but the door was not opened.

Then was this oracle heard by him :—

"Hear, oh ! Garga, why the gods have been displeased with you. How can they like a man who conspires against the life of his own child and tries to poison one who is helplessly dependent on him ? All your mishaps are due to your wickedness. The poison you mixed up with Kanka's food has killed the cow Suravi."

After three days' fast and vigil, did Garga hear the above oracle and he became deeply affected by repentance. He lamented saying, " By wrong belief, have I done a great sin. Yea—all my virtues have gone for naught ! Wickedly did I think of killing my own daughter and attempted to poison one who is the very soul of candour and spotless as an angel ! I mixed poison with his food. I have destroyed the life of Suravi—the cow of the temple. And what should I do by way of atonement ? Shall I destroy myself by entering into the fire ? The great crime of killing the cow is mine. How can I get rid of it and be clear in the eyes of the gods ? "

He again shut the door of the temple and observed fast for another three days and nights. Again the oracle was heard; it said "Pick up the withered flowers gathered by Lila, which you threw away as unholy and worship the gods with them and you will be free from all sin."

The Brahmin wept as he gathered the flowers brought by Lila, which he had cast away. He wept too when he worshipped the gods with them. Thus did he become free from the crime of cow-killing.

He now fully understood that the wicked Brahmins had plotted against Kanka and Lila, and that through their contrivance Kanka was made to leave the house.

Convinced of the innocence of Kanka and Lila and of the wickedness of the Brahmins, Garga called his disciples to him and ordered them to go in quest of Kanka and bring him back. Ll. 1-78.

16. The Two Disciples sent to search Kanka.

Bichitra and Madhava were two youths requested by Garga to go abroad in quest of Kanka. Garga said when they were ready to depart, "Long has he been brought up in this home like our son. How can I now live without him? Dear as the bird Hiraman was he, who constantly pleased my ears with his sweet talk—Alas! he has fled away! You have all along loved him as your brother. Now for his sake and for my sake find him out. It is for my fault that Kanka is now homeless. If you meet him say that I have sworn by my life that I will not keep this life without him! Tell him moreover that there is none in this house to look after the calf Patuli, to take it to the meadows and feed it! Tell him that the bird Hiraman and Suka though they cannot speak, have given up food for grief,—that my garden which once smiled like the moon, is now covered with darkness, and that this hermitage of ours has grown dismal as the cremation ground. So long as you do not return, I will not leave this temple—If you cannot find him out I will starve myself to death. . If you meet him, take him by the hand and say, "He whom you called your father is covered with remorse and shame and prays for forgiveness from you."

They bowed to him and left the village to seek out Kanka whom they loved as brother.

Lila from her lonely chamber heard all that passed by.

Ll. 1-36.

17. How Lila bore her Loneliness.

Lila ate but little and spent many a night without sleep. She spread a part of her *sadi* on the ground and there lay like one unable to rise. Sometimes in the morning when the sun peeped through her windows, she prayed to him with joint hands. "Oh! Sun, you rise in the east and wander in your airy path, all day long. In the course of your travel you see all the lands. No spot is there, however dark, where your rays do not penetrate. You know, oh! God of Light, where he is staying now. When you will see him again, be pleased to tell him about me and do not fail to light up his path for his quick return."

Sometimes she would gently walk to the riverside and send her silent prayers to the boatman: "You ply your boat and visit many places, oh! brother boatman. If you happen to meet him, bring him back to our shores, tell him that my days appear to me long, and my nights seem as if they will never end. Alas my grief makes them so! Tell him, besides, that my life cannot go on long in this way."

She addressed the river and said, "Oh you of high lineage—born of the mountains! Take compassion on the sorrowful one! You know how dearly we loved each other, how we passed our days and nights in gay talks! You wander through many lands, do you not, oh river, hear the sound of his flute! If you meet him, tell him a word for me. How can he live, parted from me?"

The silent river, the trees and all listened to her pathetic appeal. Their heart melted in pity. But how could they show their sympathy outwardly?

Thus the inanimate objects became her companions, and with them she communed in deep sorrow. She prayed to the sky, which with the thousand eyes of stars, saw every corner of the earth. She said, "I was asleep in the night and a thief came and stole the precious stone which I valued most! Had I the wings of a bird, I would have gone to him." If a bird happened to sit on the branch of a near tree, Lila hastened to it and weeping made enquiries if it had seen Kanka, saying, "You have come here from a long distance, perchance you saw him!" Then she addressed her own Hiraman and Suka in the cage and said: "He loved you dearly. Did he not say anything to you by way of farewell?" She would touch the birds by her soft hands and caress them with tears, saying, "I will follow you, dear ones, if you will show me the path. He tended you with so much care and could you forget such a one? He loved you so much; did he not leave his address with you?" She set the birds free from the cage and said again: "Go where he has gone. If you happen to meet him, sing a song to tell him of my sorrows." Ll. 1-108.

18. A Tale of Six Months' Sorrows.

In the month of March the whole garden smiled with full-blown *malat* and *bakul* The bees hummed over *malati* flowers and Lila addressed them and said, "Tell him, O bees, if you meet, that the *malati* creepers that he had planted with his own hands, have borne flowers. Would he not visit his garden to see them?"

In April the heat of the air became intolerable and she wept for him all day long thinking how Kanka fared in a distant land in such a season. The flowers and leaves wore a golden hue and the groves constantly resounded with the hum of bees. The cuckoos sat on boughs and the bees on flowers. She asked them to carry her message that the flowers now withered in the garden as there was none to pluck them. Her own garlands woven without the aid of a thread faded daily. Alas! how cruel it was for him to keep away in such a month!

In May the sweet smell of the *gandharaj* and the red petals of the *jaba* spread a charm over the land. The cuckoo sang farewell notes to the spring. The new leaves on the tops of trees were a source of delight to the eyes. And she wept remembering Kanka.

The month of June came with its present of gay flowers and fruits. The mangoes, the jack and the blackberries ripened on the boughs of trees. Every day new birds with painted wings visited their garden, sang new notes and flew to new lands. When the heat became intense she spread her own *sadi* and lay on the cool ground thinking of Kanka all the while.

In July the rains descended to the earth like a maiden with a golden vessel in her hand. She sprinkled life-giving water over the earth, and the grass and plants again took a lively green hue. The shallow rivers became suddenly replenished, and overflowed the banks. The boats with sails spread on, marched to distant lands. "Will they not give me the tidings of Kanka?" She asked herself and sighed.

Then came August. The clouds roared in the sky and the lightnings flashed. The peacocks danced displaying the colour of rainbow in their gorgeous tails. The *kadamba* flowers—the crown of the rains—bloomed on all sides, and the smell of the *ketaki* sweetened the air.

Then behold the month of September that looked like a woman with a pitcher of water on her head. The overflowing rains carried weighty stones onward by their force. The lotus bloomed in the water and spread its smell in the air. The *Dom* women went about in distant lands in their long boats, busy in making their cane baskets. The *Chatak's* cry was heard at intervals praying for drops from the clouds. Whilst the bird *Papia*, wet with September floods, with thunder over his head, persisted in his attempts to please his love by crying, "O bride speak"[1] all day long. "Who is your bride, O bird, and to whom do you make your appeal? Your laments touch my heart and feign would I express my own sorrows to you if I could have you alone for a moment."

Thus did Lila pass six long and weary months grieving over Kanka.

Bichitra and Madhab would come back with Kanka. That was her one hope on which hang the thread of her life. Raghusut, the poet says, "O damsel, Providence is against you."

Bichitra and Madhab have returned; nowhere could Kanka be found.

She heard of their coming back. Vain hopes deluded her. She saw them and said in a soft and whispering tone, "You have come but where is my brother Kanka?"

Ll. 1-90 (abridged).

19. The Disappointing News.

They said sadly, "Dear sister, we travelled over many lands. Often did we pass sleepless nights. We suffered a great deal in the way and we searched many a far region. But nowhere could we get any clue.

[1] The sweet note of *Papia* mimics the sound of the Bengali words "বউ কথা কও" or "O bride speak" hence the bird is called in the country-side by its more familiar name "O bride speak."

"First we went to the east up to Sylhet. Then we followed a river through the Surma Valley that we met with in the way. We went to Kamrup and there saw the temple of Kali, where goats and buffaloes are sacrificed every Tuesday and Sunday. From there we turned to west and visited Nadia the birthplace of Chaitanya. But our long search has gone for naught. We fear, Kanka does not live. Had he lived we would have certainly met him."

Then the two youths came to Garga and bowed to him. He made enquiries about Kanka. They said, "Friend of childhood and companion of youth, he is dearer to us than life. If we could get him back, sacrificing our very life, we would perhaps do so. We searched him to the utmost of our power, but no trace could we get."

20. Garga sends Them Back.

Then Garga told them, "No, no, this reply does not please me. Anyhow you must get him back. This is the reward that I want from you for the pains I took to teach you for so many years. When he will come back, I will go with him and live in wild forests infested with tigers and other beasts of prey far off from all habitation of men. For me death seems to be in sight. But peacefully could I die if he would be near my death-bed. O my dear pupils, Bichitra and Madhab, go again and try by all means to find him out. I will give you a suggestion. He was devoted to Chaitanya. There follow those paths where the sound of the anklets of his feet in his mystic dance is heard, and you will be able to trace him out. Where his followers play on tabors and cymbals, and the sky becomes resonant with the music—go thither and you will be perhaps able to trace him out. There where even the birds that fly in the air sing tne name of Krishna and the sound of the great music throws such a spell as to make even the rivers flow against their course—

there where the dust raised by the feet of his followers has covered, as it were, the very sky above,—thither should you go and try your chance."

Bichitra and Madhab at the order of their Guru started for distant countries again. But hear what happened in the meantime. Ll. 1-32.

21. The Rumour.

There ran a rumour all over the country that Kanka was drowned in a river on his way. They spoke in whispers, and if any one asked they stopped ; but without asking the report often came to one's ears. Alas, who will tell Lila if really he is dead! She could not know the truth and wept all the day, lying on her bed. The sun rose as usual, and in the evening the moon peeped through her windows. Nothing seemed to have changed. Only Kanka was not near her. If she asked the moon and stars, they hid their face in the clouds, the air sometimes spoke in inaudible whispers, chilling her very life-blood, "He is no more, he is no more." In her bed she would not have a wink of sleep, or if ever she slept for some moments she dreamt that Kanka's body was floating on the waters : and then she would awake with a start.

Some time passed again in this way and Madhab returned. She saw him come alone and dared not ask the tidings of Kanka. He came to her and said in a tone of despair: "Dear Lila, dear sister, I could not get any information of him though I tried my utmost. What shall I say to my preceptor ? Long have I searched him, but all in vain." Then Lila softly asked him, "Have you heard any rumour about him ?" And he replied in deep sorrow, "I do not know whether the rumour is true or false, but people say that he was drowned in last July. He was going to visit Chaitanya on a merchant's vessel by the river Pagla, when a great storm overtook the boat. It sank and with it our dear brother Kanka."

22. Lila in Death-bed.

"Take me where he has gone" bemoaned Lila. From that day she ceased to touch food. All alone she sat day and night and wept. Her dazzling beauty faded away. Autumn came and went and the cold season set in. She lay down on the bare floor covering herself with her thin *saḍi* and wept the whole night. "More than a brother was he to me, alas, we shall meet no more. What a pity, that he was drowned in a river and I could not see him, while drawing his last breath! My mother died when I was a mere child and what I suffered God alone knows. My father reared me up with great care, but woe to me, my loving father became to me my enemy afterwards. Innocent am I, yet people spread false stories about me. O, Sun and Moon you have witnessed and must proclaim the truth after my death."

Thus did she lament. One full year passed in this way. Madhab returned, but Kanka was not found. Raghusut says, "No way is there to save the poor girl's life." Her youthful charms had, ere this, been a wonder to all. But just as the autumnal frost kills the whole array of lilies, those charms have now entirely faded away. The curls of her hair once surpassed in beauty the waves of the Ganges, but now her tresses looked like shrivelled threads of jute. When she walked her hair almost touched the ankles, but now uncared for it became torn and knotted, and in her bed lay near her pillow like an unseemly heap. Her charming face showed a death-like pallor and looked like the full moon in the jaws of the clouds. Her beautiful eyes became sunk and death sat in their hollows. The lips no more showed their wonted lovely red. She had once looked like a lovely creeper, but behold her now withered and shrivelled like the leaf of the sugar-cane! The dazzling rainbow has disappeared behind the clouds.

Then one day the bird flew away from the cage to the unknown regions. The poet Raghusut says, "Such is this world. Who will say why one feels so much sorrow for another?" Ll. 1-58.

23. The Last Scene.

Seated near the corpse Garga lamented, "Sleep no more, dear Lila, lift your eyes and see your brother coming. Is it right that you should leave me thus? Who will give me food when I am hungry? Who will fan me when I shall return home fatigued in the heat of the sun? Who will knidle the evening light in my house; and who will gather flowers for me to worship Siva? How can I bear to live all alone in this house? Your dear birds—Hiraman and Shuka—are there. Who will take care of them? The pitcher is there, who will fill it with water? Alas, dear one, all your hopes are gone! You are here on the river-bank—on the cremation ground, leaving all that you loved. My end too is near. Look at me only once, and open your eyes to see me, so that I may bid you my last farewell."

* * *

Hearing all from Bichitra, Kanka hurried homeward. When he returned he saw every room dark in the house; then he ran to the cremation ground, he saw there Garga lamenting aloud.

His laments seemed to move the very trees which let fall their leaves and flowers as a token of sympathy. The sky seemed to be overcast with clouds and the earth looked aggrieved at his sorrow.

There on the bank of the river, Garga and Kanka met. Just as a tree is all ablaze when lightning falls on it so became Garga, at the sight of Kanka with the fire of his grief. He clasped him to his breast with loud wailings. "Where were you Kanka all this time? The last word that Lila uttered was your name. She was only eight years old when her mother died and I brought her up all these years with care. She has left me now. Thus is the image brought to the temple for worship, but thrown away before the priest could offer his *puza*. But who can fight against fate! Go home and throw away all the gods from my temple, burn the house and know it for certain that to-day ends all my connection with this world."

The very gods of heaven shed tears at Garga's laments. The river tried softly to soothe him by the sound of her ripples. The birds of the forests wept, sitting mutely on boughs. The poet Raghusut says, "Even stone melted at his sorrow."

To cool his burning heart, Garga went to Puri with Kanka. Five of his disciples, most attached to him, accompanied him there and left all connection with their family.

Ll. 1-70.

KAJALREKHA

PREFACE

Kajalrekha is a folk-tale full of marvellous incidents and instances of super-human powers exhibited by men. In real life no still-born baby was ever pierced by needles and arrows; no child without life and nourishment ever grew up from infancy to youth and, on the first day of its gaining consciousness, talked the human language without having had any opportunity to acquire it; no shoal ever sprang up in the sea as the result of a curse, and no parrot except in the Panchatantra and other works of fancy, ever foretold future events with absolute certainty like a prophet. These and other similar details make this story a typical folktale.

But in our country, it is often found difficult to fix a clear line of demarcation between fact and fiction, especially in the regions of poetry and religion. The Buddha is a historical figure, but there are so many legends that have been attributed to him by popular faith that he shines as a demi-god, appealing to the imagination and the credulity of the Buddhists precisely in the same manner as the legendary gods Siva of the Sivaites and Visnu of the Vaisnavas do to the followers of their respective creeds. Mythology often rises to the level of history by incorporating human elements in the conception of gods presented in life-like vividness, and history not infrequently sinks into pure fiction by amalgamation of wonderful tales beyond the boundaries of human belief.

The same is the case in regard to this folk-tale. Kajalrekha's character, though presented through the coloured glass of poetical imagination, does not appear a whit less real than that of Mahua, Malua and other heroines of our historical ballads.

The country was full of self-sacrificing loving women. They burnt themselves alive on the funeral pyres of their husbands out of intense love, and people admired this martyrdom; and Malua, Mahua and Sunai committed suicide having been driven to that extreme step by love and renunciation. In the folk-lore, in the popular literature and in their songs the writers could not help introducing this one grand theme of exalted womanly virtues which invested even their imaginary productions with a glow of life and truth. Imagination here owes its inspiration to the underlying historical facts.

It is, in fact, difficult for us to conceive Kajalrekha on other lines than assigned to the historical characters of Malua, Chandravati and Lila. She is verily their cousin, linked to them by inevitable ties of family likeness, bearing the hall-mark of the same great virtues. All barriers between history and fiction melt away and Kajalrekha, Kamala and others, heroines of fiction and of actual life, claim from us the same degree of admiration, standing before us in an equally life-like pose and vividness of reality. The purity and holiness of female life was a real factor in the country, and hence it was reflected in poetry and in life, in folk-lore and in history with equal effect.

The stories of Malanchamala, Kanchanmala, Sankhamala and Rupmala show an essential similarity in this respect to those of Kajalrekha and Jiralani. They are all folk-tales. But it must be emphasised that these stories have all come from Mymensing,—the chosen place of wonderful and ideal womanhood. It is here also that Malua, Mahua and Kamala actually lived and inspired the poets who wrote the historical ballads. We thus see facts on one side of the picture and fiction on the other, and in both the type is common; one is drawn from actual life—its names, references to locality and even details are all real, while the other under the thin veneer of imaginary situations and unreal nomenclatures represent facts not less potently or vividly than the historical songs.

Characters like the above, I should say by way of a little digression, are still to be found in this province of Bengal. They make their utmost sacrifices not because any poet will sing of them or that they will be applauded. They wish to hide their sacrifice from others, content with the reward of that inner approval which comes from the heart and is called conscience. Kajalrekha's sufferings are almost Christlike. Before I read this poem I had no idea of the true import of Christ's saying "Resist no evil." Kajalrekha is a personification of this doctrine. Yet it is not her lack of moral strength or heroic element of character that makes her submit to her lot without a resistance. She is the very princess of heroines by her patience preserved to the last in shutting her lips in expectation of the opportune hour. She scarcely blames any one however heinous or cruel, but stands like the very picture of patience and forbearance. Possessed of fine suceptibilities of the tenderest of womankind, she exercises a wonderful control over the dominating impulses which in her trying situations would naturally prompt ordinary persons. No priestly canons or artificial restrictions influence such characters. They suffer a good deal, but no one will be able to say that they suffer under compulsion or that it is a superstitious convention of social life that makes them slavishly cling to their husbands. Their heart is "subdued even to the very quality of their lords." No outward force, not even the highest culture can save a person from the inevitable sorrows which true love brings in its train. The suffering of a person in love inspires true poetry. What the mother suffers for the child contains in it elements of the divine spirit of protection. In nuptial love this is not the less apparent. If we call it weakness or unworthy of praise, we take away all seriousness and majesty from life which sinks into the level of the commonplace and the inglorious.

In the earlier stages of their life, some of these characters have appeared a little frivolous. Kamala's conversation with Chikan—the milkwoman is almost offensive by its crude humour. Jiralani's first impression on seeing her lover verges on indiscreetness. But if we pass on to the hour of their trial at the next stage we see that their light-hearted gaities were mere pleasantries, indulged in by those who are of a naturally cheerful temperament.

When danger comes—an extreme destitution or despair confronts them—they suddenly assume all the majesty of martyrs of the first rank and show their sterling qualities by remarkable sacrifices, never acting under impulse or temporary excitement, but all the same, taking a determined and resolved attitude for maintaining their honour.

What appears light or even frivolous in the beginning of the story, startles us by its adamantine strength towards its end, for which we were not quite prepared. In this respect these characters bear some resemblance to Nora in Ibsen's "Doll's House," who when she first appears to us, strikes us by her lightness and gaiety and takes us by surprise towards the end by displaying a strength of character and seriousness which hitherto lay unsuspected in her character, like a reserved force unexpectedly brought to meet the exigencies of a critical hour in the battlefield.

Dr. Stella Kramrisch says that what strikes her most in these ballads of Mymensing is the fact that folk-lore and art have sometimes become one in them. Foreign scholars, who look on our matters from outside without sharing our prejudices, sometimes show a sounder and better judgment than we ourselves do in regard to our literature and art. Folk-lore, ever since Grimm brothers drew attention to it in the early part of the 19th century, has been a subject of serious study with European scholars. But more or less folklore is taken as a subject which captures the imagination of the children by the romantic nature of its narration and as a never-ceasing fountain of curiosity. To the scholar, the poetic value of a folk-tale lies in showing the extreme simplicity of the untutored mind, while as works of antiquity, it shows better than all historical records, the gradual evolution of the human mind from primitive ideas to the unrestrained imaginativeness of the Middle Ages. The linguistic value of the folk-lore of a nation bearing in it evidences of social, religious and other points involved at particular periods of their growth, has also attracted many scholars. It is helpful besides in tracing the ways of the common human mind at different stages of its development, showing an interchange of ideas between different nations living at more or less distance from one another and giving rise to scientific problems as to the ways of communication that existed in the early periods of history.

But when folk-lore takes the form of true poetry, and when not merely rousing the curiosity of the child or the scientific enquiries of scholars, it gives vivid pictures full of life and romance possessing all the genuine interest of exquisite poetry and leaves indelible impressions on the minds of the readers by its lofty ideals, it certainly becomes art and deserves a unique place in literature. Such a place, I feel bound to claim, is due to the folklore of Mymensing.

Kajalrekha, though a folk-tale, draws its essential elements from the soil itself. Mention of some localities of Mymensing, references to some peculiar customs of that district all go to show that it is a flower which bloomed in that celebrated garden of flower-like songs and ballads—Mymensing. Though the exile of the heroine may be regarded by outsiders as an instance of incredible cruelty and a fanciful creation of the author of the folk-story yet there is no doubt that such cruelties really existed in the country and were not a pure product of imagination. People here had, only a short time ago, such a deep-rooted faith in the prophecy of astrologers that they often treated children with unspeakable cruelties, nay, even murdered them if the astrologers predicted any serious mishap to occur in future owing to hostile planetary influence. Even so late as the 16th century Raja Pratapaditya of Jessore was about to be murdered in his childhood by his father Vikramaditya who blindly believed in the astrologer's words, but was saved by the intervention of his uncle Basanta Ray. Women and children who mostly represent mute innocence in society, were at the mercy of these false prophets. Alas ! how many children were thrown into the Bay by the hands of their own mothers, their tenderest and best guardians on earth ! There was no law in the land to save the poor babies from the most unnatural and grim superstition. This cruelty is born of superstition, and does not indicate any innate defect in the human side of the individuals perpetrating the crimes. The folk-tale is therefore suggestive of grim facts that actually existed in our society and is its true index.

This story is written in the prose dialect spoken in the eastern districts of Mymensing, but there are many metrical verses with which it is interspersed, and these form by far the most interesting portion of the folk-story. They are mostly in the *payár* metre, only in one instance there is a specimen of the *tripadi* (Chap. XX, Ll. 5-10). This folk-tale is not told here for the first time. It is known in the whole country-side and was compiled some years ago by Babu Dakshinaranjan Mitra Majumdar in his *Thákurmár Jhuli*, though under a different name and disagreeing with the present narrative in some of its main incidents. The total number of lines constituting the poetical portion of the tale is 472 of which 10 lines are in the *tripadi* and 462 in the *payár* metre. The story has been divided by me into 21 chapters, though as collected, no such division existed in the original. Babu Chandra Kumar De recovered the story on the 13th of Kartic, 1329 B. E., from a village in the Netrakona sub-division.

The trouble will ever arise in the minds of foreign readers as regards the 12th or 13th years in a girl's life mentioned in the ballads as causing great anxieties in parents for her marriage. The development of womanhood in this tropical clime of ours is quicker than elsewhere. Girls are found to give birth to children often in their 13th or 14th year.

DINESH CHANDRA SEN.

7, Bishwakosh Lane,

Bagbazar, Calcutta, 12th March, 1923.

KAJALREKHA

I

In the southern districts of Khaliajuri (Mymensing), there was a merchant named Dhaneswar. He had one son and one daughter. The merchant became immensely rich by the grace of God. His daughter was now in her tenth year and she was called Kajalrekha (*lit.* streak of the black paint collyrium). She was exceedingly handsome; when she smiled it seemed pearls and diamonds shone from her face, beaming like a full-blown water-lily drifted by a stream during the rains His son was only four years old and was named Ratneswar (*lit.* Lord of gold). It was an unlucky time, the Goddess of fortune forsook the merchant, being annoyed for some reasons.

Now hear what followed. Ll. 1-12.

II

By gambling the merchant lost all that he had. His servants, horses, elephants and all his wealth were gone. Losing all by his addiction to wicked dice-play he turned a *Fakir* and wandered about the country.

The only treasures that he had on earth were his son and daughter. So great was his misfortune that of his 12 merchant vesssels, he had not one left. Ll. 1-8.

III

Prose : The merchant Dhaneswar lost everything by playing at dice. His servants, horses and men were now all gone. His daughter attained her marriageable age. Anyhow she must be married. His ill fame as one addicted to dice-play soon spread in the country and no one came forward to marry the daughter of one addicted to such a wicked practice. At this stage a *sannyasi* came to his house. He made the gift of a *Suka* and of a finger-ring to the merchant and said, "This bird is known as *Dharma-mati* (*lit.* saintly-minded). If you act under its directions, you will be able to recover all your lost property." The merchant was very glad and kept the bird with care. The *sannyasi* took leave of him and went away.

One day the merchant asked the *Suka*.

Verse : "Tell me, oh dear parrot, when will my evil days come to an end. My golden palace is now in ruins,—all my valuable furniture is gone. I have not a couch left. I sleep on the bare floor.

"I have no cup, not even a pitcher for water, I drink water from the tank with my hands. I wander about the country like a *Fakir*. My father had left me a stable full of horses and elephants, but such is my lot that I have now not one there. I have a daughter and an only son in this house. They are like its two solitary lamps. But I have no means, oh bird, to feed them.

THE SUKA.

"Do not cry in this way, oh merchant, your evil days will be soon over ; sell the ring of luck that you have got and with the money get your broken ships repaired. Bring skilful artisans for the purpose. You should reserve some of this money as capital and with this go on trading. Visit the eastern countries crossing the great swamps called *howars*, and rest assured, you will earn enough in one year, that will enable you to go on for twelve years in a princely style.

Ll. 1-18.

IV

Prose : Now hear what the merchant did next. He sold the ring of luck in the market and got all the broken sea-going vessels of his father's time repaired by good artisans. He then started for the eastern countries. By the blessings of God, he got back all that he had lost. The merchant became again a master of horses and elephants, servants and officers, and his wealth became so great that he had hardly a space left in his treasury where he could store it. The pleasure-houses which his ancestors had erected in the midst of the tanks, were now thoroughly repaired. One could count the dust grains and the stars of the sky but not the wealth of this merchant.

V

Verse : Now placed far above want again in this way, one anxiety troubled his mind. Kajalrekha, his daughter, was yet unmarried. She had just stepped into her 12th year and been fast approaching that age when she should be married. The merchant was puzzled by this problem and consulted the bird as to the course he should adopt.

Ll. 1-6.

VI

Prose : The *Suka* heard all that he said and advised as follows : " You have now got over your mishap in one way but evil of another kind is in store for you. It will take a long time before you can be free from it. This daughter of yours is destined to be married to a dead husband. Do not keep her in your palace. Send her as an exile to the forest." The merchant bagan to weep as he heard this prophecy and advice of the bird saying, " Cursed be my luck! This daughter is my pet child. How can I bear to see her married to a dead man?" He cried, "alas! alas!"

Prose: "Parents train up their daughters to offer them to suitable grooms. With what heart shall I send this pet daughter of mine, as an exile to the forest? When she was a mere child, her mother died and I reared her up with utmost care. An evil luck is mine. From one danger I fall into another."

The bird said. "There's no help."

VII

Prose: What did the merchant do? On the pretext of going on sea-voyage for trade, he made one of his ships ready and set out with his daughter. Travelling against the tide for some days he came in sight of a place covered with dense wood. The ship cast anchor there and the merchant entered the forest with his daughter. They walked many a mile and Kajalrekha felt greatly depressed in spirit.

VIII

THE MERCHANT'S SOLILOQUY.

"How am I to banish you, oh my dear child? With unconvered back in the winter exposing myself to biting cold, I warmed you with the warmth of my bosom. What pains did I not take to bring you up! Now I have come here to send you to the forests and no more to think of your marriage. It seems my evil days will never leave me." Ll. 1-12.

IX

Verse:

Chorus: "Oh my father, where are you going to lead me?"

"You came with the object of trade but how is it that your ship is anchored here, and why have you entered this deep forest? If it were in your mind that you would banish me why did you not allow me to live at our home with my brother and others for a few days more? I don't know why you have come to this forest. My suspicion is that you will banish me here. Ask, oh my father, ask the trees, plants and creepers of the forest, where was it ever heard that a father banished his child in this way! The stars of the sky, the moon, the sun and the planets are the guardians of virtue; they know what happened in these four ages. Ask them, oh father, where was it ever heard that a child was banished at the advice of a forest-bird? This river traces her noble lineage from the mountains and goes to meet the high seas. She is a witness of all that happened in the past four ages. Ask her where was it ever heard that trusting to the words of a wild bird a daughter was banished in this way!"

Ll. 1-16.

X

Prose: They proceeded on and on till they reached the very depths of that jungly land. There was no human being in that forest, nor were there any beast or bird. They saw there an old temple in a dilapidated condition shut from inside. The father and daughter sat on the stair-case a while for taking rest. The mid-day sun was sending its burning rays and Kazalrekha was greatly oppressed by hunger and thirst.

KAJALREKHA.

Song: "My feet cannot walk anymore, oh where is my mother gone! alas where is my dear brother now? Ill luck pursues me day and night, oh father, give me a drop of water to allay my thirst."

Prose : The merchant said, "Wait a moment. I will see if there's water anywhere near!" So saying he left the place.

When her father had gone away, the girl rose from her seat and looked around the place. Then she touched the door of the temple with her gentle hands and lo, it opened at her touch. She entered the temple and the door became mysteriously bolted again. Kazalrekha tried her best but she could not open the door. Meantime, the merchant returned with a cup full of water and called her aloud, "Oh Kazal—open the door," but he received no reply. After a while he perceived that his daughter was saying something from inside. He again called her saying, "Come out, daughter, here is water for you." Alas! Kazal was now a prisoner in the temple and this her father could not know. There the girl explained everything to her father who tried his best to open the door. But he could not. Next he tried to break it open. This also he could not.

XI

Verse : The merchant said in a loud voice, "Oh my darling, what is it that you see in the temple?" She wept and said, "It is the corpse of a prince I find lying on a couch. A lamp fed by butter is burning day and night. The body of the prince I find is pierced by hundreds of needles and arrows."

The merchant again called her aloud and said, "Oh my darling, the inevitable decree is written on your forehead, what can I do to avert the calamity which awaits you? Now you see the prophecy of the bird is fulfilled to the letter. Providence is against you. How can I find for you a good bridegroom? Being your father, I am going to ask you to marry this dead prince. What a pity! How shall I return home leaving the treasure of my heart here! Now listen to me, dear daughter of my heart, the corpse of the prince that you see near you is your husband. Sun and moon and the presiding gods of this forest, bear witness. From to-day I shall give up all affection from my heart. Bear my words in mind. If you are a chaste woman you will be able to restore this dead young man to life. I depart now. We shall never meet again. I bless you. May you restore your husband to life and be allowed to return. Keep the shell-bracelets of luck in your hands for ever."

The father and the daughter wept. The animals of the forest shed silent tears. The girl was left alone in that depth of the forest. The father's heart broke and the girl was seized with terror. Alas, it was not even their good fortune to see each other's face at the time of final parting.

Ll. 1-24.

XII

Prose: The merchant went away. Kajalrekha was left in that temple and she continued to cry and weep there all alone with the corpse near her. Her father, the only companion in the forest, had cruelly forsaken her. She approached the bed of the dead prince and with tears overflowing her eyes, lamented thus.

Verse: "Awake, oh beautiful prince, unlucky as I am, glance but once at me. I never saw you in life before. My father, however, has declared you as my husband. His heart is hard. He has left me in this condition. For three days and nights I have taken no meal. Your looks are handsome and bright like the moon. It appears, the shadows of death are on you. You look as if the morning sun is hid under the clouds. Who has, alas! brought you to this condition and left you a dead corpse in this lonely place? How cruel must be your parents! The lamp of their house surely thou wert, yet they had the heart to leave you here in this plight. Are they as heartless and insincere as my father so as to cast off all affection from their mind and suffer you to rot in this forest? Whoever you are, oh my lord, I have been told that you are my husband. So long as I live, I am yours. Trust me, open your lips to speak to me and open your eyes to look at me. Awake and give me reply. Don't, I pray, deceive me any more in this way.

"Alas! like poor Behula, I have been offered to the dead by my father." Ll. 1-20.

XIII

Prose: After sometime the door of the temple opened of itself. Kajalrekha wonderingly observed an ascetic enter the temple. The father and daughter had tried their utmost but could not open the door. At the mere touch of the *sannyasi* it became wide open now. Kajalrekha was astonished at this and thought within herself "This *sannyasi* will be able to restore my husband to life."

She bowed at the feet of the *sannyasi* and began to cry. The *sannyasi* consoled her and said, "Fear not, oh maiden, this dead youth was a prince and I have brought him here. Take off one by one the needles from his body. When all the needles have thus been taken off, then remove the two needles from his two eyes and apply to them the juice of these leaves that I give you. But take care, many more miseries are in store for you. *Don't resist evil nor try to escape the inevitable decree of fate by force.* This dead prince is your husband but bear my advice in mind, until the bird '*Dharma-mati*' introduces you to him, do not tell him who you are, however much you may suffer. If you violate my advice you will turn a widow."

Saying so the *sannyasi* went away.

It took Kajalrekha seven days and seven nights to pick out one by one the needles from the body of the dead prince. These seven days she fasted; she did not come out of the temple for all this time. On the eighth day the body of the husband was quiet free from the needles. The two only remained in his eyes. She came out of the temple and went in quest of water to take her bath.[1] Walking some distance she saw a tank; on each of the four sides there was a landing *ghat* made of stone. The water of the tank was of the hue of pomegranate juice. She came down and went into the tank to bathe. Just at this time she beheld an old man, followed by a girl 14 years of age, crying out. "Is a female servant wanted?" She appeared to be a rustic girl without anything special in her features.

The man approached Kajalrekha and asked her if she was in need of a female servant. She asked him, "What is this girl to you, my good man?" He said, "She is my daughter. Extreme poverty has driven me to this point. I am going to sell her. I went everywhere in the neighbouring villages but none would buy her. Then I met a *sannyasi* who told me, "A princess dwells in yonder forest, most probably she is in need of a female servant."

"I think you are the princess of whom the *sannyasi* has told me."

Then Kajalrekha began to think thus within herself: "There was one cruel father in this world who banished his daughter to this forest. But here is another more cruel than that, one who has come to sell his daughter on the plea of poverty. Surely this girl is born to misery as I am."

Feeling sympathy for her and expecting to find in her one who would share her miseries, Kajalrekha bought her from her father at the price of her golden bracelet.

Song: "As a fruit of her own evil action in her past life she was banished to the forest. Now she purchased a servant with her bracelet and named her Kankan-dashi or "Maid of the Bracelet."

[1] As her hasband was to be restored to life now, she wanted to clean herself by a bath and present herself as his bride in the temple.

Then she pointed out to the maid the old temple and said, "Go there, you will see the corpse of a prince but do not be frightened. You will find some leaves under his pillow. Make some juice with them. I shall instantly come back and apply the juice to his eyes removing from them the two needles. This will give him life again." When she said this, her left eye quivered, which was a sign that she did not do well by disclosing this secret to the 'Maid of the Bracelet.'

Verse : When to the Maid of the Bracelet she had said so, a sudden terror seized her and her left eye quivered.

The maid went a few steps onward and turned back to see the path. All kinds of devilish thoughts came into her head in the meanwhile.

She picked out the two needles from the Prince's eyes and applied the juice to them as she had heard. At once the prince rose up from his bed regaining life. The Maid of the Bracelet said, "Now, prince, marry me."

The prince did not know who she was, but all the same he took an oath then and there, saying—"Since by your grace I have regained my life, I take the oath that I will marry you." A second oath he took saying, "Here do I touch your body and swear that you will be the lady of my heart, since it is you who has given me my life." A third oath he took saying, "Here do I swear." Let Dharma (God) be witness. From to-day you will be the Queen of my palace. My whole kingdom, my nobles, kinsmen and officers gave me up. The people are happy in their homes leaving me, their king, a corpse, in this forest all alone. It is your kindness to which I owe my life. I swear therefore that there is none in this world who will be as dear to me as you." Ll. 1-18.

XIV

Prose: He never cared to know who her parents were, nor enquired what caste she belonged to. He

The Maid of the Bracelet

" At this moment with her clothes all wet after bath, Kajalrekha entered the temple."

Kajalrekha, p. 263

promised to marry her solely because she was the giver of his life.

Song: "In that temple burnt a lamp fed by sacred butter, the prince touched it and swore."

Prose: At this moment with her clothes all wet after bath, Kajalrekha entered the temple. Entering she was surprised to find her husband restored to life.

Verse: "Kajalrekha looked at him with joy. He was bright as the moon free from eclipse. He looked glorious like the morning sun. She glanced at him with eager eyes from head to foot. The prince was also struck with her surprising beauty. He had never seen a woman as handsome as she.

She was at the dawn of her youth, she sparkled like a precious diamond. He said sweetly to her, "Wherefrom do you come, oh girl? What is your name? Who are your parents and where is your home? Why do you wander about in this forest? Be gracious and give me a reply. Your father is cruel and mother no less so. How could they allow you to leave home and come all alone to this deserted place?"

The Maid of the Bracelet came forward and intervened at this stage saying, "I have purchased her by my bracelet. Her name is Kankan-dasi (the Maid of the Bracelet)."

Thus the queen became a slave and the slave a queen. It is all due to her evil action (in some past life) that made Kajalrekha wretched from birth. Ll. 1-18.

XV

In the palace of the prince Kajalrekha passes her days as a servant. She fetches water from the tank, dusts the rooms, washes clothes, and night and day serves the false queen. But inspite of all her devotion and sense of duty that queen is not pleased with her. She is abused by her on some pretext or other every time.

The false queen always watched her with suspicion and kept her under strict surveillance lest she disclosed the truth to anybody. The prince, however, observed all this very closely. He became enamoured of her for her excellent modesty, her sweet conversation, her courteous and good manners, above all, for her beauty which was like the radiance of the moon.

The Prince.

"Who are you, oh beautiful one, where is your home? What is your name and who are your parents? Tell me the truth and give me these details about you. You work here as a servant but this evidently does not suit you. My own suspicion is that you are a princess. By some stroke of evil fate you have been reduced to this condition. Your beauty puts the glorious moon to shame. Do not, oh maiden, deceive me, but let me know the truth." Ll. 1-18.

Kajalrekha.

"I am the 'Maid of the Bracelet.' Your wife has purchased me with her bracelet. I was in the forest, passing my days in great misery. Here you have kindly placed me above want by giving me my daily meals and clothes."

"I have no father, no mother, no brother, oh my lord. Like a cloud drifted by the wind I wander about as one who is utterly helpless."

Prose: Though thus the prince put her many questions every day he failed to get any definite reply. By this time the false queen made his life intolerable by her wicked ways and manners, by her crudeness of self-praise and long talks. The prince loved Kajalrekha in the heart of his heart. He was so much struck with her beauty and other qualities that he became maddened by a curiosity to learn who she really was. He considered his wealth, his empire and capital all meaningless and vain without her. He could not sleep in the night nor take his usual meals. He had no heart in his work. The world seemed void in his eyes.

One day he called his old minister to him and said, "I am going away on a journey for nine months, to visit other countries. During this time try your best to get all information about this girl who calls herself the Maid of the Bracelet."

He took leave of the minister and went to the false queen and asked her if she should like him to bring her anything from the foreign countries which he was going to visit. The false queen expressed her wish for a cane basket, a winnow, a flat tray, a rice-husking pedal made of *amli* wood, a nose-ornament made of bell metal, and a pair of brazen anklets.

The prince felt a disgust at all this and went to Kajalrekha (now the Maid of the Bracelet). At first she said, "I don't want anything. I am quite happy at your house, I have no want here." But the prince insisted on her asking something of him, saying, "You must ask something of me; something that you like best." Kajalrekha said, "I have no want here I told you, but really if you want to get something for me, please purchase the bird of the name of '*Dharma-mati*' for me."

The prince had no difficulty in getting the trinkets for the false queen. Of course it took him no time to discover what metal she was made of. He was however weary and sick at heart not being able to secure the bird *Dharma-mati* for Kajalrekha inspite of his efforts. He wandered from one country to another, from the jurisdiction of one prince or merchant to that of another, and thus six months passed.

After three months more he would have to return to his capital and of these also two months passed. At this point he arrived at the town of Kajalrekha's father. There he had it announced by beat of drum that he was willing to purchase a bird named *Dharma-mati.* The merchant Dhaneswar wondered as to who might be the man who wanted the bird of such a name. He knew well that his daughter alone knew of the bird. He was convinced that whether she passed her days in happiness or in sorrows, it mattered not, but it must be she and none other who had sent a man to purchase the *Suka.* So Dhaneswar decided his course and offered the bird to the Needle Prince as he was called, who was highly delighted to secure it for Kajalrekha whom he wanted to please by all posible ways and means.

XVI

On returning home the Needle Prince gave to his false queen what he had brought for her, and he handed over the parrot to Kajalrekha but said nothing to either. Now, listen to what had occurred during his absence from home.

The minister, whenever there was some difficult point in state affairs to be solved, referred it both to the false queen and Kajalrekha for their opinions.

The former had no idea in any matter but often gave orders off-hand; in one instance her order was so imprudent that it caused a material harm to the state, but the minister, shewing her every respect due to her position, did not oppose her wishes but carried them out. On one occasion a great danger threatened the state. The minister could not find any means to avert it. He sought the advise of Kajalrekha. Her advice proved so wholesome and wise that the danger was easily got over. Now, the minister stated all these to the Raja privately. The Raja knew beforehand what turn things would take in his absence but said nothing. The minister suggested that for a further trial about the respective merits of the two ladies, the Raja should invite a few friends to a dinner at his palace and the duties of the kitchen should be entrusted to both of them separately. On the first day such duty should devolve on the queen and on the next on "the Maid of the Bracelet."

The false queen prepared sauce with *chalta*[1]—a hot drink with *deua* (the fruit of *Artoocarpus Lacucha*), a plain salad of *Kachu*[2] in which she forgot to put salt. The prince in shame, hung his head down when the food was served to his friends. The next day the Maid of the Bracelet was entrusted with the charge of the kitchen.

Verse: She rose early in the morning and took her bath; with a pure body and mind she entered the kitchen. She bound her hair into a knot and put on a short handy cloth. She had the kitchen washed by the water of the Ganges. She prepared the spices with a delicate hand pressing them on a stone and kept ready a paste of powdered rice. The stems of the *mankachu* (an esculent root) were cut to pieces. She prepared a broth of pigeons and curries of various kinds of fish. She then made fine cakes with sugar and thickened milk which when placed on the plates invited appetite by their sweet flavour. The arch-shaped cake called the *Chandrapooli* which looked like the crescent moon was next prepared. Various drinks of excellent taste and flavour were placed in golden cups. *Chai*, *Chapari* and *Poa* were the delicacies of the district and she showed a great skill in their making. The cake called *Khir Puli* inside which was thickened milk sweetened by sugar was a delicacy highly tasteful and was much enjoyed. There were beautiful seats made of jack-wood which were placed on the floor cleaned and washed with care.

She put the fine *shali* rice on golden plates and in their corners placed pieces of lemon elegantly cut to give a taste to the food. In golden cups she kept thickened milk and curd; and ripe bananas from which the skin was taken out, were ready on a golden plate. Then golden vessels filled with cold water were reserved for washing the face and hands

[1] *Dillenia speciosa.*

[2] An esculent root.

and she prepared nice betels with catechu made of the sweet smelling juice of the flower of the screw-plant and these she placed in a golden betel-box.

After doing all these she remained in the kitchen for a while. Ll. 1-24.

Prose: The trial did not end here but went on. The night of the Lakshmipuja day called the *Kojagar ratri* or the night for keeping vigil, when the harvest goddess is worshipped, the prince at the advice of the minister asked the queen and Kajalrekha to decorate the courtyard with *alipana* paintings. The king said, " Some of my friends will be present, so try your best to make the paintings beautiful." The false queen drew legs of the raven and the crow, the foot-steps of the crane ; a store-house of the mustard seed and ears of corn.

How and What Kajalrekha painted.

Verse: She kept handfuls of rice of a very fine quality—the *shali*—under water until they were thoroughly softened. Then she washed them carefully and pressed them on a stone. She prepared a white liquid paste with them and first of all she drew the adored feet of her parents which were always uppermost in her mind. She next drew two granaries taking care to paint the footsteps of the harvest goddess in the paths leading to them, and she introduced at intervals fine ears of rice drooping low with their burden. Then she drew the palace of the great god Siva and his consort Parvati in the Kailas mountains. In the middle of a big lotus leaf she painted Visnu and Lakshmi seated together, and on a chariot drawn by the royal swan she painted the figure cf Manasa Devi from whom all victories proceeded. Then she drew the figures of witches and the Siddhas who could perform miracles by tantrik practices and next of the nymphs of heaven. She drew a *Sheora* grove (*Trophis Aspera*) and under it the figure of Banadevi (the Sylvan deity). Then she painted Raksha Kali—the Goddess who saves us from all dangers. The warrior-god Kartikeya and the writer-god Ganes she drew next with their respective *bahanas* or animals they rode. And then Ram and Sita and Lakshman were drawn by her admirably. The great chariot Puspaka—the areoplane was sketched in her drawings and the gods Yama and Indra were also introduced in this panorama.

She next painted the sea, the sun and the moon and last of all an old dilapidated temple in the middle of an woodland with the picture of a dead prince inside it. She drew all figures excepting her own. The figures of the Needle Prince and of his courtiers were all there—but not any of her own.

When the painting was finished she kindled a lamp fed by sacred butter and then she bowed down with her head bent to the ground.

Ll. 1-24.

XVII

Prose: The Raja with his friends, ministers and other officers went first to see the paintings of his queen and then saw those of Kajalrekha. They were unanimous in coming to the conclusion that she surely belonged to some respectable family. In this way various trials went on.

Now, the girl often approaches the parrot and unloads her heart by weeping before it. She puts to the bird questions about her father and brother and asks when her miseries will come to an end.

Song: "Tell me, oh bird, all that has taken place in my father's home since I left it. How are my parents ? For ten years I have been in strange lands suffering great sorrows. For all this time I have not had the good fortune of seeing them but once.

" My younger brother was dear to me as my life. I see his face now and then only in my dreams in the night. All this was written in my forehead, so how could I avoid it ? My father banished me to a forest. There I met a dead prince. For seven days and nights with infinite pains I picked out the needles from his body and then what sorrows were reserved for me! I purchased a maid-servant with my bracelet. She became the queen and I her servant. Oh, wise bird, you have been present in this world from the Satya Yuga.[1] Tell the truth, when will the weight of my miseries be removed?"

Ll. 1-14.

The Reply of the Bird.

Song: "Don't cry, oh maiden, do not lament any more. In the depth of night shall I tell you all that you wish to know."

When it was passed mid-night, the girl called the bird aloud and said, "The night is far advanced. Are you awake, dear friend? It will be dawn ere long."

"In my father's house there are innumerable servants but as ill luck would have it, I work here as a servant myself. In my father's house there are excellent mats,—the *shital patis* of artistic workmanship, fine couches and bedsteads but as ill luck would have it, I sleep here on the bare floor. My father used to buy for me flame-coloured *sadis* of silk, here do I wear short and coarse *sadis* made by the country weavers. With my own bracelet, dear bird, I purchased a maid-servant. She has become the queen and I her servant. You are wise, oh bird, present in this world from the Satya Yuga. Tell me when the night of my woes will be over!

The Bird.

"Do not cry, oh maiden, do not lament, I will tell you everything regarding your father's house. Ever since you were

[1] The bird *Dharma-mati* was believed to be of a hoary old age living for all the four great divisions of time—the Satya, the Treta, the Dwapara and the Kali-yugas.

banished ten years ago, your father has not gone on sea voyage for trade. These ten years your father has been passing his life under the shadow of a great grief. He has grown blind by shedding tears night and day. The citizens weep as they talk of you. The servants of the house stop their work as they remember you. From the day you have been banished the elephants and horses of the stable do not touch grass or water when your name is mentioned.

"The sun is not bright in the day and the moon looks pale by night in grief, and the wild birds sing their saddest lay from the boughs of trees. No lamp can dispel the darkness of the fair palace. This, in short, is the story of your father's house. Ten years have passed and there are yet two years during which you will continue to suffer. After this time happiness is in store for you. Ll. I-44.

XVIII

Prose: In this way the maiden speaks every night of her hopes and sorrows to the bird. She asks the question over again as to when her evil days will be at an end. The bird soothes her by sweet words as best as it can.

Thus passed some days more. Now another incident took place at this moment.

The prince had a friend who was a guest at his house at the time. This friend was convinced that Kajalrekha must have been a princess. He was so much impressed by her beauty and noble qualities that he became maddened with love. He lost all sense of right and wrong. Night and day he thought over his plans to take away the maiden from that place to his own palace and there marry her. He took the false queen into his confidence. The Needle Prince also was so much enamoured of Kajalrekha that he ceased attending court and stayed in the inner apartment for the pleasure of talking with her.

He was quite indifferent to his false queen, who felt herself greatly wronged and devised plans to remove Kajalrekha from the palace by some means or other. The friend of the prince and the false queen put their heads together and developed some plans. They were convinced that if they could succeed in creating a suspicion in the mind of the prince against Kajalrekha's character, he would surely banish her.

Kajal slept in a room all alone with the bird *Dharma-mati* for her only companion. Taking the advice of the friend of her husband the false queen covered the gateway leading to Kajalrekha's room with a thin layer of vermilion and the friend stepped over the spot leaving four marks of his feet on it. It just appeared from these foot-prints as if a man had gone into and come out of the room. Now the false queen charged Kajalrekha with misconduct and persuaded the prince to believe her story by an eloquent speech. The friend also joined her and endorsed all she had said and thus produced a strong conviction in the mind of the prince as to Kajalrekha's guilt. In great wrath did the prince call on Kajalrekha and ask for an explanation.

She wept and said :—

Verse : "I sleep alone in my room. Alas! who is such a bitter enemy of mine as to have fabricated this story!

"I call the angels of heaven to bear witness to my conduct; the moon and the stars were awake in the night and witnessed all that happened: I call on them to bear witness. The parrot is my witness. The lamp of my room burns steadily with wakeful eyes in the night. I call on it to bear witness! I call on the Night itself to give evidence. The parrot remains in its cage in the room all night. Bring it to your royal court and ask what it knows. Let him tell the truth. Ll. 1-8.

Prose : The parrot was in its golden cage and he was brought before the Court.

Verse: "Tell us, oh wise bird, on oath before God, was the maiden all alone last night? Tell us if she is chaste or not? In this court which has always followed the maxims of truth and justice—tell the truth, we cite you as witness."

The Bird.

"Oh prince, I don't know what I should say. I have no memory of what took place last night. She is unlucky and hence has been involved in a bad case. She is guilty in that sense, so you may banish her to a forest."[1] Ll. 1-16.

Then the prince asked his friend to take her with him and banish her to some desert island in the sea.

Kajalrekha.

Verse: "The guilty one begs leave of you, oh prince! From to-day I shall no more be in your palace. Remember me, esteemed prince, as one who served you for some time and forget and forgive all my faults. You may forget me, no matter. My prayer to God is that He may grant me the fortune of seeing you but once at the time of my death." She took leave of the false queen—her eyes were blinded with tears. She could not see the path. She said, "I have committed many faults, esteemed queen, forgive them and remember me—once your servant."

She took leave of the parrot. Her incessant tears fell on the earth like rain. She came on board the ship calling the sun and the moon to bear witness to her innocence. The citizens assembled there and cried, "Alas! alas!" Ll. 1-14.

[1] The bird Suka with its prophetic eyes foresaw that his evidence would not be believed and that more sufferings awaited the lot of the girl. Hence he did not stand against fate but gave an equivocal answer.

XIX

Prose: It was a vast sea—its coasts or limits could not be seen. The ship came into the midst of this great water. Then the friend of the Needle Prince said to the maiden :—

Verse: "My home is at the city of Kanchanpur. My father is a great man—a millionaire. I have innumerable horses and elephants in my stable. Nine lakhs of cows graze in our pastures, our wealth is immense and the prows of our ships are plated with gold. We have pleasure-houses in the midst of our tanks, there are rich canopies, curtains, bedsteads, couches, and other valuable furniture in our palace, I have not yet married, I am a bachelor. Be kind unto me, fair maiden, and fill in the gap in my house consenting to be my bride. All the servants and maid-servants of the house will minister to your wishes. If you agree, I will lead the ship towards my fair city."

Kajalrehka.

"You are a friend of the prince and I am but his maid-servant; owing to my ill luck am I doomed to exile. He has sent me with you wishing you to banish me. Being the son of a king, why should you marry a maid-servant?"

The Prince.

"You were a servant, but now I will make you my queen. Once but come to my palace and you will see.

My palace shines with gold and there the couches and bedsteads are made of solid gold. You will be delighted to see my father's city.

THE MAIDEN

"Hear, oh prince, the tale of my sorrows. My father took me to be a guilty one and banished me.

Then I became a servant in a Raja's palace. He has banished me taking me to be a guilty one. So I have come here with the burden of scandal on my head. Why not throw me into these deep waters. Covered with shame as I am I will not show my face to any human being. Ll. 1-26.

Prose: The prince did not listen to the maiden's laments but ordered his ship to be straightway taken towards his city. She began to cry saying:

Verse: "Alas! where are my parents at this evil hour? There is none to help me even if I die of a broken heart. My husband took me to be a guilty one and banished me.

"For my evil actions in some past life I am born to misery and am wretched for life. This wicked man has raised his hands to hurt a person who is already dead. If I am a chaste woman, let there spring up a shoal in the sea at my words." Ll. 1-16.

Instantly a shoal sprang up in the deep sea and the ship struck on the sands. The captain and the oarsmen all said, "This maiden is a witch. It is *for her* that things have come to this pass. We must get rid of her."

The prince was thus obliged by his men to land her on the sands. As soon as she got down from the ship, it floated again. The friend of the Needle Prince had no other recourse left but abandon her there inspite of his great unwillingness to do so.

Song: Let us for a while turn the topics from Kajalrekha to the merchant Ratneswar.

After a few days of what happened above, Dhaneswar died. Ratneswar then proceeded on sea-voyage for trade with his father's ships. Now travelling in different countries the young merchant was on his way back to home. His ships encountered a great storm and were obliged to cast anchor on the sandy shore where Kajal was barely alive. She sustained her life for six months living upon the green reeds that grew there. The night passed and the young merchant espied one morning a beautiful damsel in that lonely shoal. He could not recognise her as his own sister, and Kajalrekha too could not recognise her brother as she had left home when he was merely four years old. After a good deal of persuasion Ratneswar prevailed upon her to come to his ship and accompany him to his home. When they reached the city of their parents, Kajal at once knew it to be their home and remembered the palace and everything in it. But she said nothing to any one and silently wept in her room all alone.

Verses: There the horses and elephants in the stable are as before, but the parents of unfortunate Kajalrekha are no longer in this world.

"The big halls and compartments of the palace look empty and void in my eyes, for my parents have left these for ever. Here in this room I used to sleep on the couch—in the arms of my mother. Here too I dreamt sweet dreams in nights full of pictures of happiness. Yonder is that room in which my mother used to serve me milk and butter; unlucky am I to have lost my dear mother. Where is my dear father Dhaneswar to-day? Won't you come, dear papa, and see your daughter who has returned home after twelve long years. Alas, no mother, no father have I in the house, not even the parrot I loved. Big halls looking grim and lonely confront my eyes on all sides."

Days passed in this way and one full month she spent weeping.

One day the young merchant Ratneswar came to her and said, "Oh my moon-faced friend, you were on the other side of the milk-white sea, my ship has brought you down to this country of ours saving you from death.

The crocodile and the big sea-fish would have eaten up your fair limbs had I not brought you here with utmost care and affection. Neither have I married nor have you, I suppose, done so. Just think of youth which is fleeting. With your consent and kind permission may I not hope to be united with you! I have neither father nor mother living. This palace looks empty and void. If you give your consent to-day I may marry you to-morrow. In fact, I have already made some advance, I have invited my kinsmen and friends who are already in the palace and the priest is ready too, to link us together in nuptial bonds; musical parties with their instruments have also assembled here. Now, make yourself happy by consenting to my proposal. We have a large number of maids and nurses in the palace, they will be all your servants, carrying out your slightest wish; you will pleasantly rest on the couch, I will offer you betel from the betel-box and they will offer you meals of fine *shali* rice in golden plates."

KAJALREKHA.

"You want to marry me, but I have one condition. If you can fulfil that I shall consent to your proposal.

"You want to marry me, but you do not know to what family I belong and who my parents are. Before any introduction, you wish to marry me. I may be a Hadi or a Dome.[1] Nobody knows it. You will not then obey the Sastras which forbid such a union."

RATNESWAR.

"Your face, fair damsel, shines like the moon. I am convinced that you are not a Hadi or a Dome. Tell me who your parents are and where is your home? How did you happen to be in that lonely sea-beach? Give me these

[1] Hadis and Domes are the lowest classes, the "untouchable ones," in the Hindu Society.

particulars, but whatever it be, I assure you, I have resolved to marry you."

Kajalrekha.

"I am not able to give you the particulars you want to know for the simple reason that from my tenth year I have been a wanderer in the forest leaving all touch with home. There is, however, a parrot in the palace of the Needle Prince, who will relate to you the whole story of my life. It is this bird who will act as my match-maker. If you want to marry, bring the bird up here and then settle everything.

Ll. 1-52.

XX

Prose : The merchant instanly sent his men to bring the parrot from the palace of the Needle Prince. They started for the city of that prince with a ship full of gold and jewels.

Now, after having banished Kajalrekha the Needle Prince became like one mad. He left his city and visited many countries in quest of her. He marched from one country to another, from one sea to another, but all in vain pursuit. He thus wandered about on board his ship many weary days and nights. When he was absent from his capital, the men sent by Ratneswar visited his city with their ship full of gold and jewels. The false queen was tempted by the high price they offered for the bird *Dharma-mati* and sold it to them.

They were right glad at the bargain and returned home with the parrot. Then it was proclaimed by Ratneswar by beat of drum that he had brought a sea-nymph from the milk-white sea and that he was going to marry her. The next day, people were struck with wonder at this report. The most surprising part of it was the announcement that a wild bird of the forest would relate before all the incidents of the sea-nymph's life. The attractive report drew people of all classes to the merchant's house. Many Rajas and princely merchants, and millionaires assembled there to witness the wonderful spectacle.

In due time a parrot was brought before the spectators in a golden cage, the doors of which were kept open at the desire of the bird.

We forgot to mention that the Needle Prince, the husband of Kajalrekha, was also present in the assembly.

At this stage of the affairs, the parrot flew up from the cage and took its seat at its top from which it gave the following account of the ancestry and other things relating to Kajalrekha.

Verses: " My name is *Dharma-mati* (*lit.* the pure-minded) I am a parrot as you see me. Listen, oh my distinguished audience, to what I am going to relate.

In the southern districts there lived a merchant named Dhaneswar who was a millionaire. He had a son and a daughter and by the grace of the Goddess of Fortune, he flourished in all respects. The girl was ten years old, she was a matchless beauty; when she smiled it seemed diamond and pearls sparkled. She looked fresh and lovely as a water-lily drenched in rain. The son was only four years old. They called him by the name of Ratneswar or the lord of gold and his body shone as gold itself. The girl was unlucky from her birth and became subject to great woes in life. The merchant asked me one day as to where he could get a suitable bridegroom for her. I am the bird *Dharma-mati*; true to my name, I could only speak the truth. I calculated the destiny of the girl and found that she was to be married to a dead prince.

For twelve years she would continually suffer from great sorrows. I also found that if the merchant would keep his girl in his palace, great mishaps would befall him. I advised him accordingly to banish the girl to some forest; that was the only condition by which she could expect her miseries to come to an end after twelve years. The merchant at my suggestion took his daughter and went on board one of his ships and took me also along with him in his travel. After going a great distance we saw a forest having many Mahua trees in it. It was a deep jungle covering a vast area and without any boundary line. For three days the girl ate nothing. She was, in fact, about to die from starvation. The father left her near an old temple and went to fetch water. When the father went she looked on all sides and then opened the door of the temple and entered it. Just then the merchant returned with a cup of water and called her aloud but she was a prisoner in the temple. The door could not be opened. It seemed to be made of steel and the bolts themselves seemed to be of the same strong metal.

So the merchant had no other course left to him than to return home leaving the daughter there." Ll. 1-38.

Prose: Here the bird flew up and taking its seat on the roof of the second floor delivered the following message:

"I will now change the topic from that of Kajalrekha to that of the Needle Prince.

In the town of Champa, there was a merchant prince named Hiradhar. He had no child. He was called '*Atkur*' (a hateful name given in the countryside to one who is without any child). He had none in the house who would keep the lamp of his line burning in his palace after his death.

He worshipped many a god but none of them granted him the boon of a son for which he prayed to them. But hear, oh my learned audience, what happened to this prince next. A *sannyasi* came to the palace sometime after and predicted that God had at last been kind to the king and would soon vouchsafe unto him a son of extraordinary beauty and talents. Saying this the *sannyasi* offered him a mango and directed that his queen should eat it. The queen ate the fruit and after ten months gave birth to a dead son.

The *sannyasi* was called for and he advised the Raja to pierce hundreds of needles into the body of the dead baby. Thus he has been known as the Needle Prince. After this, the *sannyasi* asked the Raja to keep him in a forest all alone.

In a dismal solitude in the depth of a great forest a temple was built and the dead prince was placed in it. Though it was a still-born baby, by the grace of gods it grew up in beauty like the bright moon. The prince lay like a corpse all the while but his body attained its youthful development in proper time. At this time Kajalrekha went there. Her father had banished her and commanded that as it was her evil lot she should marry a dead man.

She wept and wept and her tears would melt a stone. In fact, she washed the body of her dead husband with them. For seven days and seven nights she sat on the bed of the prince and picked out the needles from his body. These seven days and seven nights she fasted and on the eighth day she went to bathe in the tank leaving the two needles of his eyes untouched and the medicine that was to give him life near the bed. Just at that time a man from a city came there and wanted to sell his daughter.

She purchased the maid-servant with her bracelet for her prince but the servant now became the queen and she her servant."

The bird then related one by one all the incidents of her husband's palace and the sorrows and miseries she was subjected to by the cruel Maid of the Bracelet now raised to the status of the queen. The bird retailed all that happened as a result of a conspiracy made by the friend of the Needle Prince and how by his wiliness the latter lost all power of judgment and sent her to exile. When he said this, the tears of the bird incessantly flowed from his eyes and choked his voice. This wicked friend had wanted to marry Kajalrekha by force. Because she was chaste her tears moved the great sea itself to compassion and it bore in its bosom a sandy shoal."

After saying so far the bird flew up in the air and while still flying he addressed the audience and said:

"To-day the twelfth year of her suffering is complete. Ratneswar, her brother, wants to marry her." Saying these words the bird disappeared in the sky.

The Needle Prince, who was there did not know if Kajalrekha was dead or alive. In the presence of all he began to cry being overpowered with grief.

Ratneswar was put to great shame. He was repentant and left the place (court) to hide his shame. He went to his sister bowed down to her with respect and affection, with a hundred apologies.

Ll. 1-58.

XXI

Prose: Thus they now knew one another and the parrot *Dharma-mati* went straight to heaven.

With great pomp the marriage of Kajalrekha was formally celebrated with the Needle Prince and the latter, after staying there a few days, returned to his city.

He kept Kajalrekha concealed in the ship and entered his palace alone. Then he ordered a large deep hole to be made in the compound. The false queen—the Maid of the Bracelet—wanted to know the reason. The Needle Prince told her that Ratneswar, the prince of the southern districts, was about to attack the city. He is bent on plunder. So he was going to take refuge inside this hole with all the valuables of his treasury. The Maid of the Bracelet as soon as she heard this, did not wait to hear anything more or seek opinion from others, but went straightway into the hole with her ornaments, before any one had gone there.

Then at a signal from the prince, his servants at once filled up the hole with earth.

DEWANA MADINA

OR

ALAL—DULAL

PREFACE

Dewana Madina is a remarkable ballad. It is interesting for many reasons. Firstly the language never rises above *patois.* The author Mansur Baiyeoti, whom I take to be one of the best of our peasant-poets, was thoroughly illiterate and sang the song in the language which his mother had taught him. The poet is a child of nature in a very literal sense of the word. He was gifted with the power of close observation of human nature and has spun out the subtle and tender emotions of the human heart with an effective mastery over the pathetic style. It may be said that he is not indebted to any culture save what he got from his little rural world.

The value of his poetry is unique, for nature is the sole teacher here. Though without the proper artistic sense, songs of this class have always a tendency to run wild, there is certainly a beauty in the panorama of views presented to the eye by a wilderness contrasted with an artistically made garden that shows the gardener's design and the prunings of his knife.

In the beginning of the story there is the tale of a female bird that killed the young ones of her co-wife. It is a pure folk-tale. A story like this is mentioned in my Folk Literature of Bengal (pp. 165-166).

The ballad is a historical one and records an event of great pathos that took place in the Dewan family of Baniachong about 200 years ago, when Sonafar was the ruling chief in that city. But these rural bards, as I have said elsewhere, often dovetail folk-stories into historical ballads apparently with the motive of making a greater impression on the people to whom such stories were already familiar. The speech of the Begum at the beginning of the tale contains much of the folk-element. There is a lack of all sense of proportion on the part of the poet in making the dying Begum give such a long address from her death-bed. The story would have been improved by a little pruning here. The laments of the children, afraid of a watery grave, might have been aptly curtailed. In fact the first portion, as we find it to be the case in most of these ballads, is one of wearisome length, monotonous and full of commonplace and stale expressions. The interest of the plot, however, gathers from the 5th canto when the brothers escape death and are taken care of by the merchant Hiradhar, and where Alal deserts his old home at the persuasion of his brother.

The poet is, as I have said, a master of tender expressions. The *baramashis* of all Hindu writers, while occasionally displaying a wealth of lyrical poetry, are generally stereotyped and artificial, where the poets are anxious to display the whole stock of their culture and lose sight of the thread of the narrative. The famous *baramashi* of Fullara is certainly a masterpiece and makes a very poignant appeal to the reader's mind. But there also, the Sanskritic element, introduced for the purpose of display, jars on the ears as in the line "জান্নু ভান্নু কৃষান্নু শীতের পরিত্রাণ."

Here in this ballad the *baramashi* of Madina possesses a supreme interest which, I am afraid, may be missed in my poor translation. The words are mostly culled from pastoral associations. Most of these, I fear, will not be understood by our Sanskrit scholars. The words are so common among our teeming agricultural population, that it is certainly not a matter for glorying on the part of the Sanskritists of Bengal that they do not understand them because they are vulgar. This language of ours is not a monopoly of the Sanskrit-knowing people; on the other hand, if we are to prize those words in our language which have the greatest force and are most effective, we must go to the cottages of Bengali peasants and not to the *tols* of the pundits. This ballad proves, beyond all doubt, that the language of the people which we have hated so long, shows the true nature of our vernacular and is a storehouse of its most powerful instruments to a greater extent than the finished classical style of the learned folk. Unless we prepare a lexicon which includes the words of the countryside, all attempts at compiling vocabularies of Sanskrit words and their meanings only will but serve to expose us to the charge of slavish imitation of ancient classics and betray our sad ignorance of the real linguistic deficiencies of our tongue. Haughton and a few European writers of Bengali vocabularies attempted, a century ago, to compile their works on a truly Bengali basis. But we have not advanced a step from where they left us a hundred years ago.

The *baramashi* in this ballad has not one line which can be improved or cut out. Its beauty lies in the rustic language, the unmatched tenderness and beauty of which it is difficult to convey in a translation. This song, like many others of the class, shows us the true type of Bengali woman,—Hindu or Muhammadan it makes little difference. Madina is more adorable to us than even Savitri or Sita, being essentially a Bengali character. Our traditionally ideal women have a classical dignity which, however noble it may be, keeps them at a little distance from the truly Bengali home. But in the rags of a peasant girl, with her daily labours in the field,—with her cooking, winnowing and husking of the rice and helping her husband in transplanting the green plants or in watering the fields or selling the *shali* crops,—this busy unlettered woman,—who seems to be one with the commonplace, rustic housewives to be met with every day in the cottages of the peasants,—has proved to the world in this ballad the sincerity, the devotedness and the tender emotions of a woman's heart more powerfully than most of the characters of our modern romantic novels. I am specially proud of the fact that Madina is a Muhammadan girl and the poet a Muhammadan;—for this ballad undisputedly proves that some of the best gems of our literature are gifts from our Muhammadan brethren and the restrictions so long attributed to our literature as possessing essentially a Hindu character is finally removed by the discovery of ballads like these. Its language and spirit both prove that it belongs to the Bengali home and that there is nothing exotic in it. It has also shewn that there is essentially no difference between a Hindu and a Muhammadan and that both are the true offspring of their dear motherland—having characteristics in common which prove their nature to be the same though clothed in different garbs.

Madina the true woman is not only great in her devotion, but also great in her absolute trust in her husband's love. And all these traits of character possess a singularly human interest as they are true presentments of nature and not the products of theories born in the fancy of clever writers.

Kajalkanda is a village of which frequent mention is to be found in the ballads of Mymensing. The village does not seem now to exist. Baniachong was a great city in Sylhet although it is now reduced to a mere village. Its ancient traditions of the great powers of the Dewans of the place extending over Lour and other administrative towns of the southern part of the district are still fresh in people's minds, and Babu Achyut Charan Tattvanidhi has devoted an important chapter of his elaborate work on the history of Sylhet to the recounting of the glories of the ancient city. I shall, however, have occasion to deal with the historical facts about the Dewans of this place later on in connection with some of the other ballads.

Dewana Madina is complete in 730 lines. I have divided the poem into 8 cantos. Jalal Gayen, whose name occurs on the last page, was one of the singers and should not be mistaken for the author of this song. The ballad cannot be less than 200 years old.

DINESH CHANDRA SEN.

7, Bishwakosh Lane,
Bagbazar, Calcutta, 22nd August, 1923.

DEWANA MADINA

I

"Swear to me, my dear husband, that you will not marry again if I should die now. Death, methinks stands at my threshold. My days are fast approaching their end. I have utterly broken down. The shadows of death are already on me. The deep pit of the grave, it seems to me, is soon to be my resting-place.

"In this house of mine, I leave my Alal and Dulal—twin brothers, to your care. No riches are more precious to their unhappy mother than these children. I make them over, my dear husband, to you. They are mere babes. They still live on mother's milk and are perfectly helpless. Here do I offer them unto you. The sun and the moon and our eyes be my witness. I leave the pet-birds of my heart to your care. The Koran and the holy scriptures be my witness. Alal and Dulal have none else to look after them save you in this world. The rivers and canals, the forests and hills, the birds of the sky, I call upon all to be my witness while leaving my sacred trust to you. Unhappy that I am, I cannot take them up in my arms. Stretch thine to protect the innocent, the helpless ones."

When she said this, incessant tears blinded her eyes. She stretched her feeble hands and drew the babies to her breast and sobbed out "Oh my poor ones!"

"Look at them, they are like two innocent buds—dearer far than any gold. How helpless they are! My dear husband, out of compassion for them, do not marry again. A co-wife is a dangerous person, my children will suffer greatly if you take another wife. To her, my children will be like thorns which she may try first of all to remove.

"I will relate to you, dear husband, the story of a co-wife.

"On the southern side of yonder tank in the leafy bough of the *hizal* tree a pigeon and its mate had made their nest. Night and day they sat together and cooed sweetly, happy in each others company. It seemed as if they knew not what sorrow was. Thus they went on for some years; and then on an unhappy day the female bird died leaving two eggs. The male bird had great trouble with the eggs. It could not leave the nest for a moment but sat there night and day, hatching them. Unable to leave the eggs lest any harm should befall them, the pigeon could not go out to collect its food and had not a moment of sleep during the night.

"Having hatched the eggs with every care, it at last found one day that two young ones had come out of them. The bird was alone and in great trouble for want of a helpmate.

"Who will go out for food and who guard the young ones in the nest?" Finding itself extremely helpless, it saw no other way to save his own life and that of the young ones, than to take a mate and this it did after a short time.

"The male bird said to its mate, 'I am going out for food. You are to stay here and make the little ones comfortable with the warmth of your bosom. I have reared them up at very great pains. Look after them well. When they grow up they will in turn be of great help to you. People water the plants with care when young but when they grow up they yield sweet fruit.'

"With this advice to its mate, the male bird flew away in quest of food. The female one now reflected as follows:

"'My enemy of a co-wife has died leaving these two thorns in my way. When they grow up evil will fall on my luck.

"'Where was it ever heard that a child born of a co-wife proved kind and sympathetic? In the end, I apprehend, there is much woe reserved for me. When I shall be a mother, these will be the natural enemies of my children. There will always be quarrels in the house on their account. How foolish would it be for me to take care of these! It will be like nursing snakes with milk. I am not going to bring evil to my doors myself. I must kill the enemies with my own hands. When my husband returns home with food, it is proper that we should divide it between ourselves only. If they are allowed to live they will take the food from my mouth. Such enemies as these should not be allowed to live. With my beak I must tear off the heads of these two unwelcome beings that have come here from some unknown regions to seize upon all the good things collected by us with toil.'

"Having thus resolved the bird caught the two young ones by the neck and smashed them on a stone. When they were killed, she threw their bodies far away into a forest. Just then the male bird returned home with food."

"When the female bird saw her mate, she began to cry. Wonderingly did the other bird ask the reason of her grief. The new wife said, 'What shall I say, my dear lord! You left our nest and the young ones to my care. Immediately after you went away a vulture came flying through the air and swept them away by force from my breast. The helpless things have, alas, thus lost their lives. That is why I am crying.'

"The pigeon began to cry at this report saying, 'Oh my poor young ones, what trouble did I not take to bring you up! What a cruel shaft has pierced my heart! Alas! where are the poor things gone, my heart is as if set on fire.'

"The bird cried bitterly in this way whilst the new wife secretly laughed triumphant at her success in attaining her wicked object.

"A co-wife can have no sympathy for my children. So, oh my husband, I repeat my prayer which is the last one I shall ever make in my life. Do not take another wife but have compassion on the poor children."

She stopped here and after a few days she left this false home of ours and returned to her own true abode.

Ll. 1-98.

II

Dewan Sonafar lamented the loss of his wife bitterly. Alal and Dulal were lost in grief. He lay long prostrate on the bare ground and sobbed out, "Alas! Alas!" It is the mother who alone feels for the child. To her the child is as her life-blood. Who else can have such affection and tender care? The Dewan took the two motherless children in his arms and struck his head with his hands in grief. "Alas, they have depended on their mother's milk, how shall I be able to save them from death? When they call aloud, 'Mamma, Mamma' and cry, it seems as if an arrow pierces my heart. How am I to give them food? She has killed three of us and not merely died herself. What offence did I give you, dear Begum, that you have taken such a terrible vengeance in leaving me! I am the Dewan of the far-famed city of Baniachong and am the lord of immense riches. My granaries are full of crops but what doth all this avail me? Even a street beggar is happier far than myself. What good will my high rank and great riches serve, if the tears of my eyes do not cease night and day! Who will enjoy all this wealth? My palace is emptied by her death. Why, oh dear, why did you aim this terrible shaft at my soul and how could you have the heart to give such pain to your dear husband? You were the lamp that dispelled the darkness of my house. You were the pet bird in the cage made of the ribs of my heart. I would have killed myself when you died, but I had not the heart to do so when I thought of the children.

Thus the Dewan smote his breast with his hands and lamented. The neighbours tried their best to soothe him by sweet words but they failed. All work stopped. His happy home was rent with sorrow. The presiding deity of the house, seemed to leave him. His settled home became unsettled and drifted hopelessly like a straw floating at the mercy of an adverse current. His state affairs remained unattended as he lay overwhelmed with grief.

"What, alas, is the good of all this outward prosperity, if there be no joy in the heart!" says Mansur Baiyati—the poet, much moved.

The ministers were alarmed at this state of things and they approached the Dewan one day. The Prime Minister addressed him and said, "Listen to me, oh master, Your Honour's house of long-standing fame is going to be ruined. Marry again and resume thy household duties and those of the state. Why should all be lost for the sake of one person?"

The Dewan said with tearful eyes: "My poor children are mere babies. It rends my heart to see their sad plight. If I marry again, that will add to their sorrows which are already too great. A step-mother can never like the children of her co-wife. She regards them as thorns in her way. For their sake, above all, I cannot entertain the idea of marrying a second time. Alal and Dulal are my very life-blood. How can I think of adding woe to their woes which are already heavy enough. Besides, the Begum gave them over to me as a sacred trust and made me swear at her death-bed that I would not marry again. Far it is from my mind to think of marrying again for my own happiness. What happiness can I possibly enjoy if Alal and Dulal die of a broken heart? That I live to-day is because of the great solace I get from seeing them. I cannot hand them over to a witch of a second wife."

The Vizier took the liberty of insisting on his point again saying, "It is no good grieving in this way. All step-mothers are not of the same mettle. Cases are known where step-mothers have been ready to sacrifice their lives for the children of their co-wives. We promise that we will take care of the young princes. If the step-mother proves unkind, what harm can she dŏ ? In that case we will look after them. Your Honour should marry for the sake of yourself and for the welfare of this house of long-standing fame.

The Dewan thought over the matter, and at last seemed convinced. He reflected, "What's the good of my allowing the house to be ruined ?" He thought. "If there be no one to look after the household, my Alal and Dulal will never know the joys of home life. They will always be miserable and I will have to carry my great grief to the grave. I will keep these children to myself and will give my new wife no opportunity to harm them."

The Dewan thus seemed inclined to marry. Meantime, the minister and other officers continued to urge their point till at last the lord of Baniachong gave his consent. No time was lost and the marriage was soon arranged and celebrated.

Ll. 1-16.

III

After the marriage, the Dewan kept the little children in his own custody, watching them like a treasure. They were not allowed to go to their step-mother. They were kept altogether in a separate apartment cut off from their step-mother's quarters. He caressed and constantly embraced them and busied himself in ministering to their comforts. The new wife became jealous of his great attention to the children and thought, "He is always busy with the children of his former wife and is full of tenderness for them. He does not care to take any notice of me. If I have children, they will share the treatment I am receiving from him. The sons of his dead wife will continue to be dear to him as his life. By my soul I can no longer tolerate this sort of thing."

She thought the matter over again and devised means to remove the cause of her distress. "These children are causing me pain every day like a fish-bone sticking in the throat. I find no pleasure in eating my meals. As long as I am not able to remove these boys from this city there will be no peace in my soul nor any good luck for me.

"If I tell the tale of my heart's pain to him, the heartless Dewan will get angry and drive me from the palace. There is only one way to save the situation. I must have recourse to stratagem."

She then settled her plan and called the Dewan to the inner apartment. When he came, she began to cry. The Dewan asked the reason of her grief and she sobbed out, "What fault have I done, my lord, that you have kept Alal and Dulal completely cut off from me. What reason is there for you to believe that I am their enemy? You have no confidence in me because I am their step-mother. You regard all step-mothers to be of the same nature. I feel greatly humiliated at the idea that my neighbours will all be thinking uncharitably of me. If the boys are not allowed to come to me, they will spread a scandal that I maltreat them. I have got no child, is it not natural for me to feel a longing to see the boys? Why do you stand thus in the way of my happiness? My heart always feels pain for the children and I cannot bear my grief any more. Can you believe that Alal and Dulal are dear to me as my life? I always feel anxiety on their account. What do they eat, what do they do—these questions naturally come to my mind every day. In the palace so many dainties are brought every day. Believe me, I do not relish any of these, sad at the thought of my Alal and Dulal. I preserve the best food for them and hang that up carefully in the *sika* expecting every day that they will come to me. When that food rots I throw it away in great disappointment. All my pain will be assuaged if I am allowed to see them. Kindly therefore, oh my lord, bring them here this very afternoon. If you do not comply with my request, then know that I will commit sucide. I do not care to live with this insult done to me.

Saying this she began to sob and cry vehemently. The heart of the Dewan melted in great compassion, and he said, "I am very happy, dear lady, at what you have said. I feel that I have given you pain without reason. My former wife offered me these two boys as a great trust and I have ever kept them close to my bosom like a mother in compliance with her last wishes. Her words were, "See that they do not suffer the least pain in any respect." Each time I see them, her words are fresh in my memory. For this, I cannot bear to part with them for a moment; they are constantly by my side. Nowhere are they allowed to go alone. You are always busy supervising household duties, hence I do not send them to you, dear lady, least you be disturbed. I keep the boys with me fearing lest I should add to your burden by sending them to you."

The Begum said sweetly in slow words, "Had I any child myself, would that, dear lord, add to my trouble? A mother always takes care of her child inspite of all her household work. If the child is unhappy she does not care for work. I assure you, the presence of the boys will, in no way, interfere with my duties in the house. Kindly do not, I pray you, stand against my wishes." Saying so she clasped her husband's feet and sobbed tenderly. She played her part so well that even stone would melt at her tender appeal. The Dewan affectionately wiped away her tears with his own hands and promised to send his sons to her the next morning. The Dewan then took leave of her with sweet words and after accepting some betels offered by her with sweet courtesy.

When the Dewan had gone away she laughed within herself, saying "Now, I have succeeded in my project and I must at once proceed to remove these thorns once for all from my way. By force or fraud I must carry out my wishes. He has promised to send the boys to-morrow morning. All right, I must decorate the house to give them a fitting reception. I will show such affection as will fill the heart of the people with wonder. They will be struck by the treatment I shall show to the co-wife's children. They will say, "The step-mother loves the children of the late Begum with her whole heart,"— so that should I afterwards tear off their heads with my nails, no one would believe it."

She began now to decorate the house for the reception of the children. She did this so well that no one could detect a flaw. She ordered for them dainties and sweetmeats of a great variety and of the first quality and placed them in due order in the drawing room; she herself cooked rich meals and before it was dawn got everything ready.

She then awaited the coming of the lads just as a crane with saintly bearing and closed eyes walks by the side of a tank in expectation of small fishes.

"She sat in an expectant attitude like a cat with her paws ready for the prey,"—says Mansur Baiyati, the poet.

When she thus awaited the coming of Alal and Dulal, her maid reported that the Dewan was on his way to her apartments. He was seen coming the next moment, followed by his two sons Alal and Dulal. The lads were dressed gaily. How handsome they looked! Even the nymphs of heaven would be attracted by their lovely figures. In an instant they were before her and saluted her respectfully. She drew them close to her bosom and kissed them tenderly. She then herself served the dishes she had prepared. Alal and Dulal were highly pleased with her preparations.

They now stayed there for days together and their step-mother prepared new dainties every day and offered them choice things. She served all food herself and remained standing before them when they took their meals. She did not lose sight of them for a moment and her kind treatment so charmed them that they did not leave her side for a day. No more were they seen walking in the streets holding the hands of their father. They forgot the pain of their mother's death and were well pleased with every thing in their step-mother's apartment.

Ll. 1-132.

IV

So did they pass their time happily again, but the Begum was all the while thinking how she could succeed in removing them from the palace. For she took them to be her bitterest enemies inspite of everything. She did not disclose her secret intention to any one. By sweet words she had conquered all hearts, so no one suspected her foul design. The people admired this rare and excellent trait in her character, and wondered how a step-mother could have so much affection. Generally such children are hated and cruelly treated and if an opportunity presents itself a step-mother does not even feel any scruple in murdering them in cold blood. But here the case was quite different. If she found a thing tasteful she did not eat it herself, but gave her own share to the children.

This extremely kind treatment to the children charmed the soul of the Dewan. He now ceased taking care of them having placed them in the sole charge of the Begum. He looked after the affairs of the state and felt greatly relieved.

Time rolled on in this way. The lady's mind was ill at ease planning all the while how she would get rid of the boys. One day in August she saw the waters of the new flood flowing on all sides in beautiful transparence, and a plan struck her at the sight. "In the new waters the boat-race is a pleasant sport. How swiftly does a boat run over long distances all buried under water! If these boys hear of this amusement they will surely feel an enthusiastic desire to see the race. Then I will appoint a person to drown them in the river."

After planning in this way she sent for the public executioner and privately discussed the matter with him.

She said to the latter, "I consider you a sincere well-wisher of mine. If you will do one thing for me, I will reward you with a gift of 20 *puras* of land duly executed by a document. You are to keep this strictly secret and swear to me that you will do so." The executioner promised to do as she desired, and said, "If I get 20 *puras* of land, there is no work in the world which I cannot do and of this I assure you, most esteemed lady." Then she whispered to him her foul intention and he agreed to carry out her wishes. He returned home. The Begum then gave orders to a carpenter, promising him a good reward, to prepare a pleasure-boat of the "*Mayurpankhi* type" (the prow of which was like a peacock). Alal and Dulal were to go by this pleasure-boat to see the boat-race. The *Mayurpankhi* became ready and the princes were dressed in suitable attire. All kinds of edibles were placed in the boat. The public executioner sat at the helm and played the part of the captain. He rowed the boat and it entered the vast river. No city, no village could be seen near by. Then the executioner came to the princes and said, "Pray to God now, for your last hour has come. I am like death unto you. You two are to die in my hands. I am to drown you in this river now. Strange, that you could not perceive the wicked design of your step-mother! your case now is hopeless. For, I am to be rewarded with 20 *puras* of land." Alal and Dulal were seized with terror at this strange news and began to lament and strike their breasts in utter grief. "We could not perceive the motive of the step-mother. Alas! if we had had the least inkling of this, we would have fled to some forest and lived like two Fakirs there. Alas! where is our mother gone and where is our dear father now at this hour! we are going to lose our lives in this abject manner. We do not find fault with you, oh captain, in this matter. You are appointed to carry out orders. From our birth we have been miserable and have suffered greatly. You may still grant us life if you have compassion on us. There will be none in the palace to light the evening lamp if we die. There is none to sympathise with our father in his great distress. She has been able to do all this because she is our step-mother. Says Mansur Baiyati, the poet, "The wickedness of a step-mother is proverbial." "If our mother had had," they lamented, " a sister, she would have taken care of us and protected us at the hour of danger with her life. If our father had had a sister she would have kept us like treasure near her bosom. If our mother had had a sister-in-law, she would have watched us night and day and would not have allowed us to step out of the house. Alas ! we had none in the house except the step-mother."

Alal clasped the feet of the executioner and said, "Kill me but set Dulal free" and Dulal said, "Torture me to death any way you like but save my brother's life." The executioner said, "A plague on you ! I will kill both." Then they fell at his feet praying for mercy and cried so piteously that even a stone would have melted at their sorrow. Then the executioner reflected, "If I leave them here far away from home, their lives would be saved and they would certainly not visit the palace again after this. Why should I commit this heinous crime if I can safely spare two innocent souls."

With twelve ships a big merchant was coming that way on the river from the opposite direction of the tide, in order to purchase rice. The public executioner called out and explained to him privately something about the boys. The merchant took the boys into his custody, and the executioner then returned home.

There is a village named Kajalkanda on the bank of the Dhanu. There lived a well-to-do peasant named Hiradhar who was a whole-sale dealer in paddy. He sold a hundred *puras* of raw paddy every year. There was not another dealer as great as he in the locality. The merchant purchased rice from Hiradhar and sold the two boys to him. Alal and Dulal lived there with Hiradhar and though they were princes they had to tend cows in the pastures the whole day and undergo great hardships being allowed food only twice. Alal in great sorrow fled away from the place.

Ll. 1-112.

V

On the banks of the Dhanu lived Dewan Sekender, the lord of 12 forests and 13 inhabited areas. The Dewan was very fond of hunting. In fact when he hunted birds, he lost all sense of the outside world. He was one day wandering in the forests hunting birds in large numbers and happened to espy the lad (Alal) under a tree. He was pleased with his handsome looks and took him to his palace. The lad proved of great service to him, doing all kinds of work, but if his master offered him wages, he would not accept any. The Dewan suspected that the boy belonged to some noble family, but when he asked him any question about his parentage, Alal observed a scrupulous silence, and this troubled the Dewan Sahib very much. When, however, he insisted on paying him wages the boy would say, "Where is the hurry, my lord, for it? I will take them all at one time, let them accumulate. I will seek money in proper time. Kindly do not fail to pay me then." There was no work, however hard, that Alal was not prepared to do for the Dewan. He did his duties with his whole might even at the risk of his life. Every one praised him for his whole-hearted service to his lord.

The Dewan suspected the boy to be the scion of a high family and was even willing to offer him one of his two daughters, Mamina and Amina. But his difficulty was apparent; until he knew of his parentage, how could he do that? If he asked Alal, he would by no means admit that he belonged to a high family. He would simply say that he was the son of a very ordinary person. But how could such a boy be born of an ordinary man?—the Dewan thought and would never believe it. He was ever more troubled in his mind as he thought over the question.

Twelve years passed away in this way and one day Alal wanted his wages that had accumulated during the long time. The Dewan wanted him to state in what shape would he like to accept them.

ALAL.

"There is a city called Baniachong. It is my wish that I should build my house in the beautiful lands adjoining that city. Kindly give me 500 men to do this work and along with these workers 200 soldiers to safeguard my interest there. The Dewan of that place is Sonafar. If need be I will fight with him and build the house."

Dewan Sekender consented to his request and gave him the help he desired.

Ll. 1-42.

VI

Now, be pleased to hear something about the city of Baniachong. Dewan Sonafar bitterly lamented the loss of his sons after they had been sent away from the city by his wicked Begum. They were like the ribs of his heart. "Oh, how cruel for them to leave the world prematurely! They have left no token by which I may soothe my soul!"—he cried constantly and became reduced to a skeleton. During his last years his wife caused him great trouble by her bad treatment. She, however, bore him one son. Leaving them the Dewan one day went to his own true home. The young prince succeeded him in the *Gadi*, but the noble house became ruined at Sonafar's death. His Begum appointed new ministers and officers after her choice dismissing the old ones. These new officers twisted their moustaches in a fashionable way and did not do any work. They, however, regularly drew their salaries. When things were in this state Alal came to the city with his men. He appointed 500 day labourers to build his house in the suburbs of the city and two hundred soldiers surrounded the place and guarded it. Day and night the work went on incessantly without any obstruction.

When the report of this reached the city of Baniachong, the ministers and other officers of state were highly enraged. They sent a man to Alal calling for due *Najar* and and rent. Alal dismissed the man without paying anything with these words," I am building this house in the lands of my father, what nonsense do you speak about *Najar* and rents ? " Some soldiers were sent to bind him hand and foot and drag him to the Court.

Next followed a hard contest between Alal's men and the soldiers of the city. The latter were taken by surprise and defeated. Alal took possession of the palace and became Dewan in the place of his father.

The soldiers and other men of Dewan Sekender received due rewards and returned to their own town. On getting the report of all this, Sekender sent a proposal to Alal offering him the hands of one of his daughters. He did not stop there but himself paid a visit to Baniachong and insisted on the proposed match. Alal said in reply, " There is a brother of mine who lives somewhere in the country, I am feeling a great pain in my heart for him. If I can get him back, I will marry. We are two brothers and we will marry your two daughters. But first let me search and find him out."

After this, Alal went alone in quest of his lost brother. He disguised himself as a very humble person and wandered from place to place. Many a river did he cross, many jungles and marshes. And though he suffered great privations and anxieties he could by no means secure any information about his brother.

One day he sat to take rest under a fig tree near a marsh. Near about him played the cow-boys who had let their charges graze at large in the pastures around.

They sometimes played and then sat and sang together. So sweet was their song that it pleased the ears. After some stray songs, they sang a ballad in chorus which was to this effect. A Dewan had two sons. His begum died leaving them helpless. The Dewan took a second wife. This wicked woman, on some pretext, sent the boys to the river in order to drown them. There by the grace of God, however, their lives were saved. A peasant took them into his care. The elder brother fled away to some city and the younger one cried day and night but could find no clue as to where he had gone."

When Alal heard this song, tears began to flow from his eyes without restraint. Then he approached the cow-boys and asked, "Who has taught you this song, my good lads?" They said, "The man who taught us this song has not come to-day with us to tend the cows. In yonder peasant's house he lives. If, sir, you wish to see him you may go by this path."

Going to the house pointed out by the cow-boys Alal met Dulal. They stood face to face and had no difficulty in recognising each other.

Alal.

"Oh my brother, you are dear to me as life, come with me to enjoy jointly the state of our father. I have settled everything about our marriage. On returning home let us marry and be settled in life."

Dulal.

I have married a peasant's daughter. She has borne me a son. I have named him Suraj-Jamal. My father-in-law has given us some small land as a dowry. How can I think of leaving my wife and son! Madina, my wife, is dear to me as life. It will be unfair to leave her; and how can I, dear brother, do such an unrighteous act?

ALAL.

" But if you give her a letter of divorce it will not be unfair. You will be clear in the eyes of God. If you live here, our social status will be lost. What is the good of this life if one loses one's position in society ?"

When Dulal heard all this he thought over the matter for some time in his mind and called for his brother-in-law, Madina's brother. He related the whole story to him and gave him a letter of divorce to be made over to his sister. He did not wait to take leave of Madina or see her once before his departure but accompanied his brother, and both of them returned to Baniachong with a gladsome heart.

Dewan Sekender heard of their return and came to Baniachong to settle the date of marriage. Alal and Dulal were dressed in their best attire and they marched at the head of a grand procession. Elephants, horses and camels, archers, sportsmen and soldiers armed with long sticks went in due order. Alal and Dulal were seen in their shining dress in the midst of the procession. Behind them went the drummers beating drums. Alal and Dulal arrived at the house of Dewan Sekender and duly married his two daughters. Mamina was married to Alal and Amina to Dulal. The rites were performed according to the rules laid down in the scriptures. They returned home, discharged the duties of the state and lived happily.

God has now brought a change over their fortune and their sorrows are at an end.

Ll. 1-94.

* * * *

VII

When beautiful Madina got the letter of divorce, she laughed at it taking it for a mere joke and would not believe it at all. "It is impossible that my husband should leave me as long as he lived. It is a mere trick to try my devotion. How can he forget his own Madina whom he loves with his whole soul? He will not be able to live parted from me for any length of time. Surely he will come back after a few days."

She anxiously awaited his return. Every morning she arose from her bed with the thought, "Surely he will come to-day"—and then put off her expectations to the next day. Thus many days passed between expectations and disappointments. To-day she prepares cakes with palm fruits and the next day busies herself in preparing fried rice. One day she makes curds of a superior quality, which she carefully keeps in store for him. With excellent rice of *shali* crops she prepares fine *chira* which she places in a clay vessel. This she keeps in a hanging rope-shelf expecting his return. Every day she prepares dainties to the best of her power, longing for his quick return. But alas, the dear husband of her heart does not come back! Good fish she has reserved in the tank and the best of chicken in her yard in expectation of him. But he never returns to his house! "Alas, what fault have I done to you that you have so cruelly left me!"—she said to herself, and thus six long months passed. She is now in great agony of heart and does not see any way out of her distress. "My son Suraj Jamal is dearer to him than life. I will send him to that city where he has become the Dewan. In weal or woe through all changes I am his partner in life. Impossible that he will leave or forget me. In due time he will surely take me to him." Still feeding herself with hope in this way she called her brother to her presence one day and said, "I have no secret to impart to you, dear brother. Go with my darling child Suraj and bring a message from my husband. Tell him everything about me and hear what he has to say." Saying this she sent him to Baniachong and the child Suraj accompanied him.

Near the great bungalow with twelve gate-ways they met Dulal in the path. Dulal, of course recognised them but said to them in whispers, "Don't stay here. Return to your home. I shall be greatly distressed and lowered in the estimation of my men if you stay here any more. You have some agricultural lands. Go live upon those. Don't come back to this city of Baniachong. There you will live comfortably. Here do not, I pray, humiliate me in the eyes of my people by your presence. Do not tarry a moment and for my sake do this. I shall be put to great shame if my people come to know of all this."

Greatly disappointed at Dulal's words they returned home with sad hearts. Suraj was in great pain and wept all the way, and related the story to his mother with tears. Sad was she at what she heard. She sobbed out to herself, "Oh Allah, what is this that you have written in my forehead? Like a bird that came from the jungle, he has fled away to the jungle. The pet bird—dearer than life, has gone away carrying off all the joy of my heart, nay my very life with him. My heart has become like a stone in having to bear this severe stroke of misfortune and live alone in this house."

"For a single day you could not, my dear, live parted from me! How have you the heart now to treat me in this way?" Then came a train of associations to her mind.

"In the good month of November, favoured by the harvest-goddess, we both used to reap the autumnal paddy in a hurry lest it should be spoilt by flood or hail-storm.

"My dear husband used to bring home the paddy and I spread them in the sun. Then we both sat down to husk the rice. Oh my husband, dear as my life, how could you be so cruel as to forget the past and go far away? In December when our fields would be covered with green crops, my duty was to keep watch over them with care. I used to fill his *hooka* with water and prepare tobacco;—with this in hand I lay waiting, looking towards the path, expecting him! Ah my dear husband, where are you now! I am dying for you. Can't you feel in your heart what I am suffering?

"When my dear husband made the fields soft and muddy with water for transplantation of the new rice-plants, I used to cook rice and awaited his return home. When he busied himself in the fields for this purpose, I handed the green plants over to him for replanting. How warmly did he praise my alacrity in all this work! How could you have the heart, my husband, to forget the past. I burn with grief as I recollect these small things. Was it a mere passing dream that you helped me to dream? Will everything vanish leaving me the memory of your cruelty alone?

"In December the biting cold made us tremble in all our limbs; my husband used to rise early at cock-crow and water the fields of *shali* crops. I carried fire to the fields and when the cold became unbearable, we both sat near the fire and warmed ourselves. We reaped the *shali* crops together in great haste and with great care. How happy we were when after the day's work we retired to rest in our home."

When she recollected, these little things tears flowed from the eyes of Madina unchecked.

"How could you be so cruel, my husband?" She said to herself again and again. "Here do I cry alone for you. He used to cut and remove the straw and the thorny plants, and I brought water to the fields. Both of us would thus work together in the day-time. Such a dear lord has left me, the unfortunate one! How will it be possible for me to live? There is not another woman in the whole world as miserable as myself. Alas! who is it that has set fire to my fields of ripe crops? What is the good of this cursed life? The cage is here but my bird has fled away."

Thus she cried day and night and passed her days in great unhappiness. She gave up taking her meals and always said, "Alas! alas!" Then she became insane. She spoke incoherent words. Sometimes she laughed and sometimes she cried and often she clapped her hands and sang.

She hardly took any food and became reduced to a skeleton. Her beauty faded away, her form lost its loveliness. After all this one day all her sorrows came to an end. She was a nymph of heaven and went to her own abode. Near her dead body lay poor Suraj Jamal—the hapless child ; his face floated in tears.

The neighbours assembled and dug a grave for her. They read the usual texts from the scriptures and buried her after performing the customary rites.

Ll. 1-112.

VIII

Having dismissed his darling son Suraj from his presence, Dulal reflected, " He is dear to me as my life-blood. How cruel of me to give him up! How is it possible for me to give him up and how is it possible for me to live parted from my beautiful Madina! What will she say when she hears of my treatment? Surely she will feel great pain. She who sacrificed every comfort of her life in order to win my love is deserted by me for no fault. Oh! with what heart shall I give her up? She was dear as my life, the ever-trusted partner of my sorrows. Alas! how heartlessly have I deserted her! Her father had offered her hand to me in the hope that I would make her happy. With this object in view he made me heir to all his lands and property. I have given pain to my dear Madina. An ungrateful wretch am I to have done so; and my place will be in hell for this piece of treachery. For the pleasures of this world which will last only for a day, I have courted eternal hell. No, I must not do this. I am going to fall at her feet and crave her pardon."

He thought in this way and disclosed his thoughts neither to his new wife nor to his brother Alal. He started from home one day all alone without taking his men or any soldiers with him.

When he set out he heard a sneeze from behind. So he stopped a while and then started again. He saw an oilman before him and on the right he saw a fox heavy with its young ones. Overhead he heard ravens croaking, and a vulture startled him with its shrill cry. When he saw all these bad omens he thought within himself, "I do not know what is in my luck to-day; why is it that I see all these inauspicious signs?"

Gradually he came near his old home. He saw the pet cow of Madina standing on the way. Evidently she was not served with grass or water. She was lowing. He was sorry to see her in that condition. Then he recollected the past. When Madina was only six, she used to visit the houses of her neighbours but always with Alal. For a moment she would not part with him. In the month of April, her mother let the bird Bulbul fly up to the sky and she ran to Alal and asked him to help her to catch it. When the bird was caught, they put it in the cage and reared it with care.

He saw the empty cage. It lay uncared for in the compound and the pet bird of their childhood piteously moaned from the house-top. He said to the bird, "Why is it, dear bird, that your eyes look red? Is it for Madina that you have wept? Alas, will you tell me, dear bird, where she has gone!"

Last May, they had both planted young mango plants. He and Madina used to water them every day. There were the plants eaten up by cattle. Surely no one had taken care of them.

Their pet cat mewed in the house and the cows lowed in the shed. "They are all here but where is she—the joy of my eyes?"

No one seemed to be in the house. Over the straw-roof of that lonely cot, the ravens croaked "*ká—ká.*"

The Weeping Willow of the Graveyard

"The boy covered his eyes with one hand and with the other pointed to the grave."

Dewana Madina, p. 311

He called Madina aloud. No one was there to give him any response. Then he searched for her on all sides.

When Suraj Jamal, who lay in a corner of the house, half-dead with grief, heard his father's voice, he came out and saw him. Dulal asked him, "Where is Madina?" The boy covered his eyes with one hand and with the other pointed to the grave. Then the child sat down helplessly on the bare earth and began to cry for his mother.

Dulal went near the grave and lay prostrate on it. He sobbed out, "Oh my God, what a judgment has fallen on me? I have killed my wife myself. My place should be in the worst of hells. Here in this world there is no place for me."

"Oh my Madina, dearer than life, arise and speak to me, I will not give pain to your heart any more. If I could get you back, my darling, I would treasure you in my bosom and for a moment never leave you. Arise and speak to me. If you will not, take me to where you have gone. I am now put to great shame for having done this foulest deed. Leave this grave and return to me. How can I live in this world without you? If you will not be kind to me nor love me as you used to do—still take me to you. Is it not true that you could not live parted from me for a moment! Now I beseech you, give me a place at your feet. I cannot bear my great sorrow. I am guilty in your eyes, it is true, but how can you forget your own Suraj? He cries for you day and night. He is wasted for want of food."

He turned a Fakir and wept day and night in great sorrow. "It seems as if the ribs of my heart had been taken away These fine trees that adorn the earth, and the stars of the sky look dark as dark night to my eyes. The river has run dry. The stone has melted. Oh! where shall I find her again? where shall I go? I am not going back to the city of Baniachong. This earth is sacred to me. Here shall I stay the rest of my life on this grave of Madina.

"Oh ye men, tell my brother Alal who is dear to me as life that the unfortunate Dulal will not return home. I was a Fakir in my early years and I shall turn a Fakir again. My heart has been rent in twain for Madina.

"If I had not written that letter of divorce nor married again, she would not have left me! I committed a perfidious act for the sake of Dewanship. For the dust of this earth I have given up a true diamond.

"From infancy she had been my darling. She would turn mad if for a moment she did not see me. For twelve years we lived together. Now this world is a hell to me without her."

So did Dulal lament over his lot. He built a small straw-house over the grave of Madina and lived like a Fakir there. He left his Dewanship and became an ascetic. He did not return to Baniachong. Now, my friends, take heed, the last of all is the grave.

Stone melted at the sorrows of Dulal. Jálál Gáin, the singer sings this tragic song.

Ll. 1-124.

GEOGRAPHICAL NOTES

Regarding the places mentioned in the Ballads and those connected with their Singers (See Map).

ai ... ... In the Sub-division of Kishorganj, on the river Bahadair 10 miles to the South of Jahangirpur. (Malua p. 43). The native village of Hiradhar,—father of Malua.

7 miles to the north-west of Kendua (See Preface to Malua, p. 35).

Ashujia the native village of the singer Shibu Gayen. 8 miles to the north of Kendua.

Baghrar Hawor ... ... In the Sub-division of Netrokona, Dewan Bhabna (Preface, p. 145). Traditionally known to be a rent-free gift to Baghra by the Dewan Shahebs.

Bamangaon ... ... In Susang. South of the Garo-hills. (See Preface to Mahua, p. iii.)

Bamankandi, Badiár Dighi, Uluakandi and Thakurbaḍir bhitá. East of Talar *Haor* in the Netrakona Sub-division. The three last were the wards of the village of Bamankandi (Mahua, pp. 2, 4, 9). The village of Bamankandi has disappeared with its wards. But there are still mounds of earth traditionally known by these names.

Baskhai ... ... In the Sub-division of Kishorganj, probably written as Bangshai in the text by the mistake of the scribe, near the river Sutia (Malua, Bengali text, p. 92) 5 or 6 miles from Arulia. There is an old *kancha* road leading from Baskhai to Arulia the native village of Chand Binod.

Basati the native village of	the singer Abdul Gayen.
Biprabarga or Bipragram " "	the poet Kanka. (Lila and Kanka p. 216). See Kanka's Vidyasunder.
Boragaon " " ...	Narayan Deb, one of the earliest writers of the Manasa-cult.
Devpur " " ..	Kenaram's uncle. (Kenaram, p. 170). In the Sub-division of Kishorganj, 18 miles to the north-east of the [illegible]-quarters.
Dhalaikona *bil*	See Preface to Malua (p. 36) and Introduction (p. xciv).
Dhola *bil*	In Netrokona, 12 miles to the north of Jahangirpur,—the marsh to which the Dewan was led by Malua.
Galáchipa the native village of	of Abdul Gayen, author of the ballad Monhar Khan Dewan in the Sub-division of Kishorganj, 1½ miles to the west of Head-quarters.
Haluaghat	In the Sadar Sub-division, Mymensing. Probably the native place of Manik Chakladar of 'Kamalá.' (See Intro., p. xcv.)
Ingua, Katar, Gopal Nagar ...	See Preface to Malua (p. 35) and Introduction (p. xcvi).
Jahangirpur	In the Sub-division of Netrakona about 32 miles to the south-east of the Head-quarters. (Malua p. 68). The town of Dewan Jahangir.
Jahangirpur, the native village of	Hiraman Mali (sweeper)—singer; in Netrokona.
Jaliar *Haor*	In Kishorganj. Here Dwija Bangshi was attacked by Kenaram (Kenaram Canto IV, l. 2).
Jigatola the native village of	Jagir Gayen, a singer of the ballads. There are two villages of this name, one 8 miles to the south of Netrokona and another 32 miles to its north in Susang.

Kajal Kanda	Probably same as the village Kájla on the Dhanu. (See Dewana Madina, p. 300).
Kalika the native village of	the singer Bipin Gayen, a Kayastha, about 30 miles to the north of the town of Mymensing.
Kavi Chandrapur „ „ ...	Azim Gayen, a singer of the ballads. Near Kendua.
Mashua „ „ ...	Ramsankar Dhopa (washerman)—singer. It is in the Sub-division of Kishorganj.
Padamsri „ „ ...	Pasani Bewa, a singer of the ballads. Near Jahangirpur (See Preface to Malua, p. 34).
Panch Pirer bhita ...	Near Biprabarga. The place where the Pir had built a mosque. (Kanka and Lila, p. 210.)
Patwaire or Patuar ...	In the Sub-division of Kishorganj about 12 miles to the west of the Head-quarters—the native village of Dwija Bangshi and Chandrávati.
Pukhuria „ „ ...	Hari Patni (boatman). It is in the Sub-division of Netrokona.
Raghunathpur and Haliura ...	See Preface to Kamala, p. 106, and Introduction, p. xcv.
Rangchapur	Mentioned in "Bhelua Sundari" (in Perg. Khaliajuri, in the Sub-division of Kishorganj).
River Kangsa	South of the Garo-hills. (Mahua p. 14) Naderchand and Mahua met each other on the banks of this river after their long separation.
River Dhanu	In the Sub-divisions of Netrokona and Kishorganj (Perg. Khaliajuri) a branch of the Meghna. (Dewana Madina p. 301).

River Phuleshwari ...	Near Patuar (See Preface to Kenaram, p. 165). The river into which Kenaram threw all his wealth.
River Raji or Rajeshwari ...	Near Kendu in Netrokona—on the banks of which the dead body of Lila was cremated.
Sachail the native village of	of Bipin Gayen, in Kishorganj.
Sanchail " " ...	Raban Gayen in Kishorganj, 16 miles to the north of Kishorganj.
Thakurkona " " ...	the poetess Sula Gayen. In the Subdivision of Netrokona.

INDEX

OPINIONS

"HISTORY OF THE BENGALI LANGUAGE AND LITERATURE" (IN ENGLISH)

By

RAI SAHIB DINESH CHANDRA SEN, B.A.

Published by

CALCUTTA UNIVERSITY

Price—Rs. 12. Demy 8vo, pp. 1030, with illustrations.

HIS EXCELLENCY LORD HARDINGE OF PENSHURST in his Convocation Address, dated the 16th March, 1912, as Chancellor of the Calcutta University:—

"During the last four years also the University has, from time to time, appointed Readers on special subjects to foster investigation of important branches of learning amongst our advanced students. One of these Readers, Mr. Sen, has embodied his lectures on the History of Bengali Language and Literature from the earliest times to the middle of the 19th century in a volume of considerable merit, which he is about to supplement by another original contribution to the history of one of the most important vernaculars in this country. May I express the hope that this example will be followed elsewhere, and that critical schools may be established for the vernacular languages of India which have not as yet received the attention that they deserve."

HIS EXCELLENCY LORD CARMICHAEL, GOVERNOR OF BENGAL, in his address on the occasion of his laying the foundation stone of the Romesh Chandra Sarswat Bhawan, dated the 20th November, 1916:—

"For long Romesh Chandra Dutt's History of the Literature of Bengal was the only work of its kind available to the general reader. The results of further study in this field have been made available to us by the publication of the learned and luminous lectures of Rai Sahib Dineshchandra Sen. * * In the direction of the History of the Language and the Literature, Rai Sahib Dineshchandra Sen has created the necessary interest by his Typical Selections. It remains for the members of the Parishad to follow this lead and to carry on the work in the same spirit of patient accurate research."

SIR ASUTOSH MOOKERJEE, in his Convocation Address, dated the 13th March, 1909, as Vice-Chancellor of the Calcutta University:—

"We have had a long series of luminous lectures from one of our own graduates, Babu Dineshchandra Sen, on the fascinating subject of the History of the Bengali Language and Literature. These lectures take a comprehensive view of the development of our vernacular, and their publication will unquestionably facilitate the historical investigation of the origin of the vernacular literature of this country, the study of which is avowedly one of the foremost objects of the New Regulations to promote."

SYLVAIN LEVI (*Paris*)—"I cannot give you praises enough—your work is a *Chintamani*—a *Ratnakara*. No book about India would I compare with yours......Never did I find such a realistic sense of literature... ..Pundit and Peasant, Yogi and Raja, mix together in a Shakespearian way on the stage you have built up."

BARTH (*Paris*)—"I can approach your book as a learner, not as a judge."

C. H. TAWNEY—"Your work shows vast research and much general culture."

VINCENT SMITH—"A work of profound learning and high value."

F. W. THOMAS—"Characterised by extensive erudition and independent research."

E. J. RAPSON—"I looked through it with great interest and great admiration for the knowledge and research to which it bears witness."

F. H. SKRINE—"Monumental work—I have been revelling in the book which taught me much of which I was ignorant."

E. B. HAVELL—"Most valuable book which every Anglo-Indian should read. I congratulate you most heartily on your very admirable English and perfect lucidity of style."

D. C. PHILLOT—"I can well understand the enthusiasm with which the work was received by scholars, for even to men unacquainted with your language, it cannot fail to be a source of great interest and profit."

L. D. BARNETT—"I congratulate you on having accomplished such an admirable work."

G. HULTZUH—"Mr. Sen's valuable work on Bengali literature, a subject hitherto unfamiliar to me, which I am now reading with great interest."

J. F. BLUMHARDT—"An extremely well-written and scholarly production, exhaustive in its wealth of materials and of immense value."

T. W. RHYS DAVIDS—"It is a most interesting and important work and reflects great credit on your industry and research."

JULES BLOCH (*Paris*)—"Your book I find an admirable one and which is the only one of its kind in the whole of India."

WILLIAM ROTHENSTEIN—"I found the book surprisingly full of suggestive information. It held me bound from beginning to end, in spite of my absolute ignorance of the language of which you write with obviously profound scholarship."

EMILE SENART (*Paris*)—"I have gone through your book with lively interest and it appears to me to do the highest credit to your learning and method of working."

HENRY VAN DYKE—(*U. S. A.*)—"Your instructive pages are full of new suggestions in regard to the richness and interest of the Bengali Language and Literature."

C. T. WINCHESTER—(*U. S. A.*)—"A work of profound learning on a theme which demands the attention of all Western scholars."

From a long review in the TIMES LITERARY SUPPLEMENT, London, June 20, 1912—"In his narration, as becomes one who is the soul of scholarly candour, he tells those, who can read him with sympathy and imagination more about the Hindu mind and its attitude towards life than we can gather from 50 volumes of impressions of travel by Europeans. Loti's picturesque account of the rites practised in Travancore temples, and even M. Chevrillon's synthesis of much browsing in Hindu Scriptures, seem faint records by the side of this unassuming tale of Hindu literature—Mr. Sen may well be proud of the lasting monument he has erected to the literature of his native Bengal."

From a long review in the ATHENÆUM, March, 16, 1912—"Mr. Sen may justly congratulate himself on the fact that in the middle age he has done more for the history of his national language and literature than any other writer of his own or indeed any time."

From a long review in the SPECTATOR, June 12, 1912—"A book of extraordinary interest to those who would make an impartial study of the Bengali mentality and character—a work which reflects the utmost credit on the candour, industry and learning of its author. In its kind his book is a masterpiece—modest, learned, thorough and sympathetic. Perhaps no other man living has the learning and happy industry for the task he has successfully accomplished."

From a review by Mr. H. BEVERIDGE in the Royal Asiatic Society's Journal, Jan., 1912—"It is a very full and interesting account of the development of the Bengali Literature. He has a power of picturesque writing ... his descriptions are often eloquent."

From a long review by S. K. RATCLIFFE in "India," London, March 15, 1912—"There is no more competent authority on the subject than Mr. Dineschandra Sen. The great value of the book is in its full and fresh treatment of the pre-English era and for this it would be difficult to give its author too high praise."

From a long review by H. KERN in the *Bijdragen of the Royal Institute for Taal* (translated by Dr. Kern himself)—"Fruit of investigation carried through many years ... highly interesting book ... the reviewer has all to admire in the pages of the work, nothing to criticize, for his whole knowledge is derived from it."

From a review by Dr. OLDENBERG in the *Frankfurter Zeitung*, December 3, 1911 (translated by the late Dr. Thibaut)—"It is an important supplementation of the history of modern Sanskrit Literature. The account of Chaitanya's influence on the poetical literature of Bengal contributes one of the most brilliant sections of the work."

From a review in DEUTSCHE RUNDSCHAN, April, 1912—"The picture which this learned Bengali has painted for us with loving care of the literature of his native land deserves to be received with attentive and grateful respect."

From a review in LUZAC'S ORIENTAL LIST, London, May-June, 1912—"A work of inestimable value, full of interesting information, containing complete account of the writings of Bengali authors from the earliest time...It will undoubtedly find a place in every Oriental Library as being the most complete and reliable standard work on the Bengali Language and Literature."

From a review in the INDIAN MAGAZINE, London, August, 1912—"For Mr. Sen's erudition, his study, patriotism, his instructive perception of the finer qualities in Bengali life and literature, the reader of his book must have a profound respect if he is to understand what modern Bengal is."

From a long review in the MADRAS MAIL, May 9, 1912—"A survey of the evolution of the Bengali letters by a student so competent, so exceptionally learned, can hardly fail to be an important event in the world of criticism."

From a long review in the PIONEER, May 5, 1912—"Mr. Sen is a typical student such as was common in mediæval Europe—a lover of learning for learning's sake...He must be a poor judge of characters who can rise from a perusal of Mr. Sen's pages without a real respect and liking for the writer, for his sincerity, his industry, his enthusiasm in the cause of learning."

From a long review in ENGLISHMAN, April 23, 1912—"Only one who has completely identified himself with the subject could have mastered it so well as the author of this imposing book."

From a review in the EMPIRE, August 31, 1918—"As a book of reference Mr. Sen's work will be found invaluable and he is to be congratulated on the result of his labours. It may be said that he has proved what an English enthusiast once said that 'Bengali' unites the mellifluousness of Italian with the power possessed by German for rendering complex ideas."

From a review in the INDIAN ANTIQUARY, December, 1912, by F. G. PARGITER: "This book is the outcome of great research and study, on which the author deserves the warmest praise. He has explained the literature and the subjects treated in it with such fulness and in such detail as to make the whole plain to any reader. The folk-literature, the structure and style of the language, metre and rhyme, and many miscellaneous points are discussed in valuable notes. The tone is calm and the judgments appear to be generally fair."

BANGA SAHITYA PARICHAYA

OR

TYPICAL SELECTIONS FROM OLD BENGALI LITERATURE."

BY

Rai Sahib Dineschandra Sen, B.A.

2 vols, pp. 1914, Royal 8vo, with an Introduction in English running over 90 pages, published by the University of Calcutta.

(*With 10 coloured illustrations. Price Rs. 12.*)

SIR GEORGE GRIERSON—"Invaluable work .....That I have yet read through its 1900 pages I do not pretend, but what I have read has filled me with admiration for the industry and learning displayed. It is a worthy sequel to your monumental History of Bengali Literature, and of it we may safely say "*finis coronat opus*." How I wish that a similar work could be compiled for other Indian languages, specially for Hindi."

E. B. HAVELL—"Two monumental volumes of old Bengali Literature. As I am not a Bengali scholar, it is impossible for me to appreciate at their full value the splendid results of your scholarship and research, but I have enjoyed reading your luminous and most instructive introduction which gives a clear insight into the subject.

I was also very much interested in the illustrations, the reproduction of which from original paintings is very successful and creditable to Swadeshi work."

H. BEVERIDGE—"Two magnificent volumes of the Banga Sahitya Parichaya......I have read with interest Rasa Sundari's autobiography in your extracts."

F. H. SKRINE—"The two splendid volumes of Banga Sahitya Parichaya I am reading with pleasure and profit. They are a credit to your profound learning and to the University which has given them to the world."

From a long review in THE TIMES LITERARY SUPPLEMENT, London, November 4, 1915—"In June, 1912, in commenting on Mr. Sen's History of Bengali Language and Literature, we suggested that that work might usefully be supplemented by an anthology of Bengali prose and poetry. Mr. Sen has for many years been occupied with the aid of other patriotic students of the mediæval literature of Bengal in collecting manuscripts of forgotten or half-forgotten poems. In addition to these more or less valuable monuments of Bengali poetic art, the chief popular presses have published great masses of literary matter, chiefly religious verse. It can hardly be said that these piles of written and printed matter have ever been subjected to a critical or philological scrutiny. Their very existence was barely known to the Europeans, even to those who have studied the Bengali Language on the spot. Educated Bengalis themselves, until quite recent times have been too busy with the arts and sciences of Europe to spare much time for indigenous treasures. That was the reason why we suggested the compiling of a critical chrestomathy for the benefit not only of European but of native scholars. The University of Calcutta prompted by the eminent scholar Sir Asutosh Mookerjee, then Vice-Chancellor, had already anticipated this need it seems. It had shrunk (rightly, we think) from the enormous and expensive task of printing the MSS. recovered by the diligence and generosity of Mr. Sen and other inquirers and employed Mr. Sen to prepare the two bulky volumes now before us. The Calcutta Senate is to be congratulated on its enterprise and generosity."

From a review in the ATHENÆUM, January 16, 1915—"We have already reviewed Mr. Sen's History of Bengali Language and Literature and have rendered some account of his previous work in Bengali entitled *Banga Bhasa O Sahitya*. Mr. Sen now supplies the means of checking his historical and critical conclusions in a copious collection of Bengali verse......Here are the materials carefully arranged and annotated with a skill and learning such as probably no one else living can command."

From a review by Mr. F.G. PARGITER in the Royal Asiatic Society's Journal—"These two portly volumes of some 2,100 pages are an anthology of Bengali poetry and prose from the 18th to the 19th century and are auxiliary to the same author's History of Bengali Language and Literature which was reviewed by Mr. Beveridge in this Journal for 1912 ......The Vice-Chancellor of the Calcutta University who was consulted, decided that the best preliminary measure would be to make and publish typical selections. The University then entrusted that duty to Babu Dinesh Chandra Sen ; this work is the outcome of his researches. There can be no question that Dinesh Babu was the person most competent to undertake the task and in these two volumes we have without doubt a good presentment of typical specimens of old Bengali literature......The style of the big book is excellent, its printing is fine, and it is embellished with well-executed reproductions in colour of some old paintings. It has also a copious index.

THE VAISNAVA LITERATURE OF MEDIÆVAL BENGAL

[Being lectures delivered as Reader to the University of Calcutta.]

BY

RAI SAHIB DINESH CHANDRA SEN, B.A.

Demy 8vo 257 pages

WITH A PREFACE BY

J. D. ANDERSON, Esq., I.C.S. (*Retired*)

Price Rs. 2 only.

SIR GEORGE GRIERSON.—"Very valuable book......I am reading it with the greatest interest and am learning much from it."

WILLIAM ROTHENSTEIN.—"I was delighted with your book, I cannot tell you how touched I am to be reminded of that side of your beloved country which appeals to me most—a side of which I was able to perceive something during my own too short visit to India. In the faces of the best of your countrymen I was able to see that spirit of which you write so charmingly in your book. I am able to recall these faces and figures as if they were before me. I hear the tinkle of the temple-bells along the ghats of Benares, the voices of the women as they sing their sacred songs crossing the noble river in the boats at sunset and I sit once more with the austere Sanyasin friends I shall never, I fear, see more. But though I shall not look upon the face of India again, the vision I had of it will fill my eyes through life, and the love I feel for your country will remain to enrich my own vision of life, so long as I am capable of using it. Though I can only read you in English, the spirit in which you write is to me so true an Indian spirit, that it shines through our own idiom, and carries me, I said before, straight to the banks of your sacred rivers, to the bathing tanks and white shrines and temples of your well remembered villages and tanks. So once more I send you my thanks for the magic carpet you sent me, upon which my soul can return to your dear land. May the songs of which you write remain to fill this land with their fragrance ; you will have use of them, in the years before you, as we have need of all that is best in the songs of our own seers in the dark waters through which we are steering."

(From a long review in the TIMES LITERARY SUPPLEMENT, 2nd August, 1917.)

The Vaisnava Literature of Mediæval Bengal—By Rai Sahib Dineschandra Sen. (Calcutta :—The University.)

Though the generalisation that all Hindus not belonging to modern reform movements are Saivas or Vaisnavas is much too wide, there are the two main divisions in the bewildering mass of sects which make up the 217,000,000 of Hindus. and at many points they overlap each other. The attempts made in the 1901 Census to collect information regarding sects led to such unsatisfactory and partial results that they were not repeated in the last decennial enumeration. But it is unquestionable that the Vaisnavas—the worshippers of Krishna—are dominant in Bengal owing to the great success of the reformed cult established by Chaitanya, a contemporary of Martin Luther. The doctrine of Bhakti or religious devotion, which he taught still flourishes in Bengal, and the four lectures of the Reader to the University of Calcutta in Bengali here reproduced provide an instructive guide to its expression in the literature of the country during the sixteenth and seventeenth centuries. The first part of the book is devoted to the early period of Vaisnava literature, dating from the eleventh century.

The Rai Sahib is filled with a most patriotic love of his nation and its literature, and has done more than any contemporary countryman to widen our knowledge of them. His bulky volume recording the history of Bengali Language and Literature from the earliest times to the nineteenth century is accepted by Orientalists as the most complete and authoritative work on the subject.

There is refreshing ingenuousness in his claim, "my industry has been great," and the "forbearing indulgence" for which he asks if he has failed from any lack of powers, will readily be granted in view of the enthusiasm for his subject which somewhat narrows the strictly critical value of his estimates, but does not impair the sustained human interest of the book.

Chaitanya clearly taught, as these pages show, that the Krishna of the Mahabharata, the great chieftain and ally of the Pandava brothers, was not the Krishna of Brindaban. The latter, said the reformer, to Rupa, the author of those masterpieces of Sanskrit drama the Vidagdha Madhava and the Lalita Madhava, was love's very self and an embodiment of sweetness : and the more material glories of Mathura should not be confused with the spiritual conquests of Brindaban. The amours of Krishna with Radha and milkmaids of Brindaban are staple themes of the literature associated with the worship of the God of the seductive flute. But Mr. Sen repeatedly insists that the love discussed in the literature he has so closely studied is spiritual and mystic, although usually presented in sensuous garb. Chaitanya who had frequent ecstasies of spiritual joy ; Rupa, who classified the emotions of love in 360 groups and the other authors whose careers are here traced were hermits of unspotted life and religious devotion. The old passionate desire for union which they taught is still dominant in modern Bengali literature not directly Vaisnava in import. As Mr. J. D. Anderson points out in his preface, the influence of Chaitanya's teaching may be detected in the mystical verses of Tagore."

From a long review in the TIMES LITERARY SUPPLEMENT, 26th April, 1918 :—

"This delightful and interesting little book is the outcome of a series of lectures supplementing the learned discourses which Mr. Sen made the material of his "Vaisnava Literature of Mediæval Bengal" reviewed by us on August 2, 1917.

It is an authentic record of the religious emotion and thought of that wonderful land of Bengal which few of its Western rulers, we suspect, have rightly comprehended, not from lack of friendly sympathy but simply from want of precisely what Mr Sen better than any one living, better than Sir Rabindranath Tagore himself, can supply.

It is indeed, no easy matter for a Western Protestant to comprehend save by friendship and sympathy with just such a pious Hindu as Mr. Sen, what is the doctrine of an *istadevata*, a "favourite deity" of Hindu pious adoration. In his native tongue Mr. Sen has written charming little books based on ancient legends, which bring us very near the heart of this simple mystery, akin, we suppose, to the cult of particular saints in Catholic countries. Such for instance, is his charming tale of "Sati," the Aryan spouse of the rough Himalayan ascetic God Siva. The tale is dedicated, in words of delightfully candid respect and affection, to the devoted and loving wives of Bengal, whose virtues as wives and mothers are the admiration of all who know their country. Your pious Vaisnava can, without any hesitation or difficulty, transfer his thoughts from the symbolical amorism of Krishna to that other strange creation-legend of Him of the Blue Throat who, to save God's creatures, swallowed the poison cast up at the Churning of the Ocean and bears the mystic stigma to this day. Well, we have our tradition legends, mysteries, and as Miss Underhill and others tell us, our own ecstatic mystics, who find such ineffable joy in loving God as, our Hindu friends tell us, the divine Radha experienced in her sweet surrender to the inspired wooing of Krishna. The important thing for us, as students of life and literature is to note how these old communal beliefs influence and develop that wonderful record of human thought and emotion wrought for us by the imaginative writers of verse and prose, the patient artists of the pen.

When all is said, there remains the old indefinable charm which attaches to all that Dines Chandra Sen writes, whether in English or his native Bengali. In his book breathe a native candour and piety which somehow remind us of the classical writers familiar to our boyhood. In truth, he is a belated contemporary of, say, Plutarch, and attacks his biographical task in much the same spirit. We hope his latest book will be widely (and sympathetically) read."

J. D. ANDERSON Esq.—retired I.C.S., Professor, Cambridge University:—I have read more than half of it. I propose to send with it, if circumstances leave me the courage to write it. a short Preface (which I hope you will read with pleasure even if you do not think it worth publication) explaining why, in the judgment of a very old student of all your works, your book should be read not only in Calcutta, but in London and Paris, and Oxford and Cambridge. I have read it and am reading it with great delight and profit and very real sympathy. Think how great must be the charm of your topic and your treatment when in this awful year of anxiety and sorrow, the reading of your delightful MS. has given me rest and refreshment in a time when every post, every knock at the door, may bring us sorrow.

I write this in a frantic hurry; the mail goes to-day—in order to go back to your most interesting and fascinating pages.

HISTORY OF THE BENGALI LANGUAGE AND LITERATURE.

Extract from a long review by SYLVAIN LEVI (Paris) in the "Revue Critique," Jan 1915;—(translated for the Bengalee).

"One cannot praise too highly the work of Mr. Sen. A profound and original erudition has been associated with a vivid imagination. The works which he analyses are brought back to life with the consciousness of the original authors, with the movement of the multitudes who patronised them and with the landscape which encircled them. The historian, though relying on his documents, has the temperament of an epic poet. He has likewise inherited the lyrical genius of his race. His enthusiastic sympathy vibrates through all his descriptions. Convinced as every Hindu is of the superiority of the Brahmanic civilization, he exalts its glories and palliates its shortcomings, if he does not approve of them he would excuse them. He tries to be just to Buddhism and Islam; in the main he is grateful to them for their contribution to the making of India. He praises with eloquent ardour of the early English missionaries of Christianity.

The appreciation of life so rare in our book-knowledge, runs throughout the work; one reads these thousand pages with a sustained interest; and one loses sight of the enormous labour which it presupposes; one easily slips into the treasure of information which it presents. The individual extracts quoted at the bottom of the pages offer a unique anthology of Bengali. The linguistic remarks scattered in the extracts abound in new and precious materials. Mr. Sen has given to his country a model which it would be difficult to surpass; we only wish that it may provoke in other parts of India emulations to follow it."

THE FOLK LITERATURE OF BENGAL

BY

RAI SAHEB DINESH CHANDRA SEN, B.A.,

Published by the Calcutta University. Demy 8vo pp. 362.

With a foreword by W. R. Gourlay, M.A., I.C.S., C.I.E., from a long review in the TIMES LITERARY SUPPLEMENT, MAY 13, 1920:

"Those who are acquainted (we hope there are many) with Mr. Sen's other works, the outcome of lectures delivered to Calcutta University under-graduates in the author's function as Ramtanu Lahiry Research Fellow in the History of the Bengali Language and Literature, will know exactly what to expect of his present delightful excursion into

Bengali Folk-lore. Mr. Sen thinks in Bengali, he thinks Bengali thoughts, he remains a pious Hindu, though his Hindu ideas are touched and stirred by contact with many kindly and admiring English friends. He is the better fitted to explain Bengal to the outer world, for he loves his native province with all his heart. He has no doubts as to the venerable origins, the sound philosophy, the artistic powers, the suggestive beauty, all the many charms of the Bengali Saraswati, the sweet and smiling goddess, muse and deity alike, the inspirer and patron of a long line of men of literature and learning too little known to the self-satisfied West.

A Hindu he remains thinking Hindu thoughts, retaining proud and happy memories of his Hindu childhood and of the kind old men and women who fed his childish imagination with old-world rhymes, with the quaintly primitive Bengali versions of the stately epics of Sanskrit scripture, with tales even more primitive handed down by word of mouth by pious mothers, relics perhaps of a culture which preceded the advent of Hinduism in Bengal. What makes Mr. Sen's books so delightful to us in Europe is precisely this indefinable Hindu quality, specially Bengali rather than Indian, something that fits itself with exquisite aptness to what we know of the scenery and climate of the Gangetic delta, where Mr. Sen was born, and where he has spent the life as a schoolmaster in Eastern Bengal, a land of wide shining meres and huge slow-moving rivers where the boatman sings ancient legends as he lazily plies the oar and the cowherd lads on the low grassy banks of Mehgna and Dhaleshwari chant plaintive rhymes that Warren Hastings may have heard as he "proceeded up country" in his spacious "budgerow."

All these pleasant old rhymes and tales Mr. Sen loves with more than patriotic emotion and admiration and this sentiment he contrives to impart to his readers, even through the difficult and laborious medium of a foreign language."

JULES BLOCH—"I have just finished the romantic story of Chandrabati (given in the Bengali Ramayanas). May I congratulate you on the good and well deserved luck of having discovered her after so many others and having added that new gem to the crown of Bengali Literature.

I cannot speak to you in detail of your chapters on the characteristics of the Bengali Ramayanas and on Tulsidas. I had only to learn from what you say and thank you for helping me and many others to get a little of that direct understanding and feeling of the literary and emotional value of those poems in general and Krittivas in particular. I hope your devotion to Bengali Literature will be regarded by a growing popularity of that literature in India and in Europe; and also that young scholars will follow your example and your direction in continuing your studies, literary and philological."

SIR GEORGE GRIERSON—"I must write to thank you for your two valued gifts of the "Folk Literature of Bengal" and "The Bengali Ramayanas." I delayed acknowledging them till I had read them through. I have been greatly interested by both, and owe you a debt of gratitude for the immense amount of information contained in them.

I add to this letter a few notes which the perusal of your books has suggested to me. Perhaps you will find them useful.

I hope that you will be spared to us to write many more such books."

DR. WILLIAM CROOKE, C.I.E., EDITOR OF "FOLK LORE"—"I have read them ("Folk Literature of Bengal" and "The Bengali Ramayanas") with much interest. They seem to me to be a very valuable contribution to the study of the religion and folk-lore of Bengal. I congratulate you on the success of your work and I shall be glad to receive copies of any other work which you may write on the same subjects."

H. BEVERIDGE—"Of the two books I must say that I like best the Bengali Ramayanas. Your book on Bengali folk-lore is also valuable" (from a letter of 12 pages containing a critical review of the two books).

From the Times Literary Supplement, April 7, 1921.

"The Bengali Ramayanas" by Rai Saheb Dinesh Chandra Sen (published by the University of Calcutta).

The Indian epics deserve closer study than they have hitherto received at the hands of the average Englishmen of culture. Apart from the interest of the main themes, the wealth of imagery and the beauty of many of the episodes, they are storehouses of information upon the ancient life of India and a key to the origin of customs which still live. Moreover they show many curious affinities to Greek literature which suggest the existence of legends common to both countries. The Ring of Polycrates is reproduced in other conditions in the "Sakuntala" the *Alcestis* has its counterpart in the story of Savitri, and the chief of Pandavas descends into hell in the manner of Odysseus though on a nobler errand.

The main theme of these lectures is the transformation of the old majestic Sanskrit epic as it came from the hands of Valmiki to the more familiar and homely style of the modern Bengali versions. The Ramayana, we are told, is a protest against Buddhist monasticism, the glorification of the domestic virtues, proclaiming that there is no need to look for salvation outside the home. The Bengali versions, which reducing the grandeur of the heroic character, to the level of ordinary mortals, bring the epic within the reach of the humblest peasant; they have their own virtues, just as the simple narrative of the Gospels has its own charm, though it be different in kind from that of Isaiah's majestic cadences. Thus in the Sanskrit poem "Kaucalya" Rama's mother is sacrificing to Fire when she hears of her son's exile; she does not flinch, but continues the sacrifice in the spirit of Greek tragedy, merely altering the character of her prayer. In the Bengali version she becomes a woman, giving vent to lamentations, such as one hears every day in modern India. In the Nibelungenlied one sees the same kind of transformation from the old Norse sagas to the atmosphere of mediæval chivalry.

The author approaches his subject in that spirit of reverence which is the due of all great literature and to him, Valmiki's Ramayana is the greatest literature in the world. The fact does not blunt his critical faculty: rather does it sharpen it, for, as he says in the preface, "historical research and the truths to which it leads do not interfere with faith," neither do they stand in the way of admiration. He sees more in the Ramayana than the mere collection of legends into a Sanskrit masterpiece from which various versions have been made from time to time. He shows us how, as the centuries proceeded, each successive version was influenced by the spirit of the age, how the story became adapted to the purposes of religious propaganda, how in the interests of the Vaisnava cult the hero Rama became the divine avatar of Vishnu, even at the risk of absurd situations. He takes us through the age of the Sakti influence, of Ramananda's philosophy and its revolt against Mahomedan iconoclasm, of the flippant immorality of the eighteenth century. "These Bengali Ramayanas," he says, "have thus quite an encyclopædic character, comprising along with the story of Rama, current theologies, folk-tales and the poetry of Ramayan is a yellow primrose, but it is something more, * * * * To the student of folk-lore these lectures are to be recommended as an earnest and loving study of a fascinating subject."

Rai Bahadur Dineshchandra Sen's Folk Literature of Bengal.

From the "REVISTA TRIMESTRALE DI STUDI FILOSOFICIE RELIGIOSI—"The University of Calcutta continues with every alacrity, the fine series of its publications thus testifying to the high scientific preparation (issuing out) of those indigenous teachers. This volume devoted to the popular tales of Bengal constitutes a contribution of the first rank to such a subject. The tracing of the History of the Bengali language and literature in this University is one of the most well deserved studies of Bengal. To it is due, in fact, the monumental and now classical History of the Bengali Language and Literature (1912);—in which, so far as our studies go, we value most the accurate estimate of the influence of Chaitanya on that lit rature—accompanied by the grand Bengali Anthology Banga Sahitya Parichaya, 1914, and then above all the pleasing and erudite researches on Vaishnab literature and the connected religious reform of Chaitanya.

A world wholly legendary depicted with the homely tenderness in most secluded locality of Bengal and half conceived in the Buddhistic epoch with delicate phantasy and fondness; the world in which Rabindranath Tagore ultimately attained his full growth is revived with every seduction of art in the luminous pages of this beautiful book. The author came in touch with this in his first days of youth when he was a village teacher in East Bengal and he now wishes to reveal it by gathering together the most secluded spirit and also the legend collected in four delicious volumes of D. R. Mazumdar, yet to be translated.

A spirit of renunciation in the devotion of wives in the love of tender and sorrowful ladies, in eagerness for patient sacrifice carry us back, as we have said, to the Buddhistic epoch of Bengal; it rises as an ideal of life and is transmitted to future generations traversed by the Mussalmani faith which also is pervaded by so many Buddhistic elements. Malancha, the sublime female incarnation of such an ideal—whose legend is translated in the last pages of this volume—the Lady wholly spiritual, a soul heroic in its devoted renunciation, mistress of her body who reveals in herself qualities that essentially belong to idea, a creature of the soul, shaped by the aspiration to come into contact with the external world. Malancha loses her eyes and her hands but so strong is her desire to see her husband that her eyes grow again and such is her desire to serve him that her hands also grow again.

In the popular narration the prose often assumes a poetic movement and metrical form. The archaic language that reminds us of remote antiquity is converted into lyric charm and becomes knotty in the prose, making us think pensively of the Vedic hymnology that entered the epic of Mahavarat.

[Translated from the Original Italian.]